palgrave advances in
byron studies

Palgrave Advances

Titles include:

John Bowen and Robert L. Patten (*editors*)
CHARLES DICKENS STUDIES

Phillip Mallett (*editor*)
THOMAS HARDY STUDIES

Lois Oppenheim (*editor*)
SAMUEL BECKETT STUDIES

Jean-Michel Rabaté (*editor*)
JAMES JOYCE STUDIES

Peter Rawlings (*editor*)
HENRY JAMES STUDIES

Frederick S. Roden (*editor*)
OSCAR WILDE STUDIES

Jane Stabler (*editor*)
BYRON STUDIES

Nicholas Williams (*editor*)
WILLIAM BLAKE STUDIES

Forthcoming:

Larry Scanlon (*editor*)
CHAUCER STUDIES

Anna Snaith (*editor*)
VIRGINIA WOOLF STUDIES

Suzanne Trill (*editor*)
EARLY MODERN WOMEN'S WRITING

Palgrave Advances
Series Standing Order ISBN 1–4039–3512–2 (Hardback) 1–4039–3513–0 (Paperback)
(*outside North America only*)

You can receive future titles in this series as they are published by placing a standing order.
Please contact your bookseller or, in the case of difficulty, write to us at the address below
with your name and address, the title of the series and the ISBN quoted above.

Customer Services Department, Macmillan Distribution Ltd, Houndmills, Basingstoke,
Hampshire RG21 6XS, England

palgrave advances in byron studies

edited by
jane stabler
university of st andrews

First published 2007 by
PALGRAVE MACMILLAN
Houndmills, Basingstoke, Hampshire RG21 6XS and
175 Fifth Avenue, New York, N.Y. 10010
Companies and representatives throughout the world

PALGRAVE MACMILLAN is the global academic imprint of the
Palgrave Macmillan division of St Martin's Press LLC and of
Palgrave Macmillan Ltd.
Macmillan® is a registered trademark in the United States,
United Kingdom and other countries. Palgrave is a registered
trademark in the European Union and other countries.

ISBN-13   978–1–4039–4592–1 hardback
ISBN-10   1–4039–4592–6 hardback
ISBN-13   978–1–4039–4593–8 paperback
ISBN-10   1–4039–4593–4 paperback

This book is printed on paper suitable for recycling and
made from fully managed and sustained forest sources.
Logging, pulping and manufacturing processes are expected to
conform to the environmental regulations of the country of origin.

A catalogue record for this book is available
from the British Library.

Library of Congress Cataloging-in-Publication Data
Palgrave advances in Byron studies / edited by Jane Stabler.
      p. cm — (Palgrave advances)
Includes bibliographical references and index.
ISBN-13: 978–1–4039–4592–1 (cloth)
ISBN-10: 1–4039–4592–6 (cloth)
      1. Byron, George Gordon Byron, Baron, 1788–1824—Criticism and
interpretation. I. Stabler, Jane.

PR4388.P35 2007
821'.7—dc22
                                                              2007060014

10   9   8   7   6   5   4   3   2   1
16   15   14   13   12   11   10   09   08   07

Printed and bound in Great Britain by
Antony Rowe Ltd, Chippenham and Eastbourne

contents

notes on contributors

Steven Bruhm is Professor of English in the Department of English at Mount St Vincent University, Halifax. His books include *Gothic Bodies: The Politics of Pain in Romantic Fiction* (1994), *Reflecting Narcissus. A Queer Aesthetic* (2000) and *Curiouser: on the Queerness of Children* (2004). He is working on a study of the Gothic Child.

Peter Cochran is the editor of the *Newstead Byron Society Review*. He has lectured on Byron in London, Oxford, Cambridge, Newstead, Glasgow, Liverpool, Versailles, Moncton, Gdansk, Salzburg, Yerevan and New York, and published numerous articles on the poet. He is author of the Byron entry in the *New Cambridge Bibliography of English Literature*, and of the entries on J.C. Hobhouse and E.J. Trelawny for the new *Oxford Dictionary of National Biography*.

Paul M. Curtis teaches English Language and Literature at l'Université de Moncton and has published several articles on Byron, digression and wordplay. He has also edited the volume of Selected Proceedings from the 30th International Byron Conference, *Byron and the Romantic Sublime* (2005).

Caroline Franklin is Professor of English at the University of Wales, Swansea. Her books include *Byron's Heroines* (1992), *Byron, A Literary Life* (2000) and *Mary Wollstonecraft, A Literary Life* (2004). At present she is editing *Women's Travel Writing, 1750–1850*, forthcoming from Routledge.

She-Ru Kao (also known as Pamela Kao) has recently received her PhD from the University of Bristol. Her research explores the depth and complexity of Byron's dramatic characterization with the help of Freudian psychoanalysis and investigates Byron's anticipation of some Freudian joke techniques in *Don Juan*.

Peter J. Kitson is Professor of English at the University of Dundee. He has published widely in the field of Romantic period literature. Recently he has published (with Tim Fulford and Debbie Lee) *Literature, Science and Exploration in the Romantic Period* (Cambridge, 2004) and *Romantic Literature, Race and Colonial Encounter, 1770–1830* (Palgrave USA) is forthcoming in 2007.

Ghislaine McDayter is Associate Professor in the Department of English at Bucknell University. She has written extensively on the early generation of Romantic poets, and has edited two collections on Romanticism. She is currently completing her book, *Convulsions in Rhyme: Byron and the Birth of Celebrity*.

Timothy Morton is Professor of Literature and the Environment at the University of California, Davis. He is the author of *Ecology without Nature: Rethinking Environmental Aesthetics* (Harvard, forthcoming), *The Poetics of Spice: Romantic Consumerism and the Exotic* (Cambridge, 2000), and *Shelley and the Revolution in Taste: The Body and the Natural World* (Cambridge, 1994).

David Punter is Professor of English and Research Dean of the Faculty of Arts at the University of Bristol. He has published books, articles and essays on the Gothic, romanticism, literary theory, psychoanalysis and the post-colonial, including an essay on Byron's *Don Juan*. His most recent book is *Postmodernism and Contemporary Writing* (2005), and he has three further books forthcoming: *Modernity*, *Metaphor*, and *Rapture*.

Philip Shaw is Reader in English Literature at the University of Leicester. His *Waterloo and the Romantic Imagination* was published by Palgrave in 2002 and his volume on the Sublime, for Routledge's New Critical Idiom, appeared in 2006. He is currently working on a project dealing with representations of war in Romantic and Victorian literature and art.

Michael Simpson is Lecturer in the Department of English and Comparative Literature at Goldsmiths' College, University of London. In addition to his work on Romantic drama, theatre, literature and criticism, he is currently completing a co-authored study of post-colonial drama titled *Crossroads in the Black Aegean: Oedipus, Antigone and Dramas of the African Diaspora* (Oxford, forthcoming). He has also begun a study of Romantic distraction, which he hopes to finish one day.

Jane Stabler is Reader in Romanticism at the School of English, University of St Andrews. Her books include the Longman *Byron Critical Reader* (1998) and *Byron, Poetics and History* (Cambridge, 2002). She is working on a study of the way the poetic conversations of the Byron-Shelley circle influenced the next generation of English poets in Italy.

Nanora Sweet teaches English and Women's and Gender Studies at the University of Missouri-St Louis. She co-edited *Felicia Hemans: Reimagining Poetry in the Nineteenth Century* (Palgrave, 2001) and publishes widely on Hemans's early work. Her poetry chapbook *Rotogravure* has just appeared, and her *Hemans and the Shaping of History* is in progress.

Susan J. Wolfson is Professor of English at Princeton University. She is the author of several essays on Byron and other subjects in the age of Romanticism. Her article here is adapted from a chapter in her most recent book, *Borderlines: The Shiftings of Gender in British Romanticism* (2006).

chronology

Childe Harold's Pilgrimage III; meets the Shelleys; begins *Manfred*

1817   *Manfred* published; begins *Childe Harold's Pilgrimage* IV; composes *Beppo*

1818   *Beppo* published; *Childe Harold's Pilgrimage* Canto IV published; begins *Don Juan*

1819   Begins *Prophecy of Dante; Mazeppa* published; *Don Juan* I and II published anonymously

1820   Pope-Bowles controversy (–1821); resumes work on *Hints from Horace*; writes *Marino Faliero*; involved with the Carbonari

1821   Begins *Sardanapalus* and *Cain*; *Don Juan* III–V published; writes *The Vision of Judgment*; 'Letter to John Murray Esqre' published; *Marino Faliero* and *Prophecy of Dante* published together; begins *The Two Foscari; Sardanapalus, The Two Foscari* and *Cain* published together

1822   Brief collaboration with Leigh Hunt and Shelley on *The Liberal*; *Werner* published by Murray; *The Vision of Judgment* published by John Hunt in *The Liberal* after split from John Murray

1823   *Heaven and Earth* published in *The Liberal*; *Don Juan* VI–VIII, IX–XI, XII–XIV; *The Age of Bronze* and *The Island* published by John Hunt; Byron leaves Italy for Greece

1824   *Don Juan* XV–XVI and *The Deformed Transformed* published; Byron dies 19 April

a note on the texts/list of abbreviations

All references to Byron's writings are to the following editions except where otherwise stated:

BLJ: Leslie A. Marchand, ed. *Byron's Letters and Journals*. 13 vols. London: John Murray, 1973–94.

CPW: Jerome J. McGann and Barry Weller, eds. *Lord Byron. The Complete Poetical Works*. Oxford: Clarendon Press, 1980–93.

CMP: Andrew Nicholson, ed. *Lord Byron. The Complete Miscellaneous Prose*. Oxford: Clarendon Press, 1991.

References to the *ottava rima* and Spenserian stanza poems are by canto, stanza and, where necessary, line within stanza. References to verse narratives are by volume, page and line number. References to shorter poems are by line number only. References to dramas are by act, scene and line number. References to prose writings are by volume and page number for *BLJ* and *CPW* and by page number for *CMP*.

introduction
reading byron now

jane stabler

In 1944 when the scholar Truman Guy Steffan began looking, there was no catalogue of Byron manuscripts. Steffan hunted them down piece by piece and began the process of transcription. The prevailing image of Byron in the mid-1920s was of a rapid and careless composer: Byron had not fared well in the era of New Criticism with its conspicuous quest for verbal density and multi-layered ambiguity. To those critics Byron was seen as 'a little superficial,' like his hero Don Juan (XI, 51, 1), and too direct to be properly difficult. There was nothing that New Critics and their immediate successors could do with him and their frustration was often vented in sharp dismissals of the 'inability to think' which accompanied the 'aplomb of the improviser' (Robson 1973, 145, 141). Steffan found, however, that his 'preliminary transcription of the manuscripts piled up such a vast number of cancellations and rejected readings that most of them could not be crammed into an interpretative monograph about Byron's mind and art on the composition of *Don Juan*' (Steffan 1957, I, vii).

With this discovery, the image of Byron's throw-away habits of composition might have proved unsustainable had it not been for a curious accident of publication: Steffan's full account of Byron's 'deliberate artistry' was not published until 1957, when it appeared as part of the variorum edition of *Don Juan* jointly edited with Willis W. Pratt. In the same year, Leslie A. Marchand published his magisterial and still unsurpassed three-volume *Byron: A Biography*. Public attention rapidly focused on the details of Byron's life and character rather than his manuscript revisions – especially as 1957 also saw the publication of G. Wilson Knight's *Lord Byron's Marriage*, with its exploration of reasons for the separation scandal and its treatment of the poetry as a source of biographical confession or clue: 'His poetry ... hints at what it may not say' (Knight 1957, 286).

Steffan's massive editorial endeavour might have checked the popular image of Byron as a poet who dashed off screeds of poetry in between bouts of lovemaking, horse-riding, or pistol practice but for Steffan's own punctiliousness: his measured determination not to overlook 'awareness of [*Don Juan*'s] defects' (Steffan 1957, I, ix) reaffirmed many of Byron's popular biographical characteristics. Observations such as 'it is Byron's physical and mental energy that makes him dash through these many runs of parallel amplification and comic accumulation' (294), could hardly fail to chime with the long-received image of the poet dating from, for example, Francis Jeffrey's perception of 'a perpetual stream of thick-coming fancies' and workmanship that was 'frequently abrupt and careless' (Rutherford 1970, 99, 100). Steffan endorsed Canto I as ideal for anthologies because in it Byron 'does not let commentary drift and amble in his most casual or laziest manner' (Steffan 1957, I, 186). Insisting on the autobiographical, 'volubly confessional' (284) colour of the poem, Steffan presented Byron's habits of composition as both impetuously energetic and languidly idle. His own intellectual and moral preference for what is 'solid and sustained' made him critical of what he regarded as the poem's flaws, 'when content is thin or dissipated' or when energy is 'dispersed' (295–6).

This mid-twentieth-century consolidation of Byron's 'dashing' reputation made it easy in the next decade for the Yale School Critics to continue to disregard Byron as 'the joker in the pack' and to omit him from the thorough and reverential investigation of 'High Romanticism' (William Blake, William Wordsworth, Samuel Taylor Coleridge, John Keats, Percy Bysshe Shelley) then underway. Taking full account of Steffan's scholarship, Paul West wrote of Byron in 1963: 'if we are embarrassed we must leave him alone. This is not Keats or Shelley but the aristocratic lame voyeur ... He is a serious writer ... but he is also one of those writers whom it is easy to overestimate' (West 1963, 3, 10). This condescending, faintly disappointed tone typifies the dominant critical work of the mid-twentieth century when T.S. Eliot's fascinated repugnance to Byron's physical appearance merged with critical disdain for the 'distressing bulk' of his poetic output (Eliot 1975, 261).

It took another massive editorial effort – that of Jerome J. McGann's Clarendon edition of the poems (1980–93) – to establish Byron's poetry as a field that afforded detailed and serious scholarly consideration (although, of course, the very commissioning of such an edition was a sign that fresh critical evaluation of Byron's work was already underway).

Embarked upon in 1971 and accomplished with impressive speed in not much more time than Steffan and Pratt took for the variorum *Don Juan*, McGann's seven-volume edition finally gave scholars an up-to-date standard complete poetical works that they could work from (if not actually afford to own). A selective close-up view of the details of Byron's modes of composition was also supplied in the Garland Manuscripts of the Younger Romantics facsimile series (1980–). The final volume of Marchand's edition of Byron's *Letters and Journals*, which began in 1973, came out in 1994, and the publication of Andrew Nicholson's *Complete Miscellaneous Prose* in 1991 meant that from the mid-1990s, scholars had standard editions for all of Byron's literary and epistolary output. At the same time, the New Critical assumption that works of literature transcended history and the literary marketplace was increasingly challenged by new editorial and critical theories.

As Peter Cochran discusses in Chapter 2, McGann's edition of Byron's poems was marked by his belief in the social nexus of textual production. Perhaps unexpectedly, fresh emphasis on the contextual conditioning of literature set readers free from the mesmeric figure of the poet. During the 1980s the presence of the Byronic hero in his own works was eclipsed as history, politics and economics swam into the foreground of critical attention. Daniel P. Watkins, Marilyn Butler and Jerome McGann advanced the controversial notion that Byron's Oriental Tales were figurative projections of the political situation in England, Ireland, or Napoleonic Europe. In these diligent allegorical readings, we can detect a critical desire to impart the complexity always felt to be lacking in Byron's texts by reading the intricacies of selective context back into the text.

This New Historicist critical manoeuvre inevitably makes the critic the absolute arbiter of meaning because she or he interprets not only the words on the page, but the space in the margins as well – what the text excludes as well as what it contains. McGann's Preface to volume III of the *Complete Poetical Works*, for example, alerts readers to 'the political dimensions of all Byron's poetry [...] even works which may not seem, to a superficial view, concerned with social or political issues'. McGann's historical certainty condemned as 'superficial' all readers who remained sceptical about the existence of exact political referents for *The Corsair* or *Lara*. Growing academic interest in post-colonial approaches to literature from the mid 1990s, however, means that the Oriental Tales are now seen again (as they were in the first place) as poems about Western encounters and fascination with the East. In the present collection, Peter Kitson charts the growth and subtle revisions of post-colonial views of orientalist texts since the popular inception of this form of critique with Edward Said's *Orientalism* (1978). Kitson's chapter shows Byron's Turkish Tales to be among the more complex representations of Islamic culture in the Romantic period and he agrees with critics such as Saree Makdisi (1998) who see Byron's depiction of the East as an alternative to Europe rather than as an imperial extension of it.

Less controversial than his symbolic contextual readings of Byron's Eastern Tales is McGann's more general theory about the material condition of texts. 'The point,' he said in his essay 'What is Critical Editing?', 'is that authors (and authorial intentions) do not govern those textual dimensions of a work which become most clearly present to us in bibliographic forms' (McGann 1991, 58). Byron himself would agree with this position as when he protested to his publisher about the censorship of the hero's last line, 'Old man! 'tis not so difficult to die' in the first edition of *Manfred*. Byron wrote to Murray in August 1817: 'You have destroyed the whole effect & moral of the poem by omitting the last line of Manfred's speaking—& why this was done I know not.' (*BLJ* V, 257). He would have had a good idea that Murray cut the line because its intimations of an easy non-Christian death might have offended Murray's 'customers among the orthodox', but editorial interference with the manuscript is, as we shall see, not the only factor that can affect the meaning of a poem.

Study of the evolution of Byron's texts led McGann to suggest that contextual 'bibliographic codes' played just as much of a role as linguistic literary codes in creating the meaning of a poem. To demonstrate this position, he invokes Byron's poem about the separation scandal in 1816, 'Fare Thee Well!' McGann points out that this poem existed in at least three versions: a first private printing, which was Byron's way of getting at his wife, Annabella; an unauthorized newspaper publication, which formed part of an editorial attack on Byron, and an authorized book publication in which Byron attempted to regain control over his composition. All three poems, McGann asserts, contain an identical lexical content, but the circumstances of their publication ensure that they acquire different meanings for each set of readers (McGann 1991, 59). As well as the three versions of the poem McGann mentions, there were other newspaper printings (for example Leigh Hunt's defensive one in the *Examiner* on 21 April 1816, the date the Deed of Separation was signed), and a host of epistolary and poetic responses. Lockhart has the controversy recently in mind when he describes Byron's boarding school fans: 'Perhaps her *Ladyship* was in the wrong after all.—I am sure if I had married such a man, I would have borne with all his little eccentricities'

(Rutherford 1970, 183). Ghislaine McDayter deals with this phenomenon in more detail in Chapter 6 and Caroline Franklin examines some of the literary responses to 'Fare Thee Well!' in Chapter 4.

Attention to 'print culture' – the play of bibliographic codes, the circulation of different editions, piracies and reviews of all these versions of the text – has greatly enriched Romantic scholarship in the last decade. Battles over copyright and unauthorized stage production were a few of the entanglements Byron and his publishers experienced before 1824. After Byron's death, poems to him, continuations of his unfinished poems and reconfigurations of him in the pages of nineteenth-century novels added to the fantastic growth of 'Byromania' that had begun while he was alive. These range from the adulatory (for example, Byron's appearance as Lord Raymond in Mary Shelley's *The Last Man*) and the slighting (as when a duodecimo volume of Byron falls out of Esther's work-basket in *Felix Holt, the Radical*, much to the disapproval of the hero). We have more reception material about Byron than any other Romantic poet, but as William St Clair has recently warned:

> When records are plentiful, it is easy to slip into the belief that they are a reliable record of actual acts of reception. It is easy to forget that, however many of such reports are found and collected, they can never be, at best, anything beyond a tiny, randomly surviving, and perhaps highly unrepresentative, sample of the far larger total acts of reception which were never even turned into words in the mind of the reader let alone recorded in writing. (St Clair 2004, 5)

Nevertheless, studies of Byron's reception have burgeoned in the years since Jon P. Klancher's *The Making of English Reading Audiences, 1790–1832*, which showed how readers internalized the opinions of the reviewers, and Lee Erikson's *The Economy of Literary Form: English Literature and the Industrialization of Publishing, 1800–1850*, which pointed out that the popularity of poetry as a commodity during the Napoleonic Wars was bound up with the scarcity and expense of paper.

Compared with the transcendental interests of critics like M.H. Abrams, Harold Bloom and Robert Gleckner, study of Romantic poetry now seems increasingly dominated by the realm of the material. The academy is seriously interested in bread and circuses: food studies and the recovery of the popular stage in late eighteenth and early nineteenth-century England and America and are two of the most colourful new developments in Romantic studies in recent years. Food studies in Romanticism may be said to have started with Timothy Morton's work in *Shelley and the*

Revolution in Taste: The Body and the Natural World (1995), followed by *The Poetics of Spice: Romantic Consumerism and the Exotic* (2000). Following the physiological connotations of 'taste' which were opened by Morton (1995), Denise Gigante's study, *Taste: A Literary History* (2005), reconsiders cannibalism in the shipwreck scene of *Don Juan* and links this with the confluence of appetite and taste in the Byronic vampire figure. In Gigante's multi-layered reading, consumption of human flesh intimates a libidinal bond between men and the dynamics of consumer capitalism. Morton's chapter in the present collection contains a tangential discussion of images of digestion in *Manfred* as part of a wider critique of contemporary ecological thought. Like Nanora Sweet's investigation in Chapter 11 of the language of 'peopled' space in *Childe Harold's Pilgrimage* Canto IV, Morton detects an impulse towards sociality in *Manfred* which he reads as an instance of hard-won environmental consciousness, at odds with Manfred's familiar reputation for misanthropy.

Contemporary critical interest in popular culture and the construction of the celebrity means that instead of being something of an embarrassment (as it was for Paul West), Byron's biography and all its intersections with dining clubs, feminine epistles, actresses, pugilists, animals, and trinkets – from illustrated anthologies to tea services – partake of cultural significance and are capable of being read. Jerome Christensen provides a dense critique of Byron as commodity in *Lord Byron's Strength: Romantic Writing and Commercial Society* (1993) and James Soderholm's *Fantasy, Forgery, and the Byron Legend* (1996), builds on this by revising the usual biographical marginalization of the contributions of women who helped to write Byron's life and fame. In his recovery of the work of Elizabeth Pigot, Caroline Lamb, Annabella Milbanke, Teresa Guiccioli and Lady Blessington, Soderholm presents Byron's market value as the result of a successful collaboration between multiple feminine backers and co-producers.

Frances Wilson's study *Byromania: Portraits of the Artist in Nineteenth- and Twentieth-Century Culture* (1999) gathers diverse strands of the growing popular reception field, embracing the representations of Byron in the novels of Caroline Lamb, Benjamin Disraeli and Dame Barbara Cartland, plays such as Tom Stoppard's *Arcadia,* and films like Ken Russell's *Gothic.* A chapter on 'Byron and his Portraits' by Christine Kenyon Jones explores the visual impact of Byronism, heralding new interdisciplinary interest in Byron in art history. Annette Peach's *Portraits of Byron* (2000) provides the equivalent of a standard edition of visual images of the poet and the richness of this field of enquiry is evident in John Clubbe's *Byron, Sully and the Power of Portraiture* (2005) which devotes over three hundred pages to Thomas Sully's 1826–28 copy of Richard Westall's 1813 portrait. While much of the reception history to date has been on published responses to Byron, scholars will soon be able to devote serious attention to the manuscript collection of fan mail sent to Byron and stored in the archive of his publisher, John Murray (about to be placed on open access in the National Library of Scotland).

The reverberations of what Thomas Babington Macaulay described as 'the British public in one of its periodical fits of morality' continue to sound to the present (Rutherford 1970, 298). Six years after the publication of Marchand's *Life* and the Steffan and Pratt Variorum edition, Paul West remarked wearily that, 'biographers are still skirmishing, to the neglect of his poems' (West 1963, 14). Continuing fascination with Byron's sexuality is evident in three recent biographies by Phyllis Grosskurth, *Byron: The Flawed Angel* (1997), Benita Eisler, *Byron: Child of Passion, Full of Fame* (1999), and Fiona McCarthy, *Byron: Life and Legend* (2002). The titles of the first two give some indication of the authors' determined efforts to rake over the ashes of the separation scandal. More attuned to the matrix of life and writing, Caroline Franklin's *Byron. A Literary Life* (2000) is a formidable scholarly act of compression; Drummond Bone's volume on Byron in the *Writers and Their Work* series (2000) is an even more distilled treatment of the major works in the context of the life.

The interdisciplinary nature of the modern literary academy has brought about rewarding fusions of literature with geography and history as in Diego Saglia's *Byron and Spain* (1996) and Stephen Cheeke's *Byron and Place: History, Translation, Nostalgia* (2003). Intertextual analysis has richly complicated the conversations between Byron, his contemporaries, and the literary tradition. Thanks to William Brewer, Paul Douglass, Jonathan Gross, Susan Oliver, Ralph Pite, James Soderholm, Jeffrey Vail, Joanna Wilkes and Susan Wolfson, we now understand much more about the literary relationships between Byron and Percy Shelley, Caroline Lamb, Lady Melbourne, Walter Scott, Dante, Thomas Moore, Madame de Staël and Felicia Hemans. In this collection, both Caroline Franklin and Nanora Sweet consider Byron's annotations to Madame de Staël's *Corinne*: Caroline Franklin sees Byron's libertine parody of female sensibility while Nanora Sweet traces a more complex pattern of allusion to and dialogue with *Corinne's* triumphal mode.

Byron's cultural presence in a changing Europe has been thoroughly documented and reassessed in Richard Cardwell's compendium on *The Reception of Byron in Europe* (2004). This study points out that Byron's widespread influence in nineteenth-century Europe was founded mainly on a French prose translation of his works that 'removed much of the saucy wit and ... left out the aesthetic and rhythmical effects of the verses' (Cardwell 2004, I, 4). The European dimension of Byron's reputation has received attention from the new interest in international relations and conflict studies evident in Philip Shaw's *Waterloo and the Romantic Imagination* (2002), and his edited collection, *Romantic Wars: Studies in Culture and Conflict, 1793–1822* (2000). In the latter volume, Simon Bainbridge meditates on the extraordinary fecundity of Byron's imagining of sieges from *The Siege of Corinth* to the Siege of Ismail cantos in *Don Juan* and the siege and sacking of Rome in *The Deformed Transformed*.

An intriguing side effect of Bainbridge's book-length study, *British Poetry and the Revolutionary and Napoleonic Wars: Visions of Conflict* (2004), is to reveal the extent to which Byron's imagining of the suffering individual as opposed to the collective, patriotic experience of war, might allow his work to fall within the category of 'feminine romanticism'. In her seminal essay on 'The Gush of the Feminine', Isobel Armstrong marks out attention to the Peninsula War as a predominantly female concern: 'The war in Spain (1808–12) ... preoccupied women in a way it did not engage their male contemporaries' (Armstrong 1995, 17). Renewed attention to the early cantos of *Childe Harold's Pilgrimage* by Simon Bainbridge, Richard Cronin, Philip Shaw and Diego Saglia, however, throws this assumption into question. Philip Shaw devotes close scrutiny to Byron's intertwining motifs of love and death in the Peninsula War in Chapter 10 of this volume and his commentary on Byron's account of 'Paynim turban and the Christian crest' 'Mix'd' alike (I, 34, 9) in *Childe Harold's Pilgrimage* Canto I offers a suggestive link with Kitson's reading of the apocalyptic ending *The Siege of Corinth* where Christian and Muslim soldiers perish in the final explosion together and the sardonically detached narrator watches the mingled ashes 'shower like rain' (*CPW* III, 354; l. 991).

In 1994 Claude Rawson's study, *Satire and Sentiment 1660–1830: Stress Points in the English Augustan Tradition*, identified war as a problem for Augustan poetics because the 'hallowed forms of epic' needed to be protected from contemporary 'military squalor' (Rawson 1994, 123). According to Rawson, mock-heroic became the inevitable recourse of the satirist and Byron in particular 'bruises Homeric dignity' (123) in his production of an alternative or 'debased' form of Augustanism (99). Byron's relationship with classical literature clearly stands in need of reassessment and Frederic Bogel, Gary Dyer, Steven Jones and Christopher Yu have provided valuable studies which place Byron in the long, intricate tradition of neo-classical British satire, especially Horatian satire. In *The Difference Satire Makes: Rhetoric and Reading from Jonson to Byron* (2001), Bogel sees indeterminacy in the poet's relationship with Horace and a number of 'blending strategies' and 'interpenetrative structures' in *Beppo* that all reaffirm Anne Mellor's 1980 Schlegelian definition of Romantic Irony as a process of 'permanent parabasis' (Bogel 2001, 196, 202, 208).

On the other hand, Christopher Yu's study *Nothing to Admire: The Politics of Poetic Satire from Dryden to Merill* (2003), identifies a much more stable political voice in Byron's Horatian satire. Yu's Byron offers 'a reinvention of Augustan skepticism toward social convention' (Yu 2003, 86). This Byron is not at the mercy of print culture or pandering to the market, but mounting a stern, defiantly anachronistic attack on the 'historical apathy and myopia that constitute the modern conditions of knowledge' (88). In Yu's reading, the playfulness of satire generates a cultural force for effective liberal opposition rather than the empty Whig rhetoric which Malcolm Kelsall's influential 1987 reading discovers as the basis for Byron's politics, or the discreditable libertine passivity that James Chandler finds in *England in 1819* (1998).

The revival of interest in reading genre more closely is connected with a more general renaissance of interest in form. The groundbreaking works in this area since the arrival of McGann's standard edition are by Susan Wolfson, Richard Cronin and Michael O' Neill. O' Neill's interest in the consciousness of Romantic poems is based in exemplary local encounters with individual poems and a line-by-line wrestling with meaning to produce fine critical distillations of the poet's thought. His work on Byron in *Romanticism and the Self-Conscious Poem* (1997) crystallizes the difference between reading Byron and reading 'Byron' into his own works:

> To read Byron biographically is to over-simplify; what does need to be recognized is that the poem [*Childe Harold* Canto III] depends for its effect on our knowing that Byron knows that we know that he is writing his canto in the aftermath of the separation scandal; creativity may result in the escape from self into text, but the text frequently persuades us we are in touch with the self that wishes to die to itself and end up as text. (O'Neill 1997, 115)

Wolfson and Cronin are both more interested in the historical dynamics of form: Cronin's chapter on Byron in *The Politics of Romantic Poetry: In Search of the Pure Commonwealth* (2000) looks at all the factors which make *Childe Harold* Cantos I and II a Whig poem of bewilderment and incoherence. Wolfson's chapter on Byron in *Formal Charges: The Shaping of Poetry in British Romanticism* (1997) anticipates Cronin's revision of heroism in a reading of the couplet form of *The Corsair*. She challenges McGann's view of Byron as a Romantic poet inextricably caught in an illusory belief in the imagination, suggesting instead that Byron 'uses the aesthetic materials of poetic form not to forge an un- or pre-critical illusion, but to produce [a] "self-conscious and critical" level of understanding' (Wolfson 1997, 135). Her chapter ends with an ingenious discussion of the tension between the masculine rhymes of neo-classical decorum and the 'scandal' and 'perplexity' of Gulnare's power over Conrad (160). Enfolding the disciplines of formal and gendered readings, Wolfson's chapter encapsulates the richness of the two critical areas at the forefront of the exponential increase in Byron studies over the last decade.

Of all the canonical Romantic poets, Byron benefits most obviously from the burgeoning field of gender and sexuality studies. Following Andrew Elfenbein's suggestive literary exploration of Byron's poetry as works of coded homosexual significance for poets and novelists in the late nineteenth century, Eric Clarke and Abigail Keegan have produced dedicated studies of the markers of homosexuality in Byron's writing. Charles Donelan engages in a different aspect of Byron's opposition to the early nineteenth-century suppression of vice. Building on Moyra Haslett's work in *Byron's Don Juan and the Don Juan Legend* (1997), he begins with the outrage prompted by the invocation of Don Juan as a hero. Following Clarke and Franklin, Donelan uses the work of Michel Foucault to place *Don Juan* in a culture of increasingly repressive and segregated gender relations. His book identifies 'fantasy' as one aspect of Byron's textual 'play' and argues that the poem 'does not defend promiscuity or sexual licence', but that it 'does defend the liberty of such licence for the daydreaming imagination, and allies this liberty to literature's capacity to reflect on a judge daydreams' (Donelan 2000, 176). By placing a hero from fantasy into a 'carefully delineated historical context' (176), Donelan suggests that Byron prepares for his own intervention in the Greek War. As with Yu's work mentioned above and Curtis's chapter in the present collection, the politically compromised Byron who emerges from the new historicism of the 1980s, caught in McGann's 'Romantic Ideology', has here been replaced with a writer whose deconstruction of fixed identity offers something of a model for contemporary culture.

Gender is at the forefront of several of the chapters in the present collection: Steven Bruhm examines the way that Juan's dancing is gendered in Chapter 1 and suggests that Byron's use of the male dancer in his poems offers resistance to conventional norms of masculinity and sexuality. In Chapter 12 Susan Wolfson gives full consideration to the instability of gender in *Don Juan* and interrogates the sexual, political nuances of the poem's spectrum of gender play, masquerade and travesty. The testing question of the extent to which Byron's texts subvert or reinforce orthodox codes of gender and sexuality also receives attention in Caroline Franklin's 'Byron and History' in Chapter 4 in which she revisits her important research on the literature that informed Regency sexual mores in *Byron's Heroines* (1992), and extends her discussion of the politics of libertinism. In Chapter 8 David Punter and Pamela Kao deploy a systematic Freudian reading to re-approach Byron's 1822 play, *Werner*, allowing the reader to reassess Byron's textual anxiety about father-son relationships: this essay works fruitfully in conjunction with the Freudian analysis Philip Shaw uses as a starting point in Chapter 10.

Critical interest in the performative elements of gender inevitably rediscovers the complexity of Byron's self-projection (which was frequently noticed by his contemporaries), creating an intriguing link with the world of the theatre. Byron's ability to perform to various audiences receives detailed attention in Paul Elledge's study of the oratorical tradition of Harrow School, *Lord Byron at Harrow School: Speaking Out, Talking Back, Acting Up, Bowing Out* (2000), and he traces the ways in which this inflected Byron's self-presentation in the House of Lords and upon the international stage. Re-examining the theatre of war, Simon Bainbridge focuses on the dramatic element of Byron's identification with a Promethean Napoleon in *Napoleon and English Romanticism* (1995). On a different performative front, Deborah Forbes's study *Sincerity's Shadow: Self-Consciousness in British Romantic and Mid-Twentieth-Century American Poetry* (2004) looks afresh at the way in which sincerity is 'staged' in Romantic and post-Romantic poetry, linking Byron and Anne Sexton as 'charismatic' writers whose poetic personalities are generated in a 'provocative relationship with an audience' (Forbes 2004, 121).

Theatre studies has been one of the liveliest arenas for the recovery of forgotten Romantic period writers: Byron shadows much of this scholarship because of his collaborative management work behind the scenes in Drury Lane and his unwitting contribution to the spectacles that were offered to the theatre-going public. Michael Simpson's book, *Closet Performances: Political Exhibition and Prohibition in the Dramas of Byron and Shelley* (1998) reconsiders Byron's mode of closet drama in *Manfred, Marino Faliero, Sardanapalus, Cain, The Two Foscari* and *Heaven and Earth*. These plays, he argues, constitute a meta-theatrical debate about political censorship and the power of the plebeian audience. In this collection Michael Simpson pays attention to Byron's hitherto neglected theatrical 'Addresses' in Chapter 9, suggesting that they confront questions about the political identity of the Drury Lane Theatre while holding at bay an anxiety about theatre land's replication of slick commodity art for potentially riotous audiences.

Simpson's invocation of Elaine Hadley's work on melodrama allows us to connect his investigation of the theatrical address with Peter Kitson's post-colonial reading of Byron's verse narratives: in both essays, Byron appears to be producing a critique of imperialism by bringing empire home. Simpson's suggestive redefinition of Byron's historical plays as early post-colonial tragedy reveals the changed perspectives brought by new critical currents after Richard Lansdown (1992) rehabilitated Byron's historical dramas as genuine political interventions.

Approaching performativity from a different angle, Steven Bruhm and Paul Curtis assess the nature of Byron's performance for the reader (Chapters 1 and 3). Both these chapters begin with the often overlooked Preface to *Don Juan* in order to re-examine the significance of the dance that Byron describes: for Bruhm, dance is one of the ways in which Byron can approach the awkward physicality of the male body; for Curtis, dance figures the lexical play of digression where what is peripheral 'pulls us in' (63). Scholarly examination of the ways in which we as critics and readers demarcate what is peripheral and/or obscene in Byron studies is evident, too, in Ghislaine McDayter's examination of nineteenth- and twentieth-century Byron voyeurism in Chapter 6.

There is no room in this necessarily brief introductory survey to include the many brilliant articles that have appeared on Byron in the last decade or so – fortunately, many of them are taken up and discussed in the chapters that follow. The eclecticism and range of recent work on Byron is a sign that his influence is increasingly measured by authors and subjects outside the canonical Romantic and traditionally literary fields of investigation. The vitality of a revisionary 'pull of the peripheral' is evident throughout this volume, combined with judicious reconsiderations of the topics that have always preoccupied Byronists. From this readers will realize that Byron's advance is, at the same time, completely assured and wholly unpredictable.

works cited and suggestions for further reading

Armstrong, Isobel. 'The Gush of the Feminine'. *Romantic Women Writers: Voices and Countervoices*. Eds Paula R. Feldman and Theresa M. Kelley. Hanover and London: University Press of New England, 1995.

Bainbridge, Simon. *Napoleon and English Romanticism*. Cambridge: Cambridge University Press, 1995.

——. '"Of war and taking towns": Byron's siege poems'. *Romantic Wars: Studies in Culture and Conflict, 1793–1822*. Ed. Philip Shaw. Aldershot: Ashgate, 2000. 161–84.

——. *British Poetry and the Revolutinary and Napoleonic Wars: Visions of Conflict*. Oxford: Oxford University Press, 2004.

Bogel, Frederic. *The Difference Satire Makes: Rhetoric and Reading from Jonson to Byron*. Ithaca, NY: Cornell University Press, 2001.

Bone, Drummond. *Byron. Writers and Their Work*. Tavistock: Northcote House, 2000.

——. ed. *The Cambridge Companion to Byron*. Cambridge: Cambridge University Press, 2004.

Brewer, William D. *The Shelley-Byron Conversation*. Gainesville: University Press of Florida, 1994.

Butler, Marilyn. 'The Orientalism of Byron's *Giaour'*. *Byron and the Limits of Fiction*. Eds Bernard Beatty and Vincent Newey. Liverpool: Liverpool University Press, 1988. 78–96.

——. 'Byron and the Empire in the East', *Byron: Augustan and Romantic*. Ed. Andrew Rutherford. Basingstoke: Macmillan, 1990. 63–81.

——. 'John Bull's Other Kingdom: Byron's Intellectual Comedy', *Studies in Romanticism* 31:3 (1992): 281–94.

Cardwell, Richard, ed. *The Reception of Byron in Europe*. 2 vols. London: Thoemmes Continuum, 2004.

Chandler, James. *England in 1819: The Politics of Literary Culture and the Case of Romantic Historicism*. Chicago and London: University of Chicago Press, 1998.

Cheeke, Stephen. *Byron and Place: History, Translation, Nostalgia*. Basingstoke: Palgrave Macmillan, 2003.

Christensen, Jerome. *Lord Byron's Strength: Romantic Writing and Commercial Society*. Baltimore, MD: Johns Hopkins University Press, 1993.

Clarke, Eric O. *Virtuous Vice: Homoeroticism and the Public Sphere*. Durham, NC: Duke University Press, 2000.

Clubbe, John. *Byron, Sully and the Power of Portraiture*: The Nineteenth Century Series. Aldershot: Ashgate, 2005.

Cronin, Richard. *The Politics of Romantic Poetry: In Search of the Pure Commonwealth*. Basingstoke: Macmillan, 2000.

Donelan, Charles. *Romanticism and Male Fantasy in Byron's Don Juan: A Marketable Vice*. Basingstoke: Macmillan, 2000.

Douglass, Paul. *Lady Caroline Lamb: A Biography*. Basingstoke: Palgrave Macmillan, 2004.

——. *The Whole Disgraceful Truth: Selected Letters of Lady Caroline Lamb*. Basingstoke: Palgrave Macmillan, 2006.

Dyer, Gary. *British Satire and the Politics of Style, 1789–1832*. Cambridge: Cambridge University Press, 1997.

Eisler, Benita. *Byron: Child of Passion, Fool of Fame*. New York: Knopf, 1999.

Elfenbein, Andrew. *Byron and the Victorians*. Cambridge: Cambridge University Press, 1995.

Eliot, T.S. 'Byron'. *English Romantic Poets: Modern Essays in Criticism*. Ed. M.H. Abrams. 2nd edn. London: Oxford University Press, 1975.

Elledge, Paul. *Lord Byron at Harrow School: Speaking Out, Talking Back, Acting Up, Bowing Out*. Baltimore, MD: Johns Hopkins University Press, 2000.

Erikson, Lee. *The Economy of Literary Form: English Literature and the Industrialization of Publishing, 1800–1850*. Baltimore, MD: Johns Hopkins University Press, 1996.

Forbes, Deborah. *Sincerity's Shadow: Self-Consciousness in British Romantic and Mid-Twentieth-Century American Poetry*. Cambridge, Mass.: Harvard University Press, 2004.

Franklin, Caroline. *Byron's Heroines*. Oxford: Oxford University Press, 1992.

——. *Byron: A Literary Life*. Basingstoke: Macmillan, 2000.

Haslett, Moyra. *Byron's Don Juan and the Don Juan Legend*. Oxford: Clarendon Press, 1997.

Gigante, Denise. *Taste: A Literary History*. New Haven and London: Yale University Press, 2005.

Grosskurth, Phyllis. *Byron: The Flawed Angel*. Toronto: Macfarlane, Walter and Ross, 1997.

Jones, Steven E. *Satire and Romanticism*. New York: St Martin's Press, 2000.

Keegan, Abigail F. *Byron's Othered Self and Voice: Contextualizing the Homographic Signature*. New York: Peter Lang, 2003.

Kelsall, Malcolm. *Byron's Politics*. Brighton: Harvester, 1987.

Kenyon Jones, Christine. 'Fantasy and Transfiguration: Byron and His Portraits'. *Byromania: Portraits of the Artist in Nineteenth- and Twentieth-Century Culture*. Ed. Frances Wilson. Basingstoke: Macmillan, 1999.

Klancher, Jon P. *The Making of English Reading Audiences, 1790–1832*. Madison, WI: University of Wisconsin Press, 1987.

Knight, G. Wilson. *Lord Byron's Marriage: The Evidence of Asterisks*. London: Routledge & Kegan Paul, 1957.

Lansdown, Richard. *Byron's Historical Dramas*. Oxford: Clarendon Press, 1992.

Levine, Alice and Robert Keane. Eds. *Rereading Byron: Essays Selected from Hofstra University's Byron Bicentennial Conference*. New York: Garland, 1993.

MacCarthy, Fiona. *Byron: Life and Legend*. London: John Murray, 2002.

Makdisi, Saree. *Romantic Imperialism: Universal Empire and the Culture of Modernity*. Cambridge: Cambridge University Press, 1998.

Marchand, Leslie A. *Byron: A Biography*. 3 vols. New York: Knopf, 1957.

McGann, Jerome J. *The Textual Condition*. Princeton, NJ: Princeton University Press, 1991.

Morton, Timothy. *Shelley and the Revolution in Taste: The Body and the Natural World*. Cambridge: Cambridge University Press, 1995.

——. *The Poetics of Spice: Romantic Consumerism and the Exotic*. Cambridge: Cambridge University Press, 2000.

Newlyn, Lucy. *Reading, Writing, and Romanticism: The Anxiety of Reception*. Oxford: Oxford University Press, 2000.

Oliver, Susan. *Scott, Byron and the Poetics of Cultural Encounter*. Basingstoke: Palgrave Macmillan, 2005.

O'Neill, Michael. *Romanticism and the Self-Conscious Poem*. Oxford: Clarendon Press, 1997.

Oueijan, Naji B. *A Compendium of Eastern Elements in Byron's Oriental Tales*. New York: Peter Lang, 1999.

Peach, Annette. *Portraits of Byron*. The Walpole Society. Vol. 62, 2000.

Pite, Ralph. *The Circle of Our Vision: Dante's Presence in English Romantic Poetry*. Oxford: Oxford University Press, 1994.

Rawes, Alan. *Byron's Poetic Experimentation: Childe Harold, the Tales, and the Quest for Comedy*. Aldershot: Ashgate, 2000.

Rawson, Claude. *Satire and Sentiment 1660–1830: Stress Points in the English Augustan Tradition*. Cambridge: Cambridge University Press, 1994.

Robson, W.W. *'Don Juan* as a Triumph of Personality'. *Byron, Childe Harold's Pilgrimage and Don Juan: A Selection of Critical Essays*. Ed. John Jump. London: Macmillan, 1973.

Rutherford, Andrew, ed. *Byron: The Critical Heritage*. London: Routledge & Kegan Paul, 1970.

Saglia, Diego. *Byron and Spain: Itinerary in the Writing of Place*. Lewiston, NY: Mellen, 1996.

Said, Edward. *Orientalism* (1978). New York: Vintage, 1979.

Sharafuddin, Mohammed. *Islam and Romantic Orientalism: Literary Encounters with the Orient*. London: Tauris, 1994.

Shaw, Philip, ed. *Romantic Wars: Studies in Culture and Conflict, 1793–1822*. Aldershot: Ashgate, 2000.

——. *Waterloo and the Romantic Imagination*. Houndmills, Basingstoke: Palgrave Macmillan, 2002.

Simpson, Michael. *Closet Performances: Political Exhibition and Prohibition in the Dramas of Byron and Shelley*. Stanford, CA: Stanford University Press, 1988.

Soderholm, James. *Fantasy, Forgery, and the Byron Legend*. Lexington: University Press of Kentucky, 1996.

St Clair, William. *The Reading Nation in the Romantic Period*. Cambridge: Cambridge University Press, 2004.

Steffan, T.G., E. Steffan and W.W. Pratt, eds. *Byron's Don Juan, A Variorum Edition*. 4 vols. Texas: University of Texas Press, 1957.

Sweet, Nanora and Julie Melnyk, eds. *Felicia Hemans: Reimagining Poetry in the Nineteenth Century*. Basingstoke: Palgrave, 2001.

Vail, Jeffrey. *The Literary Relationship of Lord Byron and Thomas Moore*. Baltimore, MD: Johns Hopkins University Press, 2001.

Watkins, Daniel P. *Social Relations in Byron's Eastern Tales*. London: Associated University Presses, 1987.

West, Paul, ed. *Byron. A Collection of Critical Essays*. Englewood Cliff, NJ: Prentice Hall, 1963.

Wilkes, Joanne. *Lord Byron and Madame de Staël: Born for Opposition*. Aldershot: Ashgate, 1999.

Wilson, Frances. *Byromania: Portraits of the Artist in Nineteenth- and Twentieth-Century Culture*. Basingstoke: Macmillan, 1999.

Wolfson, Susan J. *Formal Charges: The Shaping of Poetry in British Romanticism*. Stanford, CA: Stanford University Press, 1997.

——. 'Hemans and the Romance of Byron'. *Felicia Hemans: Reimagining Poetry in the Nineteenth Century*. Eds Nanora Sweet and Julie Melnyk. Basingstoke: Palgrave, 2001. 155–80.

Yu, Christopher. *Nothing to Admire: The Politics of Poetic Satire from Dryden to Merrill*. Oxford: Oxford University Press, 2003.

1

byron and the choreography of queer desire

steven bruhm

In the Preface to Cantos I and II of *Don Juan*, Byron invents a complex and parodic narrative structure through which he asks his readers to visualize the story he is about to tell. The Preface opens with a slap at Wordsworth's 'unintelligible' note to his equally unintelligible poem 'The Thorn', where Wordsworth suggests that his poem's narrator is '"the captain of a merchantman or small trading vessel"'. Byron then one-ups his rival: he requests of his own reader a 'like exertion of imagination' to suppose that *Don Juan* will be narrated by a 'Spanish gentleman in a village in the Sierra Morena' or, if we prefer, an English gentleman who has spent time in Spain and thus knows the language well. From here, Byron complicates the scene of storytelling with precise detail:

> at some distance a groupe of black-eyed peasantry are dancing to the sound of the flute of a Portuguese servant belonging to two foreign travellers who have an hour ago dismounted from their horses to spend the night on their way to the capital of Andalusia;—of these, one is attending to the story and the other, having sauntered further, is watching the beautiful movements of a tall peasant girl whose whole soul is in her eyes and her heart in the dance, of which she is the magnet to ten thousand feelings that vibrate with her own. (*CPW* V, 83)

Nor is this foreign traveller the only observer of the dance: two French prisoners vie with each other to catch sight of her, one of whom, the speaker of the Preface tells us, becomes part of that 'magnet to ten thousand feelings'. Despite the wounds he sustained in battle, 'his eyes sparkle in unison and his fingers beat time against the bars of his prison to the sound of the Fandango, which is fleeting before him' (83).

16

Oddities abound here. First, the Preface suggests that the entire epic narrative of *Don Juan* can best be understood as a structured opposition between storytelling and dance, as if dance, the particular art form named and minutely imagined by the speaker, were somehow the type of expression most counter to or separated from narrative. The foreign travellers divide themselves: one listens to the story being told by the Spanish gentleman and one leaves the site of storytelling to watch the dancing girl. That separation is confirmed in the next paragraph when, the speaker tells us, 'Our friend the story-teller—at some distance with a small elderly audience—is supposed to tell his story without being much moved by the musical hilarity at the other end of the village green' (83). That the dance is all-engrossing to the more errant traveller, who seems to care not one whit for the Spanish gentleman's story, is itself replicated in the detail of the French prisoner: this unfortunate soul is able to forget 'a sabre cut [on his forehead] received in the recent skirmish' and instead lose himself in the rhythm of the fandango and in the erotic beauty of the peasant girl dancing before him. Dancing becomes a metaphor for the erotic fascinations that pervade *Don Juan*, fascinations that frequently stymie the narrator in the epic. But the precision of the detail regarding the dance—right down to the mention of the fandango, a Spanish dance form that found one of its first stage expressions in Angiolini and Gluck's 1761 ballet, *Don Juan* (Craine 2002, 173)—suggests that there might be something about dance per se that removes it from general metaphor and makes meaning in its particularity. Dance, it would seem, registers for Byron an extremely eloquent performance of erotics, yet one whose eloquence is opposed to that of epic narrative, or perhaps any verbal utterance.

The second noteworthy oddity of this Preface contradicts the first, or at least contradicts our efforts to see in the Preface a serious and significant effort to fashion a poetics within or against the art of dance. The intensely elaborate narrative/dance template by which the speaker would have us read *Don Juan* is, we must remember, a parody. The speaker sets up his opposition thus: 'The Reader who has acquiesced in Mr W. Wordsworth's supposition that his "Misery, oh Misery" [in 'The Thorn'] is related by the "Captain of a small &c.", is requested to suppose by a like exertion of Imagination that the following epic narrative is told by a Spanish gentleman...' (*CPW* V, 82). And then, 'Having supposed as much of this as the utter impossibility of such a supposition will admit, the reader is requested to extend his supposed power of supposing as far as to conceive that the Dedication [of *Don Juan*] to Mr Southey, and several stanzas of the poem itself, are interpolated by the English editor' (84). The narrative frame is undercut at every turn here, since it – both in Wordsworth and in *Don Juan* – presupposes an impossible act of imagination, one that appears ridiculous or unintelligible to a reader of Byron's sensibilities. And so, while the imagined or 'supposed' scene of the dancing girl counterposed with the storyteller is the generative node of understanding *Don Juan*, that supposed scene is satirically undermined by its metonymic relation to Wordsworth's meretricious poetry and Robert Southey's meretricious politics. Thus, my second oddity: the narrative splitting that will mark the Byronic narrator throughout *Don Juan*, the narrative splitting between erotic indulgence and narrative proficiency, is both crucial to appreciating Byron's poetic pleasures in the poem and impossible to imagine or sustain. By casting his narrator outside the erotic action of the poem, Byron both establishes a solitary, aggressively self-contained speaker and aligns that speaker with Wordsworth and Southey, the former providing the paradigm for an imagined narrator, the latter representing the separation of sexuality from poetic output, a separation that culminates in the famous 'dry Bob' remark of the 'Dedication'. The Preface has set us up for the dance but refuses to allow us to take a single step without tripping.

My purpose in this sustained rumination on the Preface to Cantos I and II of *Don Juan* is to present the major terms by which I want to consider a quality of observation and expression in Byron that I see as queer – if not genitally homosexual, then certainly inspiring a mode of observation, expression, and embodiment that will become, throughout the nineteenth and twentieth centuries, unmistakably affiliated with the homosexual.[1] I want to push into some of the later cantos of *Don Juan* as well as into Byron's earlier poem 'Waltz: An Apostrophic Hymn' the concerns that Byron sets up in the Preface – concerns regarding the intersection of dance observation, storytelling, and parody. Put more precisely, I want to consider the ways in which Byron imagines the (usually, but not exclusively) female dancer as a nodal point in an otherwise markedly male homosocial continuum, the kind of continuum that Eve Kosofsky Sedgwick has theorized in her books, *Between Men: English Literature and Male Homosocial Desire* (1985) and *Epistemology of the Closet* (1990). For as Sedgwick has pointed out, the word 'homosocial' is both a social scientific term meant to denote 'social bonds between persons of the same sex', distinguishing itself from *homosexual* relations, but which also describes a mandatorily erotic relation between men, and thus 'hypothesize[s] the potential unbrokenness of a continuum between homosocial and homosexual' (Sedgwick 1985, 1). That Byron's Preface should multiply the singular male imagined by Wordsworth into at least three (if not five) males is important, I think: Byron's males exhibit erotic engagements that range from storytelling, which is separate from the erotic world of dance, to a total captivation by the erotics of dance, whether that be by the solitary observer (Byron's foreign traveller) or the male watcher in proximity to and competing with another male (the wounded French soldier in the prison). And that such a pointed multiplication of male subjectivities should be conducted under the banner of parody suggests a complex matrix of homages and disavowals, connections and disconnections at the site of dance. If, as I have been suggesting, the Preface divides the narrator's perceptive 'I' into distanced storyteller and dance *aficionado* as a way of cordoning off sexuality from narration, it simultaneously suggests a kind of erotic plethora – both heterosexual and homosocial/sexual – in the moment of dance observation. It is this erotic plethora, I want to suggest, that constitutes Byron's thoughts on dance, the queer resonances that spill into them, and ultimately the rhetorics of impossibility and loss that attend the male subject as he sets himself the task of narrating the very erotics that dance might deploy.

In a letter of 7 May 1813, Byron wrote to Lady Melbourne that 'I have an invitation to a *city* or rather *citizen's* ball where I wish to see the young people unmuzzled—& as Hobhouse is going—who is a Cynic after my own heart—I shall be regaled with his observations—which may be safely made as we are both spectators—I *can't* dance—& he *won't' (BLJ* III, 46–7). This detail, another example of men watching dancing in Byron's *oeuvre*, suggests what has been rather a commonplace in thinking about Byron and dance, a commonplace Lady Caroline Lamb was one of the first to articulate: that Byron's lameness made him extremely impatient with and dismissive of dance as a physical activity in which he could not participate.[2] But what's more important for my purposes here is the way the Byron and Hobhouse of this passage constitute an 1813 prototype for the Victorian bachelor as Eve Sedgwick defines him. For Sedgwick, the Victorian bachelor is the domesticated urbanite's answer to the kind of male homosexual panic experienced by the Gothic hero of the previous literary era. This figure, she writes,

> personifies the most deflationary tonal contrast to the eschatological harrowings and epistemological doublings of the paranoid Gothic. Where the Gothic hero had been solipsistic, the bachelor hero is selfish. Where the Gothic hero had raged, the bachelor hero bitches. Where the Gothic hero had been suicidally inclined, the bachelor hero is a hypochondriac. The Gothic hero ranges from euphoria to

despondency; the bachelor hero, from the eupeptic to the dyspeptic.
(Sedgwick 1990, 189)

While readers of *Manfred*, *Cain*, or *The Corsair* will have no trouble aligning Byron's heroes with Sedgwick's definition of the Gothic, they will also see the speaker of *Don Juan* as something closer to the domesticated Victorian bachelor, with his petty cattiness, his hypochondriasis, his wry detachment. Wry detachment, but also *sexual* detachment. As Sedgwick writes, 'the disruptive and self-ignorant potential for violence in the Gothic hero is replaced in the bachelor hero by physical timidity and, often, by a high value on introspection and by (at least partial) self-knowledge' (190); consequently, the Victorian bachelor often presents himself as having no commerce with genital sexuality. And while such a representation hardly characterizes Byron in general, it does describe Byron at the dance. Hence his attendance *at* – but refusal to participate *in* – the citizen's ball where he and Hobhouse will indulge their cynicism about the young and unmuzzled, will regale each other with observations from a safe distance, and will not dance. Andrew Elfenbein has argued that Byron left a legacy of homosexual relations on which self-selected Victorian authors could capitalize in order to align themselves with Byron's cult (Elfenbein 1995, 207); but he also left a legacy of a less genital but more discursively bitchy queerness that we can trace throughout the Victorian period in the dance *aficionado* and opera buff (Thackeray's speaker in 'De Juventute', the bachelor heroes of *Dorian Gray* or *Trilby*), all the way up to contemporary queer (auto)biography (Michael Moon on Maria Montez, Kevin Kopelson on Nijinski, Wayne Koestenbaum on anyone in a pretty dress) – not excluding my personal favourites, Waldorf and Statler, the exquisitely mean old queens who sat in their box during *The Muppet Show* and carped at the quality of the performances. It is this quality of bitchery, of distanced men feeling eupeptic or dyspeptic before a scene of dance, that I want now to consider more closely in Byron, with an eye to discussing how the mechanics of dance intersect with a pronounced queer pleasure in commentary and observation.

In all of Byron's extended passages on the dance, he filters scenes of erotic engagement and plenitude through a distanced narrator-observer, the Sedgwickian bachelor figure whose performances at the scene are intellectual and critical rather than choreographic and embodied.[3] Nowhere is this clearer than in Canto XII of *Don Juan* where Juan and the narrator arrive at the Regency Ball and, like the two foreign travellers of the Preface, immediately split up, depending on their willingness to participate in the dance. While Juan quickly moves onto the dance floor (more on this later), the Byronic flâneur/narrator prefers to 'win a corner, / ... Where he may fix himself, like small "Jack Horner", / And let the Babel run round as it may, / And look on as a mourner, or a scorner, / Or an approver, or a mere spectator, / Yawning a little as the night grows later' (*Don Juan* XI, 69, 2–8). The image of the dance observer as 'a mourner, or a scorner' had been established earlier, in Canto III, when the piratical father Lambro returns to his island after a long absence to find his village engaged in merry-making. 'Seeing a troop of his domestics dancing / Like dervises, who turn as on a pivot, he / Perceived it was the Pyrrhic dance so martial, / To which the Levantines are very partial' (*Don Juan* III, 29, 5–8). In this spectacle of dancing, marked by a plenitude of sound, colour, and movement, he finds 'a group of Grecian girls, / ... Link'd hand in hand, and dancing' – a 'virgin throng' that 'would set ten poets raving' (III, 30, 1–8). Lambro too will rave, but not poetically. He perceives dancing bodies juxtaposed with food and drink, making of them sensual commodities to be consumed by everyone but the patriarch himself, and soon learns that this is the celebration to mark the end of mourning for him after his supposed death. While the narrator deems this Dionysian celebration of life an 'innocent diversion / For the imagination or the senses, / ... All pretty pastimes in which no offense is' (III, 35, 1–4), for Lambro, it induces anger and melancholy. It is 'A thing to human feelings the most trying, / And harder for the heart to overcome, / ... To find our hearthstone turn'd into a tomb, / And round its once warm precincts palely lying / The ashes of our hopes' (III, 51, 2–7). If dance in *Don Juan* – and in Byron's *oeuvre* generally – signals a world of eroticism and fullness of bodily pleasure, it also signals the degree to which the observer is separate from that world. While Juan is off having sex with Lambro's daughter Haidée, Lambro feels the loss of all the privileges and potencies that attend a paterfamilias. In a chain of metonymic associations, dance transmogrifies the condition of patriarchal power into one of absence and loss.

Or so it does in a conventionally 'straight' reading of Byron, with all his attendant abjections and sadnesses. But as I have been suggesting, Byron rarely reads dance – and men within dance – straight. In the earliest sustained discussion of dance in Byron's work, his 1812 'Waltz: An Apostrophic Hymn', Byron deploys the kind of satire I noted in the Preface to make distinct points about politics – both national and sexual – with the kind of queer bitchery we saw when he and Hobhouse went to the dance. Narrated by one Horace Hornem, Esq., 'a country gentleman of a midland county' (*CPW* III, 22), 'Waltz' depicts the arrival of Hornem and his family in London for the season where they attend a ball given by the Countess of Waltzaway. Here he finds a new dance recently imported from the Rhine, and while he apostrophizes on its charms, we are also told that he (like Byron) can't actually perform the dance: 'Now that I know what it [the waltz] is, I like it of all things, and so does Mrs. H; though I have broken my shins, and four times overturned Mrs. Hornem's maid in practising the preliminary steps in a morning' (23). Now overturning the maid may be part of the goal, but barking the shins is not, and so Hornem decides he will stop attempting to dance and will write about it instead: 'having a turn for rhyme, tastily displayed in some election ballads and songs, … I sate down, and with the aid of W.F. Esq. [that is, William Fitzgerald] and a few hints from Dr. B[usby]…, I composed the following Hymn' (23). That Hymn – or rather, mock-hymn – locates Byron's cutting satire within a naively obtuse and distanced observer of the dance, a storyteller who will meditate on the meanings of the waltz's semiotics in order to praise (and for Byron to condemn) its implications.

As Gary Dyer has cogently argued, this poem is founded upon a paradox that makes no sense for the seasoned reader of Byron. On the one hand, the poem is a scathing critique of the Prince Regent's love of waltzing, his ability not only to succumb to its fashion but to recreate that fashion in England, and the perfidious political opportunism such fashion-mongering affords the turncoats who courted him (Dyer 2005, 4ff). Hornem seems to be one of the Prince Regent's fans, and accordingly praises the waltz, emphasizing its *newness*: 'Blest was the time Waltz chose for her debût; / The Court, the R——t, like herself were new' (ll. 161–2). But behind this praise we can hear the more cynical Byron who recognizes that not much has changed:

> New face for friends, for foes some new rewards,
> New ornaments for black—and royal guards…
> New mistresses—no—old—and yet 'tis true,
> Though they be *old*, the *thing* is something new. (ll. 163–72)

The poem's thinly veiled scorn for the Prince of Wales and his Hanoverian allegiances perfectly accords with Byron's own Whig politics. While the ballroom scene, this 'something new', recycles old friends, old politics, and old mistresses, it also bespeaks a sense of profound *loss*: the loss of Whig ideals as the Prince Regent rewarded the 'blackguards' who had supported his father, George III; the loss of an English poetic and dramatic voice to 'Ten plays—and forty tales of Kotzebue's' imported from Germany (l. 72); the loss of Irish jigs and Scotch reels of which Byron was very fond.[4] Indeed, for all its newness, the waltz produces in the speaker a sense of Byronic melancholy similar to that of *Childe Harold* and *Don Juan*: 'Morals and minuets... /...all have had their days' (ll. 182–3).

What's strange to find in a Byron poem, though, is that these lost morals are sexual as well as political. In the address to the Publisher, Hornem indicates that he is going to the Countess's Ball 'expecting to see a country-dance, or, at most, cotillions, reels, and all the old paces to the newest tunes. But judge of my surprise, on arriving, to see poor dear Mrs. Hornem with her arms half round the loins of a huge hussar-looking gentleman I never set eyes on before, and his, to say truth, rather more than half round her waist, turning round, and round, and round...' (*CPW* III, 23). Hornem's good-natured surprise notwithstanding, the poem suggests that women get caught up in the erotic movements of the waltz until 'Her mind with these is gone, and with it go / The little left behind it to bestow' (ll. 246–7). [5] Thus, the other part of the contradiction that Gary Dyer has noted: the loss of any sense of female constancy and self-restraint. The erotically engaging waltz fosters adultery and sexual freedom, a sense of license that also falls under satirical dismissal, as if Byron were adopting a Puritan high road in his poem (Dyer 2005, 3). Indeed, the dismissal of waltzing as sexually licentious seems to align the poet with the moralizing cant of his day. In 1810, for example, a correspondent signing herself 'A Lady of Distinction' offered the following evaluation of the waltz:

> with regard to the lately-introduced German waltz, I cannot speak ... favorably. I must agree with Goethe, when writing of the national dance of this country, 'that none but husbands and wives can with any propriety be partners in the waltz'.
>
> There is something in the close approximation of persons, in the attitudes, and in the motion, which ill agrees with the delicacy of woman, should she be placed in such a situation with any other man than the most intimate connexion she can have in life. Indeed, I have often heard men of no very over-strained feeling say, 'that there are very few women in the world with whom they could bear to dance the german waltz'. (Lady 1813, 154)[6]

Such conduct advice was not at all uncommon. According to Jane Desmond, 'the waltz was regarded as too sexually dangerous for "respectable" women in North America and Europe when it was first introduced in the nineteenth century. The combination of intoxicating fast whirling and a "close" embrace was thought to be enough to make women take leave of their senses. Some advice books for women even claimed waltzing could lead to prostitution' (Desmond 1997, 32). For Dyer's reading of 'Waltz', though, it's not simply the close embracing that's key to the poem's satire, but rather the taking leave of the senses, a threat which could be seen not only in women but in men like the Prince Regent, whose sexual appetites often led him by the nose (Dyer 2005, 11). In this reading of the poem, then, waltzing becomes a scathing critique of the way mindlessness in hetero-sexed appetite can have scandalous political consequences.

While Dyer is certainly right to suggest the poem's condemnation of a *thoughtless* sexuality embodied in the waltz (we'll see this later in *Don Juan*), we can also take farther the complicated sexual engagements in the poem itself. Ultimately, we can make sense of its shifting grounds by closely reading the final stanza, where Horace turns his inability to dance, and Byron his satirical persona, to a particularly queer end. Having let the satirical mask slip enough to condemn the waltz's superficiality outright, Byron then has Horace rally:

> Voluptuous Waltz! and dare I thus blaspheme?
> Thy bard forgot thy praises were his theme.
> Terpsichore forgive!—at every ball,
> My wife *now* waltzes—and my daughters *shall*;
> *My* son (or stop—'tis needless to enquire—
> These little accidents should ne'er transpire;
> Some ages hence our genealogic tree
> Will wear as green a bough for him as me)
> Waltzing shall rear, to make our name amends,
> Grandsons for me—in heirs to all his friends. (ll. 248–57)

Not unlike Byron himself, Horace watches others dance because, as he has already disarmingly told us, he is very bad at it himself. And that both wife and daughters should be waltzing confirms for Horace and for us that he risks wearing the horns of cuckoldry that his last name implies. After all, when he arrived at the ball expecting to find innocent country dances, he instead found his wife pressed into the loins of another gentleman. Moreover, his dancing 'son' appears not to be his at all, but the product of a 'little accident' that should have never transpired. Despite his name, Horace seems more horned than horning. But in a curious way, Horace also has the power to bestow the horns of cuckoldry on others, if only by proxy. Any anxiety the poem registers regarding sexual license in the waltz is calmed by the illegitimate son's imagined sexual reproduction, the successful injection of doubly illegitimate grandsons into the lines of patrilineage belonging to the Hornems' more 'potent' male friends. And it is the sexual vigours of the waltz that will allow Horace's son to effect this injection. Thus, with the rise of the son on whom Horace's poetic and sexual hopes rest, we see Hornem cathect another man – a man who is and is not a bough of his own genealogic tree – indulging himself in the fantasies of this other man's sexual wealth and political power. The way Hornem puts it at the end of the poem, this sexual potency imagined and enacted *through another man* (his bastard son) is his personal revenge on his own fellows. This should remind us of the lynchpin of Eve Sedgwick's argument about the homosocial: men use sexual reproduction with women as a way to conduct precariously sexualized relations of camaraderie and competition with other men. 'Waltz shall rear' in two senses here: the dance 'sexually reproduces' (thus 'rearing' children) and it 'rises up in anger' or 'attacks' (to import the specifically German etymology of the word 'rearing'). Moreover, this is Sedgwick with a vengeance, since the erotic paradigm in 'Waltz' involves not just two men but many, choreographed by a man through another man and on to multiple men. By exploiting the sexual explicitness of the waltz and having his son fuck women, Horace will fuck the other men who may be fucking him. Here Byron brings together the curious strands by which I opened this chapter – the homosocial-cum-queer imagination and the parodic voice woven together at the scene of dance. Horace is distinctly *outside* the waltz, yet his very position as self-denigrated outsider allows him the bitchy, satirical pleasures of engagement with men, men whose debts to the heteronormative and paternal system he can both exploit and bastardize.

In tracing the overdeterminations of gender and sexual fantasy in 'Waltz: An Apostrophic Hymn', I want to anatomize the dance *aficionado* as we see him appear in the early decades of the nineteenth century. In our contemporary critical imagination, this dance critic is a distinctly *gay* figure, an arbiter of grace and beauty, who fetishizes the female dancer because he wants to *be* that female dancer – elegant, beautiful, feminine. To the degree that it's accurate, this image of the male dance observer's transgendered identification begins in the Romantic period. Writing in the context of ballet criticism, dance scholar and theorist Felicia McCarren puts the case this way: 'The ballet public of the 1840s was constituted by a preponderantly male mixture of ... those who had entrée backstage, in the *coulisses* of the [Paris] Opéra, and those who wished they had. The competitive adoration of the dancer, tempered by misogynistic undercurrents, is apparent in tandem with a *dandyesque* homosexual identification with her' (McCarren 1998, 71). What's ultimately at stake here, McCarren says, is visual power: 'The visual experience of the dandy at the Opéra, shaped by concerns of power and pleasure, emphasized uninterrupted viewing and visual possession of the dancing image in conjunction with the homosocial atmosphere of the loges' (83). While McCarren is writing here of the Paris Opéra and the world of the ballet, much the same can be said for the world of the social dance, such as that of the waltz in the ballrooms of London. I don't want to ignore the practical differences between stage ballet and social dance, but it is worth noting that the early nineteenth century had not codified the distinction between the 'high' art of ballet and the 'lower' or less academically interesting world of the dance floor. In fact, given that nineteenth-century ballerinas were often likened to syphilitic prostitutes and that the coveted backstage of the Opéra was a place to procure a sexual patron for the evening, the perceived difference between the balletic stage and the thoroughly base music hall was really more a matter of degree than of kind. Within this highly sexualized field, then, the queer reader wants to know: how did the homosocial, dandyesque gaze of the newly emergent dance critic see the dancing *male* body? If Mrs Hormen's attitude directs her husband's gaze to 'the loins of a huge hussar-looking gentleman,' what exactly does Horace see when he looks at those loins?

The first answer to my question is: nothing. Ostensibly, if the nineteenth-century dance critic had his way, he would not have seen the male body at all. During the decades from the late eighteenth century to the 1840s, stage dance underwent a startling transformation. Whereas the ballets of the 1780s starred male performers who often performed female roles *en travesti*, the Romantic period in dance systematically banished the male from the stage – or at least reduced him from principal performer to the role of a scaffold on which to hang the prima ballerina's virtuoso performances. Here, for example, is dance critic Jules Janin writing on 24 August 1832:

> we are hardly partisans of what are called the grands danseurs. The grand danseur seems to us so sad, so heavy! ... He corresponds to nothing, he represents nothing, he is nothing. Talk to us of a pretty dancing girl, who deploys at ease the grace of her face, the elegance of her figure, who shows us all the treasures of her beauty in such a fleeting way; thank God I understand that marvellously well.... But a man, a horrible ugly man, as ugly as you and I, a vile empty rabbit, who jumps around without knowing why, a creature expressly made for carrying a musket, a sabre, and wearing a uniform! for this to

dance as a woman would do, is impossible! (Janin 1840, 3, quoted in McCarren, 85)

So too Théophile Gautier, impresario extraordinaire of the Romantic ballet and creator of one of its first and greatest works, *Giselle*: 'Really there is nothing worse than a man displaying his red neck, his great muscular arms, his legs with beefy calves, and his whole heavy virile frame shaken by jumps and pirouettes' (Gautier 1899, quoted in McCarren, 87). The point here is not whether men can dance, it's how they *look* while doing so. According to Ramsay Burt, it was not the activity of male dancing but the spectacle it created that was 'nervously dismissed' in the Romantic ballet (Burt 1995, 13). Not surprisingly, by the 1840s stage gender had changed so much that male roles in ballets were characteristically performed by women *en travesti*, the effect of the all-female cast being much more pleasing to the spectatorial eye than the lumps and bumps of the male physique. Women made better men than men.

Given this historically curious move to drive men off the stage and out of the public eye, let's return one last time to Byron's 'Waltz' to consider exactly what type of male body we are seeing there. The beefy calves and virile frame that Gautier would have removed from the public view are also, of course, the hussar-looking gentleman's loins that Horace Hornem's wife is clutching. For that matter, hussars are the poem's exhibit A of masculine clumsiness and physical inelegance: for the feminine Waltz is the 'nimble nymph ... to whom the young hussar, / The whiskered votary of Waltz and war—/ His night devotes, despite of spur and boots, / A sight unmatched since Orpheus and his brutes' (ll. 15–18). Such brutes include not only the 'clumsy cits [who] attempt to bounce, / And cockneys [who] practice what they can't pronounce' (ll. 157–8), but also the Regent himself, who offers a rather unattractive 'princely paunch' to his lady's touch (l. 195). If Horace Hornem has read his Sedgwick and wants to sexually infiltrate these men through the homosocial/homosexual prowess of his son, he's also read his Gautier and Janin, and would prefer these rather unattractive bodies not be seen at all. We don't know how the hussar dances, but we do know that he doesn't look good doing it.

Which is all well and good for dismissing clumsy cits and paunchy princes, but what if you're the seductively attractive Don Juan and your observer is the endlessly fascinated narrator of your life story? The description of Juan dancing in Canto XIV of *Don Juan* is remarkable for its differences from male dance in 'Waltz':

> Chaste were his steps, each kept within due bound,
>   And elegance was sprinkled o'er his figure;
> Like swift Camilla, he scarce skimm'd the ground
>   And rather held in than put forth his vigour;
> And then he had an ear for music's sound,
>   Which might defy a Crotchet Critic's rigour.
> Such classic *pas*—sans flaws—set off our hero,
> He glanced[7] like a personified Bolero... (*Don Juan* XIV, 39)

On the surface of it, Byron's compliments on Juan's dancing are backhanded: Juan is a good dancer because he's not British, he's foreign, and 'all foreigners excel / The serious Angles in the eloquence / Of pantomime' (XIV, 38, 1–3). Unlike the calculating British person, 'He danced without theatrical pretence, / Not like the ballet-master in the van / Of his drill'd nymphs' (38, 6–8), which is to say he danced 'With emphasis, and also with good sense' (38, 4). Moreover, Juan is presumably a good dancer because he's male. The waltz, we are told elsewhere, may be 'The only dance which teaches girls to think' (XI, 68, 3), because it forces them to keep an eye out for the possible marital connections and assignations they might make on the dance floor – not to mention the ones they should avoid. Not so Juan: he

> Must steer with care through all that glittering sea
>   Of gems and plumes, and pearls and silks, to where
> He deems it is his proper place to be;
>   Dissolving in the waltz to some soft air,
> Or proudlier prancing with mercurial skill.... (XI, 70, 3–7)

And finally, Juan is a good dancer because, unlike his author's countrymen and women, he recognizes no separation from the dance. His classic *pas*, sans flaw, sets him off (no little Byronism there!), but sets him off to *be* the dance his is dancing, a personified bolero, an ontology rather than a mere performer of choreography. Like Yeats who can't tell the dancer from the dance, the Byronic dancer (un)becomes what he performs.

And in this (un)becoming, sex and gender matter. As with the other scenes of dance I've been discussing, Juan's performance is a *chaîné* of paradoxes: he must 'steer with care' at the same time that he 'dissolves'; his natural, anti-theatrical theatricality must avoid the gendered rigidity of the ballet master and his drilled nymphs, at the same time that it embraces both mastery and effeminacy; he must be purposefully rigorous about restraining his masculinity, *holding in* rather than *putting forth* his vigour. Only in this masculine assertion of antimasculinity can he be chaste and elegant, like Virgil and Alexander Pope's Camilla or like a ballerina skimming the ground. This strangely liminal ontology is what allows him to 'dissolve' in the waltz – as it was feared women would do as the incessant spinning around made them lose their sense and self-control – or 'proudlier prance', shooting his masculinity over the top like Mick Jagger, Bette Midler, or any other self-assured drag queen. As a dancer, Juan transgresses the typical image of the male, with all his lumps and bumps, and instead choreographs a type of male performance that, while gesturing to eighteenth-century codes of elegance and breeding, self-consciously maps a new, *un*self-conscious performance of femininity. Queerly, Juan seems closer to the ballerina *en travesti* here than to any conventionally imagined 'grand danseur'. It's little wonder, then, that we should hear the narrator complain of being nonplussed, of being unable sufficiently to narrate this effect: 'The *'tout ensemble'* of [Juan's] movements wore a / Grace of the soft Ideal, seldom shown, / And ne'er to be described; for to the dolour / Of bards and prosers, words are void of colour' (XIV, 40, 5–8).

While Juan's dancing may display 'a grace … seldom shown and ne'er to be described', the narrator does a pretty good job of describing it. Indeed, it is in the description of Juan dancing – of Juan *as a male dancer* – that we leave the satiric or parodic world of dance commentary that Byron has consistently shown throughout his discussion on dance. Juan, we are told, 'had an ear for music's sound, / Which might defy a Crotchet Critic's rigour', but it's precisely the relationship between Juan and his 'crotchet critic' that is the ultimate subject of this passage. The double-speak of parody that dismissed Wordsworth and Southey in the Preface, and that undermined Horace Hornem's authority in 'Waltz', here gives way to a different kind of double-speak, one based in homage and adoration rather than dismissal. 'Crotchet' is, of course, a pun: Byron is using the word in its musical significance meaning a quarter note, thus suggesting Juan's perfection in his musical rhythm; but he's also using it in the sense of perverse and unfounded crankiness, the crotchetiness of bachelors as they carp from the wings. Juan's elegance and grace disarms the queer bitch's critique and fosters in him an admiration for this moving, dancing male body, one that deviates from the anti-danseur fashion developing in the 1820s. Or, significantly, that plays into it perfectly: the only male dancer that Théophile Gautier had any praise for, one Jules Perrot, was acceptable to the dance stage only because he was effeminate, a close approximation of the ballerinas of the day. A close approximation, but he still had that pesky bulge to give the game away. What made Perrot remarkable to Gautier is that he was effeminate *as a man*; his masculinity was crucial in determining his greatness. And the same is true of Juan: he may be adorable for holding in his masculinity and dissolving, but he's also adorable for pride and prancing. If he has the lumps and bumps of a male physique like a hussar, that's all to the good, because these lumps reveal that this is a *man* who can dance. And it's the lumps and bumps that pervade the choreographic imagination as men are being driven from the stage. After all, the waltz was scandalous ultimately because it was the first social dance to turn partners from their positions side by side to face each other, where hips and loins met, and where the observer could no longer see but could not help but image the pubic areas of each of the partners. If the dance critic/narrator of *Don Juan* can image our boy dissolving, I think we know why. When it comes to this queer critical observer, Juan puts the 'crotch' back in 'crotchet'.

Finally, this claim that words cannot describe Juan's dancing is not a simple modesty trope deployed by the narrator to satirize himself; rather, the very inability to speak or write Juan's dancing is gendered and sexualized in an important way. We may remember that the 'virgin throng' of dancers on Lambro's island in Canto III were able to 'set ten poets raving' (III, 30, 6), but Juan's 'grace' affords no such *ekphrasis*: 'words are void of colour' (XIV, 40, 8). This pronounced silence may be Byron's gesture to that perfidious word not to be uttered among Christians, the love that dare not speak its name, the continually conjured, continually erased designation of the homoerotic sodomite (see Sedgwick 1985, 94–6 and 1990, 74). It may be, but I doubt it. Byron is talking about the culturally sanctioned activity of dance, the performance that glues together the fragments of high social life. Descriptions of balls permeate *Don Juan;* they are not unspeakable in any material sense. Perhaps Byron's pronounced silence is expressing the highly recognized separation in the early nineteenth century between dancing and language, where writers on dance were increasingly feeling the impossibility of recording such a slippery, ephemeral, and corporeal art as dance.[8] This too seems unlikely. When it comes to women dancing, Byron does not hesitate to declare their representability in language. 'Ten poets rave'. There is something about the homoeros of a man dancing and a man watching that belies description while taking us beyond the (paranoid?) desire to drive men off the stage altogether.

That something can be explained by Byron's queer revision of Jules Janin and his claim that the male dancer 'corresponds to nothing, he represents nothing, he is nothing'. To correspond to nothing, to represent nothing, is to suggest metonymically and antithetically a whole range of somethings, a swath of possibilities for choreographic and corporeal erotics that cannot be conscripted in advance. The male dancer refuses to signify a conventional masculinity, a conventional sexuality, a conventional relationship between the dancing spectacle and his/her crotchet critic. (And it was this refusal and unconventionality that kept men relatively unimportant in nineteenth-century stage dance until Nijinsky ... but that's another queer story.) In performing this refusal, the male dancer produces with his critical male observer a visual field governed by the ten thousand magnetic pulls we saw in my opening quotation. In Byron's *oeuvre*, this magnetism is established by a separation between he who dances and he who writes. For in the final analysis, we must remember that Juan has never written poetry because 'His duties warlike, loving or official, / His steady application as a dancer / Had kept him from the brink of Hippocrene' (XI, 51, 5–7). His observer/critic, the Jack Horner, sits in a corner and watches the dance, claiming he is unable or unwilling to do it himself. When it comes to dancing Byron may situate himself as the dyspeptic bachelor in the box, but his captivated and shameless consumption of the male dancer has its own erotic poetics, poetics that are as articulate as dancing itself.

notes

1. Here I part from earlier work, including my own, that seeks to find and theorize same-sex genital contact in Byron's life and then read the implications of the contact in his work. See in particular Louis Crompton's *Byron and Greek Love*, Jerome Christensen's *Lord Byron's Strength* (especially chapter 3), and chapter 1 of my *Reflecting Narcissus: A Queer Aesthetic*. In '"One Half What I Should Say": Byron's Gay Narrator in *Don Juan*', Jonathan David Gross comes closer to my own interests later in this essay when I consider the erotics of the relationship between Juan and his narrator. While I'm interested in tracing a different phenomenon in Byron's discursive strategies, and while I'm uncomfortable with Gross's ahistorical use of the word 'gay', I think Gross's argument can be read nicely with mine in identifying Byron's peculiarly disruptive sexual strategies.
2. Frances Wilson, in the notes to her edition of Lamb's novel *Glenarvon*, writes that 'While the *Morning Post* called Lamb a "correct and animated waltzer", Lamb claimed that due to Byron's limp, "he had made me swear I was never to waltz"' (Lamb 1995, 369 n. 70). Wilson is quoting Elizabeth Jenkins's 1932 biography of Lamb (Jenkins 1932, 149).
3. In *Reflecting Narcissus* I consider the conflation of the homoerotic voyeur with the bitchy critic in Byron's play, *The Deformed Transformed*.
4. In 1816, when Byron was travelling through Switzerland with John Cam Hobhouse, he records a scene in a public house in Brientz: 'The whole town of Brientz were apparently gathered together in the rooms below—pretty music—& excellent Waltzing—none but peasants—the dancing much better

than in England—the English can't Waltz—never could—nor ever will. One man with his pipe in his mouth—but danced as well as the others—some other dances in pairs—and in fours—and very good' (*BLJ* V, 103).

Byron didn't hate the dance, he just hated the way the *British* – and British Society – danced. Foreigners of the lower classes, he tells us, can do it much better, because they have no self-consciousness. These foreign others dance with gusto, perceiving no separation between themselves and their movement, or between themselves and the other dancers in the democratic corps.

5. Indeed, as Gary Dyer has written of 'English Bards and Scotch Reviewers', no less than 'Satan deems waltzing too carnal even for his demons' (Dyer 2002, 6). And Byron's catalogue of pedigrees of debutants affords us another example of his bemoaning the dance as a collapse of distinction that breeds stupidity: 'Some waltz; some draw; some fathom the abyss / Of metaphysics, others are content / With music, the most moderate shine as wits, / While others have a genius turned for fits' (*Don Juan* XII, 52, 5–8).

Apart from its shots at Lady Byron and Lady Caroline Lamb, what's most notable about this catalogue is the way it is flanked by the waltz and the throwing of fits, two highly choreographed modes of women's irrational expression. It is this combination that Felicia McCarren (1998) takes up as she analyzes the conjoining of nineteenth-century dance with theories of women's madness.

6. This extreme suspicion of waltz's licentiousness was short-lived. By 1816 Thomas Wilson could observe that 'Waltzing, notwithstanding all the opposition its more extensive practice has had to encounter, is now generally considered so *chaste*, in comparison with Country Dancing, Cotillions, or any other species of Dancing, that truth looses [sic] *not a jot* of its veracity when it is affirmed, that, in most parties, where Dancing is resorted to as an amusement, Waltzing is more frequently substituted for Country Dancing, than the *latter* is for the *former*' (Wilson 1816, 154).

7. To 'glance' is to move, spring, and turn quickly or obliquely, as in a Spanish dance.

8. According to dance historian Susan Leigh Foster, 'By the late 1820s dance, although it remained joyously light, also became identified with loss. Its ephemerality impressed viewers as much as its buoyancy. This transient quality of dancing – the fact that it disappeared as rapidly as it presented itself – had never concerned late-eighteenth-century choreographers.... Now, in the wake of melodrama's functionalist distinction between speech and gesture, with a burgeoning capitalist economy through which all the arts began to circulate, and with the intensified masculinization of public space, dance took on a new role in relation to other arts. It alone lacked the capability to inscribe itself. It alone endured only in one's memory' (Foster 1996, 197).

works cited and suggestions for further reading

Bruhm, Steven. *Reflecting Narcissus: A Queer Aesthetic*. Minneapolis: University of Minnesota Press, 2000.

Burt, Ramsay. *The Male Dancer: Bodies, Spectacle, Sexuality*. New York: Routledge, 1995.

Christensen, Jerome. *Lord Byron's Strength: Romantic Writing and Commercial Society*. Baltimore, MD: Johns Hopkins University Press, 1993.

Craine, Debra and Judith Macrell. *Oxford Dictionary of Dance*. New York: Oxford University Press, 2002.

Crompton, Louis. *Byron and Greek Love: Homophobia in 19th-Century England*. London: Faber and Faber, 1985.

Desmond, Jane C. 'Embodying Difference: Issues in Dance and Cultural Studies'. *Meaning in Motion: New Cultural Studies of Dance*. Ed. Jane C. Desmond. Durham, NC: Duke University Press, 1997. 29–54.

Dyer, Gary. 'The Politics of Waltzing'. Unpublished paper, 2005.

Elfenbein, Andrew. *Byron and the Victorians*. Cambridge: Cambridge University Press, 1995.

Foster, Susan Leigh. *Choreography & Narrative: Ballet's Staging of Story and Desire*. Bloomington, IN: Indiana University Press, 1996.

Gautier, Théophile. *L'histoire De L'art Dramatique En France Depuis 25 Ans*. Leipzig: Hetzel, 1899.

Gross, Jonathan David. '"One Half What I Should Say": Byron's Gay Narrator in *Don Juan*'. *European Romantic Review* 9.3 (1998): 323–50.

Janin, Jules. *Journal des débats politiques et litteeraires*, 1840.

Jenkins, Elizabeth. *Lady Caroline Lamb*. London: Gollancz, 1932.

Koestenbaum, Wayne. *The Queen's Throat: Opera, Homosexuality, and the Mystery of Desire*. New York: Poseidon, 1993.

Kopelson, Kevin. *The Queer Afterlife of Vaslav Nijinsky*. Stanford, CA: Stanford University Press, 1997.

Lady of Distinction. 'The Mirror of the Graces'. *From the Ballroom to Hell: Grace and Folly in Nineteenth Century Dance*. Ed. Elizabeth Aldrich. Evanston, IL.: Northwestern University Press, 1813. 154.

Lamb, Lady Caroline. *Glenarvon*. London: J.M. Dent, 1995.

McCarren, Felicia. *Dance Pathologies: Performance, Poetics, Medicine*. Stanford, CA: Stanford University Press, 1998.

Moon, Michael. *A Small Boy and Others: Imitation and Initiation in American Culture from Henry James to Andy Warhol*. Durham, NC: Duke University Press, 1998.

Sedgwick, Eve Kosofsky. *Between Men: English Literature and Male Homosocial Desire*. New York: Columbia University Press, 1985.

——. *Epistemology of the Closet*. Berkeley, CA: University of California Press, 1990.

Steffan, T.G., E. Steffan and W.W. Pratt, eds. *Lord Byron: Don Juan*. New York: Penguin, 1987.

Thackeray, William Makepeace. 'De Juventute'. *Roundabout Papers and the Second Funeral of Napoleon*. New York: Harper & Brothers, 1911. 68–83.

Wilson, Thomas. 'A Description of the Correct Method of Waltzing'. *From the Ballroom to Hell: Grace and Folly in Nineteenth-Century Dance*. Ed. Elizabeth Aldrich. Evanston, IL.: Northwestern University Press, 1816. 154.

Yeats, W.B. 'Among School Children'. *The Collected Works of W.B. Yeats, Volume I: The Poems*. Ed. Richard J. Finneran. New York: Scribner, 1997. 219–21.

2
byron and the politics of editing

peter cochran

A writer as important as Byron should have had more honour done to his manuscripts by editors than has been the case. Two invaluable series – *Manuscripts of the Younger Romantics* and *Shelley and his Circle* – have put many of the manuscripts in the public domain; but the amount of attention paid to them by editors has so far been minimal. Were it not for these two series, for example, we should not be in a position so confidently to rethink the couplet to *Beppo*, stanza 5, which is, in the fair copy done by the poet himself,

> For, bating Covent Garden, I can't hit on
> A Place that's called "Piazza" in Great Britain.

This becomes, in all editions:

> For, bating Covent Garden, I can hit on
> No place that's called 'Piazza' in Great Britain.

Jerome J. McGann, in his Clarendon edition, credits Hobhouse (on no evidence: Hobhouse did not work on the *Beppo* proofs)[1] with the alterations 'which try (successfully, one must allow) to improve the sound relationships among the words'.[2] What he omits to say is that they also lessen the power of a joke, for 'to hit on' was 'to enjoy a sexual encounter at' (compare *Don Juan* IX, 77, 6). Hobhouse had, in Byron's company, enjoyed several such hits while at Venice, on, or off, piazzas: 'although your poets are shy as elephants or camels of being seen in the act of procreation yet I have not unfrequently witnessed his lordship's coupleting' he writes to Murray, on 7 December 1817.[3] He may have thought that this particular couplet came a bit too close for comfort, for

34

the Piazza Coffee House was indeed a 'meeting-place' in Covent Garden; and so, to spare the apparently continuing editorial blushes of 1818, posterity has been denied the couplet in its Byronic form ever since.

Typography is an important part of Byron's humour. Itsuyo Higashinaka first suggested a passage from *Joseph Andrews*, Book I Chapter 18, as a possible subtext for *Don Juan* Canto V stanza 139:[4]

> Her first thought was to cut off Juan's head,
>   Her second, to cut only his—acquaintance;
> Her third, to ask him where he had been bred,
>   Her fourth to rally him into repentance,
> Her fifth to call her Maids and go to bed,
>   Her Sixth to stab herself, her Seventh, to sentence
> The lash to Baba; but her grand resource
> Was to sit down again, and cry of course.—

Here is the *Joseph Andrews* passage from the third edition of 1743 (Betty the chambermaid has just thrown herself at Andrews, without success):

> Betty was in the most violent Agitation at this Disappointment. Rage and Lust pulled her Heart, as with two Strings, two different Ways; one Moment she thought of stabbing *Joseph*, the next, of taking him in her Arms, and devouring him with Kisses; but the latter Passion was far more prevalent. Then she thought of revenging his Refusal on herself; but while she was engaged on this Meditation, happily Death presented himself to her in so many Shapes of drowning, hanging, poisoning, &c. that her distracted Mind could resolve on none. In this Perturbation of Spirit, it accidentally occurred to her Memory, that her Master's bed was not made ...

The banal yet violent emotions are well conveyed by the capitals: Betty is at once as dignified as Phaedra (see *Don Juan* V, 131, 3) and as undignified as her companion in the novel, Lady Booby (see *Don Juan* V, 131, 2). It is unfortunate that, as virtually no Fielding manuscripts survive, we cannot tell how deliberate an effect this is on the author's part; in any case, no modern edition repeats the effect.

Compare Julia's speech to Alfonso at *Don Juan*, Canto I stanza 149, edited from Byron's fair copy:

> 'Did not the Italian Musico Cazzani
>   'Sing at my heart Six months at least in vain?

> 'Did not his Countryman Count Corniani,
> 'Call me the only virtuous wife in Spain?
> 'Were there not also Russians, English, many?
> 'The Count Strongstroganoff I put in pain,
> 'And Lord MountCoffeehouse, the Irish Peer,
> 'Who killed himself for love (with Wine) last year?—

Here the manuscript capitals for *Six, Countryman, Peer*, and *Wine* were all refused by the printer, and have been in all subsequent editions. The poet's intention appears to be alliterative and rhetorical rather than grammatical; but the irregularity of capitalizing adjectives and common nouns was too much for the printer in 1819.

The principle upon which mid-eighteenth-century printers operated was by no means rigid. Here, from John Smith's *Printer's Grammar* (1755) is evidence that choice was always available:

> But before we actually begin to compose, we should be informed, either by the Author, or Master, after what manner our work is to be done; whether the old way, with Capitals to Substantives, and Italic to Proper names; or after the more neat practice, all in Roman, and Capitals to Proper nouns, and emphatical words. Accordingly if the first method is to be observed, we put a Capital letter, not only to all Substantives, but also upon the following occasions; viz.
> 1. After a Full-point, that denotes the conclusion of a Sentence; but not after one that stands for a mark of Abbreviation.
> 2. To Proper names of Men and Women; which are put in Italic besides.
> 3. To names of Kingdoms, Provinces, Cities, Mountains, and Rivers; which are put in Italic besides.
> 4. To names of Arts and Sciences; as also of those that profess them.
> 5. To names of Dignity and Quality, whether Ecclesiastical, or Civil.
> 6. To names of Festivals.
> 7. To words that express the Title of the Subject.
> On the other hand; if a work is to be done in the more modern and neater way, we pay no regard to put any thing in Italic but what is underscored in our Copy; neither do we drown the beauty of Roman lower-case sorts by gracing every Substantive with a Capital; but only such as are Proper names, or are words of particular signification and emphasis.[5]

Smith's preference for 'the beauty of Roman lower-case sorts' may be guessed at; but he cunningly employs a bit of each method in his own style.

Between Smith's time and Byron's, the use of capitals underwent a drastic official change, with impatience at excessive upper-casing becoming more and more widespread. We can perhaps locate the final demise of heavy capitalization in the last quarter of the eighteenth century, by juxtaposing the two following passages. The first is from Philip Luckombe's *History and Art of Printing* (1771):

UPPER CASE SORTS. LARGE CAPITALS

Other authors ... denote their emphatical expressions, by beginning them with Capitals, whether they be of the substantive kind, or otherwise. In such case it would be kind in Gentlemen to put some distinguishing mark to their emphatical words in copy, and either underscore the word, or make some other token, which may inform the Compositor of the Author's intention; since otherwise it will be difficult for the former, in the pursuit of his business, to lay a stress upon the same word with the Author, especially if the copy is written in the common way, viz. with Capitals to substantives or without any method at all. The loss of time which the Compositor sustains by not having the emphasis of words pointed out to him, till in the Proof-sheet, is very considerable; and destroys the care the Compositor took in spacing his matter; and he seldom gets much advantage by alterations, especially in Works of small size, and large characters, where some Capitals make a great alteration, and sometimes occasion the over-running of several lines, before their driving out can be recovered.

Words or Matter, which is to be set in Capitals, should be written in Capitals in the copy, or treble underscored, in contradistinction of Small Capitals, which are double underscored; and of Italic, which is intimated by underscoring once what is to be in that character.[6]

The second is from Caleb Stower's *The Printer's Grammar* of 1808:

CAPITALS

The use of capitals has been considerably abridged of late years; and the antiquated method of using them with every substantive, and sometimes even with verbs and adverbs, is now discontinued, except in a few instances, such as Acts of Parliament. They are considered, in the present day, as necessary only to distinguish proper names of persons, places, &c. There are, however, some particular works in which authors deem it essential to mark emphatic words with a capital; in such cases, and there can be no general rule to guide the compositor, we would recommend the author always to send his copy properly prepared in this particular to the printer, or he will become liable to the charge the compositor is allowed for his loss of time in following his alterations. The method of denoting a capital, or words of capital letters in manuscript, is by underscoring it with three distinct lines.[7]

It will be seen (incidentally) that the 1771 manual treats capitals with the kind of awe one might experience when confronted by an impressive male organ and (more centrally) that the earlier printer has a more elaborate respect for the Gentlemen who are his authors – as well as an Enthusiasm for Capitals equal, we may guess, to theirs. Stower adopts a much brusquer air than does Luckombe; he speaks as a master professional dictating to amateurs, where Luckombe is a servant politely begging a little consideration from his employer ('In such case it would be kind in Gentlemen to put some distinguishing mark to their emphatical words in copy'). Printers were among the most articulate of the newly-radicalized artisans,[8] and it is interesting to see the fact reflected in the businesslike tone in which Stower naturally speaks. (For 'newly-radicalized artisan', read newly-conscious bourgeois; Luckombe does not mention any monetary loss for which the careless writer will be liable, as Stower does.) For him, the question is far less haphazardly determined than it is for Luckombe; and one cannot readily imagine Stower speaking, as Luckombe does, of the 'beauty' of capitals. It seems that Byron and Thomas Davison, Murray's printer, were divided by times which were changing, at once socially and typographically.

In his *Lectures on the English Poets* (1818), Hazlitt places the loss of capitalization in extremely interesting company, in a way which reminds us of the subtextual levelling in Stower. Of the new verse of the day, he writes:

All the common-place figures of poetry, tropes, allegories, personifica-tions, with the whole heathen mythology, were instantly discarded; a classical allusion was considered as a piece of antiquated foppery; capital letters were no more allowed in print, than letters-patent of nobility were permitted in real life; kings and queens were dethroned from their rank and station in legitimate tragedy or epic poetry, as they were decapitated elsewhere; rhyme was looked upon as a relic of the feudal system, and regular metre was abolished along with regular government.[9]

Byron's earlier works treat heathen mythology with ambivalence (except *The Curse of Minerva*, where it is too useful); but he demonstrates an allegiance to rhyme, to classical allusion, and (logically, as Hazlitt might argue) to capitals, as well:

> Oh! Nature's noblest gift—my grey goose-quill!
> Slave of my thoughts, obedient to my will,
> Torn from thy parent bird to form a pen,
> That mighty instrument of little men!   [10]
> The pen! foredoomed to aid the mental throes
> Of brains that labour, big with Verse or Prose,
>   Though Nymphs forsake, and Critics may deride
> The Lover's solace, and the Author's pride.
> What Wits! what Poets dost thou daily raise!   [15]
> How frequent is thy use, how small thy praise!

English Bards, and Scotch Reviewers (from which these are lines 7 to 16 in the fourth edition of 1810) was not printed by Thomas Davison ('that Tory of a *Printer*' in Byron's words),[10] but by T. Collins, and was not for Murray but for James Cawthorn, a less establishment-orientated publisher. It presents a picture which is to become characteristic, for the printer has created neat capitalized antitheses, where Byron is haphazard. In his printer's copy he uppercases *Quill*, not *Nature*, in line 7, *Pen* in line 9, *Verse* and *Prose* in line 12 (inking the capital over in the former) neither *Nymphs* nor *Critics* in line 13, *Lover's* but not *Author's* in line 14, and *Poets* but not *Wits* in line 15. Clearly the printer, while seeing his author's liking for capitals, felt free to interpret it in his own way.

When Byron changed publisher and printer for *Childe Harold* and the Turkish Tales, he met with still stronger professional resistance. The number of common nouns Davison seems prepared to capitalize is very small; though he will grant the dignity to abstractions as such:

> And must they fall? the young, the proud, the brave,
> To swell one bloated Chief's unwholesome reign?
> No step between submission and a grave?
> The rise of rapine and the fall of Spain?
> And doth the Power that man adores ordain
> Their doom, nor heed the suppliant's appeal?
> Is all that desperate Valour acts in vain?
> And Counsel sage, and patriot Zeal,
> The Veteran's skill, Youth's fire, and Manhood's heart of steel?

The printer's problem here (*Childe Harold* I, stanza 53) is whether *Veteran* is a common noun, as logically it should be, or whether its contextualization with *Counsel, Zeal, Youth* and *Manhood* forces semi-abstract status on it, and thus capitals. The printer's copy was made by R.C. Dallas, who only upper-cased *Rapine* and *Valour* in the fourth and seventh lines.[11] Byron had upper-cased *Young, Chief's, Rapine, Valour, Counsel, Zeal* and *Manhood*. The poet had no system of capitalization, but deployed them as the mood took him: printers evidently had to be seen to be less whimsical.

In the *Don Juan* fair copies which he made himself, Byron never follows Stower's advice in underscoring individual letters (unless they are words in themselves: 'I' at IV, 46, 4–5) and never underscores anything three times. He underscores singly for italicization and doubly for greater emphasis, receiving small caps: GOOD at *Beppo*, 74, 2; ONE and TWO at *Don Juan* I, 62, 3–4; CHASTE at I, 113, 3. But he capitalizes unambiguously, 'beginning [words] with Capitals, whether they be of the substantive kind, or otherwise', as Luckombe would permit; he capitalizes not only nouns, but pronouns (especially 'She') and indeed any word to which he wants to give emphasis – whether for a comic, emphatic, or metrical reason is not consistently clear. He often inks-over a lower case to capitalize it:

> And mischief=making <m/>Monkey from his birth (I, 25, 2)
> What men call gallantry and <g/>Gods <a/>Adultery (I, 63, 7)
> 'Day has not broke – there's <n/>No <o/>One in the street.' (I, 182, 8)
> Her <s/>Small Snow feet had Slippers but no stocking (II, 121, 8)

It will be seen that he does not follow the habit through wholeheartedly, however: one might expect *Mischief-making* at I, 25, 2, *Men* and / or *Gallantry* at I, 63, 7 and *Stocking* at II, 121, 8; but, whether from diffidence or laziness, he does not add them. However, he very often adds capitals in the transition from rough to fair copy. Thus, at III, 58, 1 the *cubless tigress* – as she appears in the rough draft – becomes a *cubless Tigress*; at III, 77, 6 Juan's *emerald aigrette* becomes an *Emerald Aigrette*; and at IV, 66, 8 *mountain mists* transmute into *Mountain Mists*. Canto III, stanza 66 is, in fair copy, very striking in this respect:

> A Beauty at the Season's Close grown Hectic,
>   A Genius who has drunk himself to death
> A Rake turned Methodistic or Eclectic—
>   (For that's the name they like to pray beneath)
> But Most, an Alderman struck Apoplectic,
>   Are things that really take away the breath,
> And show that late hours, wine, and love are able
> To do not much less damage than the table.

Here the capitals at *Season's, Close, Hectic, Methodistic* and even *Most* are added at fair copy stage, to complement the rest. Their comical facetiousess contributes to one of the poem's most important effects.

Why Thomas Davison ignored Byron's clearly indicated intentions and refused all the capitals which were not either proper nouns or at the start of lines and sentences, I do not know: perhaps he sensed Byron's three-quarters-hearted attitude to the matter; more likely he was just adhering to modern usage, or to the Murray house style. Why Byron never protested is also a mystery. In the extant *Don Juan* proofs, he only insists on the retention of two capitals (*Passion* and *Love* at I, 74, 6–7). After the severance with Murray he allowed himself some cutting asides about Davison – 'go a little cautious ... in believing his statements' (*BLJ* IX, 200); 'He is a mere Spy of Murray's depend on it' (*BLJ* X, 98); but while publisher and author were cooperating – even coldly – he voiced no complaints. I suspect that, never being wholly convinced that writing poetry was a worthwhile activity, he was indifferent about what might seem a minor matter of usage; he loathed the idea of being a professional writer, and to protest too much might lay him open to the suspicion that he thought of himself as one.

However, either he or Hobhouse relocated commas in the proof at I, 171, 8 ('*My mistress, all for*') and I, 195, 8 (*you, my Soul*) in such a way as to show a precise awareness of punctuation- as opposed to capitalization-effects[12] so he was not careless of all accidental details. (These commas *may* be the work of Hobhouse: you can rarely tell a writer by his commas. I am not convinced that either improves its line.)

Whatever the reason for Byron's indifference, the printed versions of Cantos I–V give an entirely false impression of how *Don Juan* looked immediately upon leaving his pen. In manuscript, the poem is clearly styled in an old-fashioned way – proclaiming by its heavy capitalization a backward-looking allegiance entirely in keeping with the author's acute distaste for nearly all modern verse-writing. But this effect is missing from almost all its public appearances from 1819 onwards (E.H. Coleridge in his 1898–1904 Murray edition restores some of the manuscript capitals, but by no means all).

When we come to the cantos printed by Byron's last publisher, John Hunt (a radical, detested by the Murray circle), the case is slightly altered. Here, as early as the prose preface to Cantos VI and VII, we find:

But the Minister was an elegant Lunatic—a sentimental Suicide—he merely cut the 'carotid artery' (blessings on their learning) and lo! the Pageant, and the Abbey! and the 'Syllables of Dolour yelled forth' by the Newspapers—and the harangue of the Coroner in an eulogy over the bleeding body of the deceased—(an Anthony worthy of such a Cæsar)—and the nauseous and atrocious cant of a degraded Crew of Conspirators against all that is sincere and honourable.[13]

The poem seems to tell a similar tale. Here, also from the first edition, is Canto VII, stanza 74:

> For every thing seemed resting on his nod,
>   As they could read all eyes. Now to them
> Who were accustomed, as a sort of God,
>   To see the Sultan, rich in many a gem,
> Like an Imperial Peacock stalk abroad,
>   (That royal bird, whose tail's a diadem)
> With all the Pomp of Power, it was a doubt
> How Power could condescend to do without.

We may wonder – perhaps the printer did – why *royal bird* in the sixth line is not capitalized; but the inconsistency looks convincingly Byronic. It seems as if Hunt's printer, C.H. Reynell (Hunt's brother-in-law, and, it is safe to assume, of a similar radical persuasion), is being far more punctilious, in the old-fashioned Luckombe manner, with regard to his author's liking for capitals; however, examination of the rough manuscript reveals another story, for there Byron has also capitalized *Nod* at line 1, *Sort* at line 3, and *Gem* at line 4.

With Cantos VI to XVI we are of course dealing with yet another middleman between poet and print: Mary Shelley, who was by this time employed by Byron to relieve him of the fatigue of fair-copying. In fair-copying stanza 74, above, she actually reverses several of Byron's rough draft details, and lower-cases *imperial peacock* at line 5, and both *powers* in the couplet. Byron, checking her work, then re-capitalizes them: but does not insist on his other original capitals at *Nod, Sort* and *Gem*. Reynell / Hunt accepts the result. Another example, stanza 17 from Canto VI, reveals a still more complex picture:

> That is, we cannot pardon their bad taste,
>   For so it seems to lovers swift or slow,
> Who fain would have a mutual flame confest,
>   And see a sentimental passion glow,
> Even were St. Francis' paramour their guest,
>   In his Monastic Concubine of Snow;—

In short, the maxim for the amorous tribe is
Horatian, 'Medio tu tutissimus ibis.'

In the last three lines, Byron had, line-openers aside, capitalized in rough only *Concubine, Snow,* and *Medio*; Mary Shelley, perhaps prudishly, refused the first two; Byron, in checking, not only restored them, but added a capital M for *Monastic*, two Ts for *Tu* and *Tutissimus*, and an I for *Ibis*. Reynell and Hunt accepted a *Monastic Concubine of Snow*, but rejected *Tu Tutissimus Ibis* completely! They thereby took the polish off the joke, for Byron follows on in the next stanza with *The 'tu''s too much, – but let it stand* ... and concludes his digression with a stanza of comically involuted self-reference, perhaps to cover his embarrassment at the peculiar scansion, perhaps to brazen out his misquotation – for the Latin is actually from the *Metamorphoses,* and is not Horatian at all. This analysis could be repeated; though it seems Mary Shelley had, by the time she copied Canto VIII, become better trained, for Byron inks-over rather less of her work.

When Mary had been preparing printer's copies for Davison, earlier in the collaboration, the story had been quite different: I count eighty-six letters in *Mazeppa,* and sixty-one in the much shorter *Venice An Ode* which are lower-cased in the first edition, despite clear instructions in Mary's texts as checked by Byron. Byron therefore seems surrounded by friends determined to curb his addiction to old-fashioned and facetious capitalization. Murray / Gifford / Davison are at least consistent; but Mary Shelley / Hunt / Reynell keep him dangling, accepting more upper-case sorts than the old firm did, but rejecting others, despite his clear instructions as he checks through and inks-over. The last ten cantos give us a fractionally clearer idea of what he wanted; but the bizarre conspiracy mainly persists, and the picture remains seriously unfocused.

In the midst of this strange business, an editorial policy of absolute consistency, accepting every one of Byron's capitals without reservation, seems called for. Jerome McGann, editor of the *Clarendon* Byron, has no comment to make; but in the 1989 Longman Shelley edition, Geoffrey Matthews and Kelvin Everest confront their corresponding problem thus:

Romantic writing increasingly blurs the personificatory and abstracting force of capitalization, by using capitals to mark names of things which are at once abstractions and physical realities. This tendency has deep roots and implications, and is definitely at work in Shelley's poetry. But it is a tendency unfortunately mingled with inconsistency and some casualness in his deployment of capitals, particularly in manuscripts, which on occasion makes it extremely difficult to decide which is the most preferable printed form. The general policy has been to preserve Shelley's manuscript capitals except where they are manifestly unnecessary.[14]

It is a policy which would be hard to follow in the case of those Byron poems for which no full autograph fair copy exists; fortunately, in the case of Cantos I to V of *Don Juan*, one does exist, presenting his intentions without ambiguity; and his requirements are similarly unambiguous in the ink which he expends liberally over Mary Shelley's fair copies of Cantos VI to VIII.

Now we turn to the effect of Byron's dashes in *The Vision of Judgement* (the extra 'e' is Byron's habitual spelling). The heroic but inscrutable figure of Junius in this poem is, I believe, an *alter ego* for Byron himself. In stanzas 74 to 80 of *The Vision* he creates a comic, but empathetic, impression of what it must have been like to try and read 'Byron', and to try to work out what kind of person – or emanation – he was. But the way in which he conveyed the sensations he imagined himself creating in his beholders has never been visible in print. Here is a transcription of the way, in manuscript, Byron wrote stanzas 76 and 77 (words in angle brackets are deletions):

76.

the
The more intently the Ghosts gazed <on him> less
the
Could they distinguish whose <his> features were—
The devil himself seemed puzzled even to guess—
They varied like a dream now here now there—
And several people swore from out the press
could
They knew him perfectly, and one <would> swear—
He was his father—upon which another
Was sure he was his mother's <uncl> cousin's brother
(BLOT)

77.
Another that he was a duke—or Knight—
An orator—a lawyer—or a priest—
Nabob
A <Doctor>—a Man Midwife;——but the Wight

Mysterious changed his countenance at least

in

As oft as they their <thei> minds, though <to> full sight
He stood—the puzzle only was increased—
The Man was a phantasmagoria in
Himself—he was so volatile and thin!

The dashes which Byron finds natural punctuation marks are vital for creating the atmosphere of dizziness and bewilderment as the crowds of demons, angels, and damned try to figure out which of the many possible Juniuses it is that they're looking at, and as Junius alters from moment to moment, frustrating their attempts. 'the Wight / Mysterious changed his countenance at least / As oft as they their minds': they want to create or recreate him, for they see his identity as in a sense their property; but in his non-stop metamorphosing, or self-reconstruction, he frustrates their ambition—without trying to. By just being what he is, he defeats them.

It is often said that Byron used the dash as a catch-all marker, because he wrote at speed, and expected his editors and/or printers to tidy things up. But the dash is a legitimate punctuation mark. In his 1808 *English Grammar* the American Quaker Lindley Murray writes:

The Dash, though often used improperly by hasty or incoherent writers, may be introduced with propriety, where the sentence breaks off abruptly; or where there is an unexpected turn in the sentiment: as, 'If thou art he, so much respected once – but oh! how fallen! How degraded!'[15]

The Junius passage is a huge sequence of 'unexpected turn(s) in the sentiment'. A version of the text which adhered to Byron's practice might go thus:

76.

The more intently the Ghosts gazed the less
    Could they distinguish whose the features were –
The devil himself seemed puzzled even to guess –
    They varied like a dream – now here, now there –
And several people swore from out the press
    They knew him perfectly, and one could swear –
He was his father – upon which another
Was sure he was his mother's cousin's brother,

77.
Another that he was a duke – or knight –
    An orator – a lawyer – or a priest –
    A Nabob – a Man Midwife; but the Wight
        Mysterious changed his countenance at least
As oft as they their minds, though in full sight
        He stood, the puzzle only was increased –
    The Man was a phantasmagoria in
    Himself, he was so volatile and thin!

The two stanzas bring a serious question into focus: not, did Byron expect his editors to do his punctuating for him? but, given the fact that such a job needed doing, did the way in which they did it show that they understood the poetry? R.F. Gleckner quotes Paul Elmer More confidently on this question:

> Byron was relatively reckless in matters of spelling, capitalization, punctuation, and italics ... [he] was consistently content to sprinkle his pages with dashes or otherwise erratic punctuation, and Murray's printer apparently put in points, commas, etc. whenever they seemed appropriate.[16]

The problem is that, as we shall see, what 'seemed appropriate' to the Murray printers in 1822 may not seem so to us, who have the manuscript still, in 2007.

The only manuscript of *The Vision* is a rough one, with dense erasures coexisting with whole stanzas devoid of correction. It is legible in parts, hard to decipher in others. The poem was first published on 15 October 1822, in the first volume of *The Liberal*, the journal set up from Pisa by Byron, Shelley, and Leigh Hunt. Its text was set up not from Byron's manuscript, but from an uncorrected proof with which John Murray had unwillingly furnished Leigh Hunt's brother John, the printer of *The Liberal*. Murray had shilly-shallied over publishing the work, and delivered the proof unhappily, because he was losing his most prestigious author to a detested radical. Byron did correct a proof, but it was not given to Hunt, and has disappeared.

This is the way in which the two stanzas emerge from the confused tale:

LXXVI.
The more intently the ghosts gazed, the less
     Could they distinguish whose the features were;
The Devil himself seem'd puzzled even to guess;
     They varied like a dream—now here, now there;
And several people swore from out the press,
     They knew him perfectly; and one could swear
He was his father; upon which another
Was sure he was his mother's cousin's brother:

LXXVII.
Another, that he was a duke, or knight,
     An orator, a lawyer, or a priest,
A nabob, a man-midwife; but the wight
     Mysterious changed his countenance at least
As oft as they their minds: though in full sight
     He stood, the puzzle only was increased;
The man was a phantasmagoria in
Himself—he was so volatile and thin![17]

In his essay *The Four Ages of Editing* (1987) Donald Reiman writes that
late Victorian editors

> modernized and smoothed out the texts ... and in several cases
> observed the prudential standards of the day by softening anything
> overtly radical or indecorous in the poetry.[18]

He might have said that in some cases – the one before us, for instance
– the work of softening had been done much earlier: by the first printer,
before the poem became public.

The effect of *The Liberal's* re-punctuation is to change the crowd's
feelings of amazement and bewilderment into something safer. A
chaotic sequence of failed identifications has been rendered comfortable,
unsurprising, and brought into the fold of good middle-class manners, by
having a dull Latinate syntax imposed on it. That identity is a necessary
bourgeois shibboleth, and no poet must be allowed to query it in too
much depth. Roman numerals (always the emblem of a class which
supposed itself educated) substitute for Byron's Arab numerals. The text
loses seven capital letters, and sixteen en dashes. It gains one new capital
('Devil'), a hyphen, two em dashes, and above all seven semicolons
and two colons. One past participle ('seem'd') is elided, and another

('increased') is not, even though no rhythmical advantage is to be gained from either decision. A specious order has been imposed on a profound and creative disorder.

Marilyn Butler writes that with English publishers in the early nineteenth century,

> The Enlightenment appeal to universals was insistently rebuked by an emphatic traditionalism, a fussy insistence on the rules of grammar and metre, and knowledge of the classics. In its motivation the appeal to standards of correctness was not as superficial as afterwards it tends to look, since it proclaimed that cultural authority was vested in those with a genteel and clerical education.[19]

Clerical correctness was a staple of the John Murray publishing house. Even the devil has to be afforded the dignity of a capital to his title. Though John Hunt and *The Liberal* were in theory in conflict with Murray's Tory values, their conflict did not extend into the area of punctuation. In any case, as I said, John Hunt had no access to Byron's manuscript, and had to use whatever text Murray gave him. Even in defeat, the Tory publisher still called the shots. A hint of Murray's attitude to Byron when Byron was out of the room and out of the country may be gleaned from Hobhouse's diary account, for Tuesday 28 April 1818, of what we would call the book launch for the fourth Canto of *Childe Harold's Pilgrimage*:

> we had a most singular evening and sat up till near three in the morning drinking Murray's Hock – our host very tipsy – Murray has sold between nine and ten thousand of the *Childe*. He said to me, 'Moore is a good fellow, *but he can't write* – there *is no man can like my man*.' He was drunk when he said this, and I was afraid would be overheard.[20]

We have no record of Hobhouse ever telling the aristocratic Byron about this attitude of proprietorship towards him on the part of the bourgeois Murray. If he did (and his disdainful attitude to the publisher hints at a suspicion on his part) it would have made the parting less painful. John Hunt could be idealized into a sturdy seventeenth-century parliament-man:

> he [Hunt] is a stiff sturdy conscientious man – and I like him – he is such a one – as Prynne – or Pym might be.[21]

It was harder to mythologize the conservative Murray into something he wasn't. Byron knew Murray intimately in a way he never knew Hunt and after Byron's death, Murray moved to repossess Byron's reputation.

The job of preparing the text of the Byron edition, which was included in the seventeen-volume 1832–3 Byron set, uniform with Moore's *Life* was given to John Wright (dates unknown) who was an editor who worked for Murray in the 1820s and 1830s. He performed such chores as preparing the index to the *Quarterly Review* and edited a complete Crabbe. Here is the way the stanzas we are examining emerge in his edition:

LXXVI.

The more intently the ghosts gazed, the less
    Could they distinguish whose the features were;
The Devil himself seem'd puzzled even to guess;
    They varied like a dream—now here, now there;
And several people swore from out the press,
    They knew him perfectly; and one could swear
He was his father: upon which another
Was sure he was his mother's cousin's brother:

LXXVII.

Another, that he was a duke, or knight,
    An orator, a lawyer, or a priest,
A nabob, a man-midwife; but the wight
    Mysterious changed his countenance at least
As oft as they their minds: though in full sight
    He stood, the puzzle only was increased;
The man was a phantasmagoria in
Himself—he was so volatile and thin.[22]

Wright did not have the manuscript: it was owned by an eighteen-year-old law student in Porthmadog called John Breese, and was not purchased by the Murrays until 1848. Wright thus has only *The Liberal* to work from. He preserves *The Liberal*'s Roman numerals, and most of the rest of the 'accidentals'. However, the semicolon after 'father' (itself created from an en dash) now becomes a colon. The small change adds to the unByronic formality of the proceeding. And *The Liberal*'s final exclamation mark (taken from the manuscript) is now a full stop, which makes the celestial and infernal crowds' excitement a thing of routine. Em dashes now have spaces before and after them. The text is made still more classical and respectable, and the comical drama, or dramatic comedy, is further neutralized.

Wright's edition held sway for over seventy years before Ernest Hartley Coleridge (1846–1920) produced a replacement edition for Murray between 1898 and 1904. E.H. Coleridge was son to Derwent Coleridge, himself second son to Samuel Taylor Coleridge. E.H. Coleridge went to Balliol, Oxford, and from 1872 to 1893 is described as having been a 'tutor'. For six months (January to June, 1894) he was Secretary to the Lord Chief Justice of England (a cousin). He edited selections from the notebooks, and all the poetry, of his grandfather, and wrote a biography of the banker Thomas Coutts. Not a professional academic then (the breed was not common at that time), but a Man of Letters, or a gentleman amateur, writing for *amateurs*. In 1930 the complete Murray set (including R.E. Prothero's edition of the letters) was selling at 7s 6d each, that is, for £5 5s, or five guineas.

Coleridge's version of the two Junius stanzas runs:

LXXVI.

The more intently the ghosts gazed, the less
Could they distinguish whose the features were;
The Devil himself seemed puzzled even to guess;
They varied like a dream—now here, now there;
And several people swore from out the press,
They knew him perfectly; and one could swear
He was his father; upon which another
Was sure he was his mother's cousin's brother:

LXXVII.

Another, that he was a duke, or knight,
An orator, a lawyer, or a priest,
A nabob, a man-midwife; but the wight
Mysterious changed his countenance at least
As oft as they their minds: though in full sight
He stood, the puzzle only was increased;
The man was a phantasmagoria in
Himself—he was so volatile and thin.[23]

Coleridge has access to the manuscript, as Wright had not: he gives the reader several alternative readings from it at the page-bottom; in this case, 'A doctor, a man-midwife' is tagged 'MS. erased' (it should be 'A Doctor, a Man Midwife'). But the only obeisance he makes towards manuscript

authenticity is to put the '-ed' ending back on 'seemed'. He even preserves
the inauthentic terminal full stop.

This was the standard edition until Jerome J. McGann (1937 –) was,
at Leslie Marchand's suggestion, given the job of editing a complete
Byron for the Clarendon Press, after Marchand had turned it down to
concentrate on Byron's letters and journals. British Byron scholars had
been approached, but their personalities had proved incompatible. In
1993, when it was completed, Oxford University Press were marketing
the complete McGann edition for approximately £490 – a price affordable
only to dedicated American specialists and to well endowed libraries. Later
paperbacks gave an improved text, with fewer notes and apparatus.

McGann describes his own situation when he started his Byron edition
thus:

> When I began editing Byron in 1971, I had no special editorial
> expertise. I had not sought the job, was surprised when I was asked,
> and I accepted without knowing what would be involved in such a
> task. This state of original innocence is important to realize because
> it forced me to set aside two years for studying textual and editorial
> theory and method. That course of study, moreover, was undertaken
> from a distinctly Anglo-American perspective, which effectively meant
> that I kept seeing my subject within the horizon of what has come to
> be called the Greg-Bowers (or 'eclectic') theory of editing.[24]

The innocent time of E.H. Coleridge was indeed long gone by now,
and it seemed impossible to approach such a responsible task without
a thorough acquaintance with editorial theory: this was a job for
an academic. McGann was and is a famous academic, and a famous
theorist. His dominant idea is that text is established by a process of
social collaboration:

> an author's work possesses autonomy only when it remains an unheard
> melody. As soon as it begins its passage to publication it undergoes a
> series of interventions which some textual critics see as a process of
> contamination, but which may equally well be seen as a process of
> training the poem for its appearances in the world ...
>
> In Byron's case, certain elements in this complex network assume
> particular importance for the textual critic. Throughout his life Byron
> sought editorial help with his poetry, so that people like R.C. Dallas,
> J.C. Hobhouse, Thomas Moore, John Murray and Murray's chief editor

William Gifford all exerted a significant impact upon Byron's literary work.[25]

McGann leaves out of his list of collaborators the printer, Thomas Davison. My suspicion is that it was the printer, the humble artificer, rather than the editor, the superior critical mind, who was responsible for suffocating Byron's comedy with colons and semicolons.

'Heard melodies are sweet, but those unheard are sweeter'. We may agree that text is established in the way McGann describes; but may also feel at liberty to regret the fact, and to feel happy that we still have Byron's manuscripts, with which we can reverse the 'contamination' process. The less an editor interferes, the better. It's true that Byron relied on these people; but they were a sad group of second-raters, and, with the possible exception of Moore, were all by 1822 seriously out of sympathy with the direction which Byron's poetical career was taking. Dallas was by then out of the equation; Hobhouse ignored the later cantos of *Don Juan* once he had, with a sense of doom, seen numbers I and II through the press, and ignored most of Byron's new work, until after his friend's death. For him, *Childe Harold* IV and *The Corsair* (of all things) were the summits of Byron's work. Murray always agreed with the last person who spoke; and if the opinion of Gifford had been acted on, neither *The Vision of Judgement,* nor *Cain,* nor *Don Juan,* would have been published at all.

McGann pays detailed attention to the role of cultural intermediaries and it is possible to see both the publication and the non-publication of *Don Juan* as collaborative acts. As McGann puts it:

> Between 1971 and 1987 one overriding fact grew upon me as I worked to produce the edition of Byron: that texts are produced and reproduced under specific social and institutional conditions, and hence that every text, including those that may appear to be purely private, is a social text. This view entails a corollary understanding, that a 'text' is not a 'material thing' but a material event or set of events, a point in time (or a moment in space) where certain communicative interchanges are being practiced. This view of the matter – this *theoria,* or way of seeing – holds true as much for the texts we inherit and study as it does for the texts we will execute ourselves.[26]

It is, nevertheless, a strange authoritarian theory which holds that even 'purely private' texts are social ones. If a person keeps a private diary and destroys it in the last days of his or her life, how does it ever become a 'communicative interchange'? Whatever the case there, it seems

to me that the 'specific social and institutional conditions' under which
The Vision was published were unsympathetic ones, and constituted a
hindrance to its appropriate editing and printing.

Donald Reiman writes of a conflict between

> those who accept the author's right to determine every detail in the
> text and those who believe that the social means of production, which
> initially provided the public with the text, ought to prevail over the
> isolated psyche of authors before they acceded to the careful scrutiny
> and good advice of friends, publisher, compositor, and (sometimes) the
> pointed observations of the representative of church and state.[27]

The Vision of Judgement was, of course, prosecuted, and might have been
published in a mutilated form, had not the pirates come up with the
resourceful idea of publishing a censored text, with the censored passages
printed in an appendix, which gave an account of the trial.

In his introduction to Volume VI of the Clarendon Byron (the one
containing *The Vision*) McGann writes:

> whereas the customary editorial policy in this edition has heretofore
> been to favour late over earlier readings (when it can be shown that
> Byron remained an active participant in the production process), in the
> present case the policy has been reversed. Here Byron's MS. readings
> are given presumptive authority over printed readings in substantive
> matters. A substantive reading in the original MS. will be rejected
> only when a later reading (printed or otherwise) makes a stronger
> case for itself.[28]

As shown above, Byron's participation in the production process of
The Vision had been minimal; so McGann's approach should yield fruit.
However, he says that substantive readings may be given presumptive
authority; and his implication is therefore, 'but not accidental ones'. On
the matter of terminology, Donald Reiman quotes Morse Peckham:

> The textual editor should do away with this theological terminology
> of accidentals and substantives, and talk simply and clearly about
> words, punctuation, spelling, capitalization, and whatever else he
> needs to talk about. These things are there, before our eyes; accidence
> and substance are not.[29]

In so far as punctuation often determines the tone, and thus the meaning, of a passage, the distinction and, the hierarchy, do seem to miss the point about poetry, which expresses mood as well as meaning (as does prose too, of course).

> ... he was so volatile and thin.

> ... means something quite different from

> ... he was so volatile and thin!

In the first you are stating a fact and expressing a neutral attitude towards it; in the second, you're stating the fact, and expressing a partial attitude, a subjective attitude, towards it. You're excited – bewildered – involved – empathetic, even! What you see in Junius's volatility and thinness implies something about you. You may not be as one-dimensional and dull as you thought you were!

The stanzas emerge, from the application of McGann's editorial policies, as follows:

76.

The more intently the ghosts gazed, the less
  Could they distinguish whose the features were;
The Devil himself seem'd puzzled even to guess;
  They varied like a dream—now here, now there;
And several people swore from out the press,
  They knew him perfectly; and one could swear
He was his father; upon which another
Was sure he was his mother's cousin's brother:

77.

Another that he was a duke, or knight,
  An orator, a lawyer, or a priest,
A nabob, a man-midwife; but the wight
  Mysterious changed his countenance at least
As oft as they their minds: though in full sight
  He stood, the puzzle only was increased;
The man was a phantasmagoria in
Himself—he was so volatile and thin![30]

McGann, at least, restores the Arabic numerals from the manuscript (as he does for his whole edition), and the final exclamation mark from both the manuscript and *The Liberal*. But they are small gains. In all other respects he reproduces what has gone before. He acknowledges the interest in the manuscript that other academics might feel, and goes further than Coleridge in giving all manuscript erasures, as opposed to just large, interesting ones, in his bottom-of-the-page apparatus: but he often gets them wrong. Here, the erased 'uncl' in the last line of the first stanza is expanded into 'uncle'; and 'they' in the fifth line of the second is given as 'though'. In all, there are 74 manuscript misreadings in the apparatus to McGann's edition of *The Vision*.

McGann also embarked on his edition, as he admits, at a very unfortunate time in terms of editing technology:

> in 1977 I was too far gone in the edition to take full advantage of computerized word processing as an editing tool. Once again my ignorance had closed down certain possibilities; and when I later (1984) learned about hypertexts and their powers, I had to swallow further regrets arising from my backward history.[31]

Donald Reiman began a review of the first three volumes of the Clarendon Byron, and sent copies round for comment, including one to McGann. Reiman takes up the tale:

> After some of my friends and colleagues read my review again in the light of his [McGann's] specific objections, I altered a few phrases. But these changes did not affect his basic objection, which was that my review made it sound as though Byron's poetry will have to be edited again reasonably soon.
>
> Indeed, as regards the first three volumes, that is precisely the conclusion I reached. But, I should add, I believe that all of *my* work and everyone else's will also eventually have to be replaced (though some a little faster than others).[32]

McGann's first three volumes have one drawback which almost incapacitates them. The absence of a running header to either the text or the notes makes it impossible to find one's way around them efficiently unless one is expert enough to be able to tell at a glance which poem, or which notes, one is looking at. This problem ceases with the fourth volume, and from then on the edition is much better – at least, as far as the simple problem of finding one's place goes.

McGann is disarmingly self-critical about his editorial work on Byron:

> Do you want me to itemize some of my horrid gaffes and blunders? ... The many, many times, in the Byron edition, when I cut corners in my editorial notes – because it was clear, having at last learned what scholarly editing entailed, I began to realize the true impossibility of the task I had blithely, and ignorantly, undertaken. The transcription errors.[33]

An example of McGann's 'corner-cutting' can be seen in the problems one experiences when trying to find evidence for the very interesting question of how well Byron knew the Qu'ran. The translation which he would have read is the famous one by George Sale. At *CPW* III, 419 and 420, McGann has notes to *The Giaour*, which cover Byron's own notes to lines 488 and 748, about women in paradise, and about 'Monkir' and 'Nekir'. His references are to 'George Sale, "Preliminary Discourse", *The Koran*, 59' and 'Sale's "Preliminary Discourse", *op. cit.* 101'. Then he has another reference at *CPW* III, 441, in a note to *The Bride of Abydos* – Byron's own note to line 409, about paradise itself. Here his reference is to 'Sale's *Koran*, "Preliminary Discourse", sec. I'. A look at these pages in Sale's first edition of 1734 shows nothing relevant, and neither does a look at the more user-friendly two-volume Sale published in 1812, closer to the time when Byron might have needed the book. In fact, we discover, McGann takes all three from the notes of E.H. Coleridge (see Coleridge III, 110, 121, and 197), and Coleridge uses not only an edition of Sale published in Chandos Classics in 1877, but also the 1880 Clarendon Press translation by E.H. Palmer. McGann seems not to have seen this, and does not state which edition of Sale he is using anyway. Our bewilderment is compounded when, on checking Coleridge's notes, we find, on 'Sale 59', a reference not to women in paradise but to Monker and Nakîr, and when we discover that 'Sale 101' is all about female camels. 'Sale sec. I' is in the 1877 translation twenty-five pages long.

Another note at *CPW* III, 441, about capitation tax, reads 'See the Koran, ch. IX'. The Qu'ran's ninth chapter is, in the 1880 Palmer translation, twenty pages long. McGann has again borrowed from Coleridge: see Coleridge III, 195. The normal way of referring to the Qu'ran, as with the Bible, is to chapter and verse, a courtesy which Sale does not, unfortunately, observe. McGann does this just once, at *CPW* V, 723, in a note to the line 'The holy camel's hump, besides the Koran' at *Don Juan* VI, 102, 8: his note is, 'Koran XXII, 36', which is indeed a reference to sacrificial camels, but ignores the fact that in the comic line, the camel's hump and the Koran are two separate items. In trying to annotate the first part of the line, he has annotated the second, to the illumination of neither.

Cross-checking the notes in this instance leads to some scepticism about *all* editors, and no knowledge at all about Byron's reading of the Qu'ran. McGann's notes referring to the Qu'ran seem to be written on the assumption that no one will be interested in them. For those who spent several hundred pounds buying his edition as it came out, the finding is grim, and eventually the reader learns always to check McGann against Coleridge (just as one learns always to check Marchand's edition of the Letters and Journals against Prothero's), and finally, where one can, to do what Byron told John Murray to do: 'Consult the M.S. *always*'.[34]

Every reader has to be, in the final upshot, his or her own editor.

notes

Peter Cochran's editions of *Don Juan*, *Beppo*, *The Vision of Judgement*, and other works, appear on the website of the International Byron Society.

1. There are no references to *Beppo* in Hobhouse's diary between 9 October 1817 (when he describes it as 'a description of Venice') and its publication on 24 February 1818. Byron sends it to Murray separately from *Childe Harold* IV (*BLJ* VI, 7–8).
2. *CPW* IV, 483.
3. John Murray Archive / National Library of Scotland.
4. Itsuyo Higashinaka. '*Gulbeyaz and* Joseph Andrews'. Byron Journal 12 (1984): 74–5.
5. John Smith, *Printer's Grammar*, 201–2.
6. Philip Luckombe, *History and Art of Printing*, 248–50.
7. Caleb Stower, *The Printer's Grammar*, 60–6.
8. See E.P. Thompson, *The Making of the English Working Class*, 202, 260, 503, 850.
9. William Hazlitt, *Lectures on the English Poets, delivered at the Surrey Institution*, 319.
10. *BLJ* III, 166.
11. B.L.Ms. Egerton 2027, 23.
12. See *CPW* V, 679–80.
13. *Don Juan* VI VII and VIII (1823), v.
14. G.M. Matthews and K. Everest, eds, *The Poems of Shelley*. Vol. 1, xxviii.
15. Lindley Murray, *English Grammar*, 386.
16. R.F. Gleckner, ed., *The Political Works of Lord Byron*, Editor's note.
17. *The Liberal* (1822): 28–9.
18. Donald H. Reiman, *Romantic Texts and Contexts*, 87.
19. Marilyn Butler, *Romantics, Rebels and Reactionaries*, 76.
20. B.L. Add. Mss. 47235, f. 14v.
21. *BLJ* X, 69.

22. Thomas Moore 1832–3. Vol. 12, 281–2.
23. E.H. Coleridge 1898–1904. Vol. 4, 513.
24. Jerome J. McGann, *The Textual Condition*, 19.
25. Jerome J. McGann, *A Critique of Modern Textual Criticism*, 51–2.
26. McGann, *The Textual Condition*, 21.
27. Reiman 1987, 177.
28. *CPW* VI, xiv.
29. Quoted Reiman 1987, 101.
30. *CPW* VI, 336.
31. McGann, 'Literary Pragmatics and the Editorial Horizon' in Philip Cohen, ed., *Devils and Angels: Textual Editing and Literary Theory*, 2.
32. Reiman 1987, 157.
33. Jerome J. McGann, *Byron and Romanticism*, ed. James Soderholm, 294.
34. *BLJ* VI, 71 (letter to Murray, 24 September 1818).

works cited and suggestions for further reading

Butler, Marilyn. *Romantics, Rebels and Reactionaries*. Oxford: Oxford University Press, 1981.

Coleridge, E.H., ed. *The Works of Lord Byron: A New, Revised and Enlarged Edition with illustrations*. 7 vols. London: John Murray, 1898–1904.

Fielding, Henry. *The History of the Adventures of Joseph Andrews*. 2 vols. London: A. Millar, 1743.

Gleckner, R.F., ed. *The Poetical Works of Byron*. Boston: Houghton Mifflin, 1975.

Greg, W.W. 'The Rationale of Copy-Text'. *Studies in Bibliography* 3 (1950–51): 19–36.

Hazlitt, William *Lectures on the English Poets, delivered at the Surrey Institution*. London: Taylor and Hessey, 1818.

Higashinaka, Itsuyo. '*Gulbeyaz* and Joseph Andrews'. *Byron Journal* 12 (1984): 74–5.

Johnson, John. *Typographia*. London: Longman, Hurst, Rees, Orme, Browne and Green, 1824.

Luckombe, Philip. *History and Art of Printing*, London: J. Johnson, 1771.

Matthews, G.M. and Everest, K, eds *The Poems of Shelley*, Vol. 1. London: Longman, 1989.

McGann, Jerome J. 'Editing Byron's Poetry'. *Byron Journal* 1 (1973): 5–10.

——. *A Critique of Modern Textual Criticism*. Chicago, IL: University of Chicago Press, 1983.

——. *The Textual Condition*. Princeton, NJ: Princeton University Press, 1991.

——. 'Literary Pragmatics and the Editorial Horizon'. *Devils and Angels: Textual Editing and Literary Theory*. Ed. Philip Cohen. Charlottesville: University Press of Virginia, 1991. 1–21.

——. *Byron and Romanticism*. Ed. James Soderholm. Cambridge: Cambridge University Press, 2002.

Moore, Thomas (J. Wright), ed. *The Works of Lord Byron, with his Letters and Journals, and his Life*. 17 vols. London: John Murray, 1832–3.

Murray, Lindley. *English Grammar*. York: Longman, Hurst, Rees, and Orme, 1808.

Reiman, Donald H. *Romantic Texts and Contexts*. Missouri: University of Missouri Press, 1987.

——. Reviews of Jerome J. McGann, *Byron. The Complete Poetical Works*, Vols 1, 2 and 3. *Keats-Shelley Memorial Bulletin* 34 (1983): 66–72 and Vols 4 and 5 (Autumn 1988): 89–100.

Scott, William. A Concise System of English Grammar. Edinburgh: Constable, 1809.

Smith, John. *The Printer's Grammar*. London: for the editor, 1755.

Steffan, T.G., Steffan, E., and Pratt, W.W. Pratt, eds. *Byron's Don Juan, A Variorum Edition*. 4 vols. Texas: University of Texas Press, 1971.

——. eds. *Don Juan*. Harmondsworth: Penguin, 1977.

Stower, Caleb. *The Printer's Grammar*. London: B. Crosby, 1808.

Tanselle, G. Thomas. 'Recent Editorial Discussion and the Central Questions of Editing'. *Studies in Bibliography* 34 (1981): 23–65.

Thompson, E.P. *The Making of the English Working Class*. Harmondsworth: Penguin, 1968.

3
byron and digression

paul m. curtis

I say, in my slight way I may proceed
   To play upon the surface Humanity.
I write the world, nor care if the world read,
   At least for this I cannot spare its vanity.
My Muse hath bred, and still perhaps may breed
   More foes by this same scroll: when I began it, I
Thought that it might turn out so—*now* I *know* it,
But still I am, or was, a pretty poet
               Don Juan XV, 60 (Byron's emphasis)

We begin with Byron's unconventional rhymes in this digressive stanza from *Don Juan*'s concluding sequence known as the English Cantos. Byron's 'irregularity of chime' (XV, 20, 6) draws our attention to two principal themes of the work: directly, to the speaker's acute consciousness of himself and his work in progress as well as, indirectly, to the reader's experience of reading it. The 'a' sequence of end-rhymes, *proceed / read / breed*, associates notions of poetical progress, the reception of such progress, and finally the generative power behind the poem or 'scroll' as well as the defensive reaction on the part of its satirized 'foes'. Notions of poetical progress are seldom untested in Byron's poetry, and this remains true from his youthful productions to those of his maturity.[1] The defensive reaction to Byron's satire was to the extent that even his staunchest supporters such as Hobhouse urged moderation. The 'b' rhymes, *Humanity / vanity / it, I* cleverly parody a syllogistic sequence. Humanity is the poem's frame of reference; vanity is the principal satiric target within this frame; and the terminal flourish of the 'b' rhyme embeds the poem (*it*) and speaker (*I*) almost as one, deep within the texture of the *ottava rima*.

60

This third rhyme in the 'b' sequence plays upon an idea brought to Byron's attention previously in 'Whistlecraft', by John Hookham Frere, which served as Byron's primary example for his experimental *Beppo*.[2] One rather cheeky effect of the rhyme is to reduce the pronouns into the boring bits of 'osities and ations'.[3] The comic threat of *it* and *I* becoming an *ity*, or a linguistic thing, is forestalled, however tenuously, by the comma-ed separation of the two.[4] A comma might not at all appear to be an imposing signpost of syntax; it is far less arresting, for example, than the Byronic dash. Vladimir Nabokov reminded his students, however, that good readers 'should notice and fondle details.'[5] In Byron's *it, I* rhyme, the comma forges a separation between, and splices together, the gargantuan poem and its polymathic speaker. Most remarkable is Byron's ability through rhyming wordplay to perform the identification between speaker and poem without the agency of metaphor.[6] As Byron reminds his publisher parenthetically, '(Plain truth, dear Murray, needs few flowers of speech)' (V, 101, 2). The identification and its correlative 'plain truth' *come into being* as the reader reads the stanza silently or, preferably, reads it aloud. Through sonic indirection we find directions out. The *ottava rima* requires a closing couplet, the end rhyme of which is as much about ending as it is about sound. The rhyme of the couplet carries forth the 'b' rhyme but in a crossing fashion, chiastically. The digressive daring of the stanza compensates for the clichéd rhyme *'now I know* it / *pretty poet'* which inverts and yet preserves the sounds of the previous 'b' rhyme.[7]

If beginning is the hardest thing to do, lingering over an epigraph is a pleasant if not effective way to begin (IV,1, 1). An exordium that lingers over a digression, however, invokes a structural irony which Byron often invites, as we shall see. It demonstrates as well, one hopes, the linguistic potential of Byron's digressive 'play' upon the surface of humanity. The 'play' or, to enlist a synonym, the 'drama' of the stanza is the intensity of the speaker's engagement with language within the context of digression. Digression provides Byron the linguistic perspective from which he can confront, delight in or attempt to resolve the discontinuity between world, where we perform, and words, the medium through which we verbalize this performance. By not being plotted, digression frees 'a more radical power of reference to those aspects of our being-in-the-world that cannot be talked about directly'.[8] A digression which is limited disingenuously to play upon surfaces, demonstrates rather the opposite – a copiousness, a profundity, and a self-consciousness of technique for which Byron has begun to receive critical credit. The burden of this project is to extend this work on Byron's poetics of digression by considering it as linguistic performance and, in the second instance, as an example of performative language. As a performance of performatives, Byron uses digression to multiply, even aestheticize, the ironic possibilities of form within *Don Juan*.

performance

We turn to a series of observations on digression in the effort to situate it within a broader framework of narrative rhetoric. The description of digression by Classical rhetoricians is a fascinating one, one that has been well sifted by previous critics. Even before we come to a strictly rhetorical definition we note two general types of indirection in the theory of digression: the idea of *egressio*, a fault or excess of style, which in the context of Greek Tragedy implies an ethical fall from society; and the comic stylistic excursion or the 'stepping to the side' from a linear narrative progress. Byron employs both types, of course: the one when he describes digression as a 'sin', the second when he apologizes for his lack of 'easy writing'.[9] In the history of Western literature, it seems, digression as a mode of narrative indirection is coeval with drama. However much a choral digression 'steps away' from the primary narration, it is still very much part of a performance before, we might assume, a highly engaged if not well-informed public. Before a public, then, the language of Classical digression is meant to be performed and heard immediately whereas a digression in a poem or novel is 'over'heard.

It is important to note the extent to which Byron conceived his poem in the first case as a performance, and, as we shall see presently, as performative. A brief examination of Byron's 'Unincorporated Preface' will confirm this point. The preface is on the whole, a satire in prose of Romantic poets, their poetry, as well as the theories of the imagination underpinning the poetry.[10] In paragraph four, however, Byron anticipates the narrative technique of *Don Juan*. He juxtaposes the imaginative impotence of Wordsworth's technique in 'The Thorn' (1800–05) and his 'epic narrative' about to begin. The clash between the contrasting narrative frames of reference deserves quotation in full.

The reader who has acquiesced in Mr. W. Wordsworth's supposition that his 'Misery oh Misery' is related by the 'Captain of a small &c.' is requested to suppose by a like exertion of Imagination that the following epic narrative is told by a Spanish Gentleman in a village in the Sierra Morena on the road between Monasterio and Seville—sitting at the door of a posada with the curate of the hamlet on his right hand, a segar in his mouth, a jug of Malaga or perhaps 'right Sherris' before him on a small table containing the relics of an olla podrida—the time sunset;—at some distance a groupe of black-eyed peasantry are dancing to the sound of the flute of a Portugese servant belonging to two foreign travellers who have an hour ago dismounted from their horses to spend the night on their way to the capital of Andalusia;—of these, one is attending to the story and the other, having sauntered further, is watching the beautiful movements of a tall peasant girl whose whole soul is in her eyes and her heart in the dance of which she is the magnet to ten thousand feelings that vibrate with her own. (*CPW* V, 82–3)

The passage proceeds according to an indirection associated with time – sunset. A lyrical mode ensues, not surprisingly, with the description of music and dance. The presence of the Spanish storyteller deliquesces into the background as two foreign travellers enter the scene. One, suggesting Hobhouse, listens to the 'story' of *Don Juan* the prose preface is intended to introduce. The second, and more Byronic traveller, is drawn to the sensuous dance of the tall peasant girl. The variant provided by McGann augments the intensity of the dance as performance: 'Magnet … to ten thousand feelings that vibrate <round her whose every gesture inspires a *corresponding* emotion>' (emphasis added). The paragraph begins with Wordsworth and concludes with a lyrical moment the singularity of which is consistent with many of Byron's poetical digressions, especially in the early cantos of *Don Juan*. The digression within the preface images the affective *centripetal* force of the tall girl's dance. Although the dance is peripheral to the narrative mandate of the preface, or perhaps *because* it is peripheral, the dance pulls the Byronic traveller in. If we consider the dancer and dance as allegorical pre-figures of the poem's digressions, however, the traveller's attraction to them and away from the narrator of the preface parallels the relationship of the poet/speaker vis-à-vis his material in *Don Juan*. Byron, therefore, aligns the dance as performance with digression; the centripetal force of the dance implies that digression is the axis of the poem; and the dance is a figure of the poem's serpentine progress to come.[11]

   A second strand in digression as performance has to do with the *improvvisatore* and the performance of improvised poetry.[12] Using Tommaso Sgricci as her primary example, Angela Esterhammer has recently made the point that for the romantic poets, especially Byron and Shelley, the *improvvisatore* 'stands for the real-time, responsive, public process of crafting poetry out of contingent subject-matter, habitual sound patterns, fragments of memory, and lively imagination'. Referring specifically to Byron, she argues, 'The improvisational quality of Byron's epics runs much deeper than observations about the casual or digressive tone of his poetic voice; it is a structural element of his sensibility, and constitutes one of the most profound analogues to a Continental tradition of spontaneous and performed verse.' [13] My argument departs from Esterhammer's by treating Byron's 'casual or digressive tone' as a structural element as accomplished at least as the one she accords improvisation. Furthermore, although improvisation and digression are complementary, they are also significantly different.

The undeniable source of the affective power of improvisation is its apparent spontaneity. One measure of its success, however, is the approximation of its imitation to the finished quality of written verse. As a linguistic feat, Sgricci's improvisations not only resembled but surpassed, say, the recitation of an entire verse drama which could have been memorized previously. The affective power of a written digression is also a function of its apparent spontaneity, as is the case with oral improvisation. The principal difference is that digression gives the impression of writing coming into being but without a mimetic precedent, and so it does not conform to the notion of a mimetic ideal. Although a Byronic digression might often take its cue from an allusion to the mimetic dramas of Shakespeare, digression is not mimetic. The improvisations of Sgricci could be repeated (in theory at least) due the reliance on the various poetic structures, conventions and topoi. Without these structures, conventions or topoi, the digressions of *Don Juan* defy repetition. If a digression could be repeated, it would lose its mongrel status as a stylistic fall or excursus.

One quality shared by improvisation and digression, however, is the high degree of oral presence. Whereas the orality of improvisation is ephemeral – undeniably the principal criterion for its effect – a digression in print resonates in the (inner) ear as if it were spoken.[14] Digression produces a unique and powerfully verbal world in Byron's later poetry. The world expressed through Byron's digressions appears to be one that is 'completely absorbed and possessed by the human mind' (Frye 1991, 33). The nature of digression in Byron is paradoxical, however, since the reader has the impression of 'hearing' its voice very clearly despite the fact that it issues from the page, a written and therefore visual medium.[15] On the odd occasion, the visual and the aural merge, 'I sometimes almost think that eyes have ears' (XV, 76, 1). The fundamental irony between narration and the speaking presence animating digression is central to performance and the performative. We turn now from performance, the common medium for drama and improvisation, to the nature of Byron's language in digression.

performative

J.L. Austin, in his *How to do Things with Words*, describes non-philosophical language as being either constative or performative. The criteria of truth and falsity are more easily applied to constative language since it states a fact and refers outwardly to some thing or idea. Not satisfied with the philosophical emphasis placed on constative language, Austin identified a type of language in which the utterance of a word, its meaning and its active effect were one. As Austin wrote, 'the issuing of the utterance is the performing of an action – it is not normally thought of as just saying something'.[16] Austin offers many examples one of which is the wager. The clause 'I bet you' signifies and performs the engagement between the contestants. In the introduction to her book *The Romantic Performative*, Angela Esterhammer discusses theories of Romantic linguists (Humboldt), as well as Anglo-American (Austin, Searle) and Continental speech act theorists (Habermas, Benveniste) as well as post-structuralist philosophers and critics (De Man, Derrida, Lyotard).[17] Esterhammer observes a contrast between Austin and previous Romantic linguists: 'Rather than taking the speaker for granted [as did Austin] a Romantic speech-act theory considers utterance as an event that before all else shapes the subject's consciousness, determines the subject's relationship to the world and the hearer, and changes the environment that surrounds, and includes, the one who speaks' (Esterhammer 2000, 13). Such an observation could well apply to the narrative and digressive components of *Don Juan*. In the digressive passages of *Don Juan*, the speaker rattles on 'exactly' as he'd talk (XV, 19, 7), and I have made the argument elsewhere that the frequency of performative language in *Beppo* is high.[18]

In both *ottava rima* poems, Byron tests the permutations of conversation: the speaker talks to himself, he addresses the reader, he apostrophizes. According to speech-act theory each of these examples might have multiple and simultaneous effects: on the speaker, the reader, the environment. More important than the frequency of performatives within digressive or narrative passages is the idea of digression as a type of 'utterance' that 'posits the conditions for [its] own effectiveness'.[19] The effectiveness of digression is that it reveals (or gives the impression that it reveals) to the reader a glimpse of the 'secret geometries' of the poem, the inner workings behind the façade of the performance.[20]

No matter how frequently Byron resorts to digression, digression never becomes repetitive. Each digression establishes the unique ground for its reception – be it allusive, biographical, multilingual – and each stimulates a unique response. Although each departure from narration might be broadly categorized as a digression, each digression instantiates a circuit of communication unique to itself. Regardless of the frequency of performative words in digression, therefore, the performative nature of digression resides less upon a strictly linguistic and Austinian definition than upon a broader rhetorical one. In a similar vein, Jane Stabler has commented that it is necessary 'to discuss individual instances of digressive play locally to see how their varying effects at the level of reading experience constitute meaning in the poem' (Stabler 2002, 109). Byronic digressions enact the premises they put forward as well as the conditions for their reception as they proceed. The apparent jeopardy of the unrehearsed pulls the reader centripetally into their dance upon the page as most every line moves against the grain of the poem's ostensible form and content. If we add the effect of performative language to the lingering subtext of digression as public performance, and both of these to our more broadly conceived notion of digression as performative, Byron's digressive technique accrues considerably in terms of its rhetorical energy and impact. Digression in Byron is at once the sign *and* performance of the potential of language.

An economical example of performance and performative would be Byron's 'Hail Muse! *et cetera*'. The speaker uses a Classical greeting at the beginning of Canto III, and he greets his muse with an archaic word that does what it means. The coincidence of action and meaning here augments the rhetorical immediacy of apostrophe. As Gavin Hopps has shown, the speaker reveres the classical convention and yet smirks at it by means of the Latin tag.[21] The question of convention aside for the moment, the gravitas of the Classical invocation is abbreviated by a classical phrase. The tag in Latin not only invades and evacuates the presence (of Calliope?) summoned by the invocation, it promises an imminent proliferation of abbreviations, however unspecified each of these might be. It is one thing to undercut a convention, but it is quite another for the speaker of the poem to make such an action an object of thought.[22] The first half of the opening line consumes itself in a loop of irony as the English performative 'Hail' is upstaged by the moribund Latin. However great the damage done to Classical invocation, Byron has us register positively the fierce vitality of inflicting this damage. As Jerome McGann has commented, 'Transitions between styles, lines, stanzas, and tones not only do not present a problem for Byron, they are the locus of all his opportunities.'[23] Such is the effectiveness of digression in general – its verbal action on the page often transcends convention or outperforms narrative. Although 'mental rest-stop' might be the appropriate metaphor for digression in a forensic context, in Byron's *Don Juan* digression serves to sharpen thinking – the speaker's as well as the reader's – rather than switch it off.[24]

convention, dilation, metaphor

'One may transcend any convention, if only one can first conceive of doing so.'[25] The concept of narrative 'dilation' – a rhetorical term signifying copiousness – does much to explain Byron's digressive technique. Patricia Parker applies the technique to Ariosto's Orlando Furioso, a work of great influence for Byron beginning with *Beppo*.[26] In Wordsworth's *Descriptive Sketches* occurs the simile 'The *west*, that burns like one dilated sun.' [27] In this instance, to dilate signifies the occupation of space – both physical and narrative – almost without duration. A spatial experience of the highest magnitude without a temporal component is strikingly Oriental, and to fill to excess the space of writing without time's passage is one success of Byron's digressions. Parker describes dilation as a concept of narrative possibility that finds its root in the narrative impetus of romance: 'The punning connection between a romance presented as "divertimento" [Orlando Furioso] (I. 4. 6–8) and the distractions which lure [Ariosto's] characters from the path of duty is simply another reminder that all such spatial metaphors for error have their narrative counterparts – deviation, diversion, and digression.'[28] In their seemingly boundless narrative space, errant knights such as Ariosto's love-crazed Orlando image moral, intellectual and spiritual wandering in the midst of stylistic errantry: with a proper moral it seems 'bad' rhetoric becomes good. Here all is possible and for romance at least if not for literature in general, Parker conjectures, 'romance may not be an aberration in literature but rather a revelation of its very nature, of the fact that all fictions "stray"' (Parker 1979, 48). Similarly Byron's digressions accumulate as if to reveal the truth in poetic 'error' or the logic in narrative multiplicity. The temporal mode separating narration and digression is that of the ever-present 'meanwhile' 'which creates the illusion of suspending linear time' (Parker 1979, 35). Byron's delight in deferral posits a teleology of endless wandering: Harold as a Cain-figure wandering the vastness of his literary space; Juan, a bankrupt hero from the literary past now as new as he is 'common' and drifting amidst the carnage of post-revolutionary Europe. The temporal progression towards meaning a reader of epic literature would expect does not exist on a general plane, or it exists everywhere, in the particular line.

From a different perspective, Joel Black comments on Schlegel's *Gesprach uber die Poesie* (1799–1800), '"Parekbasis" [for Schlegel] was essentially anti-rhetorical, a means of permanently dissolving the speaker-listener, writer-reader relation, and of perpetually canceling those "framing techniques" – such as the medieval devices of the dream vision, and palinode, and the modern device of the self-conscious narrator – which fiction has repeatedly adopted to differentiate itself from the "real" world.'[29] Black is correct in his estimation of digression as a technique which 'un-frames' narrative. Parekbasis in Byron is not, however, simply 'anti-rhetorical:' after all, it has the sanction of the most eminent classical rhetoricians. Instead, it exposes the tenuous relationship between the real world and a narrated one. The digressive 'fiction' is persistently more 'real' than Juan's history, and this is consistent with the epistolary Byron who 'hate[s] all things *fiction*' (*BLJ* V, 203). Digression releases the world of fact into the poem, a famous example of which is the assassination of the Commandant in Canto V, stanzas 33–9.[30] From the perspective of an egg, to use an ironic observation of Samuel Butler, a chicken is an excuse to hatch another egg.[31] Digression, moreover, gives the impression of sincerity in part because of the blunt opinions expressed regarding narrative as persuasion. The performance is purer without props.

> Few men dare show their thoughts of worst or best;
>   Dissimulation always sets apart
> A corner for herself; and therefore Fiction
> Is that which passes with least contradiction. (XV, 3, 5–8)

Dissimulation reserves part of 'her' corner for digression, no doubt; and the collaboration between the two produces an illusory transparency of narrative. Due to the ironic relationship between narration and digression, the digressive rhetoric, and not the speaker of this rhetoric, nor Byron as McGann contends, is the 'hero' of *Don Juan*.[32]

Byron's treatment of metaphor provides one example of the logic particular to his digression. The extent of Byron's metaphor often goes beyond what the rhetoricians call *allegoria*; what begins as a turn of phrase will continue with sufficient elaboration in order to usurp the narrative form within which it finds its point of departure. Otherwise described, the limits for figural language often vanish once the process of a metaphorical identification has begun; the metaphor defines its own progress as it proceeds. Examples of metaphor such as this may be designated as digressions since they fix upon a particular word or idea, pursue an analogy which seems not to inform the poem in progress, and then return once the metaphoric identification has been exhausted. This type of metaphor is radically different from the epic simile, for example. Epic simile is designed to give the impression that universal forces are at play in the midst of a particular event: such as the wind-tossed feather atop a warrior's helmet which signifies equally the continuum of nature's beauty in the midst of man's horrific inhumanity. At his old lunes, Byron's metaphors appear to 'forget' their starting point, and as Joseph Priestley pointed out, the reader has to 'begin again' upon returning to the narrative.[33]

In Canto II, stanzas 177–81, our narrator compares a coastline's ripple to a bumper of champagne. The unexpected associations that emerge non-sequentially produce an informal enquiry on what constitutes a boundary or a frame of cognition: be it physical, intellectual, or poetic. The dilation of the metaphor implies as well the dilation of the speaker's being. The clarity of his metaphoric vision comes, ironically, from within the context of inebriation. In a larger circle of reference, the clarity of Byron's vision reflects upon an English society that is drunk on power and its own self-importance.

177

It was a wild and breaker-beaten coast,
    With cliffs above, and a broad sandy shore,
Guarded by shoals and rocks as by an host,
    With here and there a creek, whose aspect wore
A better welcome to the tempest-tost;
    And rarely ceased the haughty billow's roar,
Save on the dead long summer days, which make
The outstretch'd ocean glitter like a lake.

178

And the small ripple spilt upon the beach
    Scarcely o'erpass'd the cream of your champaigne,
When o'er the brim the sparkling bumpers reach,
    That spring-dew of the spirit! the heart's rain!
Few things surpass old wine; and they may preach
    Who please,—the more because they preach in vain,—
Let us have wine and woman, mirth and laughter,
Sermons and soda water the day after.

179

Man, being reasonable, must get drunk;
    The best of life is but intoxication:
Glory, the grape, love, gold, in these are sunk
    The hopes of all men, and of every nation;
Without their sap, how branchless were the trunk
    Of life's strange tree, so fruitful on occasion:
But to return,—Get very drunk; and when
You wake with head-ache, you shall see what then.

180

Ring for your valet—bid him quickly bring
    Some hock and soda-water, then you'll know
A pleasure worthy of Xerxes the great king;
    For not the blest sherbet, sublimed with snow,
Nor the first sparkle of the desert-spring,
    Nor Burgundy in all its sunset glow,
After long travel, ennui, love, or slaughter,
Vie with that draught of hock and soda-water.

181

The coast—I think it was the coast that I
    Was just describing—Yes, it *was* the coast—
Lay at this period quiet as the sky,
    The sands untumbled, the blue waves untost,
And all was stillness, save the sea-bird's cry,
    And dolphin's leap, and the little billow crost
By some low rock or shelve, that made it fret
Against the boundary it scarcely wet.

182

And forth they wandered ... (Byron's emphasis)

In the midst of a lyric description, a metaphorical analogy associating
a ripple and the cream of champagne begins. The associative potential
of the analogy quickly displaces, even usurps, the description it is
meant to elaborate, however. The speaker pursues the analogy without
premeditation, intoxicated by its possibility, unbound by narrative
constraint. The unpredictable proliferation of champagne to 'old
wine' to 'sermons and soda-water' is comic, even thrilling, because the
progression is without precedence, the sequence of common experience,

or thematic frame of reference. Abraham Tucker, in his *The Light of Nature Pursued* (1768), describes an associative principle that would reside in 'an understanding pliable and comprehensive enough to strike out trains immediately among any collection of objects and discern their respective situations ... it would not know what irregularity was'.[34] Juan and Haidée, whose 'large black prophet eye seem'd to dilate / And follow far the disappearing sun' (IV, 22, 1–2), have been forgotten by both the reader and speaker as he yields to his digressive associations. The return from digression to narration is misleading but not misdirected. 'But to return' compels the speaker to command 'Get very drunk', calling forth Xerxes allusively, as in Canto I, for ironic moral authority. Stanza 181 parodies a genuine return to the narrative, 'I think it was the coast that I / Was just describing—Yes, it *was* the coast.' The 'ripple' which began the digression (II, 178, 1) becomes the 'little billow' (II, 181, 6). We return to Juan's narrative courtesy of a variation of the initial image.

Byron's wave-variation is all the more wave-like by hiding in the open, as it were, of the great dilatory space the reader crosses. The little billow 'fret[s] / Against the boundary it scarcely wet' (II, 181, 7–8). The image of limit, the frame that separates the sea from the shore, serves to blend the two narrative modes, 'And forth they wandered' (II, 182, 1) echoes Milton. The digression consumes four stanzas, or 32 lines, before it returns to a lyric setting time*ful* with its paradisal resonances.[35] The digression diminishes our awareness of sequence in the poem and our awareness of the time it takes to read. Altogether, time as sequence for the poem and for the reader is altered. We encounter a rhetorical 'space' of great magnitude but with few temporal indicators to use as reference points. The sudden consciousness of the difference between digression and narration produces a peculiar and pleasurable vertigo as we find ourselves between the seams of story.[36] Digression, as implied by the opening of Tristram Shandy's story, occupies 'a zone of time without the ticking of clocks'.[37] A line from *Childe Harold* IV perhaps best describes the form of time produced by digression:

> For our remembrance, and from out the plain
> Heaves like a long-swept wave about to break,
> And on the curl hangs pausing ... [38]

The stasis of the curl versus the dilatory participial 'pausing' describes the moment and momentum of digression as it enacts its premise.[39]

Our last example returns us to the title of this chapter. At 'his old Lunes' once again, the speaker of *Don Juan* in Canto XIII, stanza 12 aligns digression with fits of lunacy and forgetfulness.

> I'm 'at my old Lunes'—digression, and forget
>   The Lady Adeline Amundeville;
> The fair most fatal Juan ever met,
>   Although she was not evil, nor meant ill;
> But Destiny and Passion spread the net,
>   (Fate is a good excuse for our own will)
> And caught them;—what do they *not* catch, methinks?
> But I'm not Oedipus, and life's a Sphinx.[40] (Byron's emphasis)

With increasing frequency in the poem, Byron uses scare quotes to identify a phrase as an allusion thereby altering its status as allusion.[41] From an earlier eighteenth-century perspective, calling an allusion out reduces the intimacy of the covert collaboration between reader and poet. Byron's habit of mapping his allusions is distinct from the larger Romantic practice of allusion.[42] Byron in this example does not seek primarily to transpose aesthetic values from a previous work to *Don Juan*. Byron uses *Merry Wives* to demonstrate before the attentive reader how modalities of deceit in his digressive poetics tend to the truth. If life is a Sphinx, as the speaker contends, our riddle is to detect the deceit at work through the language of digression. The utterance of a riddle performs the engagement with the interlocutor. By signalling the verbal oddity of 'lunes', Byron challenges us to ponder the honesty of its delivery or the wariness the word implies.[43]

The reprise of Falstaff's adventures in *The Merry Wives of Windsor*, you will recall, depends upon the triple betrayal of the fat knight by Master Ford. In order to test the fidelity of his 'merry' wife, Ford assumes the identity of a Master Brook. Falstaff is easy prey to the sexual liaisons with Mistress Ford arranged by Master Brook all of which are discovered, of course, by none other than Master Ford. As is the case in *I Henry IV*, Falstaff's lack of virtue is of heroic proportions.[44] His attempts to escape detection in *Merry Wives* are as successful as his attempts on Mistress Ford's honour. In the first instance, Falstaff hides in a laundry hamper and is thrown into the Thames at Datchet Lane. In the second, he cross-dresses as the obese old witch from Brainford whom Ford has threatened previously with violence. The third and climactic attempt at dissembling takes place at Herne's Oak with Falstaff wearing a buck's head. The line Byron draws our attention to from the play is spoken by Mistress Page, a 'merry' friend of Mistress Ford. In Act IV she comments that Master Ford's fits of jealousy have surpassed the usual standard and that he is

> in his old *lines* again: he so takes on yonder with my husband; so rails against all married mankind; so curses all Eve's daughters, of what complexion soever; and so buffets himself on the forehead, crying 'Peer out, peer out!', that any madness I ever yet beheld seemed but tameness, civility, and patience to this his distemper he is in now. I am glad the fat knight is not here. (IV. ii .17–25, my emphasis)[45]

Ford feigns madness to get to the truth of his wife's fidelity. He has trapped Falstaff repeatedly, so a description of him by Mistress Page as being at his lunes means rather the contrary, that Ford's dissimulation provides access to this truth. The implication is that Byron's objective is truth which he pursues through the lunes, or irony, of his digressions. Once again, digression harkens back to its dramatic origins, alludes to Shakespearean drama and dramatizes the ironic potential of deceit.[46]

What level of deceit is possible in digression? Or, from what perspective might we label a rhetorical posture as deceitful? If Byron's digressions are deceitful, are they not, as is the case with Master Ford, truth through an ironic lens? His deployment of digression engages the reader to plumb its possibilities of deceit and delight in the ironies of its complexity. Byron digresses elsewhere on the nature of lying as performance, or 'The truth in masquerade' (XI, 37, 2).[47] The allusion to *Merry Wives* portrays lying in a much more favourable light as a way to truth. The waywardness of digression, let us be wary, never subscribes to a truth even though its purpose is truthful. Whereas 'the truth' exists exclusively in a singular form, its performance in *Don Juan* through digression is multi-form, polyvalent, yet never plural. As Byron noted previously via Horace, 'And truth and fiction with such art compounds, / We know not where to fix their several bounds.'[48]

To conclude, I have tried to account for the vitality and plenitude of Byron's digressive technique and to offer as well through the many examples additional reasons for the pleasure Byron provides his readers. Byron's 'Muse admires digression', and I have explored its 'slippery' effects through aspects of performance in *Don Juan* and through aspects of performative language.[49] Paul Ricoeur makes the simple but crucial distinction that 'every narrative is narrating something ..., yet something which itself is not narrative'.[50] I have looked into several digressions, but I have not answered the question 'what is digression?' Rather, (and without resorting to digression) I have tried to explain how this unique discourse enacts its own premises and challenges the reader with ironic possibility. Digression gives access to a more purely verbal world since this world exists without or beyond the sequential logic of the narration within which it occurs. The power of Byron's digressions resides in the evocation a verbal world that far exceeds in scope the already considerable world evoked by the narration. Byron's skill with digression surpasses the rhetorical objective of persuasion to imply the potential of what might be created through language. The apprehension of the final form of this creation is never complete, however. Digression is a release of the word-hoard through which Byron 'write[s] the world'. When asked innocently by Boswell, what is poetry, Dr. Johnson replied memorably, 'Why, Sir, it is much easier to say what it is not. We all *know* what light is; but it is not so easy to tell what it is.' If the question 'what is digression' were put to Tristram, he would repeat a previous observation, that it is the 'sunshine'.[51] Having begun the eleventh Canto of *Don Juan*, Byron wrote to Kinnaird 14 April 1823, 'You must not mind occasional rambling I mean it for a poetical T[ristram] Shandy—or Montaigne's Essays with a story for a hinge' (*BLJ* X, 150). If story is a hinge, digression is the door through which Byron admits the light.

notes

1. The critical and popular receptions of digression contemporary to Byron and since have been most ably discussed by Jane Stabler. The success of her *Byron Poetics and History* as literary criticism resides, firstly, in its astute appreciation of Byron's *poetics* of digression and what the designation implies; and, secondly, in the alternately author and reader centred applications of the fruits of her wide reading. Stabler demonstrates how the art of Byron's digressive technique evolves through his career as a function of his response to both the public and personal spheres. Bernard Beatty elucidates convincingly the complexities of poetical progress in his fine *Byron's Don Juan*.
2. William Harmon gives the name 'heteromerous' to such an augmented rhyme, 'Rhyme in English Verse: History, Structures, Functions'. *Studies in Philology* 84.4 (Fall, 1987): 373.
3. In a comic tone of self-reference, 'Whistlecraft's' proem draws attention to its narrative method with the narrator's pledge to avoid a poetic diction 'With long tail'd words [ending] in *osity* and *ation*'. John Hookham Frere, 'Prospectus and Specimen of an Intended National Work, by William and Robert Whistlecraft', in *The Works of John Hookham Frere*, ed. W.E. Frere. Vol. 2. 'Proem' Verse VI. The anonymous *Beppo* sold six times as many copies as 'Whistlecraft' in one-sixth the time. John Murray to Byron 16 June 1818, *Byron: The Critical Heritage*, ed. Andrew Rutherford, 121.
4. On the rich and complex notion of words as things see, L.E. Marshall, '"Words are things": Byron and the Prophetic Efficacy of Language'. *Studies in English Literature* 25 (1985): 801–22. See IX, 5 for a similar augmented rhyme.

5. Nabokov is quoted in Ian McEwan's eulogy in memory of Saul Bellow. See *The Globe & Mail* (9 April, 2005): R5.
6. Northrop Frye often refers to the formula of metaphoric identification as described by the phrase 'A is B'. Despite the felicity of a metaphoric identification, we are conscious of the paradox that A *is not* B. See, for example, 'The Motive of Metaphor' in *The Educated Imagination*, 32.
7. McGann notes the echo to Gay's epitaph, *CPW* V, 764. For other rhymes feigning poetic incapacity, see V, 77; VI, 17–18; IX, 74; XIII, 8; XV, 19–20.
8. Paul Ricoeur, *Time and Narrative*. Vol. 1. Trans. Kathleen McLaughlin and David Pellauer, 80.
9. *Beppo* ll, 394, 401, *CPW* IV, 144–5. Anne Mellor defines the rhetorical mode of Byron's digressions in *Don Juan* as 'confessional'. *English Romantic Irony*, 59.
10. See McGann's comments, *CPW* V, 683–5. Jonathan David Gross mentions the preface in his '"One Half What I Should Say": Byron's Gay Narrator in *Don Juan*'. *European Romantic Review* 9.3 (Summer 1998): 330. Gross contends that 'Recognizing the closeted nature of the narrator's sexuality can explain his digressive style, one of the poem's most debated features' (323). Peter W. Graham takes up the preface in his *Don Juan and Regency England*, 16–22.
11. As a serpentine movement, the dance is reminiscent of narrative progression in *The Giaour*, Byron's 'snake of a poem' (*BLJ* III, 100). Hogarth's influence on Byron's rhetorical indirection bears further examination especially with regard to the 'Serpentine line'. At the culmination of Chapter VII comes this commentary: 'The Serpentine line, by its waving and winding at the same time different ways, leads the eye in a pleasing manner along the continuity of its variety, if I may be allowed the expression; and which by its twisting so many different ways, may be said to inclose ('tho but a single line) varied contents; and therefore all its variety cannot be expressed on paper by one continued line, without the assistance of the imagination, or the help of a figure; ... where that sort of proportion'd, winding line, which will hereafter be called the precise Serpentine line, or *line of grace*, is represented by a fine wire, properly twisted round the elegant and varied figure of a cone.' William Hogarth, *The Analysis of Beauty* ed. Joseph Burke, 39. Hogarth's emphasis.
12. The *OED* cites Byron's usage of 'improvisatore'. See *Don Juan* XV, 20.
13. Angela Esterhammer, 'Spontaneous Overflows and Revivifying Rays: Romanticism and the Discourse of Improvisation', The 2004 Garnett Sedgewick Memorial Lecture, 33.
14. For the poem's speaker as a performative one, see 'Dan Phoebus takes me for an auctioneer'. XIII, 74, 4.
15. On the relation between written content and the oral form of poetry, see Frye, 'the content of written poetry is the form of oral poetry' in 'The Expanding World of Metaphor'. *Northrop Frye: Myth and Metaphor, Selected Essays, 1974–1988*, ed. Robert D. Denham, 110.
16. J.L. Austin, *How to do Things with Words*, 6–7.
17. Angela Esterhammer, *The Romantic Performative: Language and Action in British and German Romanticism*, 1–21. See as well Derrida's critique of Austin in his 'Signature Event Context' in *Margins of Philosophy*, trans. with additional notes Alan Bass, 307–30.
18. Paul M. Curtis, 'Byron's *Beppo*: Digression and Contingency'. *Dalhousie Review* 73.1 (Spring 1993): 18–33.

19. Esterhammer (2000) uses this clause in reference to Romantic linguists and their perception of utterances creating contexts and altering conventions (9).

20. Alan Hollinghurst, *The Line of Beauty*, 73.

21. Gavin Hopps, 'Hail Muse! *et cetera*'. *Litteraria Pragensia* 7.14 (1997): 69–83. On the indirection of apostrophe see Puttenham: 'Many times when we have runne a long race in our tale spoken to the hearers, we do sodainly flye out and either speake or exclaime at some other person or thing, and therefore the Greekes call such figure (as we do) the turnway or turnetale, and breedeth by such exchaunge a certaine recreation to the hearers minds.' (*The Arte of English Poesie*, 245.)

22. See similar examples: 'My Muse despises reference;' (XIV, 54, 6) 'I write what's uppermost, without delay; / This narrative is not meant for narration;' 'Leaving my people to proceed alone, / While I soliloquize beyond expression.' (III, 96, 3–4). The last example anticipates the narrative plurality of a Jasper Fforde novel.

23. Jerome J. McGann, *Don Juan in Context*, 95.

24. The metaphor 'mental rest-stop' is used by Joel D. Black, 'The Second Fall: The Laws of Digression and Gravitation in Romantic Narrative and their Impact on Contemporary Encyclopaedic Literature'. Diss. Stanford 1979. I rely upon his first chapter, 'Digression and Literary History', 12–81.

25. David Mitchell, *Cloud Atlas: A Novel*, 460.

26. The translator W.S. Rose influenced Byron's *ottava rima* style. His version of *Orlando* appeared in 8 volumes between 1823 and 1831. As Byron commented in May 1818, 'Rose is a fine fellow – and one of the few English who understand Italy—without which Italian is nothing.' *BLJ* VI, 38.

27. William Wordsworth, 'Descriptive Sketches Taken During a Pedestrian Tour Among the Alps [1850]'. *William Wordsworth: The Poems*. Vol. 1, ed. John O. Hayden, 103.

28. Patricia Parker, *Inescapable Romance*, 25. As Parker points out, 'Spatial "dilation" is linked, etymologically, with temporal "deferral" through a complex association with the Latin roots *differre / dilatore*, a connection which survives in the English word dilatory' (58). Interestingly Sir Walter Scott recalls Ariosto for his own under-appreciated digressive weave: 'Like the digressive poet Ariosto, I find myself under the necessity of connecting the branches of my story, by taking up the adventures of another of the characters, and bringing them down to the point at which we have left those of Jeanie Deans. It is not, perhaps, the most artificial way of telling a story, but it has the advantage of sparing the necessity of resuming what a knitter ... might call our "dropped stitches"; a labour in which the author generally toils much, without getting credit for the pains.' *The Heart of Mid-Lothian*, ed. John Henry Raleigh, 164.

29. Joel D. Black, 'Confession, Digression, Gravitation: Thomas de Quincey's German Connection' in *Thomas de Quincey: Bicentenary Studies*, ed. Robert Lance Snyder, 314.

30. Beatty (1985) studies this scene in his first chapter.

31. Frye (1990) refers to Samuel Butler's famous remark in 'Some Reflections of Life and Habit', 144.

32. 'The Book of Byron and the Book of a World' in *The Beauty of Inflections: Literary Investigations in Historical Method and Theory*, 291.

33. Joseph Priestley, an advocate of Hartley's theory of association, praises those digressions which occur as natural 'transitions' in the mind, and cautions against those which deviate beyond the normal association of ideas: 'If a digression be continued till we quite lose sight of the principal subject, the uniformity of the whole piese is broken, and at the end of such digression the reader hath, as it were, *to begin again*; and he may be under a necessity of looking a considerable way back, before he can recover the train of ideas he had lost, and without which he cannot proceed with the work.' *A Course of Lectures on Oratory and Criticism: 1777* English Linguistics 1500–1800. No. 126, ed. R.C. Alston, 36. Commenting on the sometimes obscure concentration of Horace or Tacitus, Ruskin writes of Byron's influence on the formation of his prose style: 'Byron wrote as easily as a hawk flies, and as clearly as a lake reflects, the exact truth in the precisely narrowest terms; nor only the exact truth, but the most central and useful one.' *Praeterita: The Autobiography of John Ruskin*, 134.

34. Abraham Tucker [Edward Search], *The Light of Nature Pursued* (London, 1768). Vol. 1, 266. Quoted in Ralph Cohen, 'Association of Ideas and Poetic Unity', *Philological Quarterly* 36 (1957): 468. Tucker's 'irregularity' anticipates line 412 in *Hints from Horace*: 'What few admire—Irregularity.' *CPW* I, 304.

35. Northrop Frye, *The Double Vision: Language and Meaning in Religion*, 49. 'We speak of the eternal presence of God as timeless, but once again the language fails us: we need some such word as "timeful" to express what the King James Bible calls the fullness of time.'

36. Jane Stabler discusses Byron's champagne metaphor in XIII, 37–8 as an example of his 'feminised digression' (166). 'Champagne' is the last word of her commentary (197).

37. The phrase is from Wallace Stevens's poem, 'Things of August' in *The Palm at the End of the Mind*, ed. Holly Stevens, 359. In 'Sterne's *Tristram Shandy*, ... the hero ascribes his misfortunes in life to his mother's having interrupted his father, in the act of coition, by asking him if he had wound the clock'. Frye 1990, 'The Responsibilities of the Critic', 131.

38. *CHP* IV, 75, 1–3. The persona is describing Mount Soractes north of Rome and in so doing enlists Horace's aid. Glossed by McGann in *CPW* II, 329.

39. Patricia Parker makes the important correlation in Romance literature between narrative *espacement* as 'deferral' wherein 'the reader has the sense of time traversed because the reading itself is so time-consuming. The continual shifting from one story to another often provides what is virtually the cartography of a single moment, like the extended space of the Renaissance illustrations where the whole plot is revealed at once. The author alone can see the warp and woof of the "cloth" he weaves (*Orlando Furioso* XIII, 81, 1–2), the sum of the frequent romance tapestries which reveal the form of an action before it happens and thus mediate between plot and person, the lofty authorial view and the character or reader still immersed in the process of time' (35).

40. See XV, 21 for the poem as a 'Conundrum of a dish'.

41. See Christopher Ricks's chapter on Byron in his *Allusion to the Poets*, 121–56.

42. Brian Hepworth discusses Romantic 'non-allusion' as occurring in a poetic line that refers more to its internal movement than to reference or 'outness',

to use Berkeley's term. *The Rise of Romanticism*, 280. On Byron's 'signalled allusions', see Stabler 2002, 104.

43. See McGann, 'Byron and "The Truth in Masquerade"', in *Romantic revisions*, eds Robert Brinkley and Keith Hanley, 194, and especially the last sentence of the essay (207).

44. In his electronic edition of the poem, Peter Cochran glosses the allusion to *I Henry IV* at Canto I, line 996 and the correspondence with *Merry Wives* at line 1139.

45. *The Merry Wives of Windsor*, ed. H.J. Oliver, 107.

46. The Arden edition rejects 'lunes' in favour of the previous Folio version 'lines'. The emendation would seem to be tailor-made for this project which considers the effects of digression upon Byron's lines in *Don Juan*. Lunes appears in Theobald's two editions of Shakespeare (1733, 1740). The sale catalogue (1816) lists 'Shakespeare's Plays, 20 vols. Bell's edition, fine paper, 1788'. *CMP* 241.

47. On the various modalities of lying and the truth, see, I, 51; XIV, 190; XV, 88.

48. *Hints from Horace, CPW* I, 297; ll. 209–10.

49. 'To the Earl of Clare', *CPW* I, 97; l. 72. For slippery, see *Beppo*, 'This story slips for ever through my fingers' (63, 2).

50. Paul Ricoeur, *Time and Narrative*. Vol. 2, trans. Kathleen McLaughlin and David Pellauer, 78.

51. *Boswell's Life of Johnson,* ed. George Birkbeck Hill. Vol. 3, 38. Boswell's emphasis. Laurence Sterne, *The Life and Opinions of Tristram Shandy, Gentleman,* ed. Ian Watt, 54–5, 'the machinery of my work is of a species by itself; two contrary motions are introduced into it, and reconciled, which were thought to be at variance with each other. In a word, my work is digressive, and it is *progressive* too, – *and at the same time*.... Digressions, incontestably, are the sunshine; – they are the life, the soul of reading; – take them out of this book for instance, – you might as well take the book along with them.' Sterne's emphasis.

works cited and suggestions for further reading

Austin, J.L. *How to do Things with Words*. Cambridge, Mass.: Harvard University Press, 1962.

Balfour, Ian. *The Rhetoric of Romantic Prophecy*. Stanford, CA: Stanford University Press, 2002.

Beatty, Bernard. *Byron's Don Juan*. London and Sydney: Croon Helm, 1985.

Black, Joel D. 'The Second Fall: The Laws of Digression and Gravitation in Romantic Narrative and their Impact on Contemporary Encyclopaedic Literature'. Diss. Stanford, 1979.

——. 'Confession, Digression, Gravitation: Thomas de Quincey's German Connection' in *Thomas de Quincey: Bicentenary Studies*. Ed. Robert Lance Snyder. Norman: University of Oklahoma Press, 1985.

Boswell, James. *Boswell's Life of Johnson*. Vol. 3. Ed. George Birkbeck Hill. Oxford: Clarendon Press, 1971.

Cohen, Ralph. 'Association of Ideas and Poetic Unity'. *Philological Quarterly* 36 (1957): 465–74.

Curtis, Paul M. 'Byron's *Beppo*: Digression and Contingency'. *Dalhousie Review* 73.1 (Spring 1993): 18–33.

Derrida, Jacques. 'Signature Event Context'. *Margins of Philosophy*. Trans. with additional notes Alan Bass. Chicago, IL: University of Chicago Press, 1982. 307–30.

Esterhammer, Angela. *The Romantic Performative: Language and Action in British and German Romanticism*. Stanford, CA: Stanford University Press, 2000.

——. 'Spontaneous Overflows and Revivifying Rays: Romanticism and the Discourse of Improvisation'. The 2004 Garnett Sedgewick Memorial Lecture. Vancouver: Ronsdale Press, 2004.

Frere, John Hookham. 'Prospectus and Specimen of an Intended National Work, by William and Robert Whistlecraft'. *The Works of John Hookham Frere*. Vol. 2. Ed. W.E. Frere. London: Basil, Montagu, Pickering, 1874.

Frye, Northrop. *The Educated Imagination*. Bloomington, IN: Indiana University Press, 1964.

——. *Northrop Frye: Myth and Metaphor, Selected Essays, 1974–1988*. Ed. Robert D. Denham. Charlottesville and London: University Press of Virginia, 1990.

——. *The Double Vision: Language and Meaning in Religion*. Toronto: University of Toronto Press, 1991.

Garber, Frederick. *Self, Text, and Romantic Irony: The Example of Byron*. Princeton, NJ: Princeton University Press, 1988.

Graham, Peter W. *Don Juan and Regency England*. Charlottesville: University of Virginia Press, 1990.

Gross, Jonathan David. '"One Half What I Should Say": Byron's Gay Narrator in *Don Juan*'. *European Romantic Review* 9.3 (Summer 1998): 323–50.

Harmon, William. 'Rhyme in English Verse: History, Structures, Functions'. *Studies in Philology* 84. 4 (Fall, 1987): 365–93.

Hepworth, Brian. *The Rise of Romanticism*. Manchester: Carcanet, 1978.

Hogarth, William. *The Analysis of Beauty*. Ed. Joseph Burke. Oxford: Clarendon Press, 1955.

Hollander, John. *Vision and Resonance: Two Senses of Poetic Form*. New York: Oxford University Press, 1975.

——. *Melodious Guile: Fictive Pattern in Poetic Language*. New Haven: Yale University Press, 1988.

Hollinghurst, Alan. *The Line of Beauty*. New York and London: Bloomsbury Publishing, 2004.

Hopps, Gavin. 'Hail Muse! *et cetera*'. *Litteraria Pragensia* 7.14 (1997): 69–83.

Lennard, John. *But I Digress: The Exploitation of Parentheses in English Printed Verse*. Oxford: Clarendon Press, 1991.

Marshall, L.E. '"Words are things": Byron and the Prophetic Efficacy of Language'. *Studies in English Literature* 25 (1985): 801–22.

McEwan, Ian. 'Ian McEwan on Saul Bellow: "We Owe him Everything"'. *The Globe & Mail* (9 April 2005): R5.

McGann, Jerome J. *Don Juan in Context*. Chicago, IL: University of Chicago Press, 1976.

—— 'The Book of Byron and the Book of a World'. *The Beauty of Inflections: Literary Investigations in Historical Method and Theory*. Oxford: Clarendon Press, 1985.

——. 'Byron and "The Truth in Masquerade"'. *Romantic revisions*. Eds Robert Brinkley and Keith Hanley. Cambridge: Cambridge University Press, 1992. 191–209.

Mellor, Anne. *English Romantic Irony*. Cambridge, Mass.: Harvard University Press, 1980.

Mitchell, David. *Cloud Atlas: A Novel*. Toronto: Vintage Canada, 2004.

Parker, Patricia. *Inescapable Romance*. Princeton, NJ: Princeton University Press, 1979.

Priestley, Joseph. *A Course of Lectures on Oratory and Criticism: 1777* English Linguistics 1500–1800. No. 126. Ed. R.C. Alston. Aldershot: The Scolar Press, 1968.

Puttenham, George. *The Arte of English Poesie*. Ashland, OH: Kent State University Press, 1970.

Rajan, Balachandra. *The Form of the Unfinished: English Poetics from Spenser to Pound*. Princeton, NJ: Princeton University Press, 1985.

Ricks, Christopher. *Allusion to the Poets*. Oxford: Oxford University Press, 2002.

Ricoeur, Paul. *Time and Narrative*. Vols 1 and 2. Trans. Kathleen McLaughlin and David Pellauer. Chicago and London: University of Chicago Press, 1984–5.

Ruskin, John. *Praeterita: The Autobiography of John Ruskin*. London: Oxford University Press, 1949.

Rutherford Andrew, ed. *Byron: The Critical Heritage*. London: Routledge & Kegan Paul, 1970.

Scott, Walter. *The Heart of Mid-Lothian*. Ed. John Henry Raleigh. Boston: Houghton Mifflin, 1966.

Shakespeare, William. *The Merry Wives of Windsor*. Ed. H.J. Oliver. London: Routledge, 1993.

Stabler, Jane. *Byron Poetics and History*. Cambridge: Cambridge University Press, 2002.

Sterne, Laurence. *The Life and Opinions of Tristram Shandy, Gentleman*. Ed. Ian Watt. Boston: Houghton Mifflin, 1965.

Stevens, Wallace. *The Palm at the End of the Mind*. Ed. Holly Stevens. New York: Vintage, 1972.

Wordsworth, William. *William Wordsworth: The Poems*. Vol. 1. Ed. John O. Hayden. New Haven and London: Yale University Press, 1981.

4
byron and history

Where history's pen its praise or blame supplies,
And lies like truth, and still most truly lies.
Lara I, ll. 187–90; *CPW* III, 220

'On the day when it shall become accepted as a canon of criticism that the political work and the political opinions of a poet are to weigh nothing in the balance which suspends his reputation – on that day the best part of the fame of Byron will fly up and vanish into air' (Swinburne 1884 [1911] 75). The aesthete poet Algernon Swinburne's 1884 pronouncement was prescient. The view that politics was inimical to art dominated the academy for the next hundred years. Modernist inspired 'new criticism' of the twentieth century embargoed historical, biographical and sociological contextualism in favour of formalist aesthetics, and found rhetorical verse such as Byron's particularly vulgar and embarrassing.[1] The structuralist and post-structuralist criticism which followed abstracted even further the play of language from its social situation. In Britain and the USA Byron became so marginalized as to be regarded as almost irrelevant to Romantic studies, even though he epitomized Romanticism for continental Europe. His poetry lacked the distilled brevity of the lyrics favoured for teaching, and was not included in the new national curriculum introduced by the Tories in 1988. Yet Byron's poetry continued to be revered and taught in secondary schools throughout the USSR and the Eastern bloc.

So when Byron returned in the 1980s as the repressed satanic side of Romanticism, politics was found in his baggage. The nineteenth-century debate on the comparative merits of the shockingly sceptical, yet politically engaged Byron and the apparently ideologically neutral but morally redemptive Wordsworth was reignited. The historical moment seemed right for a return to historicist criticism, as the end of the cold war paradoxically meant that the influence of the Marxist tradition, now rendered harmless, could be voiced in the West. But it was above all feminism which brought about the demise of a supposedly apolitical poetics in the academy, so that criticism rediscovered the ideological implications of texts. Byron's rhetoric of freedom from imperial oppression seemed newly relevant as European eastern bloc countries freed themselves from the Soviet empire, while his anti-Tory stance appealed to opponents of the West's return to right-wing conservatism after the radicalism of the 1960s and 1970s. On the other hand, his aristocratic libertinism presented a severe challenge to the political correctness of the day. It will be the task of this chapter to assess whether the concern of historicism with the nineteenth-century production and reception of Byron's poetry has changed our view of it; whether it has self-reflexively challenged our presentist critical preconceptions and preoccupations; and whether, after twenty years, it has any more to tell us.

1980s new historicism took the particular form in Romantic studies of a demythologizing sceptical stance of self scrutiny. The editor and foremost twentieth-century critic of Byron, Jerome McGann, in his contentious polemic, *The Romantic Ideology: A Critical Investigation* (1983), unmasked as false-consciousness the uncritical endorsement by critics such as Meyer Abrams and Northrop Frye of 'romanticism's own self-represen-tations' (McGann 1983, 1). Influenced by Marxism, Jerome McGann, his former student Marjorie Levinson, Paul Hamilton and leading British Romanticist Marilyn Butler, followed this with *Rethinking Historicism* (Levinson 1989) whose implied – or in Butler's case, declared – agenda included opposing the right-wing governments of Ronald Reagan and Margaret Thatcher.[2] They did so by examining how the apparently innocuous activity of teaching Romantic poetry had played its part in constructing and reproducing capitalism, in what Althusser inelegantly termed the 'Ideological State Apparatus' of education which socializes the coming generations into conservatism.[3] British cultural materialists, such as Chris Baldick, pointed out the central importance to the development of the discipline of English Literature of the construction of the Romantic canon with Wordsworth's *The Prelude* at its centre, whose turning away from revolution to solace in nature inculcated quietism.

It was no coincidence that in the year that saw many bicentenary conferences commemorating 1789, scholars of the Romantic period were fomenting revolution. A wholesale cultural revaluation, including a re-examination of the special status previously accorded to texts deemed 'Romantic', was spearheaded by feminist scholars, whose rediscovery of the leading role played by women writers of the time had made it necessary to tear up the map of the old route between the Enlightenment and Victorianism. Feminists led the way and new historicists inspired by deconstruction followed. They endorsed the opening up of the 1750–1850 archives to scrutiny: breaking down the barriers between 'literary' texts and other genres and questioning the hierarchy of 'major' and 'minor' writers set up by critics inspired by modernist aesthetics. This was enabled by the democratization of conventional bibliographical and editorial scholarship through IT – a development which new historicists Jerome McGann and Alan Liu have made the centre of both their critical practice and theory.

This very radical attack on the canon in Romantic literature was in contrast to the effect of new historicism on Renaissance studies, where, despite a comparable concern with ideological critique and the revaluing of women writers, the texts under consideration remained more traditional. On the other hand, the influence on Romantic period historicists of post-structuralism's critique of the universalism and 'humanism' of Enlightenment values was less strong. Renaissance new historicism had been inspired by Foucault to paint a darkly deterministic vision of the inescapability of power; whereas Marxist cultural materialism, drawing from Raymond Williams a view of texts as sites of contested ideologies, enabled less pessimistic takes on cultural production in British Romantic period criticism.[4] Indeed, Claire Colebrook suggests that American new historicists McGann and Levinson actually resuscitated the Enlightenment idea that historical self-awareness is a vehicle of emancipation, by their revelations of how Romantic lyrical concern with private emotion had displaced or obscured the historical conditions of production (Colebrook 1997, 12). While the intricate dialogic essays of McGann (McGann 2002), the sophisticated work of Jerome Christensen on Byron's self-representation (Christensen 1993) and Susan Wolfson's witty deconstruction of the ideology of poetic form (Wolfson 1988) testify to a postmodernist concern with the play of language in and between texts in historicist studies of Byron, versions of cultural materialism have been more prevalent (Foot 1988; Kelsall 1987, Graham 1990; Watkins 1987; 1993; Lansdown 1992; Haslett 1997).

One of the most revelatory uses made of history in Byron studies was that by Marilyn Butler (1988, 1992) and Nigel Leask (1992), who, inspired by post-colonial theory, explored the ambivalence of Byron's Orientalist verse, produced at a time when British imperialism was evolving from trade towards rule and missionary activity in India. Pioneering historicist scholarship by Crompton (1985), Franklin (1992) and Wolfson (2006) also considered for the first time the representation of gender in Byron's poetry, taking into account contemporary attitudes to homosexuality, debate over the role of women and playful Romantic transgression of gender boundaries. The very popularity of Byron's verse was a phenomenon in literary history, a major inspiration behind both the magisterial materialist analysis by William St Clair (2004) of book sales and readership in the period, and studies of the appropriation of the poet's image in nineteenth- and twentieth-century popular culture (Wilson 1999; Elfenbein 1995). The question of the censorship and piracy of Byron's poetry and the part it played in working-class radicals' arguments for a free press has featured in groundbreaking studies of popular culture before the Reform Act of 1832 (Wood 1994; Gilmartin 1996).

Byron studies were also, of course, central to McGann's frequent and important interventions in the theoretical debates within new historicism (McGann 1983, 1985a, 1985b, 1988, 2001), as he negotiated between the Scylla and Charybdis of Marxist and post-structuralist theory. His most important contribution to the debate was to question the idealism behind rigid abstractions like 'the text', which ignored the indeterminacy inevitably built in to editorial practice: no less subjective or impervious to historical change than interpretation. McGann argued that editorial, bibliographic and interpretative scholarship should not be discrete areas but should be brought to bear on each other, in order to fully acknowledge the social nature of the textual transmission of meaning. In answer to the charge that new historicism limits the generation of meaning to the originating moment of the text's production, McGann has called for a 'renovated' dialogical diachronic historicist criticism which he defines as necessarily comparative. This should take account not only of the circumstances of production of a text but also of its subsequent transmissions, in order to compare interpretations with those of the present (McGann 2002, 77, 213, 232).

In looking for the 'advances', the ways forward for historicist criticism, this integration of the practices of traditional literary scholarship with sophisticated critical analysis, is a welcome development which has already begun. Inspired by the democratization of scholarship enabled by the availability of electronic bibliographies, full text databases and hypertext editions, scholars are now breaking down boundaries within the discipline itself and taking cultural materialism to a new stage. Recently, new studies of the Romantic period have begun to appear which blend post-structuralist insights into the practice of reading with historical awareness: taking into account the history of the book; the material practices of the production, circulation and dissemination of print culture; the mediating role of literary institutions; and the concepts of taste and of genius that influenced readership (Siskin 1988; Clery 2002; Franklin 2000). This is not to 'reassert a totalizing critical idealism by assuming that a particular kind of interdisciplinary approach is inherently more "complete" than any other', by that insistence on the superiority of historicism which Ellen Pollak warned against (Pollak 1988, 285). Rather it is to open up the possibilities for a more pluralist, varied and inclusive practice.

Instead of either assuming that literary works directly reflect the time in which they were written, or taking the present as a fixed point of reference by which to measure or judge past texts, the best new historicist work understands both texts and our own critical response to them as discrete processes of imagining or reinventing the past which should be compared and contrasted. So future studies could pay some attention to Byron's own historicism and the relationship between his poetry and the romantic historiography of his time. The most cursory glance at Byron's *oeuvre* demonstrates the centrality of history to virtually everything he wrote. Epigraphs or notes to the tales often indicate a precise historical setting: for example, *The Giaour* (*CPW* III, 39–40). Harold/ Byron's journeys have him meditating on sites which are perceived as palimpsests of the recent through to the classical past, as in his apostrophe to Venice in *Childe Harold's Pilgrimage*, Canto IV, stanzas 1–19, where 'An Emperor tramples where an Emperor knelt' (IV, 12, 2). Though *The Curse of Minerva* satirized antiquarianism, Byron and Hobhouse's voluminous notes to *Childe Harold's Pilgrimage* often themselves claim scholarly authority, and the commentary on these lines corrects Gibbon (*CPW* II, 320). The Venetian plays are all – as Byron described *Marino Faliero* – 'rigidly historical' (*BLJ* VIII, 152). The author announced his intention 'to follow the account of Diodorus Siculus' in *Sardanapalus* (*CPW* VI, 17, 607) though he had also consulted William Mitford's recent *History of Greece* (1818). The appendix to *The Two Foscari* cited as sources Pierre Darù's *Histoire de la République de Venise* (1819) and J.C.L. Simonde de Sismondi's *Histoire des Républiques Italiennnes du Moyen Âge* (1807–17), which had also inspired *Marino Faliero*. McGann comments that many of the Doge's speeches in the former play were closely modelled on the historians' accounts (*CPW* VI, 628). The Biblical plays take their sources in Genesis literally and therefore ironically, in the spirit of Pierre Bayle's *Dictionnaire historique et critique* (1695–97) (*CPW* VI, 649). *Cain*, inspired by Cuvier, envisions a world degenerating over cataclysmic cycles of geological time. Historical personages are imagined speaking to the present reader in *The Lament of Tasso* and *The Prophecy of Dante*. *Don Juan* is set precisely at the period of the French Revolution, before and after the Siege of Ismail (1790), while

the narrator speaks in an ever-changing present time. In the preface to
The Vision of Judgment, Byron takes on the role of sceptical historian
weighing up the evidence: predicting that George III's '*public* career will
not be more favourably transmitted by history' than in his satire (see
also stanza 45). By way of contrast, he has the devil Asmodeus declaring
he has caught the hagiographical Poet Laureate Southey: 'at a libel—/No
less on History than the Holy Bible' (*The Vision of Judgment* 86, 7–8).

It would be pointless to multiply examples, but this brief overview
indicates to what an extent Byron was engaging with, fictionalizing and
critiquing histories. Indeed, it could be argued that Byron should be set
side by side with Walter Scott as one of the age's greatest historical writers.
This is not simply a matter of settings and sources, but because the poetry
foregrounds its historicism in its formal properties. Byron adapts genres
which stage the otherness of the past as some sort of performance, often
bringing the poet's and the reader's present (which he recognizes will soon
themselves cease to be identical) into clashing juxtaposition with it. For
example, Byron was a pioneer in the nineteenth-century development
of the dramatic monologue into a historical poetic form, in which a
speaker from the past, such as Dante or Tasso, may be judged both with
objectivity that comes from temporal or geographical distancing and yet
with sympathy evinced by his first-person confession. The audience of
the plays and monologues has greater knowledge of the span of history
than the characters, who are fixed in their own times, and views with
irony prophecies of the future by Sardanapalus (V. i. 436–42), Marino
Faliero (V. ii. 78–84), or Cain (I. i. 438–50) and their curses on their
enemies which predict posterity's judgement on them. But sometimes the
historical personage steps to the edge of the stage, like Dante who states
knowingly: 'I am not of this people, nor this age' (*The Prophecy of Dante*
I, l. 143). At the same time, the implicit comparison with Byron himself,
as a present-day exiled poet, shadows the character's words, which we are
always conscious are ventriloquized. There is often a sly acknowledgement
of the fictionalization of the past with the use of double entendres and
parallels with the present, which include the viewing of the writing and
performance of the poem itself as of historical significance. Marino Faliero
points out to a fellow Venetian the importance of relaying his story:

When the beholder knows a Doge conspired,
Let him be told the cause—it is your history. (*Marino Faliero,* V. i. 511–2)

Especially in *Childe Harold's Pilgrimage,* the poet-narrator places himself
both meditatively and literally on the stage of European history: 'Stop!—for
thy tread is on an Empire's dust!' (*Childe Harold's Pilgrimage* III, 17, 1).

There is as yet no major study of Byron's philosophy of history, though the contemplation of places of historical significance has been addressed by Stephen Cheeke (2003, 10–14), and Frederick Shilstone (1988) considers how the concept of tradition is figured in the verse. Upcoming studies need to relate a historicist poet such as Byron to the change from eighteenth- to nineteenth-century historiography, described by the structuralist theorist Hayden White as follows:

> The first phase of nineteenth-century historical consciousness took shape within the context of a crisis in late Enlightenment historical thinking. Thinkers such as Voltaire, Gibbon, Hume, Kant, and Robertson had finally come to view history in essentially Ironic terms. The pre-Romantics – Rousseau, Justus Möser, Edmund Burke, the Swiss nature poets, the *Stürmer und Dränger,* and especially Herder – opposed to this Ironic conception of history a self-consciously 'naive' counterpart. They believed in 'empathy' as a method of historical enquiry, and they cultivated a sympathy for those aspects of both history and humanity which the Enlighteners had viewed with scorn or condescension. (White 1973, 38–9)

The historicism of Byron and Scott was produced by this philosophical crisis. Both Scots, they were imbued with Scottish Enlightenment scepticism, yet simultaneously enthused by antiquarian revaluation of popular balladry and warrior culture. Scott, of course, had led the way with his *Minstrelsy of the Scottish Border* (1802). Byron followed, phonetically transcribing Albanian songs and translating Romaic Greek ballads whilst on his travels. This non-canonical popular poetry was beginning to be recognized as fascinating historical source material even if it could not be considered timeless art as were the classics, for the new historiography attempted to 'get as close as possible to the everyday past as it was experienced by contemporaries' by appropriating 'manners' and the social from the province of antiquarians and archaeologists (Rigney 2001, 123, 71). Byron followed Scott in making modern reproductions of these originals, constructing phenomenally popular historical romances in verse. The importance with which he regarded conveying everyday 'manners' may be deduced from the angry letter sent with an extra footnote on 14 November 1813 to the publisher John Murray, who had queried a Muslim character referring to the Old Testament in *The Bride of Abydos*:

> I send you a note for the *ignorant*—but I really wonder at finding *you* among them.—I don't care one lump of Sugar for my *poetry*—but for

my *costume*—and my *correctness* on those points (of which I think the *funeral* was a proof) I will combat lustily. *(BLJ* III, 165)

Romanticism as a whole would be particularly inspired by empathy with the primitive past and revulsion against scepticism. Interestingly, this is a movement which some modern historians, such as Simon Schama, and literary biographers, such as Peter Ackroyd, are now replicating, in reviving a writing style of imaginative empathy in conscious revolt against postmodernist relativity and its deconstruction of humanism (Southgate 1996, 130).

By the time he came to write *Don Juan*, however, Byron felt that the poetic pendulum had swung too far in the direction of Romantic empathy. After saturating himself in the satire of Pope, he wrote to John Murray on 15 September 1817:

> I am convinced the more I think of it—that he [Thomas Moore] and *all* of us—Scott—Southey—Wordsworth—Moore—Campbell—I—are all in the wrong ... revolutionary poetical system—or systems—*(BLJ* V, 265)

Byron's turn to irony (usually attributed to his discovery of the Italian *ottava rima* tradition) must have been also partly prompted by reading his favourite Enlightenment historians, Gibbon, Hume, and Voltaire, whose influence had produced an 'historical epistemology that was Skeptical in the extreme and ... an ethical attitude, generated by Skepticism, that was manifestly relativistic' (White 1973, 48). They considered facts as quite separate from moral or intellectual truth, so historical writing could be overtly polemical or satirical. Yet Byron was a Romantic poet, not a historian *manqué*, for he validates poetry as the higher art: responsible for actually creating cultural memory through the higher faculty of the imagination (*Don Juan* I, 5).

In attempting a mock-heroic poem of epic scale ('My poem's epic', *Don Juan* I, 200, 1), which took an androgynous boy as hero instead of a warrior, Byron mocked the masculine martial ethos which constitutes the unspoken basis of historical judgements and had produced barbarous jubilation over the carnage of Waterloo. Byron's hero is a lover not a soldier because this poem is to be a history of the private life, not a celebration of public glory (*Don Juan* I, 1–5). That sexual politics are inextricably entwined with class and power, and public with private, had been signalled by the poet's original epigraph, which Hobhouse persuaded him to replace: 'Domestica facta ... Horace' (*CPW* V, 670) for 'home affairs' was a double entendre ostensibly meaning national politics but suggesting too the politics of the family. Imagining the individual soldier's experience is not evasive of the public world of history so much as a consciously democratic corrective to the military historian's godlike stance:

> History can only take things in the gross;
> But could we know them in detail, perchance
> In balancing the profit and the loss,
> War's merit it by no means might enhance,
> ...
> The drying up a single tear has more
> Of honest fame, than shedding seas of gore. (*Don Juan* VIII, 3)

Indeed, the narrator mentions history six times in the Ismail cantos. In his asides, he often reveals himself to be personally obsessed with the intangibility of the past:

> Alas!
> Where is the world of *eight* years past? *'Twas there*—
> I look for it—'tis gone, a Globe of Glass!
> Cracked, shivered, vanished, scarcely gazed on, ere
> A silent change dissolves the glittering mass. (XI, 76, 2–6)

He sometimes apes the pedantry of the historian, declaring solemnly when setting the scene for Juan's loss of his virginity: 'I like to be particular in dates', for:

> They are a sort of post-house, where the Fates
> Change horses, making history change its tune,
> Then spur away o'er empires and o'er states (*Don Juan* I, 103, 4–6)

Then he straight-facedly declares of *Don Juan* 'this story's actually true' (I, 202, 8), challenging the reader to reconsider the basis on which historical discourse is considered to be hierarchically superior because 'objective' while literature is relegated to the merely fictional:

> If any person doubt it, I appeal
> To history, tradition, and to facts,
> To newspapers, whose truth all know and feel,
> To plays in five, and operas in three acts;
> All these confirm my statement a good deal,
> But that which more completely faith exacts
> Is, that myself, and several now in Seville,
> *Saw* Juan's last elopement with the devil. (*Don Juan* I, 203)

This faux-naive passage makes us realize how relative is our judgement on what constitutes a fact, and question whether 'history' is closer to 'tradition' than 'facts', as the word order of the line suggests. We are asked to consider the relative basis of authority we grant to 'facts', depending on their provenance: whether written in a history book, traditionally believed, printed in a newspaper, artistic representations of events, or eyewitness accounts. All could constitute evidence of sorts, but all need to be weighed with each other and all may well be subjective. In fact, the narrator later goes as far as to call 'History, the grand liar' (*Don Juan* IX, 81, 4). Though the Don Juan myth itself is to the modern mind merely outright fiction, on account of its supernatural ending, it can tell us a great deal about the kind of culture which produced so many versions of it. Like Vico, Byron is suggesting that myths can be historically understood.

By alluding to the pantomime as well as the original Renaissance tragicomedy *El Burlador de Sevilla* (1630) he claims to have seen himself (I, 1, 203), Byron obliquely acknowledges that the defiant villain has now become softened to a figure of fun: fought over by fisherwomen who 'grow quite outrageous' in *Don Juan, or the Libertine Destroy'd: A Tragical Pantominial (sic) entertainment in two acts* (1798) and tormented in hell by female furies in Moncrieff's *Giovanni in London; or, the libertine reclaimed: an operatic extravaganza in two acts* (1817). Setting his version at the time of the French Revolution, Byron is hinting that such literature which demonized the aristocrat as predator would soon cease to be produced, now that the mercantile classes had seized power and were no longer in fear. His plan to have Juan guillotined in the Terror (*BLJ* VIII, 78; Medwin 1966, 165) would, however, demonstrate how very limited is the concept of 'freedom' in bourgeois liberalism, when, in power, it enforces a regulatory Puritanism as totalitarian as that of the church.

Innumerable histories were written in the Romantic period. In the sale catalogues of Byron's library, which contain only part of his former collection, there are over two hundred history books and a further two hundred and fifty volumes of letters and memoirs.[5] As well as the classic sceptics Voltaire, Gibbon, Hume, Bayle, to the first two of whom Byron paid tribute in *Childe Harold's Pilgrimage* Canto III, stanza 105, we notice how very many modern histories he collected which relate to Europe in the late eighteenth century and revolutionary period, especially on France, Russia, Austria and Prussia.[6] Byron said of *Don Juan*: 'I *have* no plan—I *had* no plan—but I have or had materials' (*BLJ* VI, 207). The 'materials' were not only his personal experience as a libertine but also his beloved books, many of which he had parted with when he left

England and was now in the act of replacing. These helped him compose *Don Juan*, a poem set at the end of the *ancien régime* yet written in a continuous present.

Byron prided himself on his realism, and followed his historical sources, memoirs, letters, secondary accounts, so closely that he was accused of plagiarism by contemporary periodicals. For example, the *Monthly Magazine* for August and September 1821 noticed the account of the shipwreck in Canto II echoed contemporary narratives of disasters at sea. Byron actually prided himself on his research: commenting to Murray that 'not a single *circumstance* of it—was not taken from *fact*—not indeed from *any single shipwreck*—but all from different *actual* facts of different wrecks', but he felt he made his sources his own (*BLJ* VIII, 186). Indeed, he often wrote sceptically 'against the grain' of the original, especially the newest 'Romantic' histories. For example, the Ismail cantos – the centrepiece of the poem – satirically undermined the heroic glorification of war in his chief and acknowledged source: Castelnau's *Essai sur l'histoire ancienne et moderne de la Nouvelle Russie* (1820) (Vassallo 1984, 125; Boyd 1958, 148–50).[7] Whereas nineteenth-century poets, led by Walter Scott, were inspired by the Napoleonic Wars to repudiate Augustan pacifism and to paint war in idealized terms, Byron swam against the stream.[8]

As I have argued elsewhere, in rewriting the Don Juan myth as a travel poem where the treatment of women indicates the stage of culture reached by their society, Byron also borrowed but subverted the comparativist formula of two recent world histories of women, which had been in his library: *The History of the Female Sex* (1808) by Christoph Meiners and *Women, Their Condition and Influence in Society* (1803) by J.A.P. Ségur (Franklin 1992, 102–27). Byron follows a similar progressivist procedure to his historians of taking Juan from Spain first to a primitive Greek isle, then to despotic Turkey, followed by the 'enlightened despotism' of feudal Russia and finally to the limited monarchy of Britain, for the increasing status of woman was seen as an index of the civilising process by Enlightenment philosophes. He turns the premise on its head, however, by hymning the sexual freedom of Southern women compared to the pious Northerners. Comparing Haidée with Aurora: 'the difference in them / Was such as lies between a flower and gem' (XV, 58, 7–8).

Meiners and Ségur themselves had deformed the progressivist premise they had inherited from Scottish Enlightenment philosophical histories by collapsing its comparativism into a simplified, and, in Meiners's case, racist binary opposition between barbaric slavery of Eastern women on the one hand and the chivalrous protection of Northern European women in the home on the other. Writing under the shadow of the revolution, they argued that allowing French women to participate in the public sphere had gone too far in the direction of female emancipation. They both called for a return to women's 'natural' role of chaste motherhood at home. Byron's poem opens by satirizing this nineteenth-century domestic ideology in the person of Donna Inez:

> Some women use their tongues—she look'd a lecture,
>> Each eye a sermon, and her brow a homily,
> An all-in-all-sufficient self-director,
>> Like the lamented late Sir Samuel Romilly,
> The Law's expounder, and the State's corrector,
>> Whose suicide was almost an anomaly—
> One sad example more, that 'All is vanity,'—
> (The jury brought their verdict in 'Insanity').
>
> In short, she was a walking calculation,
>> Miss Edgeworth's novels stepping from their covers,
> Or Mrs. Trimmer's books on education,
>> Or 'Coelebs' Wife' set out in search of lovers,
> Morality's prim personification,
>> In which not Envy's self a flaw discovers,
> To others' share let 'female errors fall,'
> For she had not even one—the worst of all.
>
> Oh! she was perfect past all parallel—
>> Of any modern female saint's comparison;
> So far beyond the cunning powers of hell,
>> Her guardian angel had given up his garrison;
> Even her minutest motions went as well
>> As those of the best time-piece made by Harrison:
> In virtues nothing earthly could surpass her,
> Save thine 'incomparable oil,' Macassar! (*Don Juan* I, 15–17)

Then, rather than endorsing the Eurocentric agenda of his Romantic period histories, Byron's poem revalues the spontaneous sensuality of Southern women with African blood, such as Julia and Haidée, over the repression which characterizes Northern women such as Adeline or hypocritical prudes such as Inez.

I'd now like to try and bring together the historicisms of both poet and critic into a frame where they can comment on each other, and that frame is the avowed libertinism of *Don Juan*. Raymond Williams's theory of dominant, emergent and residual ideologies is useful in considering how the sexual politics in the first two cantos may have appeared to contemporary readers in 1819 (Williams 1977, 121–8). By taking a libertine as his hero, in the wake of the separation scandal, Byron was championing the sexual mores of the aristocracy, a class increasingly marginalized from the centres of power, as his own family's decline exemplified. Against such 'residual' ideology, the domestic moralism of the Evangelical middle classes had triumphed and become culturally 'dominant'. Yet the aristocrat's poem consciously reaches out to make common cause with the libertinage of the underworld, where working-class radicals peddled pornography alongside political pamphlets, for example by adapting Hone's parody of the Ten Commandments (I, 204–6), and in the Preface to Cantos VI, VII and VIII by supporting the right of free speech for James Watson, Samuel Waddington and Richard Carlile (CPW V, 296–7, 719). The Byron scandal had itself helped weaken the status of the aristocracy, just as the Queen Caroline affair, in which the notoriously profligate Prince Regent accused his wife of infidelity, was undermining the monarchy.[9] By apparently accepting and justifying the label of aristocratic libertine which had been affixed to him in the newspapers, and by setting his story in the last days of the *ancien régime*, Byron knowingly exacerbated its subversive effect. Reviewers reacted to the publication of Cantos I and II with a storm of outrage, but by the time the apostate aristocrat was unmasking the private life of the 'bon ton' in the English cantos, they were less condemnatory and doubtless 'enjoyed the spectacle of a nobleman pillorying his own class in print' (Ward 1979, 24). The 'emergent' ideology of feminism consisted at the time in championing Lady Byron as a victim of the inequity of the marriage and property laws, and turning against Byron – the libertine title of the poem was anyway a calculated disincentive to respectable women to consider themselves readers. But just how far away was the rise of feminism may be seen by the general condemnation which greeted the activism of women of all classes in favour of Queen Caroline (Clark 2004, 200), and even mid-century by the calumny which Harriet Beecher Stowe attracted by her vindication of Lady Byron and vilification of the poet.

How can the libertine text talk back to our own preconceptions today? Identifying the misogyny of past literature is easy enough for modern feminist critics, but researching the historical conditions of production may challenge any bland assumption that this confirms the hegemony of patriarchy, and likewise ask us to become aware of the implications of the historical origin of our own ideology. The libertine tradition of freethinking drew inspiration from classical philosophy and literature especially Ovid, from Rabelais and late medieval anticlericalism, and from Enlightenment scepticism (Porter 1990). Flowering after the Civil War in seventeenth-century Britain, it was shaped both by revolution and by its opposition to Puritan Christianity. In his recent study of libertines and radicals in early modern London, James Grantham Turner argues that bawdy libertine literature – far from demonstrating patriarchal hegemony – actually originated as a satiric reaction to the increased authority of women: 'a deliberate attempt to confront and neutralize women's efforts to establish their own institutions – an attempt that frequently unravels, ... by paying an unintended tribute to women's achievement' (Turner 2002, xiii). In other words, libertinism and feminism originated as a binary: a twin reaction to Puritanism and social revolution. Byron's *Don Juan* provides another example of the *defensive* nature of libertine literature in a later period of puritan revival.[10] The myth itself is a fantasy of male power over women: fetishized repetition betrays the depth of anxiety.

The portrait of Donna Inez was impelled by a desire for revenge on the poet's wife, Annabella Milbanke, and her powerful supporters in the separation scandal of 1816, but is painted, not as a likeness, but as an ideological caricature made up of female-authored literary texts.[11] Byron's portrait of Inez's calculated performance (she runs like clockwork, perfectly oiled) brings to mind the contemporary critic Diane Long Hoeveler's definition of the 'professional femininity' of the nineteenth-century heroine of female-authored Gothic fiction '– a cultivated pose, a masquerade of docility, passivity, wise passiveness, and tightly controlled emotions' which obtains power through staged weakness (Hoeveler 1998, xv). Such Richardsonian scenarios fantasize a form of 'victim feminism' by pitting the plucky protagonist against an aristocratic libertine. It is this mythologizing which Byron's poem seeks to deconstruct. By doing so he unintentionally pays a tribute to the dominance of the women writers of his day.

Byron's choice of the chauvinist Anglicans Sarah Trimmer and Hannah More as amongst Inez's favourite authors reminds us that originally the word 'libertines' described sixteenth- and seventeenth-century freethinkers or Protestants who supported religious toleration and refused to accept the social and ecclesiastical authority of one national church.[12] This aspect of libertinism is still discernible in *Don Juan* – which ridicules in the mock dedication the Lake poets, who were now using their pens to support the sacred tie between the Anglican Church and the Kingdom. Southey went on to write *The Book of the Church* (1824), and *Vindiciae Ecclesiae Anglicanae* (1826); Wordsworth published *Ecclesiastical Sketches* (1822); Coleridge wrote *On the Constitution of the Church and State* (1830).

It is a testimony to Hannah More's influence as a leader of the Evangelical movement within the Anglican Church that it is she (via her disciple Inez) who is Byron's main target in Canto 1 – not the freethinking feminist Mary Wollstonecraft – who had herself been so castigated in the anti-Jacobin press as an advocate of free love, after Godwin's *Memoirs* were published in 1798, that she was now only respected in Unitarian and radical circles. A historicist focus is not just useful in clarifying this original context of Byron's satire but should help us to reflect on our own feminist practice. For the current rehabilitation of Hannah More by present-day secular feminists, who compare her as an educationalist with Wollstonecraft, glosses over sectarian differences dividing Romantic period women writers seen as crucial at the time (Mellor 2000, Myers 1986). Byron's poem challenged nineteenth-century feminists to include sexual freedom on their agenda. It still challenges us, as modern readers, to detach ourselves from the libertine / victim binaries which shaped nineteenth-century gender politics, and to imagine a freedom for women outside the puritan heritage.

In contrast to the moralistic mother, Inez, Juan's first lover, Donna Julia, is a Rousseauistic heroine, who makes the feminist point that adulteresses are victimized by society's double standard, in her famous letter:

> 'Man's love is of his life a thing apart,
>   'Tis woman's whole existence; man may range
> The court, camp, church, the vessel, and the mart,
>   Sword, gown, gain glory, offer in exchange
> Pride, fame, ambition, to fill up his heart,
>   And few there are whom these can not estrange;
> Man has all these resources, we but one,
> To love again, and be again undone.' (*Don Juan* I, 194)

Hobhouse wrote 'Coppet to wit' in the margin of the manuscript, realizing it alluded to Madame de Staël's *De l'influence des passions* (1796), 'Love is the story of women's lives; it is an episode in that of men', and *Corinne* (1807) Book 18 Chapter 5 (*CPW* V, 680).[13] Joanne Wilkes points out that Byron's annotations to Teresa Guiccioli's copy of the novel show particular interest in this section of the novel (Wilkes 1999, 11).

Byron's parody of contrasting novelistic heroines of sense and sensibility in Canto I thus cleverly sends up the two most best-selling women novelists of the period, rivals Hannah More, and Madame de Staël. More's one novel, *Coelebs in Search of a Wife* (1809), was written in spite of its author's disapproval of fiction, specifically to counteract the nefarious influence of Staël's *Corinne*, which would go into thirty-two French editions in forty years and set the agenda for nineteenth-century women's writing on both sides of the channel.[14] *Coelebs* itself became a best-seller and went into twelve editions in the first year of publication. Both books were in Byron's library amongst scores of other female-authored novels, and though he had infuriated Staël by keeping a poker face whilst lecturing her in public that her inflated rhetoric about romantic love would encourage female immorality, he privately considered Staël a better novelist than the moralist Edgeworth (*BLJ* III, 226).

The satiric allusions in Canto I to Maria Edgeworth, Sarah Trimmer, Hannah More and Madame de Staël demonstrate the male poet's fear of the influence and authority of female novelists. *Don Juan* started life as a novel, 'Don Julian', after John Murray had urged Byron to try his hand at prose. He and Scott had already remasculinized poetry with their adventurous verse tales, superseding the older generation of female poets who had reigned supreme in the 1780s. But until Scott published *Waverley*, women continued to publish more novels than men and set the literary agenda. Even as a narrative poem, the novelistic form of *Don Juan* constitutes an attempted revival of the masculine episodic comic epic of Fielding and the self-conscious fictionality of Sterne in opposition to the female Richardsonian tradition.

Michel Feher has argued that, as well as revenge on the female reading public, the motive of libertine fiction was to explore morality (Feher 1997, 12). Byron concluded Canto I by challenging the reader to deny it was not a 'moral tale' (I, 207–9) – a claim he often repeated but which is usually dismissed as mere tongue-in-cheek. But his narrator does utilize a materialist stance to expose both the artificiality of individuals like Inez who repress the promptings of nature in order to obtain power over others, as well as the folly of Platonists like Julia whose belief in transcendent love blinds them to its rootedness in the physical. In response to More and Staël's claim that, one way or another, women are self-sacrificing victims – the poem reduces both orthodox morality and the cult of glorifying human relationships to their Hobbesian basics in the ego. Byron here follows in the footsteps of French eighteenth-century libertine fiction by challenging female sentimentalists such as Staël, successors to the precieuses, who argued that true love does exist, but who asserted that only women were capable of selfless love and constancy.[15]

Back in 1813, when idolized by women readers, Byron had in *The Giaour* produced a hero who devotes his whole life to the memory of the one and only love of his life. He was mocked by Jane Austen in the form of her Byronic Captain Benwick in *Persuasion*, whose mourning for his dead fiancée is exacerbated by his reading *The Giaour* but still evaporates after a few months after it has succeeded in making him an object of sympathetic interest to the young ladies. *Persuasion* concludes with Anne Elliot arguing against a male champion of masculine fidelity for the greater constancy of her own sex in words comparable to Corinne's (Austen 1976, 236). It's quite likely that Byron had read the novel and was responding specifically to it as well as *Corinne*, for it had been published by Murray, who had sent him a bundle of new publications at the time he was finishing the canto (*CPW* V, 680). Now the poet took a new direction in the argument by portraying even Don Juan himself as capable of true love though not monogamy. The young Juan exemplifies what Catherine Cusset has categorized as not 'active' or predatory libertinage, but 'passive' libertinage: whereby the individual is momentarily overwhelmed by desire, which may coexist with his perfectly genuine love for another, because instinct temporarily makes him oblivious of any other reality but the physical (Cusset 1998, 2).[16] The Byronic narrator could be said to idealize instinct rather than love when he explains how Juan came to forget Julia:

> that which
> Men call inconstancy is nothing more
> Than admiration due where nature's rich
> Profusion with young beauty covers o'er
> Some favour'd object. (II, 211, 1–5)

> The heart is like the sky, a part of heaven,
> But changes night and day too, like the sky. (II, 214, 1–2)

The digressive 'mobility' of *Don Juan*, is a form produced by that scrutiny of orthodox morality in which philosophical libertinism originated, where the competing demands of morality and realism produced a structural dualism. Moral relativism had led to a fragmentary and dialogic form in early French novels (DeJean 1981, 84). The Pulcian burlesque tradition in Italy, in which Byron steeped himself, was comparable in its open-ended parody of romantic heroism which refused to systematize even its own scepticism. The poem begins by satirizing Julia's belief in platonic love (I, 79–85) and gently ironizes even Haidée's spontaneous capacity for passion (II, 190–1), yet it allows each woman the tragic closure necessary to set the seal on her absolute belief in love. Because their tragedies are brought about by patriarchal enforcement of the double standard, the paradox is created that women's higher ideals may be perceived as the consolation of oppression, perhaps a 'false consciousness'. Yet, ironically, male sexual freedom precludes men from becoming heroic rebels. Only a woman can 'risk /A throne, the world, the universe, to be / Beloved in her own way' (VI, 3, 2–4).

Men are doomed by liberty to a life based on instinct and performing only comic supporting roles in the opera of love. Haidée cannot be thought corruptible: so like all nineteenth-century heroines she must die:

> Days lay she in that state unchanged, though chill
>   With nothing livid, still her lips were red;
> She had no pulse, but death seem'd absent still;
>   No hideous sign proclaim'd her surely dead;
> Corruption came not in each mind to kill
>   All hope; to look upon her sweet face bred
> New thoughts of life, for it seem'd full of soul,
> She had so much, earth could not claim the whole. (IV, 60)

Juan, meanwhile isn't permitted an aria. As in Richard Strauss's *Ariadne auf Naxos*, he is relegated to the backstage harlequinade, being shackled in the slave-ship with a troupe of opera singers discussing their performances.

To sum up, we can see that the sexual satire *Don Juan* unconsciously testifies to the growing power of nineteenth-century women in the church, education and in literature. The separation scandal which occasioned the poem was only the opening salvo in the Byron controversy: a cause célèbre successfully exploited by feminist propagandists and reactivated at intervals throughout the nineteenth century. A pamphlet war had initially broken out in 1816 with poems published in answer to pirated copies of Byron's reproachful lyric to Annabella, 'Fare Thee Well!'. For example, Mrs Cockle's 'Reply to Lord Byron's "Fare thee well"' (Newcastle: S. Hodgson, 1817, 6) portrays Lady Byron as an angel of purity praying for Byron's redemption.

> Talk not of sever'd love—of ties disjoin'd—
> What ties can fetter, or what laws can bind
> The slave of vice—of passions uncontroul'd?—
> *Proud in* his errors—in his *wand'rings bold*,—
> *Bound by no duty*—to no *feelings just*—
> Nor *man* his *friend*—nor *Providence his trust*;
> Yet blessed with gifts, which in their proper use,
> The imperishable laurel would produce-
> With *talents*, that in virtue's better way

Had shed around him glory's brightest ray;
With *wit* that might have lent a charm to sense,
Beyond the Muse's dangerous eloquence;
Warm with the sophists' fire—the sceptic's art,
To *charm* the fancy – but *corrupt the heart.*
     Perhaps, when retrospection's painful hour
Marks thy lone wand'rings on some distant shore,
When even pleasure's voice shall cease to charm;
Reflection, pointing to *one* angel form,
In blest communion with her kindred skies,
Whilst soft for thee, her whisper'd prayers arise,
Shall tell thee WHERE, with *supplicating love,*
She breathes thy pardon here, and *asks it* from ABOVE.
                                                                            C.
Newcastle, April 16th.

Mrs Cockle was a patriotic moralist very much in the Hannah More
mould, whose conduct book *Important Studies for the Female Sex*, advertised
in 1811, closed with a letter on death displaying 'all the horrors attendant
on that awful change when met by sinful infidelity' according to the
approving notice in the *Anti-Jacobin Review.*

Many *ottava rima* parodies appeared after the publication of *Don Juan*
which pictured the poet going to hell, though some wrote in support
of Byron. The anonymous author of *Faliero, or The Neapolitan Libertine*
(1823) hoped its readers would comprise both 'the Satanic and a portion
of the Evangelical school' (3). His salacious tale invoked male homosocial
bonding by pitying women for their confinement by the sexual double
standard, relishing heterosexual libertinism while castigating effeminate
'dandies' and 'mollies'. He declared:

> I hate the woman that for ever bent
> On fine descriptions of her darling preacher
> And wishing wicked sinners would repent
> Of all those follies which can never reach her. (stanza 60, 33)

The Byron controversy was reactivated in 1830 when Moore's *Life of
Byron* was published, and Lady Byron issued a rebuttal of his depiction
of her parents' role in the separation. Lady Byron was by now a phi-
lanthropist pioneer of the cooperative movement, who met but did
not approve of Robert Owen. Ray Strachey, in his magisterial history of
the women's movement, notes that she assisted charitable schemes of

feminist friends such as Mary Carpenter, Harriet Martineau and Anna Jameson.[17] Her friends cited the controversy in 1816 over the financial settlement and threat to the custody of Ada as one of the case studies exposing the inequities of the marriage laws. Harriet Martineau's obituary of Lady Byron in 1860 portrayed her as a philanthropic heroine in thrall to male libertinism. In 1869 – it is no coincidence that this was the year which saw the publication of John Stuart Mill's *On the Subjection of Women* – Harriet Beecher Stowe decided to go public that Lady Byron had confided to her that the cause of the separation was the poet's incest with his half-sister. Her article, later extended into a book, *Lady Byron Vindicated* (1870), caused a storm of pamphlets on both sides of the Atlantic. Stowe's sister Catherine Beecher was the American successor to Hannah More and instrumental in popularizing domestic ideology. For social conservatives such as Stowe, it took this extreme binary between pious victim and aristocratic libertine to make her own precarious alliance with feminism acceptable.

The battle between feminism and libertinism has been shown to be essentially a literary one, in which language has been wielded to produce weapons of false universals. In the 1970s women's movement, Angela Carter urged modern feminists to deconstruct this binary by learning from the ultra-libertine Marquis de Sade the relationship between sexuality and power. In *The Sadeian Woman* she urged us to shed our pious self-image:

> All the mythic versions of women, from the myth of the redeeming purity of the virgin to that of the healing, reconciling mother, are consolatory nonsenses [...] if a revival of the myths of these cults gives women emotional satisfaction, it does so at the price of obscuring the real conditions of life.

Yet she does not let the Marquis – and we may add Byron – off the hook. For she adds that the libertine's belief that through sex 'we touch the bedrock of human nature' is another consolatory myth.

> Flesh is not an irreducible human universal. Although the erotic relationship may seem to exist freely, on its own terms, among the distorted social relationships of a bourgeois society, it is in fact ... a direct confrontation of two beings whose actions in the bed are wholly determined by their acts when they are out of it. [...] Our flesh arrives to us out of history. (Carter 1979, 5–9)[18]

notes

1. T.S. Eliot repeated Swinburne's charge that Byron had no ear for language: 'Of Byron, one can say, as of no other English poet of his eminence, that he added nothing to the language ... I cannot think of any other poet of his distinction who might so easily have been an accomplished foreigner writing English.' *On Poetry and Poets*, 201.
2. See especially Butler's essay 'Repossessing the past: the case for an open literary history', Levinson 1989, 64–84.
3. Louis Althusser, *Lenin and Philosophy and other essays*, trans. B. Brewster (1972).
4. Jon Klancher comments that 'English Romantic writings were staged within an unstable ensemble of older institutions in crisis (state and church) and emerging institutional events which pressured any act of cultural production' so that historical reading necessitates a more complex positioning of texts against this background than the assumption of an absolutist state in new historicism. See 'English Romanticism and Cultural Production', in Veeser 1989, 77–88 (80).
5. W.H. Marshall, 'The catalogues for sale of Lord Byron's books', *Library Chronicle* 34 (1968): 24–50; 'Catalogue of the Library of The Late Lord Byron ... which will be sold at auction by Mr Evans. London, 1827.' See Elizabeth Boyd, *Byron's Don Juan: A Critical Study*, 92.
6. There are 18 references to Gibbon, 8 to Voltaire, 4 to Bayle and 1 to Hume in Byron's poetry and notes.
7. For detailed commentary on other possible sources, see also Peter Cochran's edition at <http://www.internationalbyronsociety.org/critiques.asp>.
8. On the nineteenth-century turn to the glorification of war, see Simon Bainbridge, *British Poetry and the Revolutionary and Napoleonic Wars: Visions of Conflict*.
9. In 1821 the latter scandal of the sexual double standard afforded such opportunity for radical propagandists and working-class agitators to use street politics and print culture to campaign for reform that there were fears that revolution was about to break out.
10. For a view that Byron was not a libertine, see Jonathan Gross, *Byron, the Erotic Liberal*, 3. Charles Donelan writes persuasively of *Don Juan* enacting a 'male revolt against the social conventions of nationalistic domestic manhood' in *Romanticism and Male Fantasy in Byron's Don Juan*, 15.
11. See Byron's refutation of the reviewers' charge that Inez was a satire on Lady Byron: *BLJ* IV, 477; VI, 95, 131, 257; VII, 208, 239.
12. See Benjamin J. Kaplan, *Calvinists and Libertines: Confession and Community in Utrecht 1578–1620*, 295; and on religious scepticism and the French novel, see Joan DeJean, *Libertine Strategies: Freedom and the Novel in Seventeenth-Century France*, x. As late as 1828, tracts against deists and atheists were labelling them libertines, for example: *Altamont the Libertine, or, Death-bed scenes of infidels and Christians*, whose accounts of bad deaths included the decidedly unrakish Hobbes, Hume, Thomas Paine and Voltaire.
13. 'There are sorrows within me that I shall never express, not even by writing. I have not the strength to write. Love alone can plumb these depths. How fortunate men are to go to war, to risk their lives, to give themselves up to

the passion for honour and danger! But there is nothing outside themselves which relieves women. Their lives, unchanging in the presence of misfortune, are a very long torture.' (Madame de Staël, *Corinne, or Italy*, trans. and ed. Sylvia Raphael, intro. John Isbell, 358).

14. Staël 1998, x. Compare with this passage from Hannah More, *Coelebs in Search of a Wife*, 205: 'Love and poetry commonly influence the two sexes in a very disproportionate degree. With men, each of them is only one passion among many. Love has various and powerful competitors in hearts divided between ambition, business and pleasure. Poetry is only one amusement in minds distracted by a thousand tumultuous pursuits: whereas in girls of ardent tempers, whose feelings are not curbed by restraint and regulated by religion, love is considered as the great business of their earthly existence. It is cherished, not as the "cordial drop", but as the whole contents of the cup; the remainder is considered only as froth or dregs. The unhappy victim not only submits to the destructive dominion of a despotic passion, but glories in it.'

15. Nancy K. Miller also comments on male libertine writers' appropriation of earlier feminist sentimental traditions in *French Dressing: Women, Men and Ancien Régime Fiction*, 77. Though libertinism is usually associated with eighteenth-century French aristocratic culture, its connection with the radical and disreputable underworld is explored in Peter Cryle and Lisa O'Connell, eds, *Libertine Enlightenment: Sex, Liberty and Licence in the Eighteenth Century*, 2.

16. This is in contrast to the 'active' libertinism of Laclos and Sade, which denies the existence of love.

17. Ray Strachey, *The Cause: A Short History of the Women's Movement in Great Britain*, 85.

18. Angela Carter, *The Sadeian Woman*, 5–9.

works cited and suggestions for further reading

Althusser, Louis. *Lenin and Philosophy and other essays*. Trans. B. Brewster. New York: Monthly Review Press, 1972.

Austen, Jane. *Persuasion*. Harmondsworth: Penguin, 1976.

Bainbridge, Simon. *British Poetry and the Revolutionary and Napoleonic Wars: Visions of Conflict*. Oxford: Oxford University Press, 2003.

Baldick, Chris. *The Social Mission of English Criticism 1848–1932*. Oxford: Clarendon Press, 1983.

Boyd, Elizabeth. *Byron's Don Juan: A Critical Study*. New York: The Humanities Press, 1958.

Butler, Marilyn. 'The Orientalism of Byron's *Giaour*'. *Byron and the Limits of Fiction*. Eds Bernard Beatty and Vincent Newey. Liverpool: Liverpool University Press, 1988. 78–96.

——. 'John Bull's Other Kingdom: Byron's Intellectual Comedy'. *Studies in Romanticism* 31.3 (1992): 281–94.

Carter, Angela. *The Sadeian Woman*. London: Virago, 1979.

Chandler, James K. *England in 1819: The Politics of Literary Culture and the Case of Romantic Historicism*. London and Chicago: University of Chicago Press, 1998.

Cheeke, Stephen. *Byron and Place: History, Translation, Nostalgia.* Basingstoke and London: Palgrave Macmillan, 2003.

Chernaik, Warren. *Sexual Freedom in Restoration Literature.* Cambridge: Cambridge University Press, 1995.

Christensen, Jerome. *Lord Byron's Strength: Romantic Writing and Commercial Society.* Baltimore, MD: Johns Hopkins University Press, 1993.

Clark, Anna. *Scandal: The Sexual Politics of the British Constitution.* Princeton and Oxford: Princeton University Press, 2004.

Clery, E.J., Caroline Franklin and Peter Garside, eds. *Authorship, Commerce and the Public: Scenes of Writing, 1750–1850.* Basingstoke: Palgrave, 2002.

Colebrook, Claire. *New Literary Histories: New Historicism and Contemporary Criticism.* Manchester and New York: Manchester University Press, 1997.

Crompton, Louis. *Byron and Greek Love: Homophobia in Nineteenth-Century England.* London: Faber and Faber, 1985.

Cryle, Peter and Lisa O'Connell, eds. *Libertine Enlightenment: Sex, Liberty and Licence in the Eighteenth Century.* Basingstoke: Palgrave Macmillan, 2004.

Cusset, Catherine. 'The Lesson of Libertinage'. *Libertinage and Modernity.* Yale French Studies 94 (1998): 1–17.

DeJean Joan. *Libertine Strategies: Freedom and the Novel in Seventeenth-Century France.* Columbus, Ohio: Ohio State University Press, 1981.

de Staël, Madame. *Corinne, or Italy.* Trans. Sylvia Raphael; intro. John Isbell. Oxford: Oxford University Press, 1998.

Donelan, Charles. *Romanticism and Male Fantasy in Byron's Don Juan.* Basingstoke: Palgrave Macmillan, 2000.

Elfenbein, Andrew. *Byron and the Victorians.* Cambridge: Cambridge University Press, 1995.

Eliot, T.S. *On Poetry and Poets.* London: Faber and Faber, 1957.

Feher, Michael., ed. *The Libertine Reader: Eroticism and Enlightenment in Eighteenth-Century France.* New York: Zone Books, 1997.

Foot, Michael. *The Poetry of Politics: A Vindication of Byron.* London: Collins, 1988.

Franklin, Caroline. *Byron's Heroines.* Oxford: Oxford University Press, 1992.

——. 'Juan's Sea Changes: Class, Race and Gender in Byron's *Don Juan*'. *Theory in Practice: Don Juan.* Ed. Nigel Wood. Buckingham and Bristol: Open University Press, 1993. 56–89.

——. *Byron, a literary Life.* Basingstoke: Macmillan, 2000.

Gilmartin, Kevin. *Print Politics: The Press and Radical Opposition in Early Nineteenth-Century England.* Cambridge: Cambridge University Press, 1996.

Graham, Peter W. *Don Juan and Regency England.* Charlottesville and London: University of Virginia Press, 1990.

Gross, Jonathan. *Byron, the Erotic Liberal.* Lanham, Boulder, New York and Oxford: Rowman and Littlefield, 2001.

Haslett, Moyra. *Byron's Don Juan and the Don Juan Legend.* Oxford: Clarendon Press, 1997.

Hoeveler, Diane Long. *Gothic Feminism: The Professionalization of Gender from Charlotte Smith to the Brontës.* Liverpool: Liverpool University Press, 1998.

Kaplan, Benjamin J. *Calvinists and Libertines: Confession and Community in Utrecht 1578–1620.* Oxford; Oxford University Press, 1995.

Kelsall, Malcolm. *Byron's Politics.* Brighton: Harvester, 1987.

Lansdown, Richard. *Byron's Historical Dramas.* Oxford: Clarendon Press, 1992.

Leask, Nigel. *British Romantic Writers and the East: Anxieties of Empire.* Cambridge: Cambridge University Press, 1992.

Levinson, Marjorie, ed. *Rethinking Historicism: Critical Readings in Romantic History.* Oxford: Basil Blackwell, 1989.

McGann, Jerome J. *The Romantic Ideology: A Critical Investigation.* Chicago: Chicago and London, 1983.

——. *A Critique of Modern Textual Criticism.* Chicago and London: University of Chicago Press, 1983.

——, ed. *Textual Criticism and Literary Interpretation.* Chicago, IL: University of Chicago Press, 1985a.

——. *The Beauty of Inflections: Literary Investigations in Historical Method and Theory.* Oxford: Clarendon Press, 1985b.

——. *Social Values and Poetic Acts: The Historical Judgment of Literary Work.* Cambridge, Mass. and London: Harvard University Press, 1988.

——. *Radiant Textuality: Literature after the World Wide Web.* New York and Basingstoke: Palgrave, 2001.

——. *Byron and Romanticism.* Ed. James Soderholm. Cambridge: Cambridge University Press, 2002.

Medwin, Thomas. *Conversations of Lord Byron.* Ed. Ernest J. Lovell, Jr. Princeton, NJ: Princeton University Press, 1966.

Mellor, Anne K. *Mothers of the Nation: Women's Political Writing in England, 1780–1830.* Bloomington, IN: Indiana University Press, 2000.

Miller, Nancy K. *French Dressing: Women, Men and Ancien Régime Fiction.* New York and London: Routledge, 1995.

More, Hannah. *Coelebs in Search of a Wife* (1808). Repr. Bristol: Thoemmes Press, 1995.

Myers, Mitzi. 'Impeccable Governesses, Rational Dames, and Moral Mothers: Mary Wollstonecraft and the Female Tradition in Georgian Children's Books'. *Children's Literature.* Eds Margaret Higonnet and Barbara Rosen. New Haven and London: Yale University Press, 1986. 31–59.

Pollack, Ellen. 'Feminism and the New Historicism: A tale of difference or the same old story?' *The Eighteenth Century* 29. 3 (1988): 281–6.

Porter, Roy. 'Libertinism and promiscuity' in *The Don Giovanni Book: Myths of Seduction and Betrayal.* Ed. Jonathan Miller. London and Boston: Faber and Faber, 1990. 1–19.

Rigney, Ann. *Imperfect Histories: The Elusive Past and the Legacy of Romantic Historicism.* Ithaca and London: Cornell University Press, 2001.

Shilstone, Frederick W. *Byron and the Myth of Tradition.* Lincoln: University of Nebraska Press, 1988.

Siskin, Clifford. *The Work of Writing: Literature and Social Change 1700–1830.* Baltimore, MD: Johns Hopkins University Press, 1998.

Southgate, Beverley. *History: What and Why? Ancient, Modern and Postmodern Perspectives.* London and New York: Routledge, 1996.

St Clair, William. *The Reading Nation in the Romantic Period.* Cambridge: Cambridge University Press, 2004.

Strachey, Ray. *The Cause: A Short History of the Women's Movement in Great Britain.* London: Virago, 1979.

Swinburne, A.C. 'Wordsworth and Byron'. *Nineteenth Century* 15 (April, 1884), repr. *Miscellanies*. London: Chatto and Windus, 1911.

Turner, James Grantham. *Libertines and Radicals in Early Modern London*. Cambridge: Cambridge University Press, 2002.

Vassallo, Peter. *Byron: The Italian Literary Influence*. New York: St Martin's Press, 1984.

Veeser, H. Aram. ed. *The New Historicism*. New York and London: Routledge, 1989.

Ward, J.A. *The Critical Reputation of Byron's Don Juan in Britain*. Salzburg Studies in English Literature. No. 91, Romantic Reassessment. Ed. James Hogg. Salzburg: Salzburg University Press, 1979.

Watkins, Daniel P. *Social Relations in Byron's Eastern Tales*. London and Toronto: Associated University Presses, 1987.

——. *A Materialist Critique of English Romantic Drama*. Gainesville: University Press of Florida, 1993.

White, Hayden. *Metahistory: The Historical Imagination in Nineteenth-century Europe*. Baltimore and London: Johns Hopkins University Press, 1973.

Wilkes, Joanne. *Lord Byron and Madame de Staël: Born for Opposition*. Aldershot: Ashgate, 1999.

Williams, Raymond. *Marxism and Literature*. Oxford: Oxford University Press, 1977.

Wilson, Frances, ed. *Byromania: Portraits of the Artist in Nineteenth and Twentieth-Century Culture*. Basingstoke: Macmillan, 1999.

Wolfson, Susan. 'Couplets, Self, and *The Corsair*'. *Studies in Romanticism* 27.4 (1988): 491–513.

——. '"Their She Condition": Cross-Dressing and the politics of gender in *Don Juan*.' *ELH* 58 (Fall 1991): 867–902.

——. *Borderlines: The Shifting of Gender in British Romanticism*. Palo Alto, CA: Stanford University Press, 2006.

Wood, Marcus. *Radical Satire and Print Culture 1790–1822*. Oxford: Oxford University Press, 1994.

5
byron and post-colonial criticism: the eastern tales

peter j. kitson

In recent years Romantic period studies have been transformed by the application of critical approaches deriving from post-colonial critical perspectives to the writing of the late eighteenth and early nineteenth centuries. What we describe as the Romantic Movement coincided with the beginnings of a modern British imperialism which involved the governance and exploitation of increasingly large portions of the globe as the nineteenth century wore on. It also involved the conflict with other imperial formations of the time, some expansive and others in decline; European empires such as the French and Russian, and non-European empires such as the Turkish Ottoman Empire and the Qing Empire of China. Romantic writers were not themselves imperialists in the literal sense of the term, though some of them became implicated in the imperial process; Coleridge, for instance, acted as a civil servant for the Governor of Malta, Sir Alexander Ball, and Charles Lamb and Thomas Love Peacock worked for the British East India Company. Many Romantic period writers, the Wordsworths, Coleridge, De Quincey, Austen and so on, had family who were involved in Empire in one way or another, and it certainly impinged on their consciousness as a pressing fact of life. This chapter, however, is concerned with a different sense of imperial involvement. Some recent historicist writing has charged that Romantic period writing, in its representation of other cultures and peoples, especially those of Islamic states is, in some ways, complicit or acts to further the imperial process. The work of Byron is especially interesting in this respect; in that he alone of all the canonical Romantic poets actually travelled in the Eastern Mediterranean or Levant in 1809–11 and that several of his writings originating from this experience represent the East or the Orient.

Representation of the East was familiar in the writing of Byron's time. In fact, the cultural historian Raymond Schwab described the Romantic age as the 'Oriental Renaissance' in that the European fascination with, and discovery of, Eastern languages and literatures, which accelerated in the mid to late eighteenth century, fuelled the interest of writers and their readers for Oriental subjects.[1] *Alf laylah wa laylah* or *The Thousand and One Nights* (which became known as *The Arabian Nights* were tales collected and translated by Antoine Galland from 1704 onwards. Galland's *Les Milles et une nuits* (translated into English from 1706 onwards) established a fascination with an East that was magical, paradisial, sensual, but also cruel and despotic; the abiding symbol for which was the harem or seraglio. This exoticised and often eroticized East easily became confused in the reader's mind with the actual East. Oriental fictions abounded in the eighteenth and early nineteenth centuries, the most notable being Montesquieu's *Lettres persane* (1721), William Collins *Persian Eclogues* (1742), Voltaire's *Zadig* (1748), Oliver Goldsmith's *A Citizen of the World* (1760–62), Frances Sheridan's *History of Nourjahad* (1767), Samuel Johnson's *Rasselas* (1759–60), John Hawkesworth *Amoran and Hamet* (1760); William Beckford's *Vathek* (1786), Elizabeth Hamilton's *Letters of a Hindu Raja* (1796), S.T. Coleridge's 'Kubla Khan' (composed c. 1797–98, published 1816), Walter Savage Landor's *Gebir* (1798), Robert Southey, *Thalaba the Destroyer* (1801) and *The Curse of Kehama* (1810), Sidney Owenson's *The Missionary* (1811), Thomas Moore's *Lalla Rookh* (1817), Percy Shelley's 'The Revolt of Islam' (1818), Thomas De Quincey's *Confessions of an English Opium Eater* (1821), James Moirer's *Adventures of Hajji Baba of Ispahan* (1824), and, of course, Byron's Eastern Tales of 1814–16. Not only was Orientalism a literary fashion, it permeated all cultural forms, including political discourse, architecture, visual art, music, and design in general (MacKenzie 1995).[2]

Many Orientalist texts regarded the East as a source of imaginative and creative renewal; however what was once viewed as a sympathetic engagement with the East, or alternatively dismissed as escapism and exoticism, has recently come to be considered in a much more suspect, if not sinister light. Rather than studying the East to learn about and understand other cultures, a number of post-colonial scholars and critics have claimed that European engagement with the East, and especially with Islam, is instead simply a series of recurring negative and often hostile stereotypes (Sardar 1999, 54–76). This reading of 'Orientalism' as a sustained and hostile way of looking at the East since the Crusades had been discussed in the scholarly Muslim and Arabic critiques of A.L. Tibawi, Anouar Abdel-Malek and Hichem Djait who saw in European writing about the East, the recycling of medieval images of Islam lacking objectivity, moderation or tolerance.[3] It was alleged by these critics that Europeans use the East against which to define their own self-image as rational and modern. Although a substantial body of writing had already appeared on this subject it was the Palestinian-American critic Edward Said's study *Orientalism* of 1978 which defined the idea and scope of the critique for a new generation of historically minded literary critics. Said expanded the critique in two important ways. First, he derived his methodology from the French post-structuralist historian Michel Foucault. Foucault had argued that the way we arrange knowledge and the institutions humans develop to advance learning are never disinterested or objective, but rather they are organized and arranged according to the dictates of the ruling system of power. Foucault argued that the linguistic articulation of knowledge, what he called the 'discourse', becomes an expression of power.[4] Said claimed that the discipline of Orientalism, the academic study of the East, was such a discourse and he identified this with the Italian Marxist, Antonio Gramsci's idea that the elite maintain their control over the masses by establishing a cultural hegemony to which all classes subscribe. Although locating Orientalist stereotypes back to the classical times, Said instanced Napoleon's Invasion of Egypt in 1798 as a key historical moment in the formulation of Orientalist discourse. Napoleon took with him scholars as well as soldiers to study the East who contributed to the French (and British) project to dominate the Near East politically and economically as well as militarily. Orientalism is thus a 'western style for dominating, restructuring, and having authority over the orient'.[5] Secondly, Said claimed that this political imperative was not just seen in the writings of contemporary travellers, diplomats, colonial administrators, linguists and historians but also in the work of imaginative writers and artists. Not only were novelists such as Kipling, Conrad, Chateaubriand, Nerval, and Flaubert, whose subject was often the East, guilty of furthering the project of Orientalism and Empire, but also writers such as Jane Austen, Charles Dickens, Henry James, and Thomas Hardy whose works hardly address such subjects, were similarly implicated. As John MacKenzie puts it, Said had the 'audacity to implicate the literature of sensibility, the Leavisite great tradition, in the squalor and brutality of imperialism' (MacKenzie1995, 5–6).

Orientalism thus became a grand narrative which subsumed many forms of cultural and scholarly endeavour to represent and contain the East. For Said, Orientalism is a body of knowledge as expressed through scholars and experts containing a family of ideas and a unifying set of values which describe and explain the East and its peoples and provide a method to deal with them. Writing about the East, whether scholarly or imaginative, thus creates the reality it attempts to describe, a reality bearing no real relation to the actual lived experience of the East. The Orientalist creates the Orient by assuming a European self that is rational, modern, technological, active, creative, masculine and in need of an irrational, sybaritic, passive, feminine, despotic and corrupt other to authenticate it.

Said's work was both praised and criticized in equal measure and it stimulated an extensive, sophisticated and, often, bitter debate (MacKenzie 1995, 1–19; Sardar 1999, 54–76; Macfie 2000, 1–10). His predominant concern with the literary was expanded to take into account different art forms such as popular culture, visual art, design, music, architecture and different regions, nations, cultures and peoples. Some traditional Orientalist scholars, such as Bernard Lewis and Ernest Gellner, have affirmed the objectivity and disinterestedness of the discipline; others have criticized Said for homogenizing a very disparate, heterogeneous and conflicting body of writing. Lisa Lowe has problematized the field by discriminating between French and British Orientalisms and the differing responses of male and female writers and travellers have also been adduced as further complicating the field.[6] Others such as Dennis Porter claimed that Said's totalizing discourse does not allow for any resistant counter discourse to challenge it, and Aijaz Ahmad argued that Said's Orientalism is paradoxically a product of the very European humanist tradition that he himself espouses.[7] Robert Young has also argued that if Orientalism has no contact with the 'real' how was its knowledge put into practice by an imperial project.[8] Other post-colonial theorists have criticized Said's over-reliance on the binary opposition of Self and Other. Homi K. Bhabha has argued that both the colonizer and colonized are psychologically heterogeneous and that the relationship between the two is not one of simple mastery and subservience but of strong ambivalence.[9] Mary Louise Pratt, though agreeing with Said that the writing of travellers actually produces rather than describes the things it discusses, emphasizes that there are negotiations and exchanges in the 'contact zone' between the two, coining the term 'transculturation'. It is in this contact zone that the colonizer and the colonized constitute as well as deform each other's identities.[10]

Post-colonial critiques of Romantic writers became more apparent in the late 1980s, as the claims of Said and his followers were subject to testing in more specialist literary fields. Rana Kabbani substantially upheld Said's thesis, in particular, she explored the European fascination or obsession with the harem which promised 'a sexual space, a voyage away from the dictates of the bourgeois morality of the metropolis' (Kabbani 1994, 6, 67). Nigel Leask brought Said's theories to bear on Romantic poetry in a serious and sophisticated way (Leask 1992). Leask concurred with Said that imaginative literature about the East shared, unwittingly or otherwise, in the project of knowing and dominating the East but he found Romantic writing to raise anxieties as well as certainties about the European self. Said, he claims, was right to assert the link between imperialism and knowledge about the East but wrong to see this as 'a closed system'. Leask argued that in the Eastern Tales, 'Byron's gaze, fixed like many of his fellow countrymen on the collapsing fabric of the Ottoman Empire, also turned back reflectively on his own culture as the world's dominant colonial power, and the significance of his own complicity in that power as a poet of orientalism' (Leask 1992, 4, 23). Byron's Orientalist verse is related to the simultaneous British commercial and imperial interest in the Levant in the post-Napoleonic period.

Most recent post-colonial criticism of Romantic poetry has tended to reinforce a Saidian perspective, albeit in more complex ways. Saree Makdisi furthered and complicated Said's project by placing Western responses to the East in the context of modernization; the industrial-izing, rationalizing, secularizing, technological project of European imperialism which, he argued, tends towards the emergence of a single and dominant world system, what we know as the process of 'globalization'. The origins of this process roughly coincide with the Romantic period. For Makdisi, Romanticism is a 'historical designation of a number of enormously varied engagements with the multitudinous discourses of modernization', a process it both critiques but also to which it contributes. It is in Romanticism's obsession with the pre- and anti-modern (or 'anti-modern otherness') which marks it out as involved in its critique of modernization, whether of Wordsworth's 'spots of time', Scott's Highlanders in *Waverley* or the oriental settings of Byron's Turkish Tales. Byron's Levant, he argues, is an 'anti-modern Orient', defined and structured by its own temporality. They are 'self-enclosed and self-referential enclaves of the anti-modern, each defined by its own unique structures of feeling and its own distinct temporality'; however rather than functioning as resistance to modernization such constructions serve only to reinforce the very modernity against which they are defined and affirm not contradict the process. Byron's construction of the Orient is thus 'a refuge from and potential alternative to modernity' with its own sense of space and time, equivalent to Wordsworth's 'spots of time' rather than a reflection of a real place (Makdisi 1998, 1–22, 123).

Srinivas Aravamudan problematizes Said's Manichean concern with Western Self and Oriental redefining the eighteenth-century European colonial in the context of the 'Tropicopolitan'. Aravamudan's term, which is similar in its agency to Pratt's 'transculturation', is used as a way of negotiating 'the colonized subject who exists both as a fictive construct of colonial tropology and actual resident of tropical space, object of representation and agent of resistance'. 'Tropicopolitans' are representations of colonial subjects, yet also as figurations which may 'transgress their prescribed function and reanimate cultural discourses in response to different contexts and intentions'. For Aravamudan 'Tropicopolitans' reveal 'memory traces' of trauma and are as much concerned with anti-colonial agency as colonialist representation. They involve a cross-identification of colonial and colonized and are 'troublesome tropes' that serve to 'interrupt the monologue of nationalist literary history' (Aravamudan 1999a, 4, 5, 17, 18).[11] Instead of the binaries of Said's Orientalism, Aravamudan prefers to situate writing about the Near East in the context of what he calls, 'Levantinization', or 'a creative response to Orientalisms as a plural rather than a singular category' and the dynamic interaction of Islamic and European cultures. For Aravamudan the Orient has multiple uses, some utopian and others repressive.

Post-colonial criticism agrees that Byron's construction of the East is simply that, a construction, a projection of the subject's desires and anxieties, though such critics differ as to the extent that this is complicit or resistant to the contemporary processes of empire which Byron as a liberal opposed. Most strident is Sardar's judgement that the tales are 'poems of the gratuitous violence, irrational vengeance, and cold-hearted barbarity of Turks – representing the darker side of Romanticism'. Sardar claims that Byron's Orient was 'derived from the history of Orientalism, a fictional image, a place of exotic fantasy, the kind of fantasy that Byron created about his own persona' (Sardar 1999, 46). Many critics such as Mohammed Sharafuddin, Abdur Raheem Kidawi and Naji B. Oueijan have by contrast written about Byron's extremely knowledgeable and sympathetic treatment of his Eastern subjects, stressing that, whatever the limitations of his audience, Byron's encounter with the East was not simply a product of fashionable exoticism but 'truly authentic' (Oueijan 1999, 46).[12] Others such as Marilyn Butler, Malcolm Kelsall, Daniel Watkins, Jerome Christensen, Daryl Ogden, and Jerome McGann, have discussed Byron's Eastern Tales in the context of the political and social debates that Byron participated in at home, arguing that the tales are not about the East at all but displacements of British political concerns, including the status of Ireland (Butler 1988; McGann1968; Watkins 1987).[13] Certainly Byron's interest in the East was long-standing; he claimed to have read the *Arabian Nights* and a number of accounts of the Ottoman Empire at an early age, such as Knolles, Mary Wortley Montagu and Paul Rycaut (Oueijan 1999, 63–8, 171–6).[14] He said he knew 'every event from Tangralopi, and afterwards Othman I., to the peace of Passarowitz, in 1718, – the battle of Cutzka, in 1739, and the treaty between Russia and Turkey in 1790'.[15] He was also well read in translations of Persian and Arabic poetry.

In September 1809 Byron left Britain for a two-year tour of the Eastern Mediterranean passing through Epirus, Albania, Acarnia, Morea, Attica, and Smyrna ending up in the Ottoman capital, Istanbul. As well as witnessing sublime natural scenery, which reminded him of the landscape of his childhood in the Scottish Highlands, he also encountered mosques, palaces, towers, coffee-houses, slave markets and bazaars.[16] The territory through which he travelled was then part of the declining, but still powerful, Ottoman Empire, and had been since the fall of Constantinople in 1453. The Ottomans had overrun Greece in the late sixteenth century following from their victories against the maritime Empire of the Venetian Republic. In liberal circles in Britain there was a strong sympathy for the plight of the nation with its past glories, a sympathy shared by Byron who would later lose his life in the struggle for national independence in 1824. The territory was a much-contested one; it marked the boundary between European Christendom and Islam. Additionally, as the grip of the Ottoman Empire weakened, local chieftains gained power. One such was Ali Pasha, whose fiefdom was Albania, at whose court Byron was entertained. Ali Pasha, for his own reasons of state, was then courting the British government, whose policy, after the Congress of Vienna in 1815, was to shore up the Sultan preventing the Russians and the French from absorbing his provinces: a policy which Byron despised and one which was at odds with much of British public opinion.

The Levant then was a mix of peoples, religions and political influences.[17] Byron's attitude to the region was complex, he frequently elegized the lost grandeur of Greece, despairing of the modern Greeks' ability to emancipate themselves and criticizing those European tourists who studied 'the harangues of the Athenian demagogues in favour of freedom' while oblivious to the fate of 'the descendents of these sturdy republicans' (*CPW* II, 202). The most notorious example of this being the removal by Lord Elgin, the British Ambassador to the Ottoman Porte, of parts of the Parthenon frieze with the permission of the Turkish authorities, anxious to please their British allies. Byron roundly criticized what he saw as cultural vandalism, although he also engaged in similar activities himself, albeit in a more modest way. Byron also admired the manners and characters of the Turks whom he met and whose society he enjoyed:

> —I see not much difference between ourselves & the Turks, save that we have foreskins and they have none, that they have long dresses and we short, and that we talk much and they little.—In England the vices in fashion are whoring & drinking, in Turkey, Sodomy & smoking, we prefer a girl and a bottle, they a pipe and pathic.—They are a sensible people. (*BLJ* I, 238)

He even expressed the wish, how serious we do not know, to become a convert to Islam.[18] In fact, Byron was certainly capable of using the Turks to act as a satiric foil for European politics and society in the manner of Montesquieu's *Persian Letters*:

> If it be difficult to pronounce what they are, we can at least say what they are *not*; they are *not* treacherous, they are *not* cowardly, they do not burn heretics, they are *not* assassins, nor has an enemy advanced to *their* capital. They are faithful to their sultan till he becomes unfit to govern, and devout to their God without an inquisition. Were they driven from St Sophia to-morrow, and the French or Russians enthroned in their stead, it would become a question whether Europe would gain by the exchange. England would certainly be the loser. (*CPW* II, 210)

Byron noted how in Greece, pagan temples, Christian churches and mosques all existed on the site of the Acropolis. Certainly the early nineteenth-century Levant was a multi-ethnic and culturally contested hybrid space, resistant to the binaries of Saidian Orientalist discourse.[19]

Byron's Eastern travels formed the basis of *Childe Harold* I and II (1812) and the Turkish Tales: *The Giaour* (1813), *The Bride of Abydos* (1813), *The Corsair* (1814), *The Siege of Corinth* (1816) and, more problematically, *Lara* (1814). Byron prided himself on the authenticity of these tales and the accuracy of their detail or costume. There is no doubt, however, that Byron understood the marketability of poetry on oriental subjects. In a letter of 1813 to Thomas Moore he advised the Irish poet to 'stick to the East' as the 'only poetical policy':

The North, South, and West have all been exhausted; but from the East, we have nothing but [Southey's] unsaleables ... The little I have done in that way is merely a 'voice in the wilderness' for you; and, if it has had any success, that also will prove that the public are orientalizing, and pave the path for you. (*BLJ* III, 101)

Clearly Byron was aware of what we might call the commodification of culture and of the market forces, which drive the process. As Leask comments on this letter, 'Byron speaks like a Levantine or East India merchant who has tapped a lucrative source of raw materials in a newly opened up Orient, which he feels will make a splash on the home market.' Byron is investing his cultural capital in an expanding market driven by imperial and colonial imperatives: the 'ambivalence of the Giaour's heroism ... reflects Byron's ambivalence with regard to the moral value of his own poetry, fitted to appeal to a public corrupted by commodity-fetishism' (Leask 1992, 13, 33). Certainly Byron's Tales were commercially extremely successful: *The Giaour* ran into thirteen editions and sold over 12,000 copies and *The Corsair* sold an unprecedented 10,000 copies on the first day of its publication. The critical reception of the Tales was also, on the whole, favourable, with reviewers praising the accuracy and local colour of the poems.

The first of Byron's Eastern Tales, *The Giaour* is a complex story of love, betrayal and revenge. It is set in the Turkish occupied Morea in the late eighteenth century and concerns the rivalry between two men over a woman, and two Empires, the Christian Venetian and the Islamic Ottoman, over the Eastern Mediterranean. Leila, the slave of the Turkish Lord Hassan, is beloved by the young Venetian, the Giaour. Hassan discovers her adultery and she is disposed of by a traditional Ottoman punishment; sewn in a sack and thrown into the sea. The Giaour ambushes Hassan's party and kills him in combat, afterwards retreating to a solitary retirement in a monastery, tortured by the recollection of the events in which he had participated. This extreme ritual punishment for adultery was known personally to Byron, as an anecdote of his time in Greece describes how he interceded to prevent the similar drowning of a young woman accused of the crime (MacCarthy 2002, 131–2). In the notes to the poem, Byron claims that he 'heard the story by accident recited by one of the coffee-house storytellers who abound in the Levant, and sing or recite their narratives' (*CPW* III, 423). *The Giaour* is a 'broken tale' (*CPW* III, 82; l. 1333). The narrative of the poem is told in a series of fragments from the perspectives of different narrators or voices, including the poet, a Muslim fisherman, the monk who hears the Giaour's confession, and the Giaour himself. Whether or not these voices are meant to be actual characters with their limited perspectives and knowledge, or as McGann suggests, the ballad poet impersonating them for his audience, the result is one that disrupts any straightforward moral or ethical perspective on the central enigmatic acts of love and death (McGann 1968, 142–7).[20] For Malcolm Kelsall, the predominantly Oriental perspective serves to 'make the Occident "Other" – an alien threat to be exterminated or expelled and from which the race must be purged by the murder of a woman' (Kelsall 1998, 246). The poem is heavily dependent on textual sources, which Said finds as characteristic of Orientalist writing in general, with Byron's notes acknowledging a debt to both William Henley's scholarly comments on Beckford's *Vathek* and D'Herbelot's compendium of Orientalist knowledge, the *Bibliothèque orientale* (1776).

The Giaour has been variously interpreted as a poem about the East. Marilyn Butler argues that the poem is an intervention in a current debate about the moral purpose of Empire with Byron expressing a healthy scepticism about the value of religious and missionary activity (Butler 1988); Leask sees the poem as a cultural allegory with no normative imperial standpoint in which Christian and Turk fight over the body of a woman identified with Greece itself (Leask 1992, 33); Caroline Franklin argues that Leila 'is the fought-over focus of the eternal triangle, situated between a Turkish tyrant and a debased would be Western liberator' (Franklin 1992, 75); Joseph Lew shifts the focus to Byron's alleged misogyny suggesting that the poem exploits Byron's 'nostalgia for a place not Christian, not English, and not the present, when unwanted women could be disposed of with relative impunity'.[21] Criticism has thus, by and large, focused on the clash of world views between Muslim and Christian and their struggle for the contested territory of Greece. *The Giaour* certainly manifests Orientalist traits. Like the other Turkish Tales it exploits an exotic landscape. Details of the Mosques, religious festivals ('the Bairam's feasts begun'), and culturally specific language ('high jeered', 'silver-sheaved ataghan', 'the jewel of Giamschid') (*CPW* III, 47, 51, 55; ll. 229, 251, 355, 479). It is a place of fakirs and dervishes, harems and festivals, a world where people appeal to Allah and Genies; all these details and context place the reader in an unfamiliar world, one where the poet is our guide. Byron's notes to the poem serve to reinforce the poet's authority as someone who has travelled and studied in the area, supporting Said's point that Orientalist knowledge is primarily textual rather than actual. The Greek islands, 'These Edens of the eastern wave',

(CPW III, 40; l. 15) are presented as a place of past glories rather than of
present significance:

> Clime of the unforgotten brave!—
> Whose land from plain to mountain-cave
> Was Freedom's home or Glory's grave—
> Shrine of the mighty! can it be,
> That this is all remains of thee? (CPW III, 43; ll. 103–7)

The landscape is likened to a dead body ('Tis Greece—but living Greece
no more!' [CPW III, 42; l. 91]). Immediately, Byron situates the tale in a
time frame where modern Greece is occluded to idealize a classical past.
A privileging of the Hellenic and neo-classical which, for Martin Bernal,
serves to establish a Eurocentric notion of civilization.[22] The tale is framed
by the hostility between the differing religions. 'Giaour' is a Turkish word
for 'infidel'. When the Muslim fisherman who narrates part of the poem
witnesses the Giaour for the first time he exclaims:

> I know thee not, I loathe thy race ...
> Right well I view, and deem thee one
> Whom Othman's sons should slay or shun
>   (CPW III, 46; ll. 191, 198–9)

The young Venetian, with 'his Christian crest and haughty mien' (CPW III,
48; l. 256) is clearly identified with his religious and ethnic context.

It is possible to read the poem in terms of Orientalist stereotyping.
Hassan is presented as an oriental despot presiding with jealous pride over
his harem ('Black Hassan from the Haram flies' [CPW III, 54; l. 339]); he
is a local chieftain who is violent, proud and vindictive, demonstrating
an eastern excess of passion that is often the preserve of a feminized East.
Betrayed, as he sees it, by Leila, he has little compunction in carrying
out the terrible punishment according to his laws and customs, an event
that is obliquely represented in lines 352–87 (CPW III, 50) of the poem.
This event is put in the context of an Islamic misogyny:

> Oh! who young Leila's glance could read
> And keep that portion of his creed
> Which saith, that woman is but dust,
> A soulless toy for tyrant's lust? (CPW III, 55; ll. 487–90)

Byron's note informs us that the belief that women have no souls is a
'vulgar error' and misreading of the Koran but, nevertheless, one held

by many (*CPW* III, 419). Leila is seen as a 'faithless slave' but the worst aspect of her crime is that she leaves Hassan for 'a Giaour' (*CPW* III, 56; l. 535). Hassan's rage and violence is allied with his religion:

> There sleeps as true an Osmanlie
> As e'er at Mecca bent the knee;
> As ever scorn'd forbidden wine,
> Or pray'd with face towards the shrine ...
> Who falls in battle 'gainst a Giaour,
> Is worthiest an immortal bower (*CPW* III, 63; ll. 729–32, 745–6)

In contrast to Hassan, the Giaour plays a chivalric role, and though he does not save Leila from Hassan, he exacts a vengeance for the crime. He is also conflicted and flawed. Unlike Hassan, he is not a participant in any extensive social network. After his death Hassan is deeply mourned by his mother; he receives an honourable funeral and the community of which he was the head subsequently disintegrates: 'For Courtesy and Pity died / With Hassan on the mountain side' (*CPW* III, 51; ll. 288–351). The Giaour is from the start an alienated and solitary figure at odds with the Christian faith ascribed to him. He is pictured with 'evil eye', 'like a demon of the night', tortured by the death of Leila and his own killing of Hassan, his mind brooding over 'guilty woes ... like the Scorpion girt by fire' (*CPW* III, 46, 53; ll. 196, 422–3). The Giaour's own Christianity is problematic, for the Muslim fisherman, he is an 'Apostate from his own vile faith' (*CPW* III, 59; l. 616). The second half of the poem from line 787 onwards is taken up with the Giaour's retirement to a monastery and his subsequent inner torment. Haunted by visitations of Leila and Hassan's severed hand, he finds no peace in the comforts of conventional religion. To the monks he is an outcast and pariah figure, 'some stray renegade, repentant of the change he made':

> But never at our vesper prayer,
> Nor e'er before the confession chair
> Kneels he, nor recks he when arise
> Incense or anthem to the skies,
> But broods within his cell alone,
> His faith and race alike unknown. (*CPW* III, 65; ll. 812; 802–7)

The Giaour's moral frame of reference is problematic. He believes the Friar will absolve him from the deed of murder because the man he killed 'was hostile to thy creed' (*CPW* III, 73; ll. 1038–9). More than this

he effaces any moral superiority he may have over Hassan by making
himself hypothetically as guilty:

> Yet did he but what I had done
> Had she been false to more than one;
> Faithless to him—he gave the blow,
> But true to me—I laid him low. (*CPW* III, 73; ll. 1062–5)

The Giaour is certainly a hybrid character, one who is capable of culturally
cross-dressing and ambushing Hassan's party 'in Arnaut garb' (*CPW* III,
59; l. 615). He is alienated from both Christendom and Islam, caught
somewhere in between the two. This facility to cross-dress, however,
is not necessarily a liberating thing. It is something in the Western
imagination reserved for Europeans who may impersonate culture of the
other with some skill, yet also despise its people. Famously the explorer
Richard Burton was able to dress and speak as an Arab and undertake the
Hajh, or pilgrimage to Mecca. That this skill, however, is seldom, if ever,
vouchsafed to the other culture, privileges a Eurocentric anthropological
perspective (Kabbani 1994, 58, 90–1).[23] The capacity of the Giaour to
disturb as well as reinforce cultural stereotypes identifies him with the
'troublesome tropes' of Aravamudan's Levantinization.

The triangular relationship between the Giaour, Hassan and Leila is
highly significant in post-colonial readings of the poem. At the heart
of the poem is a struggle between two men for a woman. In some ways
Leila is simply a counter in this struggle opening the poem to readings in
which the homosocial and the homoerotic predominate. The Giaour is
certainly as much obsessed by his hatred for Hassan as his love for Leila,
'The maid I love—the man I hate' (*CPW* II, 7; l. 1018). Sara Suleri has
argued that British representations of India in the nineteenth century are
heavily suffused with a 'predominantly homoerotic cast'.[24] Certainly the
Levant was for Byron a place where he could more easily indulge in the
homosexual liaisons which were an important facet of his complicated
sexual identity.[25] It was also a place where, in his Eastern tragedy about
an effeminate ruler *Sardanapalus* and the Turkish Cantos of *Don Juan*, he
could explore cross-gender and cross-cultural identities.[26] For Caroline
Franklin 'one of the most interesting aspects of Byron's poetry is both
his use of sexual stereotypes, and his experimentation with role reversal'
(Franklin 1992, 57). The special place of the harem in the Western
imagination is often remarked upon in post-colonial criticism, it is 'one
of the most powerful symbols of exoticism and Otherness associated with
the orient. It represents the antithesis of all that the West believes about

sexuality' (Sardar 1999, 57; Kabbani 1994, 67–85).[27] Leila is a slave in Hassan's harem. We are told she is 'Circassia's daughter' (*CPW* III, 56; l. 505), originating from Georgia, a place reputed by travellers and natural historians alike as the source of the most beautiful of the human races; the prize acquisitions of the harem. J.F. Lane, for instance, later made a career from painting Circassian women (Kabbani 1994, 83). Leila is imaged as the 'Kashmeer butterfly', 'a lovely toy so fiercely sought', the passive victim chased and destroyed, 'with wounded wing, or bleeding breast' (*CPW* III, 52; ll. 388–421). Certainly she has no voice or real presence in the poem. Gayatri Spivak has famously characterized British representations of the Hindu rite of Sati prior to its abolition in 1829 as 'white men are saving brown women from brown men'.[28] Spivak argues that the voice of the woman is lost in this debate between men. Others such as Leask have seen Leila as a synecdoche for the contested Greek nation, both of which are imaged as beautiful corpses in the poem. While this does make schematic sense, the racial origins of Leila also create ambiguity (Leask 1992, 29; Franklin 1992, 39–47).

The romance plot of *The Giaour* enacted against the Levantine background with its clash of cultures is repeated in all the Turkish Tales with significant variation; as McGann comments 'they are repetitive to a fault' (McGann 1968, 162). The second of the Tales, *The Bride of Abydos*, is told in a simpler narrative form. It features the story of the love of Selim and Zulieka which is frustrated by Zulieka's father, the despotic Giaffir. Again the tale is framed by a poet lamenting the lost glories of ancient Greece and of her heroes such as Achilles:

> Dust long outlasts the storied stone—
> But Thou—thy very dust is gone! (*CPW* III, 125; ll. 53–4)

The setting of the poem is more sumptuous and luxurious than that of *The Giaour*. Abydos is a place of luxury, sensuality and of Eastern paradisial gardens. Zulieka's chamber is richly furnished:

> The richest work of Iran's loom,
> And Sheeraz' tribute of perfume;
> All that eye or sense delight
> Are gather'd in that gorgeous room—(*CPW* III, 126; ll. 80–3)

The story is one of passion and revenge as Selim plots his vengeance against Giaffir who poisoned his father, usurped his lands and brought him up as his own child. As the poem progresses Selim undergoes a

transformation from effeminate prince to rebel leader, further exploring
Byronic notions of masculinity in an Eastern setting. As Franklin argues,
the main action of the tale posits the debate between the Western
bourgeois monogamous relationship desired by Selim and Zulieka and the
dynastic polygamy Giaffir seeks to impose on his daughter in marrying
her to an old ally (Franklin 1992, 47–64). Similarly, for Leask, the poem
dramatizes the limits of Byron's aristocratic Whig liberalism where Selim
is unable to 'reconcile his notion of heroism with *realpolitik* and the
revolutionary values of his pirate band' (Leask 1992, 38).

> So let them ease their hearts with prate
> Of equal rights, which man ne'er knew,
> I have a love for freedom too. (*CPW* III, 135; ll. 384–6)

More complex is Byron's third Eastern Tale, *The Corsair*, of 1814.
This returns us to the familiar narrative territory of *The Giaour* with its
conflicted central character, the Christian pirate Conrad and his arch-
antagonist, the Muslim despot, Seyd:

> High in the hall reclines the turbaned Seyd;
> Around—the bearded chiefs he came to lead.
> Removed the banquet, and the last pilaff—
> Forbidden draughts, 'tis said, he dared to quaff,
> Though to the rest the sober berry's juice
> The slaves bear round for rigid Moslems use;
> The long chibouque's dissolving cloud supply,
> While dance the Almas to wild minstrelsy.
> ...
> And revellers may more securely sleep
> On silken couch than o'er rugged deep.
> (*CPW* III, 172; ll. 29–36, 39–40)

Seyd is a 'hated tyrant' (*CPW* III, 200; l. 319) and hypocrite (unlike
the strict Muslim Hassan), who cruelly impales his enemies, sadistically
enjoying and extending their agonies, who melodramatically foams and
tears his beard with excessive rage, and whose soldiers use the captured
Greeks as target practice (*CPW* III, 177; l. 181). Once again the action
of the tale involves a female slave of Seyd's harem, who becomes the
object of two men's attentions. Byron, however, this time complicates
the romance plot by introducing two female characters, Conrad's Greek
love Medora and the more adventurous slave Gulnare. Contra Spivak,
the plot of this poem involves a brown woman saving a white man from

a brown man. Conrad is a fairly typical Byronic hero, a leader born to command yet troubled by inner turmoil (*CPW* III, 159; ll. 249–80). His one clear virtue is his love for 'his Bird of Beauty' Medora (*CPW* III, 162; l. 346). Medora, like Leila and Zuleika, is a beautiful but passive woman, convinced by the news of Conrad's death, expires. She is the first heroine of the Tales not subject to a Turkish patriarchal figure. Like Leila, she is identified with the land of Greece (Franklin 1992, 64). She represents the virtues of domesticity and peace, an anticipation of Coventry Patmore's Victorian 'Angel in the House':

> ...wilt thou ne'er
> My Conrad! Learn the joys of peace to share?
> Sure thou hast more than wealth, and many a home
> As bright as this invites us not to roam. (*CPW* III, 163; ll. 388–91)

Conrad, like the Giaour, is also able to culturally cross-dress, convincingly assuming the guise of a 'dervish' which he adopts to successfully surprise Seyd while feasting. It is while sacking Seyd's palace that the fire spreads to the harem. True to his chivalric code Conrad leaves off his assault to rescue the endangered women:

> 'Oh! Burst the Haram—wrong not on your lives
> One female form—remember—*we* have wives.
> (*CPW* III, 177; ll. 202–3)

Saving Gulnare 'the Haram queen—but still the slave of Seyd' (*CPW* III, 178; l. 224), Conrad is himself captured. Despite the promise of an agonizing death at the hands of his vindictive and jealous enemy, Conrad refuses to become involved in Gulnare's plot to treacherously assassinate Seyd while he sleeps. Gulnare's act is antithetical to the code of feminine behaviour practised by Medora and reveals her as a free and revolutionary spirit, not bound by Conrad's chivalric limitations. Refusing the roles of slave, wife and mother Gulnare is a problematic figure in the text. She is compared to the Eastern temptress Cleopatra (*CPW* III, 189; l. 550). The one kiss, 'the first, the last that Frailty stole from Faith' (*CPW* III, 208; l. 551) that Conrad bestows on her betrays Medora and breaks his own heart. *The Corsair*, at times, reads like a parody or self-examination of European Orientalism with stereotypical presentations of Turkish despots, desirable slaves of the harem, seductive oriental temptresses, chivalric heroes and faithful wives being set up only to be critiqued and abandoned. The extent to which an audience was meant to sympathize with Conrad's absurdly heroic conduct, or to be horrified or attracted to

Gulnare's adoption of an active, masculine role is not clear. How critical of classical Hellenism the sepulchral Medora's inert passivity is meant to be is also ambivalent. Certainly Byron still writes within a Eurocentric framework, exploring European attitudes to politics and other nations; it is no accident that in the poem's dedication to Thomas Moore, Byron draws an explicit parallel between the predicament of Ireland and the East where 'the wrongs of your own country, the magnificent and fiery spirit of her sons, the beauty and feeling of her daughters, may there be found' (*CPW* III, 148).

Lara (1814) is the conclusion of the series, though published two years before *The Siege of Corinth*. Byron wrote that it 'completes the series—and its very likeness renders it necessary for the others' (*BLJ* IV, 165). In the advertisement to the poem, Byron indicated that it was in some sense a sequel to *The Corsair*. We are led to view Lara as an analogous figure to Conrad returned to his European ancestral home with Gulnare, disguised as his page Kaled. From the postcolonial perspective, the poem is especially interesting because it brings the Oriental home and into the domestic arena. Lara returns from his mysterious exotic adventures to his unspecified homeland not like colonialists such as Robert Clive, rich and powerful, but haunted and alienated, 'a stranger in this breathing world, / An erring spirit from another hurled' (*CPW*, III, 225; ll. 315-6), tormented like the Giaour, by his nightmares of traumatic events. The poem is characteristically reticent about the nature of his terrors:

> Whate'er his phrenzy dream'd or eye beheld,
> If yet remember'd ne'er to be reveal'd,
> Rests at his heart. (*CPW*, III, 222; ll. 201-266)

The overtly Gothic presentation of these events anticipates later nineteenth-century colonial gothic fictions of Wilkie Collins, Rider Haggard and Conan Doyle in which the crimes visited on colonial subjects by imperial powers return to plague the metropolis in uncanny forms. Lara's alienated presence disturbs the social fabric of his home. Sir Ezzelin, who knows his former life and its apparent crimes mysteriously disappears, presumably murdered by Kaled, with or without Lara's complicity; Kaled's disposal of Ezzelin in the river, reversing the gender relations of Hassan's drowning of Leila in *The Corsair* (Franklin 1992, 86). Similarly, Kaled reverses the gender and cultural cross dressing of *The Corsair* and *The Giaour*, being a female oriental, disguised as a male page, although never regarded as anything other than foreign. The character of Kaled similarly raises issues for Lara's world. The boyishly beautiful page who 'would fix his gaze' for 'hours on Lara' (*CPW*, III, p. 232; l. 544) whom above all things he loves, raises again issues of homosexual desire played out against the backdrop of Oriental cultures. Kaled, like Gulnare, is stereotypical Oriental female, slavish to her master but wild, passionate, jealous and capable of excess. *Lara* is as much a poem about colonial guilt as about Byron's critique of aristocratic society and its feudal politics. It reminds us that deeds done at the peripheries of the European influence are not isolated and distant; but will return inevitably the homeland with devastating results.

The *Siege of Corinth* (1814) returns us to the struggle between Christian and Muslim empires of *The Giaour*. In many ways it is one of the most troubling of the Turkish Tales, with its savage and ironic suicidal conclusion (Watkins 1987, 108). It marks a much more critical engagement with the aristocratic honour code of the Giaour and Conrad. It reminds us that the key imperial power in the Eastern Mediterranean at this time was the Ottoman Empire. The poem is situated at a key boundary between Christian West and Islamic East, 'where Asia's bounds and ours divide' (*CPW* III, 347, l. 767) and it meditates on the decline of the Venetian Republic as it is expelled from the Morea (Kelsall 1998, 248–9). The exploration of the cross-cultural traveller is carried further than in the other tales, as its hero, Alp, is a renegade, a convert to Islam and leading soldier in the Turkish forces. Alp's motivation, however, is not religious but derives from wounded pride (*CPW* III, 342, ll. 606–11). Minotti, the elderly commander of the Venetian forces in Corinth, has forbidden Alp to marry his daughter Francesca after his expulsion from the Republic for offences that remain mysterious. Alp, however, is no post-colonial hybrid; he confirms the stereotype of the European who can impersonate another's culture without assimilating it. Although a 'turban girt his shaven brow' (*CPW* III, 325, l. 75) he is defined by his aristocratic pride rather than a cultural openness. Alp is motivated not by the true zeal of the convert but by 'the memory of a thousand wrongs' (*CPW* III, 325; l. 83):

> Not his the loud fantastic boast
> To plant the crescent o'er the cross,
> Or risk a life with little loss,
> Secure in paradise to be
> By Houris loved immortally:
> Nor his, what burning patriots feel,
> The stern exaltedness of zeal,
> Profuse of blood, untired in toil,

> When battling on the parent soil.
> He stood alone—a renegade. (*CPW* III 331; ll. 251–61)

Alp's pre-eminency among the Turks derives from his 'ever daring to be first' (*CPW* III, 331; l. 280). Alp's love, Francesca again resembles the effaced and passive heroines, Leila and Medora, appearing in the poem only as a ghost to warn Alp to 'dash that turban to earth' and 'sign / The sign of the cross' (*CPW* III, 340; ll. 532–3).

In the end *The Siege of Corinth* underscores Byron's faith, not in Western imperialism or in an anticipation of contemporary notions of multiculturalism, but in the Enlightenment cosmopolitanism that he held throughout his life. Such a belief was predicated on a belief in a universal human nature and cultural relativism. Cosmopolitanism was also premised on a belief in nationalisms, and, itself, a Eurocentric desire to mitigate the local and particular. Byron's symbolic enactment of cosmopolitanism, however, manifests itself in a rather gruesome way. While traversing the battlefield, Alp notices how cultural and racial differences are irrelevant in death as the 'lean dogs ... Hold o'er the dead their carnival' (*CPW* III, 336; ll. 409–10). The climax of the poem occurs in the church under which there is held the Christian's magazine of armaments. This is the occasion for Byron's secular irony as religious symbols are placed in close proximity to moments of vicious carnage, in part religiously motivated:

> Madonna's face upon him shone,
> Painted in heavenly hues above,
> With eyes of light and looks of love;
> ...
> Still she smiled; even now she smiles,
> Though slaughter streams along her aisles:
>   (*CPW* III, 352; ll. 904–6, 913–14)

When Minotti explodes the magazine Christian and Muslim alike are slaughtered:

> Spire, vaults, the shrine, the spoil, the slain,
> The turbaned victors, the Christian band,
> All that of living or dead remain,
> Hurled on high with the shivered fane,
> In one wild roar expire!
> ...
> Down the ashes shower like rain;

Some fell in the gulf, which received the sprinkles
With a thousand circling wrinkles;
Some fell on the shore, but, far away,
Scattered o'er the isthmus lay;
Christian or Moslem, which be they?
Let their mothers see and say! (*CPW* III, 354; ll. 971–5, 991–7)

It is a cosmopolitanism established through destruction and death. Postcolonial criticism would see in Byron's concluding lines the tragic dilemma of the European cosmopolitan mind. It would argue on the lines of recent critics that, 'Modernity has never fallen short of making universalist claims to world citizenship, based on the spectacular success of the Enlightenment as a pedagogical and political project' and to point out that a 'genuine desire for equality as a human norm' is combined with a 'ethnocentric provincialism.'[29] From a Saidian perspective, Byron's Enlightenment cosmopolitanism simply underwrites Orientalism; yet to accept this view in its entirety is to homogenize and flatten the debates about colonialism and empire and Britain's accommodation with other peoples and cultures. Byron's Eastern Tales and their cosmopolitan ethic belong to an assimilationist phase of Empire rather than to the rigorous anglicizing and missionary projects of the later nineteenth century. They instance the failure of cosmopolitanism where people prefer suicide, assassination and slaughter to tolerance and compromise.[30] Time bound as they are, the Eastern Tales do not simply celebrate Western values but raise troublesome questions about the relationships between cultures and the processes of economic, military and imperial expansion. If Byron's Eastern Tales focus on the tragic inability of different peoples and cultures to dispense with religious bigotry and imperial rivalry, we should allow that this is a critique of West and East alike and one which leaves us with few certainties.

notes

1. Raymond Schwab, *The Oriental Renaissance: Europe's Rediscovery of India and the East, 1680–1880*, trans. Gene Patterson Black.
2. Martha Pike Conant, *The Oriental Tale in England in the Eighteenth Century*. See Robert L. Mack, ed. *Oriental Tales* and Alan Richardson, ed., *Three Oriental Tales*.
3. A.L. Tidawi, *English Speaking Orientalists*; Anouar Abdel-Malek, *Civilisations and Social Theory*; H. Djait, *Europe and Islam*.
4. Michel Foucault, *Knowledge/Power*.
5. Edward W. Said, *Orientalism*, 3.

6. Bernard Lewis, *Islam and the West*; Ernest Gellner, 'In Defence of Orientalism', *Sociology*, 14. 2 (1980): 295–300; Lisa Lowe, *Critical Terrains: French and British Orientalisms*.

7. Dennis Porter, 'Orientalism and its problems' in Francis Barker et al., *The Politics of Theory*, 179–83; Aijaz Ahmad, *Postmodernism and Islam*.

8. Robert Young, *White Mythologies: Writing History and the West*.

9. Homi K. Bhabha, *The Location of Culture*.

10. Mary Louise Pratt, *Imperial Eyes: Travel Writing and Transculturation*.

11. See also Srinivas Aravamudan, 'In the Wake of the Novel: The Oriental Tale as National Allegory'. *Novel* 33 (1999b): 5–31.

12. Mohammed Sharadfuddin, *Islam and Romantic Orientalism: Literary Encounters with the Orient*, 214–74 224–5; Abdur Raheem Kidawi, *Orientalism in Byron's 'Turkish Tales'*; Naji B. Oueijan, 'Western Exoticism and Byron's Orientalism'. *Prism(s)* 9 (1998): 27–39.

13. See also Marilyn Butler, 'John Bull's Other Kingdom'. *Studies in Romanticism* 31.3 (1992): 281–94; 'Byron and the Empire in the East' in *Byron: Augustan and Romantic*, ed. Andrew Rutherford, 63–81; Jerome Christensen, 'Perversion, Parody, and Cultural Hegemony: Lord Byron's Oriental Tales'. *South Atlantic Quarterly* 88. 3 (1989): 569–603; Daryl S. Ogden, 'Byron, Italy, and the Poetics of Liberal Imperialism'. *Keats-Shelley Journal* 49 (2000): 114–37.

14. See Bernard Blackstone, 'Byron and Islam: The Triple Eros'. *Journal of European Studies* 4 (1974): 325–63; Harold S. Wiener, 'Byron and the East: Literary Sources of the "Turkish Tales,"' in *Nineteenth-century Studies*, ed. R.C. Bald, 89–129.

15. Thomas Moore, *The Life, Letters and Journals of Lord Byron*, ed. Malcolm Jack, 46–9.

16. For details of Byron's travels see Fiona MacCarthy, *Byron: Life and Legend*, 89–138.

17. Nigel Leask, 'Byron and the Eastern Mediterranean' in *The Cambridge Companion to Byron*, ed. Drummond Bone, 101–2.

18. 'To depart from this accursed country, and I promise to turn Mussulman rather than return to it'. *BLJ* I, 202, 89, 173; II, 53, 120.

19. See Byron's comment that 'the Greeks hardly regard [the Albanians] as Christians, or the Turks as Moslems; and in fact they are a mixture of both and sometimes neither' *CPW* II, 193.

20. See also David Seed, '"Disjointed Fragments": Concealment and Revelation in *The Giaour*'. *Byron Journal* 18 (1990): 14–26.

21. Joseph Lew, 'The Necessary Orientalist? *The Giaour* and Nineteenth-Century Imperialist Misogyny' in *Romanticism, Race and Imperial Culture, 1780–1834*, eds Alan Richardson and Sonia Hofkosh, 183 see also Eric Meyer, '"I know thee not, I loathe thy race": Romantic Orientalism in the Eye of the Other'. *ELH* 63. 3 (1991): 657–99.

22. Martin Bernal, *Black Athena: The Afroasiatic Roots of Classical Civilization*. Vol 1: The *Fabrication of Ancient Greece 1785–1985*.

23. See also Gail Ching-Liang Low, *White Skins Black Masks: Representation and Colonialism*, 202–11, 219–20.

24. Sara Suleri, *The Rhetoric of English India*, 26. See Eve Kosofsky Sedgwick, *Between Men: English Literature and Male Homosocial Desire*.

25. See Louis Crompton, *Byron and Greek Love: Homophobia in Nineteenth Century England*; see also Jeffrey L. Schneider, 'Secret Sins of the Orient: Creating a

(Homo)Textual Context for Reading Byron's *The Giaour*. *College English* 65. I (2002): 81–95.
26. See Susan J. Wolfson, '"A Problem Few Dare Imitate": Byron's *Sardanapalus* and the "Effeminate Character"'. *ELH* 58.4 (1991): 867–902; Malcolm Kelsall, 'Byron and the Women of the Harem', and Alan Richardson, 'Escape from the Seraglio: Cultural Transvestism in Don Juan'. *Rereading Byron: Essays Selected from the Hofstra University's Bicentennial Conference*, eds Alice Levine and Robert N. Keane, 166–73, 175–85.
27. See Malek Alloula, *The Colonial Harem*.
28. Gayatri Chakravorty Spivak, 'Can the Subaltern Speak' in *Marxism and the Interpretation of Culture*, eds Cary Nelson and Lawrence Grossberg, 271–313.
29. Carol A. Breckenridge, Sheldon Pollock, Homi K. Bhabha, and Dipesh Chakrabarty, eds, *Cosmopolitanism*, 5.
30. This chapter was written at the time of the events of 7th July in London where to date fifty-seven people of different faiths and ethnic origins were murdered by four suicide bombers acting in the name of Islam.

works cited and suggestions for further reading

Abdel-Malek, Anouar. *Civilisations and Social Theory*. London: Macmillan, 1981.

Ahmad, Aijaz. *Postmodernism and Islam*. London and New York: Routledge, 1992.

Alloula, Malek. *The Colonial Harem*. Minneapolis: University of Minnesota Press, 1986.

Aravamudan, Srinivas. *Tropicopolitans: Colonialism and Agency 1688–1804*. Durham and London: Duke University Press, 1999a.

——. 'In the Wake of the Novel: The Oriental Tale as National Allegory'. *Novel* 33 (1999b): 5–31.

Ballaster, Ros. *Fabulous Orients: Fictions of the East in England 1662–1785*. Oxford: Oxford University Press, 2005.

——. *Fables of the East: Selected Tales 1662–1785*. Oxford: Oxford University Press, 2005.

Breckenridge, Carol, Sheldon Pollock, Homi K. Bhabha and Dipesh Chakrabarty, eds. *Cosmopolitanism*. Durham and London: Duke University Press, 2002.

Bernal, Martin. *Black Athena: The Afroasiatic Roots of Classical Civilization*. Vol. 1: *The Fabrication of Ancient Greece 1785–1985*. New Brunswick, NJ: Rutgers University Press, 1989.

Bhabha, Homi K. *The Location of Culture*. London and New York: Routledge, 1994.

Blackstone, Bernard. 'Byron and Islam: The Triple Eros'. *Journal of European Studies* 4 (1974): 325–63.

Butler, Marilyn. 'The Orientalism of Byron's *Giaour*'. *Byron and the Limits of Fiction*. Eds Bernard Beatty and Vincent Newey. Liverpool: Liverpool University Press, 1988. 78–96.

——. 'Byron and the Empire in the East', *Byron: Augustan and Romantic*. Ed. Andrew Rutherford. Basingstoke: Macmillan, 1990. 63–81.

——. 'John Bull's Other Kingdom: Byron's Intellectual Comedy'. *Studies in Romanticism* 31.3 (1992): 281–94.

Christensen, Jerome. 'Perversion, Parody, and Cultural Hegemony: Lord Byron's Oriental Tales'. *South Atlantic Quarterly* 88. 3 (1989): 569–603.

Conant, Martha Pike. *The Oriental Tale in England in the Eighteenth Century*. London: Frank Cass, 1966.

Crompton, Louis. *Byron and Greek Love: Homophobia in Nineteenth Century England*. Berkeley, CA: University of California Press, 1985.

Djait, H. *Europe and Islam*. Berkeley, CA: University of California Press, 1985.

Foucault, Michel. *Knowledge/Power*. New York: Pantheon, 1980.

Franklin, Caroline. *Byron's Heroines*. Oxford: Clarendon Press, 1992.

Gellner, Ernest. 'In Defence of Orientalism'. *Sociology* 14. 2 (1980): 295–300.

Irwin, Robert. *For Lust of Knowing: the Orientalists and their Enemies*. London: Allen Lane, 2006.

Kabbani, Rana. *Imperial Fictions: Europe's Myths of Orient*. Basingstoke: Macmillan, 1986; rev. edn: London: HarperCollins, 1994.

Kelsall, Malcolm.'Byron and the Women of the Harem'. *Rereading Byron: Essays Selected from the Hofstra University's Bicentennial Conference*. Eds Alice Levine and Robert N. Keane. New York: Garland, 1993. 166–73.

——. '"Once she did hold the gorgeous East in fee ...": Byron's Venice and Oriental Empire'. *Romanticism and Colonialism: Writing and Empire, 1780–1830*. Eds Tim Fulford and Peter J. Kitson. Cambridge: Cambridge University Press, 1998. 243–60.

Kidawi, Abdur Raheem. *Orientalism in Byron's 'Turkish Tales'*. Lewiston, NY: Mellen, 1995.

Leask, Nigel. *British Romantic Writers and the East: Anxieties of Empire*. Cambridge: Cambridge University Press, 1992.

——. 'Byron and the Eastern Mediterranean'. *The Cambridge Companion to Byron*. Ed. Drummond Bone. Cambridge: Cambridge University Press, 2004. 99–117.

Lew, Joseph. 'The Necessary Orientalist? *The Giaour* and Nineteenth-Century Imperialist Misogyny'. *Romanticism, Race and Imperial Culture, 1780–1834*. Eds Alan Richardson and Sonia Hofkosh. Bloomington and Indianapolis: Indiana University Press, 1996. 173–202.

Lewis, Bernard. *Islam and the West*. Oxford: Oxford University Press, 1993.

Low, Gail Ching-Liang. *White Skins Black Masks: Representation and Colonialism*. London and New York: Routledge, 1996.

Lowe, Lisa. *Critical Terrains: French and British Orientalisms*. Ithaca, NY: Cornell University Press, 1991.

MacCarthy, Fiona. *Byron: Life and Legend*. London: John Murray, 2002.

Mack, Robert L., ed. *Oriental Tales*. Oxford: World's Classics, 1992.

MacKenzie, John M. *Orientalism; History, Theory and the Arts*. Manchester: Manchester University Press, 1995.

Makdisi, Saree. *Romantic Imperialism: Universal Empire and the Culture of Modernity*. Cambridge: Cambridge University Press, 1998.

McGann, Jerome J. *Fiery Dust*. Chicago, IL: University of Chicago Press, 1968.

Meyer, Eric. '"I know thee not, I loathe thy race": Romantic Orientalism in the Eye of the Other'. *ELH* 63. 3 (1991): 657–99.

Moore, Thomas. *The Life, Letters and Journals of Lord Byron*. Ed. Malcolm Jack. Michigan: Scholarly Press, 1972.

Ogden, Daryl S. 'Byron, Italy, and the Poetics of Liberal Imperialism'. *Keats-Shelley Journal* 49 (2000): 114–37.

Oueijan, Naji B. 'Western Exoticism and Byron's Orientalism'. *Prism(s)* 9 (1998): 27–39.

——. *A Compendium of Eastern Elements in Byron's Oriental Tales*. New York. Peter Lang, 1999.

Porter, Dennis. 'Orientalism and its problems'. *The Politics of Theory*. Eds Francis Barker et al. Colchester: University of Essex 1983. 179–83.

Pratt, Mary Louise. *Imperial Eyes: Travel Writing and Transculturation*. London and New York: Routledge, 1992.

Richardson, Alan. 'Escape from the Seraglio: Cultural Transvestism in Don Juan'. *Rereading Byron: Essays Selected from the Hofstra University's Bicentennial Conference*. Eds Alice Levine and Robert N. Keane. New York: Garland, 1993. 175–85.

——, ed. *Three Oriental Tales*. Boston: Houghlin Mifflin, 2002.

Said, Edward. *Orientalism*. London: Pantheon Books, 1978.

Sardar, Ziauddin. *Orientalism*. Buckingham: Open University Press, 1999.

Schneider, Jeffrey L. 'Secret Sins of the Orient: Creating a (Homo)Textual Context for Reading Byron's *The Giaour*'. *College English* 65. I (2002): 81–95.

Schwab, Raymond. *The Oriental Renaissance: Europe's Rediscovery of India and the East, 1680–1880*. Trans. Gene Patterson Black. New York: Columbia University Press, 1984.

Sedgwick, Eve Kosofsky. *Between Men: English Literature and Male Homosocial Desire*. New York: Columbia University Press, 1985.

Seed, David. '"Disjointed Fragments": Concealment and Revelation in *The Giaour*'. *Byron Journal* 18 (1990): 14–26.

Sharafuddin, Mohammed. *Islam and Romantic Orientalism: Literary Encounters with the Orient*. London: I.B. Tauris, 1994. 214–74.

Spivak, Gayatri Chakravorty. 'Can the Subaltern Speak'. *Marxism and the Interpretation of Culture*. Eds Cary Nelson and Lawrence Grossberg. Urbana, IL: University of Illinois Press, 1988. 271–313.

Suleri, Sara. *The Rhetoric of English India*. Chicago, IL: University of Chicago Press, 1992.

Tidawi, A.L. *English Speaking Orientalists*. London: Luzac, 1964.

Watkins, Daniel. *Social Relations in Byron's Eastern Tales*. London: Associated University Presses, 1987.

Wiener, Harold S. 'Byron and the East: Literary Sources of the "Turkish Tales"'. *Nineteenth-century Studies*. Ed. R.C. Bald. New York: Greenwood Press, 1940 [reissued 1968]. 89–129.

Wolfson, Susan J. '"A Problem Few Dare Imitate": Byron's *Sardanapalus* and the "Effeminate Character"'. *ELH* 58.4 (1991): 867–902.

Young, Robert. *White Mythologies: Writing History and the West*. London and New York: Routledge, 1990.

6
byron and twentieth-century popular culture
ghislaine mcdayter

> Where Keats is autumn haze and Shelley pure ether, Byron is rock—and
> the hard outcroppings may indicate geologic epochs or hot underflows
> of lava that are worth noting and understanding.
>
> William J. Calvert, *Byron: The Romantic Paradox*, 1962

In Calvert's bizarre but by no means unprecedented description of the
younger generation of Romantic poets, we are encouraged to approach
Byron's corpus, unlike the ethereal bodies of his contemporaries, as we
would a geological site: Byron's poetry is a physical residue of his presence
that has hardened and fossilized, leaving us a material object by which
to understand him. And like any geological dig, it is assumed that the
rock under our eyes is a faithful and undistorted record of a lost past.
Somehow, it is argued, we still have access to the physical *reality* of Byron
in ways that we do not to Keats or Shelley.

It is this popular fixation with the materiality of the poet that the
following chapter will examine. For while Byron himself argued that
the 'flesh is frail', the cultural power of his own flesh has been notable
precisely for its temporal and imaginative endurance. There is something
about Byron, as opposed to the other Romantics, that inspires an interest
in the *body* of the poet far more than the corpus of the poet; and, as Fiona
MacCarthy points out in her recent biography, as late as the 'twentieth
century Byron's continuing *physical* presence was felt even by those who
disliked him'[1] (my emphasis). She notes, for example, how T.S. Eliot and
Virginia Woolf expressed their distaste for the poet not because of his
poetry but because of a physical repugnance to his body. The adoring
W.H. Auden similarly 'treated Byron as if he were still alive'[2] and I can add
that, at a Byron conference at Newstead Abbey, I was informed by one of
the participants that the one thing she wanted to do before she died was

sleep in Byron's bed. Evidently there is nothing 'ethereal' about this poet in the imaginations of his readers; even when Byron 'haunts' us it is a decidedly physical manifestation of his presence that is conjured forth.

This chapter will explore the critical implications of this fascination with the corporeal nature of Byron's appeal in the twentieth century and theorize its operations. Drawing on psychoanalytic theories of fantasy and the fetish, I will argue that the powerful draw the poet's flesh still has for his readers has come to signify a marker between criticism's self-perceived 'legitimate' study of the poet and what it considers to be the fetishization/commodification of Byron as an object of desire by his fans. For if the Freudian fetish is an object that 'operate[s] entirely in the realm of the simulacrum, generating a copy or surrogate phallus for an original that never was there in the first place'[3] and the Marxist fetish is an object that has been granted an utterly fallacious secret value due its ability to signify an '*energy*, a magical transcendent power, a *mana* (whose latest avatar would possibly be the libido)',[4] then Byron's body seems to be a perfect model for them both – especially for his less sympathetic critics.[5] In such critical circles, Byron's body has come to signify precisely this false 'mana' of the fetish which exercises a mythic hold over his more unsophisticated readers. But as Jean Baudrillard has pointed out, the use of what he calls 'the fetishism metaphor' in academic circles to denigrate popular culture's investment in materiality presupposes 'the existence, somewhere, of a non-alienated consciousness of an object in some "true", objective state' which, presumably, critics alone can access.[6] The privileging of Byron's body (the perverse object of desire) over his poetic corpus (the true value of the poet) – the material over the symbolic – smacks of an infantile regression to the realm of the maternal body for these critics. Nor should this come as a surprise since, as Peter Brooks has remarked, 'the body . . . often presents us with a fall from language, a return to an infantile presymbolic space in which primal drives reassert their force'.[7] The critical assumption is that we should have grown out of such childish obsessions with the real, and focus on what really matters – the text. The Byromaniac's refusal to do so, then, is consistently viewed today as a pathology; here we find the expression of fetishism's disavowal defined by Octave Mannoni's famous articulation, 'I know, but nonetheless'.[8] That is, 'I know that Byron's physical presence, powerful though it may have been, is no longer present, but nonetheless . . . I want to sleep in his bed.'

As Brooks notes, however, this critical opposition between the material and the symbolic, the body and the sign, is misleading at best:

The earliest infantile experiences – the sense of the infant's body in relation to its mother's, its orientation in space, its first attempts to achieve equilibrium – may be foundational for all symbolism … Bodily parts, sensations, and perceptions (including the notorious recognition of the anatomical distinction between the sexes) are the first building blocks in the construction of a symbolic order.[9]

To dismiss the body as 'merely' superficial is to ignore the fact that it is in our repeated misrecognitions of the body that symbolic systems are born. To put it bluntly, in words that sound ludicrous but need to be said, there is no possibility of a Byronic text without a Byronic body.[10] *Don Juan*'s narrator might indeed warn us that 'immaterialism's a serious matter' when his hero seeks the spectral presence of the Black Monk, but Byron's own play on words reminds us that embedded *within* the 'serious' business of immateriality is the equally serious 'matter' of flesh.[11] In short, despite Byron criticism's dismissal of materiality as unworthy of study, it would be wise to remember that there are few things more 'material' than a poetic text.

of shrivelled limbs and sylvan satyrs: finding the fetish

Byron's flesh has been the subject of remarkable interest from his own time until the present day; his beauty, his limp, and his much vaunted sexual magnetism have all been the focus of endless critical attempts to reach the 'truth' of the poet. Even when examining his poetry, the critical language used is decidedly 'bodily'. Thus Grosskurth remarks with assurance that 'the necessity to penetrate the hero's façade, to reach the sensitive heart that undeniably throbbed beneath the severe exterior became the determined purpose of every young woman who copied passages into her commonplace book'.[12] The act of copying Byron's poetry out in fragments becomes either a kind of metaphoric autopsy – a 'penetrative' act that will uncover the organs of truth under the skin of social appearance – or a phallic mastery over the 'throbbing' and utterly exposed essence of Byron's being.[13]

This metaphoric penetration of the poet, of course, anticipated the real and repeated attempts to 'dig up' the truth of Byron by dissection and autopsy after his death in 1824. But even having replaced the notoriously unreliable realm of literary analysis with the presumably more stable body of medical 'fact' in our attempts to discover 'the true Byron', the contradictory reports remain bewildering. We are told by reliable eyewitnesses that Byron's lameness was in his left, his right, and both feet. His hair, we are assured is both auburn and black, his smile simultaneously open and boyish, twisted and morose. This confusion can hardly be blamed on a paucity of evidence, for we have more physical descriptions of Byron by his contemporaries than of any other Romantic poet.[14] Arguably, then, the source of the confusion concerning the poet's 'real' attributes has less to do with the unreliability of the physical evidence – Byron's notoriously 'mercurial nature' could not, after all, alter the position of his club foot – and more to do with the peculiarly libidinal nature of his readers' attempt to unveil his truth *through* his body. Byron's body 'stands' in for something far more powerful and evocative than mere flesh: it becomes the screen upon which we project our own fantasies, anxieties and desires. What we find there says volumes about what we see (or wish to see) in ourselves, and this is confirmed by what MacCarthy has recognized as a long history of 'male biographers of Byron who portrayed their subject according to the image they wished to appropriate for themselves'.[15] The many critical attempts to uncover the truth of Byron have failed precisely because what we find 'buried' is not Byron at all, but the phantasmatic embodiment of our own desire. But before examining the fetishizing practices of Byronic criticism, it is necessary to see exactly how this fantasy of the poet's body evolved and manifested itself in popular culture.

Two central events in the sexualization of Byron's flesh are important here: the exhumation and the autopsy of Byron's body. In June of 1938, the vicar of Hucknall Torkard oversaw the opening of the Byron family tomb, ostensibly to 'establish some archeological points of general interest' about a reputed crypt under the church. However, any interest there may have been in such a crypt was quickly forgotten when the coffin lid of the poet was discovered to be 'loose'. As with Calvert's description of Byron's geological importance, the vicar's interest in rock formation quickly gives way to an interest in the flesh. Rumours had been rife for nearly a century that the poet's body had been stolen, molested, or had mysteriously disappeared (the many resurrections of Byron-as-vampire in popular culture come to mind here), but the men under the guidance of the vicar, Canon Barber, decided that, while they had no authority to exhume the body, the 'truth ought to prevail' and they proceeded to open the tomb and coffin of the sixth Lord Byron for the sake of posterity.[16] What they found was the remains of a 'remarkably handsome' young man, in excellent preservation. The truth-seekers stood in 'reverential' awe of the miraculously intact body which still emanated a power unchanged in death:

> What was beneath it? ... Dare I look within? ... Reverently, very reverently, I raised the lid, and before my eyes there lay the embalmed body of Byron in as perfect a condition as when it was placed in the coffin one hundred and fourteen years ago. His features and hair easily recognizable from the portraits with which I was so familiar. The serene, almost happy expression on his face made a profound impression upon me.[17]

Barber becomes very emotional when confronted by the 'young, handsome and the most famous man of genius of his age, a name throughout Europe'.[18] The only thing to mar the perfection of Byron's presence, he tells us, is the fact that one foot is severed and lying apart from the rest of the body. The churchwarden, A.E. Houldsworth, who attends the event, however, is less interested in *this* mangled limb than in the monstrous appearance of another: Byron's penis. There was, we are told, a 'quite abnormal development' of Byron's sexual member, even in the body's embalmed state.[19] Apparently it was not enough to know that the poet's body was indeed still 'there'; something else had to be seen to be believed.

Such moments of libidinal excavation are, of course, fertile ground for the formation of the fetish, for, whatever else it is, the fetish object is always a substitute for the missing penis. For Freud, the fetish originates in the unwelcome moment of awareness when the subject first confronts maternal castration. Rather than fully accept the absence of the maternal penis and thus accept the possibility of castration, the boy of Freud's scenario replaces it with something that 'stands in for' the penis:

> In the conflict between the weight of the unwelcome perception and the force of his counter-wish, a compromise has been reached, as is only possible under the dominance of the unconscious laws of thought – the primary process. Yes, in his mind the woman *has* got a penis, in spite of everything; but this penis is no longer the same as it was before. Something else has taken its place, has been appointed its substitute, as it were, and now inherits the interest which was formerly directed to its predecessor.[20]

In the case of Byron's body we see the simultaneous attempt to reconcile castration with potency. But even *having* seen the penis, we're not quite sure *what* we see. The manner in which Houldsworth describes Byron's penile irregularity leaves us guessing as to the precise dimensions and severity of the poet's 'abnormality'. Was the poet's member abnormally *large* and thus evidence of the poet's excessive masculinity – what his critics would refer to as his 'magical potency'? Or was the abnormality a deformation, repeating the poet's lameness/castration, and thus the physical proof of the poet's sexual *in*adequacy?[21]

We begin to see here why it is of vital importance to the Byron enthusiasts that 'the truth prevail' and that it be determined whether Byron's body is *really* present in his crypt or not. The question being asked is resonant of castration anxiety: 'dare I look within?' Has 'it' mysteriously disappeared, swept away by violent and unscrupulous forces, or does it remain where we had always known it to be, intact and whole? If, as I have suggested, the fixation with Byron's body has its origin in this fetishistic power, then it can come as little surprise that, having found one of the poet's limbs castrated, the anxiety created by this lack should be immediately compensated for by the formidable *presence* of another. It is Byron's 'presence' in both senses of the word, which impresses the onlookers of the exhumation; the actual presence of Byron's body/intactness, but also the residue of his symbolic presence – his potent charm. Byron's fetishized body specifically acts as a 'token of triumph over the threat of castration and a protection against it'.[22] Byron may be gone, but his arresting presence is never fully lost – 'it' is simply shifted elsewhere. Thus, if indeed 'male biographers' have been in the habit of portraying the poet according to an image they themselves could appropriate, then any fantasy identification with the poet need not be challenged by Byron's alarming 'lack'.

A wonderful illustration of this fantasy work can be found in the journals of Edward Trelawny, a friend in Byron's later life who ostentatiously adopted the persona of one of Byron's own heroes. Trelawny studied the embalmed body of Byron in an effort to establish the 'true' nature of the poet's power, and he too focuses on the poet's 'abnormal limbs' in his attempt to do so. What Trelawny refers to as 'the great mystery' of Byron's physical abnormality is, as he puts it, 'solved' when he obtains a few stolen moments to be alone with the poet's corpse. Trelawny's description of the encounter is highly charged to say the least:

> No one was within the house but Fletcher, of which I was glad. As if he knew my wishes, he led me up a narrow stair into a small room, with nothing in it but a coffin standing on trestles . . . he withdrew the black pall and the white shroud, and there lay the embalmed body of the Pilgrim – more beautiful in death than in life . . . few marble busts could have matched its stainless white, the harmony of its proportions, and perfect finish; yet he had been dissatisfied with that body, and

longed to cast its slough ... I asked Fletcher to bring me a glass of water. On his leaving the room, to confirm or remove my doubts as to the exact cause of his lameness, I uncovered the Pilgrim's feet, and was answered – the great mystery was solved. Both his feet were clubbed, and his legs withered to the knee – the form and features of an Apollo, with the feet of a sylvan satyr.[23]

Trelawny's description of the body as a sacred relic and his lingering description of its marble luster and harmony of proportions are already thoroughly sexualized, but what is particularly telling is the fact that he too is compelled to discover the 'great mystery' of Byron's body. Like Barber, he frets about 'what is beneath' the veiled form. He waits until he is alone, tricking Fletcher to leave the room, and then peeks at the veiled 'mystery' of Byron's presence. At this moment, Trelawny experiences a version of the disavowal that the gravediggers would later record in Hucknall Torkard. Both of Byron's limbs, we are told, are withered to the knee, making the poet's presence one of a blighted God. But significantly, while such emasculation of the poet would seem to imply a qualification of his potency, this anxiety is quickly overcome by the reference to the satyr. Satyrs may have cloven feet, but they are also renowned for their thoroughly lascivious nature. Byron remains the fetish, the guarantee of potency.[24]

The remarkably phantasmatic nature of these two encounters with the poet's body is made particularly clear when we compare it to the information recorded by John Cam Hobhouse's diary after he encountered the embalmed body of his friend when it lay 'in state' in 20 Great George Street on 6 July, post autopsy. Hobhouse remarks that he too is 'drawn by an irresistible inclination'[25] to see the corpse of his friend but he is devastated to discover that the doctors performing the autopsy had so mangled the body that it was barely recognizable.[26] All of which makes us wonder about the sublimely beautiful corpse seen by Trelawny and Barber. Crane claims, echoing MacCarthy's reading of the male biographers, that Barber saw what he wanted to see in the immortalized features of the poet.[27] But in the case of Trelawny there is every possibility that the *entire* encounter was a fantasy. Trelawny not only gets the location of the club foot wrong, he does not comment upon the disfigured appearance of the corpse so upsetting to Hobhouse after the autopsy. The evidence suggests that Trelawny fantasized his entire viewing of Byron's corpse, and thus, had been unaware that the two doctors performing the autopsy in Greece had previously disfigured the body nearly beyond recognition. With this in mind, it is hardly surprising that Trelawny recorded Byron's lameness incorrectly; he was basing his recollections on memory and fantasy. Not that the doctors, despite such 'scientific' methodology, are any more reliable. As MacCarthy notes, the presiding doctor, Millingen, is so overwhelmed with 'excitement' as he views the 'beautiful symmetry' of the poet's body that he recorded Byron's left rather than right leg as the injured limb.[28]

The common feature in all these narratives of revelation and discovery is the almost uncontrollable need to 'peek' under the protective veil that covers Byron's body and discover the truth to his 'great mystery'. It is perhaps not surprising that literary criticism has condemned such past fascination with Byron's limbs as childish; the behaviour is, after all, reminiscent of Freud's 'inquisitive boy' who develops a foot fetish. Freud's child also 'peers' up skirts and under veils in his efforts to see the much longed-for 'truth' of sexual difference, and there is certainly much in the child's resulting disavowal to remind us of the response felt by Byron's 'fans' upon viewing his 'mysterious' deformity.[29] When modern Byron criticism records such examples of nineteenth-century 'Byromania', then, it is generally with a note of embarrassed condescension. Indeed, what the next section will illustrate are the ways in which 'serious' Byronists have either conveniently forgotten these earlier fetishists altogether or have simply infantilized and/or feminized them in a gesture of dismissal. This interest in the material realm is so identifiable in our culture *as* feminine (rather than as spiritual or intellectual) that the Byron fetishist has now become almost exclusively identified as female in both scholarship and popular culture. No longer can the student of Byron's body be confused with a historical 'truth-seeker'. This female fetishist, we are told, seeks something rather more tangible from Byron's body than the revelation of a point of historical interest. She doesn't want to *understand* Byron. She just *wants* Byron.

re-membering byron: film and fantasy

The representation of the Byron fetishist originates in the contemporary response to Byron's fame known as 'Byromania'. This term, coined by Annabella Milbanke, who was later to become the poet's wife, ridiculed the contemporary fascination with Byron by Regency women:

> See Caro, smiling, sighing, o'er his face
> In hopes to imitate each strange grimace
> And mar the silliness that looks so fair
> By bringing signs of wilder Passion there.[30]

'Caro', of course, refers to Byron's most notorious lover, Lady Caroline Lamb, and Annabella's point in referring to such 'Byromaniacs' is that they are so intent upon reading and possessing Byron's *body*, that they utterly misread his poetry. They forget the '*Truths* that cut so deep' making them 'to our friend's oppression kind'. More established critics of the day similarly accused Byron's female readers of being far more interested in Byron's sexual favours than in his work. John Gibson Lockhart wrote in his 'Letter to the Right Hon. Lord Byron. By John Bull' (1821) that the poet's early poetry was calculated to become 'a school-*girl's* tale' and that 'every boarding-school in the empire still contains many devout believers in the amazing misery of the black-haired, high-browed, blue-eyed, bare-throated Lord Byron'.[31] What is more, every one of these young women fantasizes about being the Lord's lover, assuming that they could have succeeded in making Byron happy where Annabella had failed. Says Lockhart's imagined 'school-girl', 'if I had married such a man, I would have borne with all his little eccentricities'.[32] Again, it would seem that not only are Byron's readers women, but they are not even very *good* readers since they are far more interested in the poet's sexual rather than poetic powers. Nor can they really be blamed, notes one critic, since 'Lord Byron possesses in an eminent degree, the facility of embodying the strong commanding passions of the soul – of being able to mould them to his own purpose – and of bringing the minds of his readers into a state of vassalage or subjection'.[33] Byron is repeatedly referred to by his critics as having a 'magical energy' or force that ensures his popularity, especially for women, who are seen as more susceptible to such auras. He has become quite literally a fetish object in the anthropological sense of the word.[34] In Baudrillard's terms he is 'a force, a supernatural property' which offers 'a similar magical potential in the subject, through schemas of projection and capture, alienation and reappropriation'.[35] For the more sanguine of Byron's critics, however, what the poet's status as fetish meant was that as soon as his *material* presence was lost in death, so too would his popularity as a poet. Thomas Babington Macaulay concludes, for example, that Byron's 'magical potency' will soon disappear once the image of the poet as a 'man, young noble and happy' has faded from memory, leaving only his poetry to posterity. Without the man to lend it his 'magic', the poetry must survive on its own merits, and for Macaulay this does not bode well, for the early works of Byron at least.[36]

But what Macaulay could not have foreseen was the invention of film in the twentieth century and its ability to resurrect that which has been lost to us. While the nineteenth century was arguably fixated with the prospect of *dis*membering Byron through autopsies, exhumations, and voyeuristic examinations in order to discover the source of his 'potency', twentieth-century popular culture has been far more interested in acts of re-membering the poet. The most prevalent example of this critical trend has, of course, been to create film and television adaptations of Byron's life and character – to provide, if you will, a replacement for the much lamented memoir left by Byron for publication after his death and destroyed in John Murray's office on 17 May 1824. Grosskurth remarks that it is at this moment of destruction that 'the real Byron' is lost to us rather than at the passing of his body: 'the carcass was not the real Byron. The vital Byron – recorder of his own life – had already been destroyed in Murray's parlour on May 17'.[37] But, *pace* Macaulay, the absence of the Byronic body does nothing to ensure the establishment of the 'true' Byronic corpus. By destroying the memoir, Hobhouse created a mysterious absence that now invited endless imaginary and fictionalized attempts to complete the corpus/corpse of Byron so tragically cut off in its/his prime. That this attempt to replenish the lack should manifest itself in film is no surprise since, as Christian Metz has argued, the screen offers us a fantasy of completion, or as he puts it, a 'prosthesis for our primally dislocated limbs'.[38] Film becomes the fantasy realm which enables us to revisit our primal trauma of loss described by the structures of psycho-analysis as the moment when we are projected from the Imaginary realm of completion into the Symbolic realm of law and subjectivity. Film for Metz, then, becomes the realm of fetishism par excellence since it is in film that we undergo the same operations of denial and disavowal enacted by the fetishist when encountering the spectacle of the mother's lack:

> A fetish, the cinema as a technical performance, as prowess, as an *exploit*, an exploit that underlines and denounces the lack on which the whole arrangement is based (the absence of the object, replaced by its reflection), an exploit which consists at the same time of making this absence forgotten... For the establishment of his full potency for cinematic enjoyment [*jouissance*] he must think at every moment (and above all *simultaneously*) of the force of presence the film has and of the absence on which this force is constructed.[39]

Byron lends himself admirably to these fetishistic operations: a limb in need of prosthetic completion and an unfinished body of work invite the kind of fantasy replacement of the absent that only film can provide. And it is precisely because of this sense of film's phantasmatic ability to complete a lack, to enact the fetish, that the films representing Byron have been so panned by Byron scholars; they celebrate a vision of Byron that is decidedly *material* and bodily in nature. There are few commentators on the Byron films, for example, who don't condemn them for their avoidance of the poet's *poetry*. Here again we find the privileging of the symbolic over the material. What should be prioritized is Byron's importance as a poet and a master of metaphoric structure, but what the films do, we are told, is trivialize the man into a physical object of desire. 'Legitimate' Byron studies gives way to Byromania and feminine fetishes.

In fact, all of the recent films on the subject of Byron suggest that they are geared to attract the same kind of 'fetishizing' female audience that Byron himself had lured during his own life. In Robert Bolt's *Lady Caroline Lamb* (1972) Byron's *Childe Harold's Pilgrimage* is shown to be carefully marketed by his publisher, John Murray, as a 'woman's book' and the poet is all but mobbed by a group of well-dressed socialites at his first London 'appearance'.[40] In *A Haunted Summer* (1988) Claire Claremont informs us that 'women faint when they see him...honestly', while at the beginning of Ken Russell's *Gothic* (1986), a group of female tourists gather together at a hotel and jostle with each other to look through a telescope trained upon the poet's window.[41] Indeed, the female gaze is so insisted upon in these films that we find repeated references to the kind of fetishistic voyeurism we have previously noted in the narratives of Barber and Trelawny. In a fascinating shift, however, the once-male voyeurs of Byron's 'beautiful symmetry' have been transformed universally into women. Byron's lovers, his wife, his prostitutes, in *every* one of these films, can be seen peering under tables and clothes in a constant harassment of the poet as they try to see his hidden limbs. In *Rowing with the Wind* (1987) by Gonzalo Suarez, Claire Claremont attempts to remove Byron's boot and is spurned with the words 'Not my boots, ever'.[42] In *Gothic*, the Claire Claremont figure similarly stoops under the table in an effort to reveal Byron's 'cloven hoof', and she too is spurned in anger, turned back from viewing any evidence of lack. In an utterly bizarre scene – arguably unnecessary from a plot standpoint – in the recent biographical adaptation of Byron's life by the BBC (2003), Hobhouse and his old friend take home a couple of prostitutes. Hobhouse is represented in *medias res*, enjoying his sexual encounter immensely as he balances a nubile young woman on his lap. The camera then pans to Byron (Jonny Lee Miller), who is shown intently reading a book at a table. In a parodic echo of *Gothic*'s depiction of Claire Claremont's under-the-table high jinks, however, there is a naked prostitute under the table, but this time engaged in the act of fellatio. The 'limbs' of Byron seem again to be conflated, for, whatever this scene may dramatize, it is clearly not a sex act in any normal sense of the word. Rather, what we find is another echo of Freud's little boy looking under the skirts of his mother in his efforts to find the elusive and missing phallus. And like the boy who enters into the realm of disavowal when confronted by the 'absence' of the penis, we too are left uncertain how to read this particular 'uncovering' of Byron's member. What, to echo Freud, do these women want? The poet's utter lack of involvement in the excavation of his body leads us to wonder whether they have found anything under the table at all, or alternately, whether the poet signifies a sexual presence of such alarming proportions as to explode all of their normal expectations. Are these women fetishizing Byron in the Freudian sense seen by Barber, Trelawny and Millingen – seeking obsessively for the truth of sexual difference in the presence of the penis – or are they rather simply seeking to possess that penis they *know* themselves to lack?

Here, of course, we run into the same problem Freud himself repeatedly confronted: what to do about the female lack? What is interesting is that Byron studies, as well as the popular imagination remembering Byron, has clearly come to the same conclusion as Freud. Women are driven by a sense of their own incompletion and physical need. But this assumption entails accepting that neither the Byron lovers in the films we have discussed nor the 'obsessive' female readers of the poet *can* be fetishists in the proper sense of the word, if only because they can never experience the state of disavowal necessary to initiate fetishism as 'a token of triumph over the threat of castration'. Women have, as Mary Ann Doane puts it, nothing to lose.[43] Criticism, then, has condemned the female 'Byromaniac' for being a 'fetishist' of Byron (debasing him into a material object of desire rather than a subject of study) while simultaneously claiming that, *as* a woman, the Byromaniac cannot properly be a fetishist (having already been castrated). And what this means, Doane astutely points out, is that women are simultaneously denied 'the ability to balance knowledge and belief and hence to maintain a distance from the lure of the image' which is the very function of the fetish.[44] This places the female 'fans' of Byron in an untenable and indeed impossible position as female subjects.

Nor has woman's paradoxical relationship to the fetish been confined to the discipline of psychoanalysis. Byron studies has long struggled over the problematic ramifications of this poet's commodification, and it is hardly news to point out that it too has been critically constructed as a gendered event. Byron is traditionally viewed as a poet 'true to himself' only in his later satires since his early Romances have been read, until recently, as examples of Byron's 'pandering' to a female audience. He supposedly sold out, became part of a literary 'factory',[45] and prostituted his art[46] for the sake of a specifically feminine readership.[47] Macaulay observed after the poet's death, for example, that 'Byron did not consider that the sway which he had exercised in literature had been purchased by servitude – by the sacrifice of his own taste to the taste of the public'.[48] Indeed, Byron's critics repeatedly claim that by relying on his carefully constructed persona in his early 'popular' work to sell his poems, the poet sold himself into the realm of commodity fetishism. Thus, as Robert F. Gleckner has noted, this commercial success may have won Byron fame during his life, but it condemned him in the eyes of modern critics:

> The judgment of the age ... was in a sense purchased in coin of the realm ... – Curiously, this judgment has produced a contrary verdict in our age. More enlightened, and rather self-righteously freed from nineteenth-century *Weltschmerz*, we have been strangely blind to all but the rampant 'Byronism', as we parrot-like continue to call it, of *Childe Harold's Pilgrimage*, the Turkish tales ... indeed, to all of the poems which are neither satiric nor antic ... most modern critics perpetuate the fashion of disdaining to comment on the poetry written prior to 1816, or of dismissing it with appropriate condescension.[49]

Byron criticism, Gleckner argues, has all too readily sacrificed serious critical examination to an 'easy understanding of content and a rather smug rediscovery of Byronic character or his "power" or "presence"'.[50] Critics speak dismissively of Byron's production of this early work, haphazardly written between dinner engagements, while his Turkish Tales continue to be read as 'degraded' coinage; they are repeatedly seen as 'a cheap appeal to a debased public taste'[51] and an 'attempt to capitalize on the taste' of the masses if only because they were pumped out of Murray's 'factory' as fast as they would sell to their enthusiastic (female) consumers.[52]

The economic language here is no coincidence; terms like 'coin of the realm', and 'capitalize' remind us immediately of the ideological underpinnings of the commodity fetish. The Byronic text, like Marx's fetish, is viewed as a commodity in which the relationship of labour to value-relation has become mystified and disconnected. In the 'factory' of Byron's Romance-production,[53] 'the commodity-form, and the value-relation of the products of labour within which it appears, have absolutely no connection with the physical nature of the commodity and the material [*dinglich*] relations arising out of this'.[54] The Byronic commodity – Byron himself in this case – is removed from its value-relation to labour, and has entered into the realm of the fetish in which it acquires the power of 'an independent being endowed magically with life'. Even Byron's close friend, Thomas Moore, was quick to reiterate the assumption that Byron's early Tales were being sold at such an unprecedented rate largely because of the poet's new status as a fetishized object of female desire:

> Nor can it be denied that, among many purer sources of interest in this poem, the allusions which he makes to instances of '*successful* passion' in his career were not without their influence on the fancies of that sex, whose weakness it is to be most easily won by those who come recommended by the greatest number of triumphs over others.[55]

The neurotic desire of the female reader is again revealed to be at the heart of the poet's success. It is not Byron's poetry that inspires these fans, but rather the suggestion that the fantasy enacted in their pages may be transformed into material, sensual reality. That the word may indeed become the thing, as Byron would have it. This was the general accusation made against the Byron fans; they were considered by contemporary critics to have formed a new 'effeminate' readership of poetry which had evolved a dangerous reliance upon the sensual rather than the spiritual powers of literature. In 1824, one anonymous critic goes on at great length to condemn this new taste of the age, as well as the poets that feed it. England, he warns, is fast sinking into a

> spirit of effeminacy: the same groveling ... propension to the soft and the beautiful in preference to the strenuous and sublime, the same proneness to wallow in the imaginary luxuries of the sense, the same gluttonous love of everything that can excite the palate of the mind – constitute the moving principle of the school of modern poetry.[56]

But while modern Byron criticism may no longer believe that such 'effeminacy' is still the dominant force in the culture, there is much to suggest that we continue to worry over an ever-increasing, and presumed puerile popular interest in the materiality of Byron rather than the sublimity of his corpus. As Ramona M. Ralston and Sidney L. Sondergard lament in their exhaustive examination of the mythic representations of Byron in film, the poet's

> artistic genius is inevitably assumed or asserted, but not demonstrated, for the image of Byron as a poet and the excesses of his Romantic lifestyle are what remain in the popular imagination, while actual

knowledge of his poetry, among any but English majors and scholars, has all but disappeared.[57]

This, it seems to me, is a significant statement that sums up much of the current attitude in Byron criticism when confronting various productions of Byromania; the new Byron 'reader' makes no pretence to *reading*. She isn't simply the bad reader she had been in the past – she now takes no interest in the text at all. Instead, she fantasizes about yet another 'lifestyle of the rich and famous', utterly disregarding the 'actual' work of the scholar who alone focuses on the word and on the poet *as* poet; this textual Byron, we are told, is worthy of examination precisely because he *transcends* the material realm and even his own body in a manner specified by MacCarthy when she insists upon the 'real' Byron as a presence embodied by his memoirs rather than his corpse. It is only the female fetishists, so commonly rendered in the Byron films, which insist upon gaining access to the poet's body – and it is perhaps not without irony that the writers of the BBC life of Byron depict the poet discarding one of his Italian lovers the moment he actually finds her *capable* of reading his poetry. As a female 'spectator' of his life, her place is not in the realm of the symbolic, but rather the material/sexual.[58]

But what, ultimately, is the difference between the reader of Byron's corpse and the reader of his corpus? Following Brooks, it is not even fully possible to read the symbolic body without going through a prior event by which we (mis)read the physical one. Indeed, in psychical terms, it is precisely this state of duality between seeing our 'real' and imagined self – the state of disavowal – that structures the operations of the fetish in the first place. The fetish, in Freudian terms, enables the subject to make the 'normal' distinctions between the self and other so lacking in the so-called 'Byromaniac'. What then to make of the vehement critical distinctions repeatedly made between the critic and the fan/fetishist? As Janice Radway points out in her astute analyses of commodity culture:

> we do not yet think clearly enough about the fact that mass culture and the middlebrow are concrete and specific challenges to our own authority as cultural custodians. Familiar evaluative assessment of mass entertainment as a form calling only for passive response repeatedly recurs, I believe, because our day-to-day praxis as academic intellectuals is itself predicated on a gendered notion of the subject and because the legitimacy of our authority depends significantly on our continuing ability to naturalize *that* subject as the norm in opposition to others.[59]

For Radway, what drives this insistence upon a rigid distinction between academic study and 'middlebrow' consumption is the fact that we, as academics, have a personal investment in its maintenance; it enables us to 'exert cultural authority over others'. Academics in our present historical moment are arguably more anxious than ever about maintaining the borders of cultural authority when, for example, students of today are introduced to Byron through 'blogs' and 'webcasts' in which Byron is represented as a cartoon ghost who returns to Victorian England to battle evil (and to indulge his sexual appetite beyond the grave).[60] If we consider that one of the many examples of Byroniana produced in recent years is a novel in which the poet's personality and identity are copied on to a hard drive in a computer, which in turn seduces the scholar/programmer into a romantic entanglement, it is perhaps understandable that critics have closed ranks and insisted upon a less libidinally invested approach to Byron studies.[61]

But as Jean Baudrillard's examination of the fetish makes clear, there is a considerable danger in constructing an artificial opposition between the fallen realm of the fetishist and the transcendent realm of the 'serious' student. For Baudrillard, the 'fetishist metaphor', so commonly used in analysis, has emerged out of 'the whole repertoire of occidental Christian and humanist ideology as orchestrated by colonists, ethnologists and missionaries' who, historically, have mobilized this term as a means by which to denigrate primitive cults; the 'fetish' cult is condemned as that which 'worship[s] certain earthly and material objects' instead of seeking Christianity's own (self-proclaimed) 'abstract and spiritual' goals.[62] 'Never having really shed this moral and rationalistic connotation,' argues Baudrillard, 'the great *fetishist metaphor* has since been the recurrent leitmotiv of the analysis of "magical thinking", whether that of the Bantu tribes or that of modern metropolitan hordes submerged in their objects and their signs.'[63] For Baudrillard, then, the careless use of this metaphor is dangerous not only because 'it short circuits analysis', (as Gleckner's above reference to the critical 'dismissal' of Byron's early 'sensual' work suggests) but also because this use of fetishism *itself* involves a fetishization of the 'conscious subject or of a human essence'.[64] That is, the so-called 'fetishist' is viewed as a being suffering from a false consciousness since she or he is seen 'to worship artificial libidinal or prestige values incorporated in the object' rather than seek a privileged, 'spiritual' truth that has not been tarnished by commodification and commercialism.[65] It is for this reason that the use of the fetish metaphor leads, ironically, to the fetishization of a human 'essence' – a transcendental subject – uncorrupted and non-alienated by the forces of commodification and commercialism. To return to Byron studies, such a privileged reverence for a 'spiritual truth' (the perceived role of the 'real' Byron critic) is neatly placed in opposition to the 'fetishist' suffering from a false consciousness (the Byromaniac).

Such a problematic usage of 'fetish' goes beyond creating a simple opposition between false and transcendent consciousness, however. As the above examination of Byron in popular culture has already shown, it *genders* these terms as well, placing the feminine firmly within the category of fallen, alienated being. If we had any doubt of this critical procedure we need look no farther than MacCarthy's biography for evidence. MacCarthy replicates this traditional portrait of the Byron fan as false-consciousness, noting that

> the correspondence [from Byron's fans] shows the remarkable capacity of Byron's more neurotic female readers to construct their personal scenarios around him, convinced by the intense emotionalism of his poetry that they are addressing 'a feeling Heart'.[66]

We are immediately reminded of Byron's cinematic audience of female listeners in *Lady Caroline Lamb* and we are encouraged immediately to disengage ourselves from this group of Byromaniacs – to identify elsewhere, with those who are not sycophants and neurotic fetishists, but true critics. Indeed the camera angles used in this scene are designed specifically to encourage a condemnation of these 'bad readers' of the poet who focus solely on Byron's physical presence. The camera pans slowly over the often gormless expressions of the women in the crowd, rarely allowing us to focus on Byron's (Richard Chamberlain) often bemused expression of contempt for those he enraptures. As a result, the camera itself forces us to identify not with the viewers/readers of women, but with an outsider who triangulates the unhealthy and obsessive dyadic union between poet and fan. We are, quite literally in terms of camera angle, *above* the crowd. The difference between us and them is the difference between the serious reader who wants to know, (or indeed already knows) the words of Byron versus those who care only about the Byronic aura. The former is the serious and well-balanced critic; the latter is a fetishist.

But even in such moments of critical distancing, we find some interesting signs of displaced desire. While it is true that we, as good critical readers, wish to place ourselves outside of the circle of adoring women, we also find ourselves with a curious bedfellow. For we are not alone in our self-conscious isolation; one more figure lurks in the shadows, ostentatiously not joining in the adoring throng, and that figure is Caroline Lamb. In the second meeting between Caro and the poet, set at Holland House, she refuses to go near the poet and is too engaged by the banter of her own adoring circle to join in with the 'crowd'. She stands apart as someone who wants to indicate that she does not consider herself to bear the same relationship to Byron as to the rest of his fans. She knows Byron *better* than this. She understands his poetic genius and, indeed, at the poetry reading we see her listening so intently to the poet's words that she is moved to tears as Byron speaks them. In short, the traditional position of the critic as someone who wishes to be seen as something other than the rather pathetic Byromaniac – as someone who truly knows and cares for Byron – puts us in the same cinematic place as his most notorious 'maniac'. The critic takes on the same self-conscious but thoroughly libidinally charged position in relation to the poet as Byron's most infamous and most critically abused lover.

The same scenario is interestingly played out in the more recent BBC television adaptation. Here, it is Annabella Milbanke who stands in for the 'smug' literary critics who feel themselves above the libidinal charms of the poet. We are shown Annabella intently preoccupied with her own 'close reading' of Byron's poetry, studiously underlining important passages that reveal elements of Byron's truth. Of course, she is revealed (no less than Lamb) to be just as fascinated and desirous of a more intimate relation with the poet's 'corpus'. What both film adaptations illustrate is that by attempting to distance ourselves from the embarrass-ingly libidinal fan, we engage in precisely the same strategies of desire *as* the fan. Crane, for example, operates on precisely this level when he attempts to represent the poet as the victim of his early commodification, and a true genius only when he turns his back on his past popularity:

> One of the most moving aspects of his last year is the way his letters and actions reveal a gradual firming of purpose, a steady discarding of the conceits and fripperies of his Italian existence, a unifying of personality, an alignment at last of intelligence and sensibility — a growth into a human greatness which mirrors the development of his literary talents from the emotional and psychological crudity of 'Childe Harold' into the mature genius of 'Don Juan'.[67]

For Crane, and many other critics, Byron's maturation as a poet and as an individual coincided with his turn from the soft feminine 'fripperies' (which presumably left him poetically 'flaccid') to 'firm' political activism. Byron's greatness is only to be achieved when he becomes 'true to himself', the non-alienated worker whose product has at last become a reflection of his labour. Thus, in 1923 John Murray (grandson of Byron's publisher) concludes that the poet in later years was 'shaking free from the Venetian toils and settling down to good and honest work'[68] while the critic Robert Escarpit blames Murray the elder precisely *for* this early unproductive and alienating toil:

> after having been engaged by Murray in his literary factory as a specialist in melancholy moods, of inconsequential revolt, powerless bitterness and mysterious exoticism, Byron later was amicably but firmly dismissed by his publisher and literary advisors when, having exhausted the poor resources of that vein, he tried to strike back through *Don Juan* towards the main stream of militant poetry which in his heart of hearts he was never to forsake.[69]

Giuseppe Mazzini is still more explicit, arguing that Byron at last achieves a transcendent status above his role as a commodity fetish because he is no longer influenced by the world at all – now 'the Byronian Ego aspires to rule *it*'. For Mazzini, Byron, 'holds his state at the centre of the Universe and from thence projects the light radiating from the depths of his own mind; as scorching and intense as the concentrated solar ray'.[70] Byron does not need to be 'excavated' for truth any more; he hurls out enlightenment from his own 'depths' and, quite literally, transcends the sordid materialism of the world around him. To return to Baudrillard, by creating such rigid oppositions as this between the spiritual and the material, we indulge in our own form of fetishism. Byron may no longer be a commodity fetish, but he has now become a different kind of fetish – a Promethean god of light.

Critics have thus been so eager to condemn the fetishized vision of Byron precisely because its operations reveal their own desiring gaze on the corpus of the poet. There is a pleasure to be had from the 'dissection' of Byron's 'beautiful symmetry' that bears a striking resemblance to the deconstruction of his texts and analysis of his poetic devices. We as critics, no less than the fetishist, enjoy the moment before the 'revelation' of the Byronic truth and savour the possibility of uncovering the 'great mystery' of his being. What we inevitably discover beneath the shroud that covers Byron is neither a hidden reality nor even a scandalous revelation. What we discover is our own anxiety about potency, integrity, and the place of desire in the act of analysis. Byron has become such an important figure in our cultural corpus since it is his body – whether commodified and 'gelded', as Byron put it, or transcendently potent – that stands in for our own.

Perhaps it is for this reason that we can never quite let sleeping poets lie. Like Annabella or my conference companion, we all want to slip in between the sheets with him, be these sheets of poetry or linen. Byron's own pleas that his epitaph be *implora eternal quiete*, 'I implore eternal peace', becomes a wry joke worthy of the poet of *Don Juan*. For what history has shown us is that we simply can't leave Byron alone, dead or alive. Like Juan reaching out in anticipation of encountering the immaterial spirit of the Black Monk, we as critics 'eager now the truth to pierce', repeatedly hit not the spirit of the poet with our grasp, but rather 'something much like flesh and blood'.[71]

notes

1. Fiona MacCarthy, *Byron: Life and Legend*, 570.
2. MacCarthy 2002, 570.
3. Emily Apter and William Pietz, eds, *Fetishism as Cultural Discourse*, 13.
4. Jean Baudrillard, *For a Critique of Political Economy*, trans. Charles Levin, 89.
5. Even Calvert's ostensibly geological vocabulary suggests the operations of the fetish since, for him, Byron's rock-like 'hardness' is decidedly phallic, his 'hot underflow' of lava representing nothing so much as the climactic evidence of his 'real' tumescent power. At the same time, the very necessity of describing the poet's presence metaphorically, as something *else* – as hardened lava rather than as the living poet – reminds us that Byron's tumescence no longer produces 'hot underflows'. It is the marker of a past 'epoch' now dead, the ossified residue of a body once alive. William J. Calvert, *Byron: The Romantic Paradox*, ix.
6. Baudrillard 1981, 89.
7. Peter Brooks, Body Works: Objects of Desire in Modern Narrative, 7.
8. Cited in Apter and Pietz 1993, 14
9. Brooks 1993, 7.
10. This is not necessarily the case with Keats and Shelley who were established as great poets by the Victorians because of their 'ethereal' nature.
11. *Don Juan* XVI, 114, 6.
12. Phyllis Grosskurth, *Byron: The Flawed Angel*, 155.
13. Arguably, such acts are no different from what Robert F. Gleckner refers to as the critic's need to 'probe beneath the admittedly forbidding surface of [Byron's] language and prosody to essential form and structure, essential theme and style'. In short, the critic no less than the fan seeks to look beneath the surface of Byron to find his 'essence'. Robert F. Gleckner, *Byron and the Ruins of Paradise*, xii.
14. Some wonderful work has been done on the 'creation' of Byron's appearance in popular culture based on the many cartoons, portraits and engravings that have been made of Byron's likeness. For further reading see, Christine Kenyon Jones, 'Fantasy and Transfiguration: Byron and his Portraits' in *Byromania: Portraits of the Artist in Nineteenth- and Twentieth-Century Culture*, ed. Frances Wilson, 109–137; John Clubbe, 'The West Portrait of Byron', *Byron Journal*

8 (1980): 22–30; "San fidele alla mia Biondetta": A Portrait of Lord Byron Formerly Belonging to Lady Caroline Lamb' *Bodleian Library Record* 14.4 (1993): 285–95.

15. MacCarthy 2002, 554.

16. Cited in MacCarthy 2002, 573.

17. Cited in David Crane, Lord Byron's Jackal: A Life of Edward John Trelawny, 363.

18. MacCarthy 2002, 574.

19. MacCarthy 2002, 574.

20. Sigmund Freud, 'Fetishism' in *The Standard Edition of the Complete Psychological Works of Sigmund Freud,* ed. and trans. James Strachey, 1950, 21: 154.

21. The term 'development' continues to be fairly ambiguous, even having examined its nineteenth-century etymology in the *Oxford English Dictionary*. The suggestion, however, is that 'development' in the late eighteenth and nineteenth centuries generally referred to 'the growth and unfolding of what is in the germ', but in its many botanical usages so prevalent during the period under discussion, 'development' also implied a movement towards organic decay.

22. Freud 1950, 21: 154.

23. Cited in Crane 1998, 135–6.

24. Trelawny, like so many of his earlier 'fans', revised his opinion of Byron's divinity in later years. In his *Letters* he would eventually come to describe not only Byron's lameness in far less complimentary terms, but also the poet himself. Thus, Byron shifts from being an 'Apollo' to being a 'weak and ignoble soul'. For a further discussion on Trelawny's ambiguous relationship to Byron and his deformity, see Leslie A. Marchand, *Byron: A Biography*, 4 vols, 1238–39 and H. Buxton Forman, ed., *Letters of Edward John Trelawny*, 265–66.

25. Cited in MacCarthy 2002, 534.

26. MacCarthy 2002, 534.

27. Crane 1998, 363.

28. As MacCarthy and others have pointed out, there is a great deal of controversy over the various stages of Byron's dissection and the accuracy of these reports. For example, while Byron's foot is recorded by Barber to have been dissected from his body, we have no record by Millingen that such a dissection was ever performed during the autopsy (MacCarthy 2002, 519).

29. '[It] is as though the last impression before the uncanny and traumatic one is retained as a fetish... Thus the foot or shoe owes it's preference as a fetish. . . to the circumstance that the inquisitive boy peered at the woman's genitals from below, from her legs up.' Freud 1950, 21: 155.

30. Ethel Colburn Mayne, The Life and Letters of Anne Isabella, Lady Noel Byron, 44.

31. John Gibson Lockhart, 'Letter to the Right Hon. Lord Byron. By John Bull' in Andrew Rutherford. *Byron: The Critical Heritage*, 182–3.

32. Lockhart, 183.

33. Anonymous, 'Uriel. A Poetical Address to the Right Hon. Lord Byron, written on the Continent: with Notes containing Strictures on the Spirit of Infidelity maintained in his Works; an Examination of his Assertion that "If Cain is Blasphemous, Paradise Lost is Blasphemous", and several other Poems'.

34. Notably, while the common understanding of the term 'fetish' (borrowed from anthropological language) suggests a supernatural power that resides in the object, the etymological origins of the word, as Baudrillard points out, suggest that the fetish was, on the contrary, something made, created, and artificial. For a further discussion see, Baudrillard 1981, 91.

35. Baudrillard, 91.

36. Thomas Babington Macaulay, Review of Thomas Moore's *Letters and Journals of Lord Byron: with Notices of his Life* (1830). *Edinburgh Review* 53 (June, 1831): 544–72.

37. Grosskurth 1997, 472.

38. Christian Metz, 'The Imaginary Signifier'. *Screen* 16.2 (1975): 15.

39. Christian Metz, The Imaginary Signifier: Psychoanalysis and the Cinema, trans. Celia Britton et al., 74.

40. *Lady Caroline Lamb*, writer/director Robert Bolt.

41. *Haunted Summer*, director Ivan Passer (Anchor Bay Entertainment, 1994); *Gothic*, director Ken Russell (Lionsgate DVD, 2002). This event is loosely based on narratives describing Byron's infamy just after his exile from England.

42. *Rowing with the Wind*, writer/director Gonzalo Suarez, English adaptation Lester Clark.

43. Mary Ann Doane, *The Desire to Desire: The Woman's Film of the 1940s*, 15.

44. Doane 1987, 12.

45. Robert Escarpit, 'Byron and France' in *Byron's Political and Cultural Influence in Nineteenth-Century Europe*, ed. Paul Graham Trueblood, 48.

46. There have been many commentaries on Byron's propensity to prostitute his art for fame by critics both past and present. Robert Southey is reported to have stated, for example, that he condemns Byron specifically 'because he had set up for pander-general to the youth of great Britain as long as his writings should endure'. Cited in W. Benbow, 'A Scourge for the Laureate in reply to his Infamous Letter of the 13th of December 1824' (London: Benbow Punter, 1824), 111.

47. It is popularly assumed that Byron had two sets of readers, one male and one female. The female readership is thought to have been formed with the publication of Byron's early work, specifically the Turkish tales, which are critically condemned by many critics as having the plot of a 'Harlequin Romance' (Grosskurth 1997, 190). The male readership is thought to have been drawn to Byron's later, satirical work. The reality of this gendered division remains questionable, but Grosskurth suggests that Byron's overwhelming female readership obscures the 'real' Byron from literary history. She notes that during his early fame, 'women were forming a circle around [Byron]; and as the ring tightened it is sometimes hard to catch more than a glimpse of him' (160).

48. Macaulay 1830, 308.

49. Gleckner 1967, xi.

50. Gleckner 1967, xii.

51. Gleckner 1967, xii.

52. Gleckner 1967, 95.

53. For the full citation see Escarpit 1981, footnote 45.

54. Karl Marx, *Capital: A Critique of Political Economy*, intro. Ernest Mandel, trans. Ben Fowkes, 3 vols, Vol. 1: 165.

55. Thomas Moore, The Life, Letters, and Journals of Lord Byron, 159.
56. Anonymous, 'The Characteristic of the Present Age of Poetry'. *London Magazine* 2 (April 1824): 427.
57. Ramona M. Ralston and Sidney L. Sondergard, 'Screening Byron: The Idiosyncrasies of the Film Myth' in *Byromania: Portraits of the Artist in Nineteenth-and Twentieth-Century Culture*, ed. Frances Wilson, 150.
58. It should be noted, however, that while Byron expressed relief that Margherita Cogni couldn't write him letters, he did frequently read Dante and Boccaccio with his other Italian mistresses.
59. Janice Radway, 'Mail-Order Culture and Its Critics: The Book-of-the-Month Club, Commodification and Consumption, and the Problem of Cultural Authority' in *Cultural Studies*, eds Lawrence Grossberg, Cary Nelson and Paula Treichler, 514.
60. Byron's ghost, even in its ethereal state, attempts to seduce the hero, William. Christopher Golden and Amber Benson, *Ghosts of Albion: The Adventures of Tamara Swift*, BBC Productions Webcast, 2003 <http:www.bbc.co.uk/cult/ghosts/intro.shtml>.
61. Amanda Prantera's novel *Conversations with Lord Byron on Perversion, 163 Years After His Lordship's death* and John Crowley's *Lord Byron's Novel: The Evening Land* are the most interesting of the many 'spin offs' that examine the use of computer technology to resurrect the Byronic presence. Notably, in both novels, the characters to be 'seduced' by Byron's mystery are academics. John Crowley, *Lord Byron's Novel: The Evening Land* (New York: William Morrow, 2005), Amanda Prantera, *Conversations with Lord Byron on Perversion, 163 Years After His Lordship's Death* (New York: Atheneum, 1987).
62. Baudrillard 1981, 88.
63. Baudrillard 1981, 88.
64. Baudrillard 1981, 89.
65. Baudrillard 1981, 89.
66. MacCarthy 2002, 162–3.
67. Crane 1998, 68.
68. Cited in MacCarthy 2002, 567.
69. Escarpit 1981, 48.
70. Guiseppe Mazzini, 'Byron and Goethe' *The Morning Chronicle* (September 1839). Cited in Rutherford 1970, 333.
71. Byron, *Don Juan* XVI, 123, 4.

works cited and suggestions for further reading

Anonymous. 'The Characteristic of the Present Age of Poetry'. *London Magazine* 2 (1824): 427.

Anonymous. 'Uriel: A Poetical Address to the Right Hon. Lord Byron, written on the Continent: with Notes containing Strictures on the Spirit of Infidelity maintained in his Works; an Examination of his Assertion that "If Cain is Blasphemous, Paradise Lost is Blasphemous", and several other Poems'. London: Hatchard, Burton and Smith, 1822.

Apter, Emily. *Feminizing the Fetish: Psychoanalysis and Narrative Obsession in Turn-of- the-Century Franc.* Ithaca, NY: Cornell University Press, 1991.

Apter, Emily and William Pietz, eds *Fetishism as Cultural Discourse.* Ithaca, NY: Cornell University Press, 1993.

Baudrillard, Jean. *For a Critique of Political Economy.* Trans. Charles Levin. St Louis: Telos Press, 1981.

Bolt, Robert. *Lady Caroline Lamb.* VHS. Prism Home Entertainment, 1992.

Brooks, Peter. *Body Works: Objects of Desire in Modern Narrative.* Cambridge, Mass.: Harvard University Press, 1993.

Calvert, J. William. *Byron: The Romantic Paradox.* New York: Russell & Russell Inc., 1962.

Clubbe, John. 'The West Portrait of Byron'. *Byron Journal* 8 (1980): 22–30.

Crane, David. *Lord Byron's Jackal: A Life of Edward John Trelawny.* London: Harper Collins, 1998.

Doane, Mary Ann. *The Desire to Desire: The Woman's Film of the 1940s.* Bloomington, IN: Indiana University Press, 1987.

Donelan, Charles. *Romanticism and Male Fantasy in Byron's Don Juan: A Marketable Vice.* New York: St Martin's Press, 2000.

Elfenbein, Andrew. *Byron and the Victorians.* Cambridge: Cambridge University Press, 1995.

Escarpit, Robert. 'Byron and France'. Ed. Paul Graham Trueblood, *Byron's Political and Cultural Influence in Nineteenth-Century Europe.* Atlantic Highlands, NJ: Humanities Press, 1981. 45–58.

Felluga, Dino Franco. *The Perversity of Poetry: Romantic Ideology and the Popular Male Poet of Genius.* Albany: State University of New York Press, 2005.

Forman, H. Buxton, ed. *Letters of Edward John Trelawny.* Oxford: Oxford University Press, 1910.

Freud, Sigmund. *The Standard Edition of the Complete Psychological Works of Sigmund Freud.* Ed. and trans. James Strachey. 24 vols. London: Hogarth Press, 1953–64.

Gleckner, Robert F. *Byron and the Ruins of Paradise.* Baltimore, MD: The Johns Hopkins University Press, 1967.

Grosskurth, Phyllis. *Byron: The Flawed Angel.* Toronto: Macfarlane, Walter and Ross, 1997.

Kenyon Jones, Christine. 'Fantasy and Transfiguration: *Byron and his Portraits'.* Byronmania: Portraits of the Artist in Nineteenth- and Twentieth-Century Culture. Ed. Frances Wilson. London: St Martin's Press, 1999.

Laplanche, Jean and J.B. Pontalis. 'Fantasy and the Origins of Sexuality'. *International Journal of Psycho-analysis* 49 (1968): 1–18.

Macaulay, Thomas Babington. Review of Thomas Moore's *Letters and Journals of Lord Byron: with Notices of his Life. Edinburgh Review* 53 (1831): 544–72.

MacCarthy, Fiona. *Byron: Life and Legend.* New York: Farrar, Straus and Giroux, 2002.

Marchand, Leslie A. *Byron: A Biography.* 4 vols. New York: Alfred A. Knopf, 1957.

Marx, Karl, *Capital: A Critique of Political Economy.* Intro. Ernest Mandel and trans. Ben Fowkes. 3 vols. New York: Vintage, 1977.

Mayne, Ethel Colburn. *The Life and Letters of Anne Isabella, Lady Noel Byron.* New York: Charles Scribner's Sons, 1929.

Metz, Christian. 'The Imaginary Signifier'. *Screen: The Journal of the Society for the Education in Film and Television* 16 (1975): 14–76.

——. *The Imaginary Signifier: Psychoanalysis and the Cinema.* Trans. Celia Britton et al. Bloomington, IN: Indiana University Press, 1977.

Moore, Thomas. *The Life, Letters, and Journals of Lord Byron.* London: John Murray, 1860.

Radway, Janice. 'Mail-Order Culture and Its Critics: The Book-of-the-Month Club, Commodification and Consumption, and the Problem of Cultural Authority'. *Cultural Studies.* Eds Lawrence Grossberg, Cary Nelson and Paula Treichler. New York: Routledge, 1992.

Ralston, Ramona M. and Sidney L. Sondergard. 'Screening Byron: The Idiosyncrasies of the Film Myth'. *Byromania: Portraits of the Artist in Nineteenth-and Twentieth-Century Culture.* Ed. Frances Wilson. London: Macmillan, 1999.

Russell, Ken. *Gothic.* DVD. Lionsgate, 2002.

Rutherford, Andrew, ed. *Byron: The Critical Heritage.* London: Routledge & Kegan Paul, 1970.

Soderholm, James. *Fantasy, Forgery and the Byron Legend.* Lexington: University Press of Kentucky, 1996.

Stein, Atara. *The Byronic Hero in Film, Fiction and Television.* Carbondale: Southern Illinois University Press, 2004.

Suarez, Gonzalo. *Rowing with the Wind.* DVD. Ditirambo, 1988.

7
byron's *manfred* and ecocriticism

timothy morton

introduction

It sounds perverse to read Byron as an ecological writer, at least in the terms prescribed by our common perception of him as the ultimate poet of existential irony. As Esther Hibbard put it, almost forty years ago, 'modern criticism has shown that [Byron] ... rebelled against the romantic concept of nature'.[1] *English Bards and Scotch Reviewers* depicts Coleridge soaring 'to eulogize an ass' (ll. 261–3), while Bowles sings 'with equal ease, and grief, / The fall of empires, or a yellow leaf' (ll. 334–5). The narrator's refreshingly blunt honesty seems indisposed to re-enchant the world: 'I like the weather, when it is not rainy, / That is, I like two months of every year' (*Beppo*, stanza 47). It is, however, these very features that enable us not only to read him ecologically, but also to use him against a too limited and ideological view of ecological literary criticism.

The poem 'Darkness' has gained an ecological resonance, as ecocriticism has discovered within and behind it a 'real', or historical-real, natural-historical event: the eruption of a volcano.[2] How fitting, then, that we start our ecological reading of Byron in precisely the opposite way: by choosing a poem famous for seeming entirely a sprout of the imagination, a piece of 'mental theatre' impossible meaningfully to embody on a stage. In so doing, we will discover that what is 'real' about ecological awareness or imagination is indeed what is most textual about it, and hence, from a narrow ecocritical view, what is most illusory will turn out to be most natural. This chapter is a reading of *Manfred*, and in particular a study of how Byron generates an unorthodox environmental awareness. All too often, ecological thinking neglects the idea of consciousness and the fact of death. Ecology even tries to erase them. These themes are held squarely

155

in full view in Byron's drama, however, which paradoxically begins to provide the basis for a fresh way of thinking ecologically.

manfred as environmental art

Manfred appears to be the ultimate Romantic psychodrama. 'Scene: a Gothic gallery. Time: midnight' is the opening stage direction. Manfred, the protagonist, spends most of the play rhapsodizing on his angst-ridden mind. This rhapsody itself involves numerous environmental figures of speech and dramatic work. It appears that even if Manfred himself is celebrating his own separate ego, he has to rely on the world around him for help. We will discover that the physical and psychic darkness evoked at the very beginning of the play has a deep ecological resonance, at least as much as 'Darkness' itself, and to greater effect, as it is more subtle and mysterious.

Other characters appear. Are they manifestations of Manfred's mind or beings from 'over there' or 'out there' – wherever 'there' is? The play is not explicit. The hesitation presents us with a dilemma. Either the very form of the play is that of solipsism, where every phenomenon is merely an objectified version of the contents of Manfred's own mind. Or precisely the opposite: the phenomena and other characters, even and especially the elemental ones, are radically 'outside' Manfred and his frame of reference, and have appeared to undermine the solipsistic power of his view. A version of the duck-rabbit optical illusion applies here: we cannot hold both views simultaneously. But the mere possibility that the elemental figures exist independently of Manfred's projection is more dangerous for the solipsist position than for the non-solipsist one. The fact that Byron chose to *dramatize* this possibility, to stage it such that a single character, Manfred, appears amidst others in a theatrical space – in short, the drama's aesthetic form – indicates that this play is a subtle challenge to solipsism. The very space of the theatre frames Manfred, puts quotation marks around him.

It is a minimalist strategy. It is almost as if Byron is trying to see just how little he needs to do to undermine the protagonist's pose. So far from celebrating the Romantic 'egotistical sublime', embodied in the figure of a Wordsworth (at least the popular image of him) or a figure in a painting by Friedrich, a lone individual straddling a chasm, *Manfred* radically frames and undermines its protagonist with the theatrical environment. In fact, the paucity of other actors simply heightens the way in which theatrical space itself, an analogue for the environment of the Alpine setting, surrounds and negates Manfred's power.

John Martin's painting of Manfred on the Jungfrau speaks this truth when it practically drowns Manfred amidst a vast chasm of rock, rendered in prismatic colours: light itself, and the paint that is its medium, almost eliminates Manfred from the scene. Marilyn Butler has observed that John Martin's work situates the Romantic author amidst the vast, alien sea of 'the people' rather than the more intimate and interactive 'public' of neo-classical discourse.[3] The rocks and swirling colours stand in, on this reading, for modern social experience in an era of emerging industry and the breakdown of patron-client conditions of artistic production. They could also stand for the transcendental thing (*Ding an Sich*) of Kantian philosophy, perceptible to human consciousness only in the negative via the aesthetics of the sublime.[4] The thing, on this reading, is a kind of abyss (Kant himself uses this word (Kant 1987, 2.A.27, B.29)). An abyss is literally embodied space: a gap between mountains, for example. It evokes in us the feeling of the infinity of abstract space itself. On this reading, the subject who contemplates this is the master of all they survey: the exhilaration inspired by the sublime causes our mind to expand into infinite space, which in turn evokes the true powers of the mind itself. But 'all they survey' is precisely nothing. This consciousness is dressed up with nowhere to go. It seems as if, even in the quintessential philosophy of mastery over nature – Kant was a great supporter of the revolutionary energy of the Enlightenment in this regard – that whatever 'nature' is secretly 'wins'. So it is in *Manfred*.

Stephen Behrendt has observed how the drama's use of dialogue establishes a sceptical frame around the characters' pronouncements – a conceptual space, if you like, a neutral medium in which certainty is held in suspension.[5] Ecological criticism is not keen to be sceptical. Indeed, it tends towards the opposite, towards sheer, sometimes naive, asseveration. Byron joins together a sense of environment with a sense of scepticism. The setting of the play is not just a backdrop to the sceptical dialogue that Behrendt elucidates. It provides us with an aesthetic experience that is analogical to scepticism. It is almost as if the environment of the play itself becomes an embodied form of scepticism. And perhaps this is indeed the true, or a true, form of the very thing we like to call 'nature'. When we try to look at it directly, it collapses into trees, cows, mountains ... cities? smoke? our perceiving mind? The list is endless, and where one stops is telling, of course. But in general, nature appears to have a 'what is it?' quality that is irreducible. In other words, 'environment' is much closer to 'theory' than it is to dogma. Notice, however, that this theoretical state of wonderment does not necessarily imply a stupefaction or hypnosis. Nor is it entirely reducible to an aesthetic experience. It has at least one foot in the scientific realm. Byron is trying to induce in us a smart ecological awareness.

There is a danger, however, in scepticism. Hegel articulates it in his narrative of progressive stages of the development of philosophy, the *Phenomenology of Spirit*.[6] The sceptic *is* in fact cleaving to a position – a paradoxical position of not having one. Thus the sceptic is caught in a contradiction. They are unable to affirm anything positive, and yet, in so doing, they *do* affirm something. The supposedly neutral medium in which they hold all ideas and beliefs in suspension is itself stained – even if their scepticism is somehow utterly pure. This unstable, contradictory character is why scepticism, for Hegel, gives birth to the next phase of mind, the 'Unhappy Consciousness', with which Hegel associates emergent Judaeo-Christianity (Hegel 1977, 126–38). Thence begins the age of reason and the next part of the *Phenomenology*'s narrative, leading up to the Enlightenment and the Romantic period.

By the time we get to Hegel's depiction of the Romantic Beautiful Soul, the world has become pretty solid again. The Beautiful Soul is not a sceptic: they *know* they are right, and the world is wrong. This is where much environmental thinking is trapped. The apocalyptic tone of the ecological rhetoric of global disaster may be very shocking, but one effect of this shock is to keep us suspended like a deer in the headlights, unable to achieve the next moment, the practical work of avoiding a global disaster. And the Beautiful Soul definitively thinks that there *is* something called Nature that is being violated by a humanity that is in some way extrinsic to it, or which has deviated from a natural path. This something is, as Ronald Shroeder puts is, radically 'dis-spirited' – spirit is 'over here', while nature is 'over there'.[7] The inwardness of *Manfred* – the whole universe becomes Manfred's mental theatre – actually goes in tandem with the brutal materialism of 'Darkness'. The spiritual inside and the material outside coexist in an emulsion, like oil and vinegar, but they do not really mix. This emulsive (non)mixture may have been what Byron had in mind when he teasingly declared to Tom Moore that he wrote the play to display the Alpine scenery.[8] The critical mind, lusting after rich aesthetic appraisals, is quick to revolt: 'there must be more to it than that'. But Bryon's remark to Moore does speak a truth about the play. The more intense the natural descriptions become, the more ethereal and spiritual they get. Manfred is capable of summing up the environment of the whole earth in a generalizing address to the sun: 'Sire of the seasons! Monarch of the climes, / And those who dwell in them! for near or far, / Our inborn spirits have a tint of thee' (III. ii. 20–2). This is all there is, and so much less than a full, rich, aesthetically variegated accounting for nature of the sort we might get in a Wordsworth or a Clare. The ethereal, vast descriptions beg the question: are we really after nature itself when we read environmental literature, or after a certain kind of (dense, particularized) aesthetic experience?

Manfred's scepticism keeps us teetering on the brink of sliding into the dogmatism of the Beautiful Soul. It is a giddy precipice, a philosophical edge as steep as the mountain peaks that serve as the actual scenery of the drama. Manfred himself appears decisively to have given up his beliefs in a happier world. He embodies in the negative the fundamentalist attitude of the Beautiful Soul, which leaves the world to rot, even in the very act of expressing great sorrow over its demise. But the drama keeps framing this solid despair in a more open atmosphere of doubt. If we follow Hegel, trying to stop scepticism turning into Romantic despair is rather like creating a dam in a stream. It does not put a stop to the stream's energy, so much as divert and contain it.

At the beginning of the second scene, Manfred 'alone upon the cliffs' expresses his inability to rest in an aesthetic experience of nature:

> Mother earth,
> And thou fresh-breaking day, and you, ye mountains—
> Why are ye beautiful? I cannot love ye. (I. ii. 7–9)

This does not appear to be a promisingly ecological state of mind. It has been common in Byron criticism to trace the 'Zeluco theme', the way in which guilt, misanthropy or gloom block an appreciation of nature.[9] Manfred's own person, however, subverts the apparent content of his words. He remains stuck on the cliffs, unable to 'plunge' to his death (I. ii. 20). He is mired in an intense contemplation of the forked nature of humanity, 'Half-dust, half-deity, alike unfit / To sink or soar' (I. ii. 40–1). He is able to give up on the dusty part of this, which his words in themselves appear to condemn. It is in this relentless clinging to the earth that Manfred hears environmental music, 'The natural music of the mountain reed' (I. ii. 48) coming from the shepherd's pipe 'in the distance' (stage direction) as it disperses through 'the liberal air' (I. ii. 50), another musical figure, since one sense of 'air' is an improvised tune. Manfred yearns to become this 'bodiless enjoyment', to vanish into the aesthetic dimension itself, like William Blake's Thel, or indeed like the Beautiful Soul, whose certainty Hegel brilliantly describes as 'changed immediately into a sound that dies away' (Hegel 1977, 399). Manfred himself threatens to become an environmental accident, and the Chamois Hunter implores him not to 'Stain … our pure vales with thy guilty blood!' (I. ii. 111). The next scene, inside the Hunter's cottage, reveals how distant Manfred is from the imaginative *Lebenswelt* of the Hunter, and how much he admires it – that is, aesthetically. This is the quintessential admiration of the Beautiful Soul for that which lies 'over there'.

The play's interest in sound effects and environmental aesthetics is not fleeting. The second stage direction in *Manfred* reads: 'A star is seen at the darker end of the gallery. It is stationary, and a voice is heard singing' (I. i). This is an instance of what the cinema theorist and contemporary composer Michel Chion calls *voix acousmatique*, a sound, and in particular a voice, that emanates from a hidden source.[10] This acousmatic sound is a predominant effect in contemporary music, and in such forms as cinema, where it is commonly audible as the voice-over, the sound of a voice that has no location on the screen. The voice-over is a voice without a body, or indeed a voice without a subject. This effect is environmental in at least two ways. It conveys a sense of the space that fills the auditorium. It is as if the sound were bathing the visual field in a surrounding liquid. The audience becomes aware of their participation in dramatic space. Moreover, acousmatic sound is necessarily synaesthetic. Because there is nothing corresponding to the sound in other perceptual fields (Manfred: 'I hear / Your voices, sweet and melancholy sounds, / As music on the waters' (I. i. 175–7), we are compelled to look (and touch, smell and taste) elsewhere. The other senses are included, paradoxically, by the exclusion of the voice from an identifiable form or sonic source. We can become distracted rather than absorbed into the aesthetic. Far from being a Wagnerian, immersive space that pulls us in to its illusion, suspending our disbelief, it is possible that *Manfred* compels us to become intellectually involved, because there is hardly anything to hold on to in the perceptual field. Possible, but not inevitable: synaesthesia could become an even more compelling from of *Gesamkunswerk*.

The first five voices are spirits who control elemental forces; the sixth dwells in night, and the seventh rules 'The star which rules thy destiny' (I. i. 50–131). The idea of the elements is itself environmental. Perhaps this was known before the 'elements' became atomic particles (the Periodic Table, and so forth). Nevertheless, there is a certain phenomenological quality about the notion of an element. It is a quality that invites us to imagine an entity not simply as an object, but as a kind of amalgam of objectivity and subjectivity, though these are inadequate words since they are mutually exclusive. Elements are phenomenological atoms: fire is what is fiery; water is wateriness; and so forth. Water is water *for* some form of sentient being. One could claim that the voices, forces that rule the elements, could refer to some kind of natural philosophical knowledge, akin to contemporary knowledge of physics. Manfred certainly appears to have power over these spirits: they are 'to thine adjuration bowed' (I. i. 58), 'at thy beck and bidding' (I. i. 133). But these spirits end up 'scoff[ing] at [Manfred's] will' (I. i. 153). What he wishes to command them to is his own forgetting – an anti-scientific gesture towards 'Oblivion, self-oblivion!' (I. i. 144). In a sense, he is asking to be overwhelmed by the elemental forces.

To seek oblivion, the opposite of the strife of the traditional poet, is also the opposite of the scientist's goal, if by *oblivion* we mean what Manfred means, which is both a subjective and an objective forgetting. 'Forgetfulness' (I. i. 136) and 'Oblivion' could be both how Manfred himself desires to have his mind wiped clean, and how he wishes to leave no trace in others' memories. For Manfred is haunted by a final voice, the voice of conscience, which speaks at the end of the first scene. This voice's diction starts off in the vein of sentimental environmental poetry common in the Romantic period:

> When the moon is on the wave
>   And the glow-worm in the grass,
> And the meteor on the grave
>   And the wisp on the morass,
> When the falling stars are shooting
> And the answered owls are hooting,
> And the silent leaves are still
> In the shadow of the hill,
> Shall my soul be upon thine
> With a power and with a sign. (I. i. 192–201)

But by the end of the speech, the voice has grown far more intense and compelling. What the voice evokes at the beginning, the night, has an existential/phenomenological quality that contains an environmental element. The night envelops everything. It is a kind of present absence. In the philosophy of Emmanuel Levinas, it is the embodiment of what he calls the 'there is' (French: *il y a*; German: *es gibt*) – the existential 'it' which we name when we say 'it is raining'. The voice is evoking the creepy presence of an absence, a sense of sheer existence that surrounds us like the night surrounds an insomniac. The acousmatic voice here becomes identified with the surrounding darkness of the night. This is a synaesthetic image, though perhaps not along the lines we were expecting. There is nothing to it. The voice is nowhere, and its analogue is something not directly named in the first stanza of its speech, but present indirectly, *anamorphically*. An *anamorphic* form is something that is in the process of losing (its) shape.

The environment always has this anamorphic property. We cannot point to it directly without it disappearing. When we point to it, it turns into this specific tree, that particular deer, a being of some kind 'over there'. It shares something, then, with the seventh spirit (Manfred's star), which Manfred compels to appear in a form. When it does manifest as a beautiful woman, Manfred reaches out to embrace it, whereupon it disappears. This is just the same as what we call 'nature'. It is never directly in the foreground, but is necessarily environing, around us, ambient. It is only possible to glimpse this ambience in a sidelong, anamorphic manner. The first scene seems to be trying to sidle up to the environment in just this way. If we name it directly, we lose its essence. Perhaps this is why it was forbidden to gaze directly upon the form of Artemis.

wilderness and the romantic ego

Just immerse yourself in the wilderness, says a certain strand of ecological discourse, and you will be redeemed in the true church of ecology. Does not the wilderness in *Manfred* actually stand for precisely the opposite – for excommunication? Manfred is able beautifully to describe nature:

> It is not noon—the sunbow's rays still arch
> The torrent with the many hues of heaven,
> And roll the sheered silver's waving column
> O'er the crag's headlong perpendicular,
> And fling its lines of foaming light along,
> And to and fro, like the pale courser's tail. (II. ii. 1–6)

The 'not noon' opens up a place and time less certain than the gothic 'night' of I. i. Is 'not noon' 11.55, as it were, or 'not-noon' – even if it were in fact 12 o'clock, the time and place are not being grasped instrumentally? On the one hand, we might claim that Manfred has set aside technology for being, in a Heideggerian manner. This will, we think, enable him to contemplate nature without the interference of human frames. On the other hand, 'not noon' is supremely linguistic – its 'don't think of a pink elephant!' sense is a rhetorical trope, apophasis. Even here, at the very beginning of this paradoxical scene, Byron inserts a radical hesitation between thinking of language, and human being, as outside or inside nature. This negatively defined moment invites an even greater degree of imaginative projection, and the reader is paid back for their audio-visual work by the following lines, which describe the coruscating effects of light interacting with water. Nature, even here, is not a place where, in Blake's words, 'man is not'.[11] The Witch of the Alps, the genius of the place, appears, and Manfred compares her 'hues of youth' with

> the rose tints, which summer's twilight leaves
> Upon the lofty glacier's virgin snow,
> The blush of earth embracing with her heaven. (II. ii. 20–2)

The Witch's very flesh becomes an ambient tint, an environmental presence. Postmodern writing has described ambience as a tint or perfume, a barely detectable trace that appears to bring a background into the foreground, while trying to retain its background quality.[12] The Witch, the figure in the foreground, is likened to the slightest of background shades. The image blends her cold, beautiful body into the background. The Witch embodies the height of Manfred's aesthetic-erotic enjoyment of the 'Earth' whose 'Son' he is (II. ii. 28). She is a figure for Manfred's existence as a being in, and from, an environment, rather than as one who transcends their environment. All he wishes to do is 'look upon [her] beauty' (II. ii. 38). This wish for abstract, Kantian appreciation is intimate and erotic, but also subject to an irreducible distance, like the one Kant himself describes as necessary for aesthetic contemplation (Kant 1987, 2.A.26). But in the image of the tinted snow, Manfred has admitted that nature can never hold still long enough for a chaste appreciation to take place, assuming that were at all possible. It is this very never-holding-still quality that Manfred wants front and centre – how to make a background feel like a foreground, without 'corrupting' its nature.

There is irony upon irony in this scene which ecological criticism must not avoid. The very aesthetic dimension that presents the world to us in its iridescent glory is also what separates us from it via an irreducible gap between the perceiving subject and the contemplated object. Manfred is quite clear that this, for him, is his last abiding wish for his relationship with the Witch, the quintessence of Alpine sublimity. So when ecological writing talks about immersing oneself in nature, it must come to terms, at least, with this passage. Manfred knows too much to allow nature to show him what to do. It would involve impossibly winding back the clock of consciousness (II. ii.158–60).

Manfred describes his immersion in nature as a retreat into isolation:

> with men, and with the thoughts of men,
> I held but slight communion; but instead,
> My joy was in the Wilderness, to breathe
> The difficult air of the iced mountain's top,
> Where the birds dare not build, nor insect's wing
> Flit o'er the herbless granite; or to plunge
> Into the torrent, and to roll along
> On the swift whirl of the new breaking wave
> Of river-stream, or ocean, in their flow. (II. ii. 60–8)

The language, syntax and length of this passage are Wordsworthian, with a twist. One senses the debt to consumerism, rather than avoiding it, in the inevitable echo of dessert in the image of the 'iced mountain' – the mountain shrinks to a confection. And consumerism *is* Romanticism, even when that Romanticism tries to escape from its grip through greater and greater subtleties of self-reflection or abstinence. The experience is of an isolated individualist, defining themselves even in their isolation against 'men, and the thoughts of men', and treating themselves to experiences, putting their identity 'in process' (as the post-structuralist language puts it). Manfred then describes the beginnings of his pursuit of science in tracing the moon through the night sky or watching lightning (II. ii. 69–74). Transcendental knowledge, and ultimate removal from earthly things (II. ii. 79–96), begins with those things themselves. The aesthetic and the scientific are intertwined. Immersion in nature connects with transcendence of it. Rather like Shelley's *Alastor*, the passage may be an allegory about the hypocrisy of a Wordsworthian wish to surround oneself with natural things, saying that it could represent a triumph of ego as much as of going out of oneself. Exquisitely aware that he curses everything he touches with his mind, Manfred is a cipher for inescapable consciousness. In Byron's world, at any rate, we cannot cut off our heads, live in the trees, and trust all will be well.

But wait – 'to look upon her beauty'? Isn't that something that Manfred, to use current California vernacular, is 'so over'? Manfred is stuck not just in irony, but in melancholia. In other words, he is not ready to digest the object that is forever lost to him, to 'incorporate' it, to use the psychoanalytic slang. Instead, he 'introjects' it: it sticks in his throat. We would assume that ugly or disgusting things might get stuck in our throat. Byron seems to be suggesting that beautiful things, even the beauty of things in themselves, gets stuck in our throat. Aesthetics is training in how to turn up one's nose, how to be disgusted. The ultimate aesthetic object, from this point of view, is vomit – something we could never digest, something that would always be stuck in our throat. Some psychoanalysts, such as Julia Kristeva, have suggested that our sense of self depends upon a primordial act of vomiting or excreting an object that, in retrospect, becomes disgusting.

Disgust, grief and pain are what we are experiencing, or about to experience, or denying that we are experiencing right now, in the current ecological emergency. Good (aesthetic) digestion depends upon there being a stable sense of background and foreground, inside and outside. When global warming is changing our climate – not the weather, but the 'phase space' of the weather, the background within which weather itself emerges – we can no longer be sure that we are able to maintain our old sense of self. Gaian utopianism – we are all immersed in matter! – is an impossible desire to return human excrement into its original food (as in the Academy of Lagado visited by Gulliver). Our genuine ecological awareness has more in common with Manfred's (and Gulliver's) disgust and inability to move from the scene of disgust. It is as if we are caught in our own headlights. Of the four humours, in the Galenic theory of the body, melancholy is said to be the one that is closest to the earth. In his very transcendence, in his striving to emerge clean from his physical experience, Manfred becomes more and more mired in matter, symbolized by the Gnostic god Arimanes: 'Life is his, / With all its infinite of agonies' (II. iv. 14–15). Melancholy is like a falling apple: evidence of a gravitational field that ties even *this* subject to the earth. And yet this very gravitational field is what ensures Manfred's victory over the spirits serving Arimanes in the second act. He already knows about 'despair' and 'humiliation' – about, that is, being brought closer to the earth (II. iv. 40–1).

irony as ecological thought

Manfred presents us with a startling paradox. Nature appears most truly as disembodied spirit(s) and as the darkness of the night. Yet conventional ecological criticism tries to name it, to gaze on it directly. At the deep-ecological extreme, nature positively excludes human subjectivity, especially one so tormented and individualistic as Manfred's. It is almost as if he embodies the existential 'feel' of Cartesian philosophy. Maurice Blanchot said the same of Pascal.[13] Manfred is the *cogito* ridden with angst. Descartes is ecological public enemy number one. He supported vivisection and promoted a dualism of subject and object that many consider to be one of the bases of ecological catastrophe. But *Manfred* does not make a straightforward distinction between subjectivity and environmental awareness. And neither for that matter does Descartes. The

Meditations begins with the idea of an environment. Descartes narrates that he is sitting comfortably by a fire.[14]

Hegel describes the emerging Unhappy Consciousness as struggling to think, to reason. The Unhappy Consciousness attempts to peel its mind away from the other, to achieve some form of 'particular individuality' (Hegel 1977, 131). But at first it can only get as far as 'devotion' towards consciousness itself. Thus 'Its thinking as such is no more than the chaotic jingling of bells, or a mist of warm incense, a musical tinkling that does not get as far as the Notion' (131). In the same way, Manfred is compelled to disentangle himself from the voices and spirits, echoes of a mystical immersion in the environment. The mystical immersion appears in the drama as the aesthetic dimension itself, as a surrounding circulation of ambient special effects. One of the common myths of ecological thinking is a Fall narrative. Once we were naively immersed in nature; now we are woefully separated. The Fall narrative reincarnates in Schiller's idea of naive and sentimental poetry. Once poetry was straightforward; now it's ironic and self-conscious. The ecological thought – the idea that everything is interconnected – is generated from the point of view of an impossible desire to get back beyond or before the sentimental. It is strictly impossible, because the desire *is* the separation, its product and its expression. *Manfred* thematizes this by having as its protagonist a man who has committed a monstrous, unspeakable crime (incest?) – the crime that is both *against* nature and supremely 'natural', that designates what human culture strives to transcend. The very namelessness of the crime, its existence as a sheer gap within the play's texture, ensures that we are within the realm of the symbolic rather than the real, of language rather than nature.

We commonly think of ecological writing as Wordsworthian through and through. By this we mean that it is sincere. This idea does injustice even to Wordsworth himself, whose finest moments are saturated with irony. Byron himself, of course, muddies the picture by lambasting Wordsworth as 'crazed beyond all hope' (*Don Juan* I, 205, 3). Being crazy is the opposite of irony. If you are so convinced that your ideas correspond with reality, then there is no gap in your view, and you are impermeable to self-consciousness, of which a mere sliver can undermine your self-containment. Ecological discourse in general is too often a discourse of evangelical rightness, justness, aptness, fitted to the world as Wordsworth says his poetics fits the world ('Prospectus to *The Recluse*,' ll. 63–6). Can irony exist in the light of environmental thought, or is it a flower of the night that will wither away in the hot, positive rays of ecological awareness?

Jerome McGann and Jane Stabler have elucidated the extent to which Byron's irony involves a perilous, Kierkegaardian dance on the volcano of nothingness.[15] *Manfred* leaves us with nowhere to stand. It is, in the words of a recent critic, a play about a non-place.[16] How much irony will this Kierkegaardian reading really tolerate? On Kierkegaard's own view, it turns out that the Beautiful Soul is destined for Hell.[17] Stabler and McGann usefully read Byronic irony as a putting-into-play of all possible subject positions, or places. *Pace* McGann, this is not so far from Kierkegaard himself. Irony, for Kierkegaard, is the highest stage of an aesthetic way of being that is unable to make the leap towards ethics. Despite putting things in play, it remains a pose, a position, an attitude. Kierkegaard discovers an irreducible gap between what he calls the aesthetic 'sphere' and the ethical one. But what if there were no gap, that in fact there were a strange, dislocated interstitial space that could not easily be described? In brief, Kierkegaard may have given up on the aesthetic too quickly. The aesthetic, ultimately the record of sentient pain and suffering, provides at the very least the fuel for the jump into the ethical sphere.[18] What if irony were not just an aesthetic pose but was in fact more like a cognitive or ethical leap? This would be very important for ecological aesthetics, for two reasons. First, it is important because pain and suffering, being a living sentient being, is the very stuff of ecology. Second, ecological discourse tends towards foreclosing ironic possibilities, to produce texts that are simply not adequate to a post-Romantic age, where irony is an inescapable fact of the ideas we have and the art forms we create. As Hegel observes, art is ironically aware of how knowledge is now always in excess of what art can do with it.[19] There is no going back to a pre-modern, pre-Romantic, pre-sentimental way of proceeding. The cat is out of the bag.

It all depends upon how we want to frame the idea of irony. Hegel, like Kierkegaard after him, thinks of irony as the demonic other of science, a corrupted knowingness full of sound and fury but signifying nothing.[20] But if irony is seeing around things, seeing the edges of things, seeing how things are non-identical, then it shares something with science. Perhaps it is even the founding moment of a scientific sequence of thinking. Irony is also the awareness of how we are caught in our frame of reference, like drowning in a glass pond. Instead of getting rid of this painful irony – instead of trying to trepan ourselves to let the self-consciousness drain out of our heads – perhaps a judo move is required. In a double twist of irony, we could recognize that this ironic awareness is itself the ecological awareness! If, as the ecological thought declares, we are all interconnected with everything – if, at bottom, *there is no problem* – then changing our state of mind would be the worst thing we could do. Painfully, and with humour, we must keep dragging ourselves back to this difficult moment of the birth of consciousness. We have not surpassed it historically, as a teleological reading of Hegel would imply. We go through it, our personal ontogeny repeating the phylogeny of the history of mind. One of the difficult things about reading *Manfred* is that it seems to remain in the same place. Manfred keeps repeating the gesture of denial and abjuration: nothing is adequate, nothing will do. It is a very awkward, painful spot in which to be. What if there were something utopian even here, something ecotopian, in a moment that looks like a sick ride on a suicidal merry-go-round? This would be wonderful news for ecological thinking. Even in the middle of ethical and ontological darkness, we can find the ecological thought.

It is as if Byron is able, through art, to force his way backwards against the current of cause and effect, towards the gate at which consciousness emerges, to plant a little seed of love and hope, even in the hard, dark soil of almost-nothingness. Byron's figures of sorrow, as McGann observes, are figures of irredeemable love rather than knowledge, and thus of relationship, like it or not.[21] Manfred's desire to own his death, to remain conscious and articulate to the last moment, addresses this.

Of course, we can recognize this soil as the very poisoned ground on which we are actually living at this moment. It is the ground that modernity, emerging from the age of reason, is successfully turning into something like the effects of a nuclear catastrophe, without even having to use nuclear bombs. Although, in fact because, it is not about being nice to sentimentalized bunny rabbits and trees with a soul, *Manfred* might help us to disarm the nuclear bomb, and live with other beings in peace.

notes

1. Esther L. Hibbard, 'Byron's View of Nature'. *Essays and Studies in English Language and Literature* 55 (1969): 1–20.
2. Jonathan Bate, 'Living with the Weather'. *Studies in Romanticism* 35.3 (Fall, 1996): 431–7.
3. Marilyn Butler, *Romantics, Rebels and Reactionaries: English Literature and its Background 1760–1830*, 39–68.
4. Immanuel Kant, *Critique of Judgment*, trans. Werner S. Pluhar, 97–140.
5. Stephen C. Behrendt, 'Manfred and Skepticism' in *Approaches to Teaching Byron's Poetry*, ed. Frederick W. Shilstone, 120–5.
6. Georg Friedrich Wilhelm Hegel, *Hegel's Phenomenology of Spirit*, trans. A.V. Miller, analysis and foreword J.N. Findlay, 124–6 (paragraphs 204–6).

7. Ronald A. Schroeder, 'Byron's "Darkness" and the Romantic Dis-Spiriting of Nature' in *Approaches to Teaching Byron's Poetry*, ed. Frederick W. Shilstone, 113–19.

8. M.S. Kushwaha, *Byron and the Dramatic Form*, 74.

9. Gerald C. Wood, 'Nature and Narrative in Byron's "The Prisoner of Chillon"'. *Keats-Shelley Journal: Keats, Shelley, Byron, Hunt, and Their Circles* 24 (1975): 108–17.

10. Michel Chion, *Audio-Vision: Sound on Screen*, ed. and trans. Claudia Gorbman, 109–11.

11. 'Where man is not nature is barren'; William Blake, *The Marriage of Heaven and Hell, The Complete Poetry and Prose of William Blake*, ed. David V. Erdman, Plate 10, line 68.

12. Brian Eno, *Ambient 1: Music for Airports* (EG Records, 1978), sleeve note.

13. Maurice Blanchot, *The Space of Literature*, trans. Ann Smock, 217.

14. René Descartes, *Meditations and Other Metaphysical Writings*, trans. and intro. Desmond M. Clarke, 19.

15. Jane Stabler, *Byron, Poetics and History*, 15. Jerome McGann, *Byron and Romanticism*, ed. James Soderholm, 116–17, 127.

16. Stephen Cheeke, *Byron and Place: History, Transition, Nostalgia*, 86–90.

17. Søren Kierkegaard, *Either/Or: A Fragment of Life*, trans. and intro. Alastair Hannay, Part A, 243–376.

18. Theodor W. Adorno, *Kierkegaard: Construction of the Aesthetic*, trans. and ed. Robert Hullot-Kentor, 40–6.

19. Georg Wilhelm Friedrich Hegel, *Introductory Lectures on Aesthetics*, trans. Bernard Bosanquet; intro. and commentary Michael Inwood, 72–4.

20. Georg Wilhelm Friedrich Hegel, *Aesthetics: Lectures on Fine Art*, trans. T.M. Knox, 2 vols. Vol. 1, 527.

21. Jerome McGann, *The Poetics of Sensibility: A Revolution in Literary Style*, 156.

works cited and suggestions for further reading

Adorno, Theodor W. *Kierkegaard: Construction of the Aesthetic*. German 1962. Trans. and ed. Robert Hullot-Kentor. Minneapolis: University of Minnesota Press, 1989, repr. 1999.

Bate, Jonathan. 'Living with the Weather'. *Studies in Romanticism* 35.3 (Fall, 1996): 431–7.

Behrendt, Stephen C. '*Manfred* and Skepticism'. *Approaches to Teaching Byron's Poetry*. Ed. Frederick W. Shilstone. New York: Modern Language Association, 1991, 120–5.

Blake, William. *The Marriage of Heaven and Hell, The Complete Poetry and Prose of William Blake*. Ed. David V. Erdman. New York: Doubleday, 1965, rev. 1988.

Blanchot, Maurice. *The Space of Literature*. 1955. Trans. Ann Smock. Lincoln and London: University of Nebraska Press, 1982.

Butler, Marilyn. *Romantics, Rebels and Reactionaries: English Literature and its Background 1760–1830*. Oxford: Oxford University Press, 1981, repr. 1989.

Cheeke, Stephen. *Byron and Place: History, Transition, Nostalgia*. New York and Basingstoke: Palgrave, 2003.

Chion, Michel. *Audio-Vision: Sound on Screen*. Ed. and trans. Claudia Gorbman. New York: Columbia University Press, 1994.

Descartes, René. *Meditations and Other Metaphysical Writings*. Trans. and intro. Desmond M. Clarke. Harmondsworth: Penguin, 1998, 2000.

Eno, Brian. *Ambient 1: Music for Airports*. EG Records, 1978, sleeve note.

Hegel, Georg Wilhelm Friedrich. *Aesthetics: Lectures on Fine Art*. Trans. T.M. Knox, 2 vols. Oxford: Clarendon Press, 1975.

——. *Hegel's Phenomenology of Spirit*. Trans. A.V. Miller, analysis and foreword J.N. Findlay. Oxford: Oxford University Press, 1977.

——. *Introductory Lectures on Aesthetics*. Trans. Bernard Bosanquet, intro. and commentary Michael Inwood. Harmondsworth: Penguin, 1993.

Hibbard, Esther L. 'Byron's View of Nature'. *Essays and Studies in English Language and Literature* 55 (1969): 1–20.

Kant, Immanuel. *Critique of Judgment*. Trans. Werner S. Pluhar. Indianapolis: Hackett, 1987.

Kierkegaard, Søren. *Either/Or: A Fragment of Life*. Trans. and intro. Alastair Hannay. London: Penguin, 1992.

Kushwaha, M.S. *Byron and the Dramatic Form*. Salzburg: Institut für Anglistik und Amerikanistik, Universität Salzburg, 1980.

Levinas, Emmanuel. 'There Is: Existence without Existents'. *The Levinas Reader*. Ed. Seán Hand. Oxford: Blackwell, 1989. 29–36.

McGann, Jerome. *The Poetics of Sensibility: A Revolution in Literary Style*. Oxford and New York: Oxford University Press, 1996.

——. *Byron and Romanticism*. Ed. James Soderholm. Cambridge: Cambridge University Press, 2002.

Schroeder, Ronald A. 'Byron's "Darkness" and the Romantic Dis-Spiriting of Nature'. *Approaches to Teaching Byron's Poetry*. Ed. Frederick W. Shilstone. New York: Modern Language Association, 1991. 113–19.

Stabler, Jane. *Byron, Poetics and History*. Cambridge: Cambridge University Press, 2002.

Wood, Gerald C. 'Nature and Narrative in Byron's "The Prisoner of Chillon"'. *Keats-Shelley Journal: Keats, Shelley, Byron, Hunt, and Their Circles* 24 (1975): 108–17.

8
byron and psychoanalytic criticism: *werner*
pamela kao and david punter

T.H. Vail Motter begins his 1935 study 'Byron's *Werner* Re-estimated', which remains the longest and arguably the most important monograph on *Werner* to date, with two extraordinary points about Byron's least reputed complete play: firstly, it has the longest stage life among Byron's plays, which amounted to 'fifty-nine years under five different actors', and secondly, it is simply a bad play (Motter 1967, 243). Following his assertions about the contradiction between the play's dramatic popularity and its lack of literary merits, Motter further points out two opposite critical attitudes towards the play: some critics ignore it without apology (e.g. Samuel C. Chew), while some German critics overestimate its importance and read into it, he suggests, 'literary "beauties" and subtleties which are not there'.

Motter himself steers clear of both attitudes and specifies that his article aims at discovering 'what *Werner* was' (as 'a theatrical document', not as 'a literary work'), 'what Byron intended it to be' (in relation to his other dramatic efforts), and 'what is its significance in the nineteenth century theatre' (Motter 1967, 247–8). He argues that in the composition of *Werner* Byron 'patently surrendered his ideals in favour of a theatrical taste which he despised, in order to woo a public for which he felt contempt' and concludes that *Werner* is 'a fittingly Byronic close to the poet's ill-fated dramatic career, a surrender and a defeat which became a defiance and a victory' (275).

The two opposite critical attitudes persist after the original publication of Motter's article in 1935 and its reissue in 1967. In his comprehensive introduction to the corpus of Byron's poetry, Marchand (1965, 105–6) devotes only one paragraph to *Werner*, claiming that 'little need be said about *Werner* as a dramatic production or as poetry'. As for its popularity 'on the Victorian stage', he concludes, 'it might better be ascribed to the bathetic taste of the age.' In the mid-1970s, when there was a renewal of interest in Byron's poetry, Blackstone and Manning vest the play with autobiographical importance, both seeming to base their arguments indirectly on Byron's own assertion in the preface that Harriet Lee's tale of Kruitzner 'made a deep impression upon me' when he first read it and that it may 'contain the germ of much that I have since written'.

To Blackstone (1975, 253), *Werner* and *The Deformed Transformed* are Byron's 'final assault of self-analysis', in which he 'is approaching the nuclear nerve of his own trauma'. He proclaims that the characters in *Werner* 'are ill-defined, like figures in a dream' and that Byron takes on the roles of both the hypnotised patient and the analyst in this psychological drama. According to Manning, *Werner* 'offers a microcosm of [Byron's] dramatic universe' (Manning 1978, 159). He argues that the tale of 'Kruitzner' confirms Byron's 'own psychodynamics' and suggests that the 'germ' mentioned in the preface relates to 'the oedipal themes at the core of Byron's work' (160).

These comments by no means exhaust the range of critical interest in *Werner*, despite the fact that it is still one of the few less trodden areas of Byron studies. We have selected and endeavoured to introduce them because they leave two threads to be picked up: one involves the play's psychological and autobiographical elements and the other its dramatic technique, described by Ehrstine as 'something of a *tour de force* in Gothicism' (Ehrstine 1976, 132).

The crossing of these two issues brings to mind Freud's 1919 essay on the 'uncanny', dubbed 'a psychologically based theory of terror' by Vijay Mishra, as opposed to the pre-Freudian sublime which 'had considered responses to the sublime through aesthetic categories of taste' (Mishra 1994, 72, 75). As Harold Bloom claims in 1977, Freud's paper 'is of enormous importance to literary criticism because it is the only major contribution that the twentieth century has made to the aesthetics of the Sublime' (Bloom 1981, 218). 'The Sublime', Bloom (1981, 218) remarks, 'is one of [Freud's] major *repressed* concerns'. Freud, at the very beginning of his paper, associates the sublime 'with feelings of a positive nature' and appears to distinguish his theory of terror from the theory of the sublime. But his subject – 'the opposite feelings of repulsion and distress,' is in reality in line with Burke's connection of the sublime with terror, with 'such situations in which some elements are felt either as painful or as threatening' (Holmqvist and Pluciennik, 2002, 719). Evaluating Burke and Freud in terms of their contribution to the reading of Gothic literature, both David B. Morris and Mishra favour the latter on the theory of terror. In his 'Gothic Sublimity', Morris (1984–85, 300) argues that Freud's theory of terror is more advanced than Burke's for a reading of the Gothic revision of the eighteenth-century sublime, of which 'sublimity is a vital, integral part ... not merely an incidental, ornamental, scenic prop'. After commenting that Burke's account of terror 'failed to examine adequately its psychological dimensions (or grounds)', Mishra also proclaims in *The Gothic Sublime* (1994, 78) that 'Freud's redefinition of terror as the return of the repressed' enables us to read the precursor text(s) of Gothic literature 'in a much more sophisticated fashion'.

As is always the case with Freud, his acclaimed theory of terror is not without its demerits and one of the criticisms comes precisely from Bloom. Freud's interpretation of E.T.A. Hoffmann's 'The Sand-Man' is, Bloom acknowledges, an 'extraordinary literary insight', which is however weakened in the latter part of the paper by Freud's reduction of the psychological origin of uncanny feelings to 'either an infantile or a primitive survival in our psyche' (Bloom 1981, 219–20).[1] Since the purpose of this essay is not to discover other possible psychological origins of the uncanny feelings, we would like to contend that the reductionism in Freud's paper does not invalidate the light it sheds on our reading of Byron's *Werner*.

Applying Freud's theory of the double, part of his contemplation on the 'uncanny', we can explore the psychological complexity of *Werner* in the context of its Gothic form. The first concern involves an examination of two 'double' figures, Werner and Ulric, and the uncanny effect they exert on the new Count Siegendorf. The second involves an investigation of the recurrent themes of exile, crime and self-justification, along with the recurrent Gothic tropes of castles and winding passages, which combine to intensify even further the reader's uncanny feelings with regard to Werner's fate. We also suggest that the repetition of images, typical in Gothic literature, is an uncanny doubling of classical dramatic ideals (the Aristotelian unity of time and place), which Byron has apparently abandoned in this final complete play.

the 'double'

Freud's investigation of the uncanny starts with a linguistic study of the German word *heimlich*, whose meaning 'develops in the direction of ambivalence, until it finally coincides with its opposite, *unheimlich*' (XIV, 347). Freud engages himself with an examination of Jentsch's theory, which ascribes the source of uncanny feelings to 'intellectual uncertainty'. He places under scrutiny Hoffmann's 'The Sand-Man', which Jentsch cites as a successful example of 'this psychological artifice' (using 'intellectual uncertainty' to arouse uncanny feelings) (XIV, 348). A different result is arrived at: the uncanny effect of the Sand-Man is achieved, according to Freud, by arousing 'an early childhood fear' and 'an infantile wish or even merely an infantile belief' (XIV, 355).

Freud goes on to discuss another masterpiece of the uncanny by Hoffmann, *Die Elixiere des Teufels*, to test its uncanny themes for 'infantile sources' (XIV, 355–6). These themes, he summarizes, are all related to 'the phenomenon of the "double"': there are identical characters with the power of telepathy, 'a doubling, dividing and interchanging of the self', and 'the constant recurrence of the same thing'. Otto Rank's fascinating book *The Double* is introduced into the discussion at this juncture.

Rank's study explores the relation of the 'double' to 'reflections in mirrors, shadows, guardian spirits, the belief in the soul', and 'the fear of death' (XIV, 356–7). He suggests that 'the "double" was originally an insurance against the destruction of the ego, an "energetic denial of the power of death"'. He argues that 'unbounded self-love', 'primary narcissism', nourishes the invention of the 'double' as 'a preservation against extinction', and that the 'double' transforms from 'an assurance of immortality' into 'the uncanny harbinger of death' after the stage of primary narcissism is surmounted.

Freud extends Rank's idea by incorporating into the concept of the double two more pieces of material that arise after the passing of primary narcissism (XIV, 357–8). One is the group of offensive things which the conscience regards as belonging to 'the old surmounted narcissism of earliest times' and which it wants to censor and repress. In 'delusions of observation', nevertheless, this critical agent 'conscience' is 'isolated, dissociated from the ego, and discernible to the physician's eye' (XIV, 357). The other is 'all the unfulfilled but possible futures' which we still preserve in our phantasy, all the crushed 'strivings of the ego', and 'all our suppressed acts of volition which nourish in us the illusion of free will'.

Freud then explores the way in which the 'double' arouses uncanny feelings. The uncanny 'is in reality nothing new or alien, but something which is familiar and old-established in the mind and which has become alienated from it only through the process of repression' (XIV, 363–4). That is to say, when the repressed returns, it is perceived as something uncanny. The double belonging to the uncanny is a creation that used to wear 'a more friendly aspect' in 'a very early mental stage'. When this early stage has long been surmounted, the double turns into 'a thing of terror, just as, after the collapse of their religion, the gods turned into demons' (XIV, 358).

werner

The theme of the double in *Werner* is tangentially touched upon in Blackstone and Ehrstine. Werner's pursuer Stralenheim is identified in the former as the doppelgänger of the eponymous protagonist of the play (Blackstone 1975, 253). Ehrstine identifies a pairing and regrouping of the four main male characters (Ehrstine 1976, 134). Werner and Gabor both enter the secret passage, both are pursued by Stralenheim, both are reduced to steal or blackmail,[2] but both are guiltless. Stralenheim and Ulric 'are aligned by the way in which they deal with the fallen world', and yet on the other hand 'Stralenheim and Werner are antagonist and protagonist, and Ulric and Gabor the pair of wandering comrades'. But a further doubling is vital to the play's uncanny effect. Werner is persecuted by Stralenheim and he is the new Count Siegendorf's double as well. Werner is a division of Kruitzner, what we might refer to as the censored chapter in his life. 'Werner' is an invented identity during the period of exile, invented to safeguard Kruitzner from Stralenheim's persecution. The change of identity from Werner to Count Siegendorf enables the latter to banish his old identity as something foreign to himself, but the suppressed old identity threatens to re-emerge when something associated with it is mentioned. For example, in his conversation with Ulric's bandit (or military) friend Rodolph (IV. i. 281–9), Werner first 'starts' at the latter's mention of 'the frontier' and then is 'agitated' at the word 'Hamburgh', the site where he has buried his old identity. Eager to disavow any connection with that city, he ends the conversation hastily.

The suppressed past returns when the cursed name 'Werner' is uttered again by Gabor in the midst of the crowd at the festive procession. As the new Count Siegendorf says about his previous name Werner,

> All
> My destinies were woven in that name:
> It will not be engraved upon my tomb,
> But it may lead me there. (V. i. 89–92)

When he is dead, the name Werner will be buried in the grave with his body, leaving no trace above ground. It would be even better if the name Werner could be buried while he is still alive, along with the ignominious theft and murder which are entangled with it. The re-emergence of this repressed yet restless name leads the new Count Siegendorf finally to his grave.

ulric

Werner, we might say, is a text structured around two doubles. Although not paired with his father in the work of either Blackstone or Ehrstine, Ulric is a substantial double of Kruitzner. Both Ulric and Werner are Kruitzner's creations, dividing his self – the former his offspring, the latter his previously assumed identity; both are originally parts of him. Peter Manning sees Ulric as one of the 'stern warrior-outcasts of the oriental tales' (Manning 1978, 168), an unprecedented victorious son (163), who has achieved autonomy in his oedipal struggle with a patriarchal figure without being punished (167). In the context of our reading of Ulric as Werner's double, it is tempting to argue that this 'unprecedented victorious son' is possible only precisely under the protective cloak of the double. The punishment for his transgression is laid on the self, who originally created this double for self-protection and wish-fulfilment.

In the time of Werner's direst need, Ulric serves as his friendly double, the insurance against his destruction in several ways and at the same time the agent of his darkest wish. When the past image of Ulric as a benevolent double cannot be suppressed and forgotten, the godsend 'double' transforms into a persecutor and the harbinger of the destruction of the entire race of Siegendorf.

Ulric is not an innocent young man blasted by his discovery of his father's wrongdoing as depicted by Kavita A. Sharma (Sharma 1982). It is true that he is swayed by Werner's argument and analysis of their emerging peril, but the temptation of Stralenheim immediately afterwards is the foremost determinant. When Stralenheim claims that Werner 'stands / Between me and a brave inheritance' (II. ii. 369–70), Ulric responds in an aside that it is parallel to Adam standing 'between / The devil and his [Paradise]' (II. ii. 386–7). Thus recognizing Stralenheim as a tempting serpent, the devil, Ulric's determination to get rid of him, which is originally motivated by Werner, is gradually strengthened and finally resolved at the end of his conversation with Stralenheim. With hindsight, the reader can clearly discern the irony behind Stralenheim's remark that 'you make me / Yours, and for ever' and Ulric's reply that 'such is my intention' (II. ii. 433–4).

The most substantial irony is that when Stralenheim tries to win over Ulric's support against Werner, he unwittingly fuels Ulric's murderous resolution with his own heartless principle in dealing with an enemy. The following dialogue is especially crucial:

STRALENHEIM. All's to be fear'd, where all is to be gain'd.
ULRIC. True; and aught done to save or to obtain it.
STRALENHEIM. You have harp'd the very string next to my heart.
  I may depend upon you?
ULRIC.   'Twere too late
  To doubt it.
STRALENHEIM. Let no foolish pity shake
  Your bosom. (II. ii. 409–14)

And thus he seals his own death warrant by confirming Werner's depiction of his evil character and encouraging Ulric to be merciless to his enemy. Ulric's composure in the face of the enemy, the disguise of his agitated mind underneath a calm exterior, and his unwavering determination to carry out a well thought-out scheme belong to an experienced bandit or soldier, not a green new convert. His is a world that Werner could never share, even though Werner used to be 'a soldier, / A hunter, and a traveller' (I. i. 33–4). While Werner loses his composure and draws suspicion upon himself throughout the play, Ulric only loses his when faced with the woman, whom he has wronged by expedient murder.

Ulric's potential for doing extreme good and evil, instead of being an inconsistent and unconvincing characterization, corresponds to the traits of other typical Byronic heroes such as Manfred and Conrad. Intriguingly, from the very beginning of Ulric's entrance on to the stage, he has been saved from answering significant questions by the interruption and assumption of other characters. The change in the length of separation from three to twelve years in the 1822 version proves crucial in justifying the father's misunderstanding of his son's character; the effect of Werner's final realization that Ulric is a 'thing of terror' is an uncanny feeling of helplessness in the face of doom, of which his following remark to Gabor is symbolic:

> Fly! I am not master,
> It seems, of my own castle—of my own
> Retainers—nay, even of these very walls,
> Or I would bid them fall and crush me! Fly! (V. ii. 6–9)

Nor is he master of his fate or Ulric's.

The figure of Ulric thus functions as Werner's double in all the three ways discussed in Freud's essay on the uncanny (XIV, 357). We shall now examine this tropology in more detail.

insurance against destruction vs harbinger of death

First of all, being Werner's son, Ulric is the natural extension of Werner's life and preservation against his mortality. As Werner is 'the last sole scion of a thousand sires' (I. i. 159), so is Ulric. By leaving Ulric with the old Count, Werner had hoped that the latter's 'anger would stop short / Of the third generation' (I. i. 95–6). In the 1815 version, Werner gives up Ulric to his father three years before the beginning of the play without confiding in his wife in exchange for 'a scanty stipend' and in order to 'secure the heritage / Forfeit in me forever' (I. i. 116, 121–2). The self-serving and pecuniary motives of Werner's rendering up of his son are obscured in the 1822 version when a symbolic motive is added. Ulric now serves both as Werner's remaining link to the old Count, signifying a possibility of reconciliation between the grandfather and the father, as well as a surrogate heir to the inheritance of the house of Siegendorf in Werner's absence if the old Count passes away. Through Ulric the race of Siegendorf will be preserved.

Though not strikingly identical to his father, Ulric resembles Werner in his features and personality to a certain extent. Although nobody else recognizes any affinity between them, Gabor comes to comprehend their relationship when witnessing Ulric washing his bloody hands after the murder of Stralenheim, and recounts this sudden realization to Werner. This recognition leads him to the assumption that he is trapped 'into this / Pretended den of refuge, to become / The victim of your guilt' (V. i. 344–6). As for Ulric's personality, one of Stralenheim's attendants, Fritz, reports that Ulric 'forms a happy mixture of his sire / And grandsire's qualities,—impetuous as / The former, and deep as the latter' (II. i. 105–7). Once again, Ulric symbolizes the possibility of reconciliation between Werner and the old Count.

Upon seeing Ulric, Werner admires this long-lost son in a narcissistic manner, reminiscent of that which Freud finds in all affectionate parents.[3] The effect of the reunion is intensified in the 1822 version, where Byron lengthens the period of their separation from three to twelve years. Werner comments on Ulric,

> Why, thou look'st all
> I should have been, and was not. Josephine!
> Sure 'tis no father's fondness dazzles me;
> But had I seen that form amid ten thousand
> Youth of the choicest, my heart would have chosen
> This for my son! (II. ii. 25–30)

Here Werner sees in Ulric an idealization of himself in terms of appearance, but in terms of character his father's fondness blinds him from taking Ulric as he is, and makes him instead interpret him as what he wants him to be.

That Ulric preserves Werner's life from extinction is realized not only in his being Werner's sole heir, but also in his rescuing his parents from poverty and, most important of all, from Stralenheim's persecution. The moment Josephine is reunited with Ulric, she exclaims that 'he comes not as a son but saviour' (II. ii. 8), another interesting addition in the 1822 version of the reunion. As Manning observes (1978, 161), Freud detects in the 'rescue-motif' the son's 'phantasy of *rescuing his father from danger and saving his life*' in order to return the gift of life to him, underlying defiance against the father in the process of achieving autonomy. Manning argues that Ulric's search for Stralenheim renders him unwittingly 'the hunter of his father' (162). But the 'rescue motif' is further extended in *Werner* into a 'rescue-and-reclaim motif' and fits in with the idea of the double in Freud and Rank, who starts as the preservation against extinction and transforms into 'the harbinger of death'.

The 'rescue-and-reclaim motif' is pronounced clearly by Ulric's justification of his murder of Stralenheim: 'As stranger I preserve him, and he *owed me* / His *life*; when due, I but resumed the debt' (V. ii. 462–3). The following extract from the first conversation between Stralenheim and Ulric, which takes place before the reunion of Werner and Ulric, is an eerie foreshadowing of the murder:

> ULRIC.   You perceive my garb
> Is Saxon, and of course my service due
> To my own sovereign. If I must decline
> Your offer, 'tis with the same feeling which
> Induced it.
> STRALENHEIM. Why, this is mere usury!
> I owe my life to you, and you refuse
> The acquittance of the interest of the debt,
> To heap more obligations on me, till
> I bow beneath them.
> ULRIC.   You shall say so when
> I claim the payment. (II. i. 177–87)

The saviour-turned-murderer motif in the relation between Stralenheim and Ulric is echoed in the relation between Werner and Ulric. Ulric never threatens Werner's life, it is true, but by a series of crimes Ulric wrecks

Werner's peace of mind, which will be forever weighed down with an excruciating sense of guilt. While Ulric restores Werner to the Castle of Siegendorf, the son gnaws into the father's soul (I. i. 47) and turns the magnificent castle into a psychic prison.

Furthermore, Ulric the heir, the symbolic extension of Werner's life, plucks himself from the withering tree of Siegendorf through his self-imposed exile and his sceptical attitude to marriage which rules out the possibility of his producing an heir. Werner is chilled when he finds Ulric to 'talk so coolly' and 'act so carelessly' with regard to his marriage with Ida (IV. i. 349–50). His love for Ida, the only woman he claims to love (IV. i. 124–5), is inhibited because of his murder of her father. He becomes agitated and pale upon hearing her talking about her father's death (IV. i. 194ff.). She dies in the end upon learning that her beloved was her father's murderer. As Werner concludes the play by mourning, 'The race of Siegendorf is past!' (V. ii. 66), the preserver of the race of Siegendorf has turned its destroyer.

wish-granter vs hangman

Secondly, Ulric is a wish-granter to his parents in a most dire situation. Although the situation would be quite different if he 'had arrived a few hours sooner' (II. ii. 17), his reappearance at the most pressing hour saves Werner from being discovered as the thief, provides the parents with money needed for their journey home, and secures their homecoming by getting rid of the 'rock in our way which I cut through' and the bolt that 'stood between us / And our true destination' (V. i. 459–61).

In encouraging the marriage of Ulric and Ida, Werner expects another wish to be fulfilled by his son. Although Werner claims to Ulric that the marriage will 'wean thee from the perils of thy youth / And haughty spirit' (IV. i. 341–2), Ulric discerns Werner's covert egoistic desire to '[unite] the future and [destroy] the past' by means of the union and he is ready to satisfy his father's wish again (IV. i. 132-33). Uncanny feelings arise when it turns out that Ulric has also realized Werner's murderous impulse to kill Stralenheim, which the latter has repressed in the midst of temptation. As Ulric justifies his crime by condemning Werner as the instigator, he argues that Werner 'invites to deeds / He longs to do, but dare not' and demands the father not to wonder how the son 'should *act* what [the father] could *think*' (V. i. 451–3).

conscience

Thirdly, while Manning calls Ulric 'the hunter of his father' (Manning 1978, 162), we would like to argue, in the context of reading Ulric as Werner's 'double', that the character Ulric materializes Werner's 'conscience'. In his self-exile from home Ulric represents Werner's petulant and rebellious youth, which the latter outgrows in his abject period of exile. Regretful of his past, Werner should have been critical of Ulric; but on the contrary he gives Ulric the highest praise. Persecuted by his own severe conscience from the very beginning of the play, Werner projects his self-criticism and self-observation onto the 'impeccable' Ulric the moment he is reunited with his son. Ulric, 'a happy mixture of his sire / And grandsire's qualities' (II. i. 105–6), incorporates the censoring eyes of both Werner and the old Count. Irresolute and passive under the sway of fate as Werner is, he endeavours only unknowingly to oppose his double, which differs from the conventional face-to-face confrontation between the self and its double.

Ulric's first appearance on the stage as his father's pursuer is heralded by his status as Stralenheim's saviour. Although in one sense Ulric is a saviour turned pursuer to Stralenheim and a pursuer turned saviour to Werner, Ulric never ceases to torture Werner's conscience. When still investigating Stralenheim's theft, Ulric calls the thief a 'villain' without knowing that he is insulting his own father to his face. Thereafter Werner projects his self-criticism on to Ulric and misreads the latter's assurance of affection as an ironic reference to his base crime of theft. He begs his son not to hate him, but it is not certain whether Ulric is referring to his knowledge of Werner's crime when he claims to know Werner better than the old Count. Werner feels greatly humiliated to have had his son discover his crime. He professes that he can see and feel Ulric's willingness to fulfil his filial duty, but yet he also feels that 'you despise me' (III. i. 237).

Ulric later capitalizes on Werner's 'delusion of criticism' and defensive attitude. After murdering Stralenheim, Ulric pre-empts any doubts and questions from Werner when they accidentally meet in the garden (III. iv. 29ff.). He pretends to suspect Werner of murdering Stralenheim and puts Werner immediately on the defensive.

Werner's counter-attack, although unconscious, is explicit. Even as he gets rid of Stralenheim with the aid of Ulric, he fights back against Ulric through the agency of Ida and Gabor. On the face of it, Werner takes Stralenheim's orphan into his care in order to assuage his sense of guilt over Stralenheim's death but Ida serves other functions as well. Werner expresses his hope, as we have seen, that Ulric's marriage to Ida will 'wean [him] from the perils of [his] youth / And haughty spirit' (IV. i. 341–2); to put this another way, Werner wishes that Ida be the cage that imprisons and tames the unruly Ulric. In addition, her most innocent remarks torment Ulric's conscience, even as Ulric's previous innocent remarks are poignant in Werner's perception. If Ulric's eyes seem always to be accusing Werner of his theft, the father avenges himself on the criticizing son by keeping Ida by Ulric's side.

Furthermore, even though Werner does not suspect Ulric of the murder of Stralenheim, he contributes to the final discovery of Ulric's crime by harbouring Gabor in the secret passage that leads to the scene of the murder. Gabor's testimony is the sole evidence of Ulric's crime, and Ulric takes it as an urgent need to silence the witness. It appears as though Werner seeks Gabor in order to take revenge on the Hungarian soldier for Stralenheim's death, but in reality the outcome is to force Ulric to plead guilty. Werner refutes Ulric's suspicion that Werner has guessed what happened on the night of the murder and his accusation that Werner is a silent accomplice (V. i. 409ff.). The way Werner describes the scene in which he sees Gabor during the pageantries intriguingly suggests that at some unconscious level Werner does suspect that Gabor is the scapegoat of Ulric's crime. He tells Ulric,

> SIEGENDORF. I look'd, as a dying soldier
>   Looks at a draught of water, for this man;
>   But still I saw him not; but in his stead—
> ULRIC.   What in his stead?
> SIEGENDORF. My eye for ever fell
>   Upon your dancing crest; the loftiest,
>   As on the loftiest and the loveliest head
>   It rose the highest of the stream of plumes,
>   Which overflow'd the glittering streets of Prague.
> ULRIC.   What's this to the Hungarian?
> SIEGENDORF. Much; for I
>   Had almost then forgot him in my son. (V. i. 120–9)

The change of Gabor's image into Ulric's insinuates that Werner may at some level know something about his son that he cannot admit into his consciousness.

recurrent themes[4]

Besides the two 'double' figures Werner and Ulric, there is another phenomenon of the double in the play: 'the constant recurrence of the same thing', which, according to Freud, includes 'the repetition of the same features or character-traits or vicissitudes, of the same crimes, or even the same names through several consecutive generations' (Freud 1990–93, XIV, 356). In *Werner* there are several striking recurrent themes and images. They are all related to the doubling of the father and son and significantly intensify the uncanny feelings already aroused by the doubling of the self and character.

The first theme, exile, is repeated several times and in effect encloses the play, which starts with both Werner and Ulric in exile and ends with Ulric's second self-imposed exile. Lying in the distant background is the exile of Josephine's Italian father, whose fate has also had a huge impact on the daughter's life. The son's identification with the father is only partial and superficial, as is the case with the other two recurrent themes; where the father fails, the son triumphs. To Werner, Ulric 'entail[s], as it were, my sins upon / Himself' by mysteriously disappearing from the Castle of Siegendorf (I. i. 92–3). Yet there is a major difference between their exiles. Werner has aimlessly wandered, struggled to survive, and regretted forfeiting the wealth, rank, and power to which he was born. Ulric, by contrast, leaves home for a purpose, finally becomes the leader of 'a thousand, ay, ten thousand / Swords, hearts, and hands' (V. ii. 45–6), and never looks back. Werner has been disinherited, but it is Ulric who denounces the father-son relation (V. ii. 34–9).

Fritz, Stralenheim's vassal, provides four different explanations of Ulric's disappearance (II. i. 114ff.). He may have left the old Count in order to search for his parents. He may have felt constrained at home, although the truth was that the old Count indulged the young heir. He may have gone to war, but peace was made soon after he left. He may have 'join'd the black bands', because of 'the wild exuberance of his nature'. The second and third speculations are immediately overruled by Fritz, whereas there is no comment on the first one. The fourth, by contrast, is pinpointed by Idenstein's disbelief in its possibility and Fritz's argument that 'there are some human natures so allied / Unto the savage love of enterprise, / That they will seek for peril as a pleasure' (II. i. 133–5).

Doubt is cast on the warm affection that Ulric exhibits towards his parents at their reunion (especially II. ii. 34–2) when we remember that he was actually involved in the 'black band' in his absence from home. The confirmation of his wild nature does not entirely exclude the possibility of filial affection, but it greatly lessens the importance of finding his parents in Ulric's agenda. Ulric is endowed with 'fierceness' like myriads of other youths born during the civil wars, who were 'bred up upon / The knees of Homicide; sprinkled, as it were, / With blood even at their baptism' (IV. i. 68–72). Furthermore, Ulric's talent for dissimulation is revealed in the scene where Stralenheim tries to persuade him to become his ally and in the scene after the murder, where he pretends to accuse Werner of murder so that suspicion would not fall on himself. His cunning art of deception compromises the authenticity of his sincerity in the reunion scene. He is, as he himself claims to Ida, 'the true cameleon, / And live but on the atmosphere' (IV. i. 219–20). He hides his true colour well, inspects the environment carefully, and waits for the opportune moment to go into action.

Crime is the second recurrent theme, and here again the identification is only superficial. As with their opposite attitudes in exile, Werner is always on the defensive and Ulric on the offensive. Werner is impulsive, temperamental and hesitant; Ulric is calm, scheming and determined. Cornered by Stralenheim in the ruined castle, Werner rushes into the secret passage with a knife, which suggests his impulse to kill the enemy. As Gabor observes, Werner is more like a 'wounded lion' which 'would turn at bay, / And rip the hunter's entrails' rather than the 'hunted deer' that Werner himself suggests (III. i. 6–9). However, no plan is ever made and he changes his mind when the impulse cools down at the sight of the sleeping enemy. Ulric, by contrast, is an eagle, who would 'overfly, or rend' nets rather than being caught in them like a thrush (III. i. 163–4). Faced with Stralenheim, the tempting, sly and poisonous serpent (II. ii. 60), Ulric the eagle circles before he swoops on its prey. The son appears to imitate the father but in reality surpasses him, which recalls the ending of *Cain* where the angel confronts Cain with the possibility that 'The fratricide might well engender parricides' (III. i. 492).

The third recurrent theme is self-justification. As mentioned above, Ulric's murderous intentions are aroused by Werner but determined in the course of Stralenheim's temptation. In the face of persuasion from both sides, Ulric proves to be a youth of independent thoughts; he is, as he claims, 'my own sovereign' (II. i. 180). Ashamed of his own disgraceful theft, Werner is agitated and rushes eagerly to his own defence, cutting short Ulric's retort. It is tempting for the audience to attribute strict moral principles to Ulric, even as Werner does when he tries to rationalize his own crime; the youth has after all just risked his life saving a complete stranger and he looks noble, selfless and upright. However, except for calling the thief a 'villain' and a 'ruffian', Ulric hardly has any chance to express his opinions in the midst of his father's enthusiastic self-vindication and eager attempt to draw Ulric into alliance with him (II. ii. 84ff.).

In a similar fashion, Ulric's circumspection successfully hides his double-dealing intent from Stralenheim; as opposed to Werner's rashness, the chameleon-like Ulric expresses his true feelings only in equivocal terms, which does not arouse any suspicion in Stralenheim at all. Instead of being blindly swayed by Werner's heated persuasion, Ulric relies on his own judgement of the situation. His flexible moral principles change in accordance with the times and with the type of enemy he faces. He deals with Stralenheim according to the latter's moral principle: 'Let no foolish pity shake / Your bosom' (II. ii. 413–14). And the timing is propitious for the murder as well; it is a time when

> The laws (if e'er
> Laws reach'd this village) are all in abeyance
> With the late general war of thirty years,
> Or crush'd, or rising slowly from the dust,
> To which the march of armies trampled them. (III. iv. 132–6)

Throughout this play characters judge and evaluate each other. Ulric, however, keeps his observations and comments to himself. If Werner's self-justification has in any way influenced Ulric, it is because it has revealed to Ulric something of his character. As Ulric confesses to Werner in the penultimate scene,

> I sought and fathom'd you—
> Doubting if you were false or feeble; I
> Perceived you were the latter; and yet so
> Confiding have I found you, that I doubted
> At times your weakness. (V. i. 419–23)

Even though he has decided to come to Werner's aid, his doubt over his father's personality stops him from sharing the murder plan. Not necessarily having been swayed completely by Werner's vehement self-justification, Ulric takes advantage of Werner's way of persuasion after confessing the murder and applies it to induce Werner's cooperation in getting rid of Gabor. By claiming that Werner is his accomplice, Ulric is seeking alliance. He fails only because Werner is too much weighed down by the thought that the strong potency of his words has actually caused death.

recurrent images

In addition to these facets of the father-son relationship, there are other recurrent themes such as the anxiety for the discovery of one's identity, hunting and persecution, as well as refuges turning into prisons. The twinning of palace and prison runs throughout Byron's writing and it appears in this play in the forms of the ruined Silesian palace and the magnificent Castle of Siegendorf, coupled with the secret passage and the disturbing visual cue of 'pageantries'.

Marvin Spevack argues that *Werner* 'contracts Byron's principles and practice' and one of the major contractions is the lack of Aristotelian unities of time and place, which Byron elsewhere upholds (Spevack 1970, xi). The two pairs of images under discussion appear to be pairs of opposites instead of counterparts. Yet they connect the two different settings in the play in a subtle way; the second image of each pair seemingly contrasting with the first one but once stripped of its grandeur uncannily turning out to be parallel to the first in essence. In other words, the second image in each pair is the first's double. And because these images are the central settings of the play, their doubling achieves the uncanny effect of the doubling of the Aristotelian unity of place.

The palace on the frontier of Silesia and the Castle of Siegendorf are in sharp contrast in terms of their appearance. The former, according to Idenstein, has been in a state of decay for twelve years (I. i. 183); the latter, according to Stralenheim, 'is the richest of the rich Bohemia, / Unscathed by scorching war' (II. ii. 372–3). Their doubling mirrors the doubling of self and character discussed above.

On one level of signification, the decayed palace represents Werner, who is wasted in body and distressed in mind after years of exile. The Castle of Siegendorf, on the other hand, represents Ulric, who is protected under the tutelage of the old Count. Intriguingly, the decayed palace and the young energetic Ulric are linked together by the number of twelve years of decay and parental absence. The magnificent and noble appearance of both the castle and the youth are misleading. Ulric, who is represented by the prosperous castle, turns out to be like the ruined palace in essence.

On another level, the decayed palace represents Werner and the magnificent castle represents the new Count of Siegendorf. While the past magnificence of the ruined palace is still present even in its remnants, Werner's dignified carriage shines through his emaciated and ragged exterior and discloses his noble origin. As the new Count cannot eschew the fact that he used to be the piteous Werner, the magnificence of the castle fails to cover the past and current rifts within the family.

The crimes and complexities that have surrounded Werner cannot be eradicated by his assumption of a new title. The new Count is haunted by Werner's sense of guilt over the theft and Stralenheim's brutal murder. As Gabor says,

When I knelt down
Amidst the People in the Church, I dream'd not
To find the beggar'd Werner in the seat
Of Senators and Princes. (V. i. 187–90)

The Count was, is, and sadly will always be 'the beggar'd Werner'. He was once persecuted with poverty, remorse and Stralenheim's chase, and now he is persecuted with poverty of soul, remorse and a sense of guilt. His new identity is like his splendid clothes for 'the appointed festival / In Prague for peace restored' (IV. i. 235–6). Underneath the clothes, 'the beggar'd Werner' can still be discerned.

In addition, these two settings are parallel in their paradoxical roles to the relationship between father and son. As the double returns as a thing of terror, so the two castles transform from safe and peaceful shelters into prisons and even graves. In the opening scene, Werner paces restlessly about the chamber in the decayed palace in which he and Josephine have been taking refuge. As far as the latter is concerned, they should be contented to be sheltered from the tempest outside; to Werner, however, no physical shelter can guarantee mental rest. Paradoxically, the harbour is soon turned into a trap, in which he, a sickly lion, is caged along with Stralenheim, a poisonous snake, until it finally changes into Stralenheim's grave. In the Castle of Siegendorf, it first appears that the much longed-for peace has finally arrived, both in the house of Siegendorf and in Prague. This place of comfort and revelry, nevertheless, is also transformed into a prison, for both father and son. Nonchalant towards the expected wedding with Ida and the festival celebrating the new peace, Ulric is engaged with the business of the black band and is eager to join his comrades as soon as possible. The Count, by contrast, is self-manacled by remorse and a sense of guilt. At the end, the castle almost turns into the grave of Gabor, is the grave of Ida, and will soon be the grave of the collapsed Siegendorf. Without any heir, the magnificent castle will soon become a ruin like the palace on the frontier of Silesia.

The second pair of images, the secret passage in the first part and the pageantries in the second part, may seem unconnected at first sight; Byron, however, links the secret passage and the pageantries by two specific visual experiences. The first is Gabor's detection of the affinity between Werner and Ulric. As quoted above, when Gabor takes refuge in the secret passage and accidentally sees Ulric after the murder, he is struck by the similarities between the features of Werner and Ulric, which inspires his suspicion of a possible alliance between them. The second is recounted by Siegendorf to Ulric. Having spotted Gabor in the church,

Siegendorf is obsessed with finding him again in the crowd when they arrive at the bridge; instead, he tells Ulric:

> SIEGENDORF.   My eye for ever fell
> Upon your dancing crest; the loftiest,
> As on the loftiest and the loveliest head
> It rose the highest of the stream of plumes,
> Which overflow'd the glittering streets of Prague. (V. i. 123–7)

As Gabor sees Werner in the murderer Ulric, Werner's attention is constantly drawn from the suspect Gabor to Ulric. The replacement of images in both cases strongly conveys the impression that these three characters' fates are 'intertwisted' and cannot be 'unravell'd', even as Siegendorf himself says (V. i. 145–7). The first visual experience suggests that Werner and Ulric are in one sense accomplices, the second suggests that Ulric may have been the real murderer instead of Gabor.

Werner says ruefully that his 'dim destiny' has involved him in 'a maze' (III. i. 145–6). This metaphor is materialized in the images of the secret passage and the pageantries, both of which convey a strong sense of fatefulness. The revelry, 'the clashing music, and the thundering / Of far Artillery,' the 'tramplings round, / The roar of rushing thousands' in the pageantries (V. i. 108ff.), are in sharp contrast with the darkness, the 'cursed pattering feet and whirring wings' of 'rats and bats' in the secret passage (III. iii. 15ff.). The latter seems to be a parody of the former. Moving along with the crowds in the pageantries, however, is as involuntary as moving in the 'Gothic labyrinth of unknown windings' (III. i. 94). The secret passage first leads Werner to the temptation of murder and theft and then leads Gabor to witnessing the murderer; the pageantries lead Gabor to Siegendorf and reveal the truth of the murder. Although it is Werner's original intention to sneak into Stralenheim's chamber through the secret passage, the second and third instances are both involuntary. The experience of entering the secret passage shared by the two hunted men, Werner and Gabor, is symbolic of their fate, which is swayed by other people's actions. When they meet again in the pageantries it is time for the chase to be ended, for Gabor by telling the truth and for Werner by final collapse.

conclusion

In this chapter we have tried to set some of Freud's concepts and some of Byron's preoccupations, as it were, in motion, in the hope that they might prove mutually illuminating. Chief among these are the 'uncanny' and the associated 'theory of terror'; the complexities of doubling; the twinned motifs of persecution and rescue; and the topic of psychological and thematic recurrence. Freud's ideas, we claim, have both a general relevance to creativity; but also a quite specific one in relation to Byron, whose work in many ways offers a prefiguration, itself uncanny, of later psychoanalytic theories.

notes

1. Freud's text runs as follows: 'Our conclusion could then be stated thus: an uncanny experience occurs either when infantile complexes which have been repressed are once more revived by some impression, or when primitive beliefs which have been surmounted seem once more to be confirmed' (XIV, 372). References to Freud's texts use *The Penguin Freud Library*, ed. James Strachey, 15 vols. References are by volume and page number.
2. Ehrstine states that 'Gabor in Act V is finally driven to bribe Siegendorf', yet 'blackmail' is a more suitable verb to use. The Hungarian is obviously claiming hush money after he finishes his witness, 'You think me venal, and scarce true: / 'Tis no less true, however, that my fortunes / Have made me both at present; you shall aid me, / I would have aided you—and also have / Been somewhat damaged in my name to save / Yours and your son's. Weigh well what I have said' (V. i. 377–82).
3. Freud writes in his essay on narcissism: 'If we look at the attitude of affectionate parents towards their children, we have to recognize that it is a revival and reproduction of their own narcissism, which they have long since abandoned'. (XI, 84)
4. This section and the next one on recurrent images were delivered by Pamela Kao at a one-day conference entitled 'New Views of Byron in Context' at Nottingham Trent University on 8 May 2004. Its original title was 'The Mirror Effects in Byron's *Werner*'.

works cited and suggestions for further reading

Barton, Anne. '"A Light to Lesson Ages": Byron's Political Plays'. *Byron: A Symposium.* Ed. John D. Jump. London: Macmillan, 1975. 138–62.

Batten, Guinn. *The Orphaned Imagination: Melancholy and Commodity Culture in English Romanticism.* Durham, NC: Duke University Press, 1998.

Brandell, Jerrold R. 'Eighty Years of Dream Sequences: A Cinematic Journey down Freud's Royal Road'. *American Imago* 61.1 (2004): 59–76.

Blackstone, Bernard. *Byron: A Survey.* London: Longman, 1975.

Bloom, Harold. 'Freud and the Poetic Sublime: A Catastrophe Theory of Creativity'. *Freud: A Collection of Critical Essays.* Ed. Perry Meisel. Englewood Cliff, NJ: Prentice Hall, 1981.

Clubbe, John. 'Byron in our Time'. *Byron Journal* 31 (2003): 11–15.

Cooke, M.G. *The Blind Man Traces the Circle: On the Patterns and Philosophy of Byron's Poetry.* Princeton, NJ: Princeton University Press, 1969.

Corr, Thomas J. 'Byron's *Werner*: The Burden of Knowledge'. *Studies in Romanticism* 24 (1985): 375–98.

Ehrstine, John W. *The Metaphysics of Byron: A Reading of the Plays*. The Hague: Mouton, 1976.

Elfenbein, Andrew. 'Byron: Gender and Sexuality'. *The Cambridge Companion to Byron*. Ed. Drummond Bone. Cambridge: Cambridge University Press, 2004.

Freud, Sigmund. *The Penguin Freud Library*. Ed. James Strachey, 15 vols. London: Penguin, 1990–93.

Gay, Peter. *Readying Freud: Explorations and Entertainments*. New Haven: Yale University Press, 1990.

Grosskurth, Phyllis. *Byron: The Flawed Angel*. London: Hodder and Stoughton, 1997.

Holmqvist, Kenneth, and Jaroslaw Pluciennik. 'A Short Guide to the Theory of the Sublime'. *Style* 36 (2002): 718–37.

LaChance, Charles. 'Naïve and Knowledgeable Nihilism in Byron's Gothic Verse'. *Papers on Language and Literature* 32 (1996): 339–68.

Lansdown, Richard. *Byron's Historical Dramas*. Oxford: Clarendon Press, 1992.

Manning, Peter J. *Byron and His Fictions*. Detroit: Wayne University Press, 1978.

Marchand, Leslie A. *Byron's Poetry: A Critical Introduction*. London: John Murray, 1965.

Martin, Philip W. *Byron: A Poet before his Public*. Cambridge: Cambridge University Press, 1982.

Mishra, Vijay. *The Gothic Sublime*. Albany: State University of New York Press, 1994.

Morris, David B. 'Gothic Sublimity'. *New Literary History* 16 (1984–85): 299–319.

Motter, T.H. Vail. 'Byron's *Werner* Re-estimated: A Neglected Chapter in Nineteenth-Century Stage History'. *Essays in Dramatic Literature*. Ed. Hardin Craig. New York: Russell and Russell, 1967.

Rank, Otto. *The Double*. Ed. Harry Tucker, Jr. Chapel Hill: University of North Carolina Press, 1971.

Rutherford, Andrew, ed. *Byron: The Critical Heritage*. London: Routledge & Kegan Paul, 1970.

Sharma, Kavita A. *Byron's Plays: A Reassessment*. Salzburg: Institut für Anglistik und Americanistik, Universität Salzburg, 1982.

Spevack, Marvin. Byron. *Werner. A Tragedy. A facsimile of the acting version of William Charles Macready*. Intro. Marvin Spevack. Munchen: Willhelm Fink Verlag, 1970.

9

byron in theory and theatre land: finding the right address

michael simpson

Would you please ensure your mobile phone is switched off? Any articulated, industrialized spectacle, whether it be a wedding, an academic conference, or a performance at Drury Lane in the early 1800s, requires certain moments of visible orchestration to effect transitions between its parts. Formal greetings, introductions, announcements and valedictions do the job. A typical evening programme at the patent theatres in London around the year 1800 would have featured two such addresses, a prologue and an epilogue, flanking the main piece. In addition to these routine addresses, there was the 'occasional address', geared to a specific event, and occasional in the two senses of such an event being rare, on the one hand, and important, on the other; great occasions tend to be occasional. In the theatre, however, unlike at a wedding, all these moments of address figure, in one respect, as less artificial and thus more natural than the main spectacle itself. By projecting themselves directly through the fourth wall and at the audience, theatrical addresses insist on their authenticity, even as they remain rigidly, and creakily, formal.

One means of accounting for this dichotomous profile of the address is to understand it as a theatrical practice, somehow naturally in place, and also as a moment of theatrical theory, formally explaining and even legislating such wider practice; since these addresses recycle certain formulae, such as the supremacy of the audience, they do possess some of the lineaments of theory. There is, of course, no shortage of theoretical regulation and description of theatre and drama in the Romantic era, but this writing more regularly takes the form of extended prefaces to editions of playtexts, such as Joanna Baillie's 'Introductory Discourses', and essays and reviews in journals, such as Hazlitt's many contributions to the

London Magazine. The theatrical address may therefore be an additional source of what has recently been termed 'Romantic theatre theory'.[1]

Debate has raged about whether Byron designed his dramas for theatrical production. No such debate is necessary, however, about the theatrical addresses that he wrote, because in several cases they were indeed recited, with Byron's blessing, in London theatres. Two of them in particular invite scrutiny: the first is titled *Address, Spoken at the Opening of Drury-Lane Theatre*, and the second *Monody on the Death of the Right Hon. R.B. Sheridan.* The first was synchronized with the beginning of Byron's association with Drury Lane, which in turn coincided with the consolidation of his literary fame, following publication of Cantos I and II of *Childe Harold's Pilgrimage.* The second address was coordinated with the end of Byron's association with Drury Lane, which was contemporaneous with the conversion of his fame into infamy and with his departure for the Continent. More than some manifestations of theatre theory, these addresses assumed a high profile, since the importance of the occasion ensured not only that they were printed, as they were being delivered over several nights, but also that they were reviewed and discussed. In addition to registering the theoretical dimension of these two addresses, this chapter will consider the theatrical occasions that informed these theoretical pronouncements about theatre and will thus allow these two occasions to illuminate one another.

My argument about these addresses will be that they provide a blueprint for reconstructing Drury Lane as a new national theatre. Figuring numerous moments of doubling, within the theatre and without, the addresses commission the theatre to test these doubles for duplicity, in what promises to become a penetrating critique of Regency society and its characteristic hyperbole and hypocrisy. In formulating this programme, the addresses promote a rehabilitated stage to vie with the newly galvanized periodical press as an instrument of reform. Since Byron, however, leaves the nation at this very moment of projected rehabilitation, in a blaze of satanic glamour, he is the one figure that cannot be fully measured by his own theatrical standard. Yet his second address, precisely by consolidating the first, enables a second blueprint of a specifically international theatre to emerge, as a double of its national counterpart. Within this cosmopolitan theatre, Byron can indeed be tracked, and there is even one of his own plays that might reconcile, albeit precariously, these two blueprints for Drury Lane.

At stake in this theoretical work is the ideological contest between the project of cultural nationalism, as prosecuted by Edgeworth and Scott, and Byron's critique of imperialism, which evolves partly in response to that grand project. The thrust of many of Edgeworth's tales and Scott's novels is to postulate the extremes of the individual self, on one side, and empire, on the other, and to figure their historic convergence as the nation itself. Self and empire are thus accommodated within the nation as a common home assembled for this very occasion. Byron's critique duly acknowledges nation, but chiefly in order to dissolve it back into the forces of ego and empire, which it is thereby not permitted to transcend.

Before developing the argument rehearsed above, we ought to dilate a little on the critical state of play. Criticism of Byron's dramatic works, when it has not blithely declared all his work 'dramatic', has identified them almost exclusively with his plays, invoking his two addresses as mere illustration, or, more frequently, as an index of his practical interest and involvement in the theatre. Despite the evidence of this involvement which they provide, the criticism has sidelined them again by taking its cue about Byron's theory of his own practice, and of other theatrical practice, from the prefaces to his plays. This relegation is not accidental since it is conditioned by the principled aversion of the prefaces themselves to theatrical exhibition, and to anything exhibited, within existing playhouses. What drives the prefaces, in turn, and underlies this occlusion of the addresses, is the antitheatricalism that Julie Carlson (1994) has vividly exposed at the heart of Romanticism. The basis, extent and limit of this antitheatricalism have been plotted within the two most dynamic critical projects currently being conducted on the drama of the Romantic era. Inspired by Carlson's groundbreaking work, the larger of these projects is that of recovering the substantial contribution of women dramatists, critics and actors and interpreting the various signs of their presence and absence. Subsequent critical work on Byron's plays, addresses and prefaces might fruitfully develop the convergence that has already happened between the criticism devoted to Baillie's closet and to Byron's closet; there may even be an interconnecting corridor to be gothically discovered here. The way for such an investigation has certainly been prepared by the sensitive work on gender performed by several feminist critics on the Byronic side: Diane Hoeveler and Susan Wolfson have written on Sardanapalus's gender-bending, and Caroline Franklin has powerfully illuminated the 'heroines' of Byron's plays.[2] Throughout Catherine Burroughs's more recent collection *Women in British Romantic Theatre*, there are intermittent moments of dialogue between Baillie and Byron, and Jane Stabler has elsewhere observed a tissue of relations between them.[3]

The other critical project on Romantic drama, which partly overlaps with the first, is exemplified by Jane Moody's enquiry into the constitution and cultural effects of 'illegitimate drama'.[4] Defined negatively, against the licensed drama of the patent theatres, this category consists of genres such as pantomime, melodrama, burletta and spectacle. The principle that defined it was the stipulation in the Licensing Act of 1737 that drama in which there was any speech must be confined, if exhibited in London, to the patent theatres. What this principle thus permitted was a space in which 'speechless' media such as spectacle, song and music could proliferate and combine to forge new dramatic forms and hybrids, unimpaired by legal and, to some extent, political regulation. Coinciding, more or less, with this critical interest in illegitimate drama of all kinds has been a considerable scholarly focus on melodrama, advanced notably in the work of Elaine Hadley.[5] Such 'vulgar' forms may seem to have little bearing on Byron's evident investment in polite drama, but the thrust of Moody's argument is that the categories of legitimate and illegitimate interpenetrate during the post-Waterloo period, when all cultural artefacts, terms and definitions are suddenly perceived as politicized and are interrogated accordingly. With both Moody's argument and Hadley's work my own argument will presently intersect.

the double act of byron's drury

As Byron's first address reopens the newly reconstructed Drury Lane in 1812, its brief is, in all probability, to avert a replication of the Old Price Riots, which had marred the reopening of Covent Garden in 1809. On this earlier occasion, audiences had protested against the new inflated prices and demanded a return to the old ticket price. In the context of this earlier catastrophe, Byron's address begins by carefully acknowledging two disjunctions: one is between the old and new Drury, and the other is between the new Drury, as a corporate operation behind the address, and the new Drury as an audience in front of the address. Let's set the scene: on 10 October 1812, the actor Robert William Elliston initiates proceedings by delivering Byron's address while dressed as Hamlet, whom he is just about to play in the main feature. Referring to the conflagration that destroyed old Drury in 1809, the address poses a question directly to the audience:

Ye who beheld, . . .
 . . .
Saw the long column of revolving flames
Shake its red shadow o'er the startled Thames,
While thousands, thronged around the burning dome,

> Shrank back appalled, and trembled for their home;
> As glared the volumed blaze, and ghastly shone
> The skies, with lightnings awful as their own;
> . . .
> Say—shall this new, nor less aspiring pile,
> Reared, where once rose the mightiest in our isle,
> Know the same favour which the former knew,
> A shrine for Shakespeare—worthy him and *you*? (ll. 5–20)

And we all say 'Yes'! There is, in fact, a space between this verse paragraph and the next, to allow the audience to respond as such, before the following paragraph opens with the echo

> Yes—it shall be—the magic of that name
> Defies the scythe of time, the torch of flame;
> On the same spot still consecrates the scene,
> And bids the Drama *be* where she hath *been*. (ll. 21–4)

That first 'yes', spoken by the audience, and replicated by the address, enacts a reconciliation between the producers and the consumers of new Drury and thereby a reconciliation between the old and the new Drury Lane, since the question of whether there is a continuity between the old and new theatre is the precise issue on which the producers are canvassing the consumers.

While this enacted convergence between producers and consumers is the means to the other convergence, it is the address itself that engineers the first reconciliation. And this device seems to have worked, at least on the first three nights, which went without a hitch. On the fourth and fifth nights, however, proceedings went histrionically awry, as two members of the audience protested at the fact that Byron's address, rather than their own, was being recited by Elliston. The backdrop to this sudden proliferation of addresses was, of course, the fact that the management of Drury Lane had originally solicited addresses for a competition to determine which might be most appropriate for the occasion. After this public relations coup, however, the management decided that none of those submitted was good enough, and commissioned Byron to supply the address instead. This plethora of addresses then increased twofold when a spoof collection, called *Rejected Addresses*, was published. The spoof was quickly succeeded by the original article, when *Genuine Rejected Addresses* appeared. To this manifold of duplicates, genuine and otherwise, Byron himself contributed a parody of one of the unsuccessful addresses.[6]

Byron's original address thus emerges from and then reactivates a host of doubles.[7]

Notwithstanding the limited success of Byron's address in precluding a second Old Price war, the management of Drury Lane engaged his services again, four years later, when Douglas Kinnaird commissioned him to provide a *Monody on the Death of the Right Hon. R.B. Sheridan*, who had been intimately associated with the theatre. Whereas Byron's first address had postulated a largely dyadic structure, between old and new Drury and between theatre and audience, which was then parodically dissolved into a hall of mirrors, the *Monody* begins where the parodies leave off, with an assertion about numerous elements, which are ultimately parts of a whole. These elemental parts are the qualities of Sheridan surviving in his plays:

> The flash of wit—the bright Intelligence,
> The beam of Song—the blaze of Eloquence,
> Set with their Sun—but still have left behind
> The enduring produce of immortal Mind. (ll. 27–30)

So this second address replicates the first, as the first claims that old Drury is perpetuated, in part, within new Drury. The second address further replicates the first precisely on the grounds that both model themselves as instrumental in the acts of replication that they portray. What this second address also rehearses is Sheridan's own monody *Verses to the Memory of Garrick*, delivered at Drury Lane much earlier, in 1779.[8] It is on the rehearsal of this earlier monody, however, that Byron's *Monody* imposes a categorical limit, replicating its form but not its content. The content denied is the argument that Garrick's performances as an actor bequeath nothing of themselves, because the mimesis of acting is so utterly ephemeral. With Sheridan's argument here, Byron's *Monody* contrasts the example of Sheridan's own work as a playwright, as it is said to preserve vital elements of him.

So far Byron's addresses seem to model the theatre as a crucible of replication, engendering doubles, or parts. His *Monody*, however, assigns another function to Drury Lane. Even as it enjoins its audience of 'Orators' (l. 101), 'Bards' (l. 105) and 'Men of wit and social eloquence' (l. 107) to emulate Sheridan's separate qualities, it projects Drury Lane as the place where such emulation can be tested, and where the attempt to recover Sheridan as a whole, by pooling such emulation, will be seen to fail:

> Long shall we seek his likeness—long in vain,
> And turn to all of him which may remain,
> Sighing that Nature formed but one such man,
> And broke the die—in moulding Sheridan! (ll. 115–18)

The bathos says it all. The parts cannot be reassembled to compose a whole. What authorizes the disappointing finality here is the fact that any reassembly of the parts is being tested at the very site where they were first manifest as parts, or, indeed, as the remarkable whole of Sheridan himself: this is Drury Lane, and so the test itself is automatically tested and validated. There is an implication, however, that the testing of any later reassembly of Sheridan's virtues, and the demonstration of its failure, in the witnessing of his plays, might motivate the different parts of the audience to redouble their effort at emulation, seeking within themselves new doubles of the relevant parts of Sheridan and then returning to Drury Lane to apply again the test of Sheridan's own works. An early opportunity to do so, indeed, was provided by the fact that Byron's *Monody* launched a Sheridan season at Drury Lane.

That those works might still inspire emulation, as well as supply the standard by which it could be found wanting, is attested by the *Monody's* account of Sheridan's most celebrated Parliamentary oration. This speech was made at the trial of Warren Hastings in 1788 and was subsequently replicated in Sheridan's play *Pizarro*, itself adapted from Kotzebue.[9] Among the twenty-four charges brought against Hastings was one that became the basis of Sheridan's rhetorical triumph: the Begums Charge centred on the allegation that Hastings had coerced the Nawab Wazir of Oudh into expropriating his own mother and grandmother of their land and treasure so that the East India Company itself might appropriate them.[10] Byron's *Monody* dramatically renders Sheridan's speech for the prosecution, endorsing the charges against Hastings's alleged colonialist excesses in India:

> When the loud cry of trampled Hindostan
> Arose to heaven in her appeal from Man,
> His was the thunder—his the avenging rod
> The wrath—the delegated voice of God!
> Which shook the nations through his lips—and blazed
> Till vanquished Senates trembled as they praised. (ll. 41–6)

Rather than merely reporting Sheridan's speech, Byron's *Monody* dramatizes it in terms of its impact on Sheridan's audience, which thereby incites a sympathetically similar response from Byron's audience. Sheridan thus comes through loud and clear.

Since Sheridan's individual virtues are available to be copied, while their composite is there as a critical ideal, Byron's *Monody* is evidently not modelling Drury Lane as a law against all doubling. Without the phenomenon of replication, after all, Sheridan's account of Garrick's acting as lost forever would apply to all cultural expression, and therefore to Sheridan's own theatrical art. Nor does the *Monody* seek, at the other extreme, to collapse difference into unity indiscriminately; that Byron's *Monody on Sheridan* takes issue with Sheridan's monody on Garrick on the very matter of replication, as we've seen, serves to distinguish them. Rather than condemning all replication or advocating it everywhere, the project of Drury Lane licensed by Byron's two addresses is a creative origination of doubles and a critical discrimination between legitimate doubles, such as new and old Drury, and illegitimate doubles, such as the officially innocent but unofficially guilty Hastings.

The epistemic scruples built into this project are evident in other divisions that we've already encountered, in addition to the contradiction between Byron and Sheridan's monodies: Drury Lane is not Covent Garden; producers and audiences of theatre are initially distinct; the two Druries are separate, in one sense, since one replaces the other; the fact that Byron's address insists on the importance of an abiding place underlying both theatres differentiates theatre from site; Sheridan's qualities are separate from one another, as are the groups within the audience identifying with them; his works do not add up to himself, but only to criteria for testing what doesn't; and, in consequence, Sheridan is distinct from absolutely everything and everybody else. Out of this matrix of qualified, segregated doubles, spanning both of Byron's addresses, emerges a comic plot that is a blueprint for a reformed stage, centred on Drury Lane. It goes roughly like this. The different voices within the address, comprising the corporate voice of the theatre and Byron's own, establish some harmony between Byron's two addresses, and this harmony exposes a contradiction between these addresses and Sheridan's monody on Garrick. This contradiction stages Sheridan's qualities as available for emulation, rather than lost forever, and the audience's imitation of them brings the two halves of the theatre together. It is this convergence that reconciles old and new Drury, and this reconciliation allows a certain accommodation between Sheridan and his works, as criteria of the emulation.

Insofar as this narrative is a programme for a reformed stage, its potential range of reference extends well beyond Sheridan and into the heart of Regency society itself. That society, after all, looks to the Prince Regent, who is a double of the King, who of course has two bodies. Does the Regent too? Well, he certainly has pretensions, and the aristocratic society that he leads parades its extravagances, especially after Waterloo. At the very moment when the periodical press takes off in an invigorating welter of 'twopenny trash', after Cobbett's innovations with his *Political Register* in early 1816,[11] Byron's *Monody,* in mid-1816, models a theatre programmed by its apprehension of doubles to expose imposture, as well as the usual suspects of vanity and folly. Such a project could be executed, to some extent, by the mordant social comedies of the Sheridan season immediately ensuing. Among the aristocratic impostures that this project might explode are, crucially, those deeply unflattering doubles of Byron forged by Lady Byron and Lady Caroline Lamb.[12] These gothic doubles had, in fact, reached critical mass after early 1816 and the very public collapse of Byron's marriage. As a consequence, the *Monody on Sheridan* was one of Byron's first exilic works.

So, as usual, Byron gets the last laugh. Bequeathing the formula for a new Drury Lane and leaving his own unwanted doubles within it, Byron, as the original, steps out of the frame and into a new realm. This realm is a posthumous life of infamy in Europe, which the new Drury Lane cannot encompass. What chiefly prevents it from doing so is indicated, perhaps, in a few lines about Sheridan in *English Bards and Scotch Reviewers*, published earlier, in 1809:

> Oh! SHERIDAN! if aught can move thy pen,
> Let Comedy assume her throne again;
> Abjure the mummery of German schools;
> Leave new Pizarros to translating fools;
> Give as the last memorial to the age,
> One classic drama, and reform the stage. (ll. 580–5)

Sheridan doesn't, of course, but his commission is clear: it is to resurrect a distinctly national drama. In the context of his failure to respond, Byron's opening address can be seen as assuming the mission itself, especially since it orbits Shakespeare so compulsively. There is further evidence of this conception of Drury Lane, as the 'national theatre', in the heavy programming of several of Shakespeare's plays, as well as Sheridan's, during the weeks after the reopening. Shakespeare's plays, of course, were contemporarily regarded as national assets because there was a broad consensus, even among writers of different political persuasions, that their inherent variety, including their status as both literature and drama, enabled them to address all parts of what thus became a single nation, united not only by these resources of the plays but also in this very consensus about their unifying power. Even though polarized political constituencies sometimes descried quite contrary agendas in Shakespeare's plays, the fact that they both did so constitutes another matter of consensus; no-one thought that the Bard was not political. On all these grounds, Shakespeare is recruited to the project of culturally consolidating Britain, in the company of Edgeworth and Scott, among others.

Despite this consensus, the notion of nation in the theatre is a charged one at this time, even if the issue of Britain as a problematically multinational nation is set aside. One word that serves to focus this charge is 'public' and it applies here in two respects. To advocate a fully national theatre, as Byron's addresses do, is to contradict the considerable lobby in favour of smaller and hence private theatres. Most prominent within this lobby is Joanna Baillie, whose preface 'To the Reader' in the third volume of her *Series of Plays* (1812) argues for three related departures in contemporary theatres: firstly, smaller stages in smaller theatres are required; secondly, a more intimate style of acting capable of communicating psychological nuance should be evolved; and thirdly, developments in theatrical lighting are necessary if such nuance, often expressed in actors' facial features, is to be visible. What Baillie envisages is the medium of cinema. In its absence, however, resources such as the facial close-up can be achieved only within theatres very different from the cavernous patent houses and other theatres modelled on them. Baillie's theory, as Catherine Burroughs has shown, is sophisticated and coherent; it is also implemented practically by Baillie's own plays, even though the ideal theatrical conditions for their production barely existed. Of especial importance for our purposes, however, is the timing of Baillie's manifesto. Coinciding with the reopening of Drury Lane, Baillie's address 'To the Reader' appears to be in debate with the new theatre and can thus be read as in dialogue with Byron's *Address*.

Against any such argument for a small, private theatre, Byron's *Address* asserts an inclusive, if incisive, national theatre, catering to a broad public by way of its Shakespearean offerings and utterly visible in its new beginning, just as it was in its spectacular demise by fire. What renders it so ultimately visible is the *Address* itself, practically performing the reopening and reflecting theoretically on how Drury Lane could not be other than it is because its differences from itself ultimately articulate its ongoing identity. The supreme irony here is the fact that Byron's own dramaturgical practice, unlike Baillie's, would, in the event, be quite inconsistent with his theory as it is expressed in both the *Address* and the *Monody*; Byronic theory within the *Address* invests in public theatre, but Byronic practice manifests itself as closet drama. If there is a general explanation of this discrepancy, it is that Byron's theory is highly theatrical, in the sense that it is directed at a particular theatre and in the sense that it is driven by specific theatrical occasions. But Byron's theatre theory, as expressed in his two addresses, is also inconsistent with itself, as we shall see.

Apart from the alternative model of private theatre, there is another factor complicating the notion of a national theatre and likewise focused on the term 'public'. This factor is the political affiliations of Drury Lane. Embodying these affinities is Sheridan himself, who was both owner-manager of Drury Lane and a Whig Member of Parliament; Samuel Whitbread, who effectively succeeded Sheridan as manager in 1811, continued this incarnation since he was also regarded as the leader of the Whigs in the Commons. These affinities extended further to several of the other public figures and businessmen who undertook the collective ownership of the new Drury Lane after the fire and who supervised its reconstruction. This political aspect of the new theatre was also perceived by the political competition, and some Tory newspapers, as Richard Lansdown has observed, detected an ambitious ideological venture in the cultural agenda of new Drury: the emphasis on Shakespeare's work was suspected as an attempt to render Shakespeare *parti pris* and thus to establish a Whiggish cultural hegemony, based on the Bard, across the whole of national culture.[13] To design a specifically national theatre is thus a controversial endeavour because, rather than despite, the fact that there is absolute consensus about Shakespeare's homogenizing powers. Who owns Shakespeare owns the rest of the nation. The public declaration in Byron's *Address* that new Drury will be a theatre dedicated to a national public can readily be understood as harbouring a secret design to privatize that public on behalf of a partial politics. More dangerous still is the possibility, hinted at in the *Address* and fully developed in the *Monody*, that Drury Lane might become an arena in which other national institutions and figures would be measured, with corrosive irony, against the doubles of their ideal selves. There is no danger to Byron himself in this arena, however. From this provocative national stage that he has helped to construct, Byron departs, effectively leaving the Committee of Drury Lane as he quits England.

the theatre of paparazzi: stalking abroad

Or does he? If we suppose that the *Monody* largely replicates the opening *Address*, then Byron indeed appears to walk off the very stage that he has elaborated; if, however, we suppose that the *Monody* does more than merely replicate the *Address*, a quite different blueprint of a theatre begins to emerge from the former text. Despite the evident continuities between the *Address* and *Monody*, there are grounds, internal and external, for distinguishing between them, precisely as the reformed Drury Lane considered so far would have us do. It is the *Monody* that vociferously proclaims this distinction. Although several voices, including Sheridan's, might be heard on the page, there is one voice that predominates on stage in 1816, and that is Byron's own. While the *Monody* was actually delivered by Mrs Sarah Davison, a well-known comic actress, the scandalous circumstances of Byron's departure amplify his contribution disproportionately, far beyond its utility in leveraging Sheridan's voice, far beyond its volume in the opening address and far beyond the level at which it can function as part of a corporate address, expressed on behalf of the theatre as a whole. The vocal parts of the *Monody* cannot be integrated into a whole, as can the vocal parts of the opening address, and, in fact, Leigh Hunt's review confirms this contradiction within the *Monody*, in an observation that would become a commonplace among Byron's reviewers:

> Lord Byron will never be skilful (sic) in addresses ... His talent does not lie so much in appealing to others, as in expressing himself. He does not make you so much a party as a witness ... With every disposition to praise the object of his verse, he will not succeed in keeping him before you; and with nothing whatsoever like egotism in the paltry sense of the word, he will chiefly be before you himself.[14]

Byron the messenger kills his own message, and in more ways than one: just as the *Monody* barely gets underway because of its compromised vocalization, so the conclusion of the *Monody*, about Sheridan being unique, is qualified by the fact that his singularity is shared, paradoxically, by Byron. These contradictions generate repercussions within the blueprint that the two addresses are elaborating. What the first reformed theatre, of carefully discriminated doubles, here helps to make manifest is another reformed theatre, organized on very different lines but depending on the first for its initial realization. Here Byron has a space.

This space, of course, is overseas, and I want to suggest that the *Monody* projects another version of Drury Lane that can follow Byron's massive personality there. How the *Monody* replicates Drury Lane in this way is in virtue of the fact that it already replicates the most celebrated monody of all, Milton's *Lycidas*. Several common factors, or analogues, suggest that

Byron's poem is citing Milton's, as we shall see. While Sheridan can thus be read as Lycidas, Byron is figured as the eloquent 'Swain' (l. 186) who is characterized at the very end of the poem as its grieving speaker. Until the final verse paragraph in Milton's poem, there has been a first-person narrator presiding, but then the narrative perspective is elevated to one remove, and that narrator and his preceding words are framed within a new third-person narrative:

> Thus sang the uncouth Swain to th'oaks and rills,
> While the still Morn went out with sandals gray;
> He touched the tender stops of various quills,
> With eager thought warbling his Doric lay:
> And now the Sun had stretched out all the hills,
> And now was dropped into the western bay;
> At last he rose, and twitched his mantle blue:
> Tomorrow to fresh woods and pastures new. (ll. 186–93)

There goes Byron, on the eve but emphatically without his Eve, turning his back on the sunset, singing his way to Italy, and thus leading the way. Whether the referent of the word 'He' (ll. 188 and 192) be the 'Swain' (l. 186), the 'Morn' (l. 187), or even the 'Sun' (l. 190), that referent becomes Byron in the relationship that the *Monody* configures with this poem. Thus cast, Byron becomes not merely an object within the *Monody*, potentially replacing Sheridan, but also an object that can be seen, heard and even followed as he alluringly recedes. Whereas Lycidas and Sheridan are dead, Byron is sensationally alive and so can be successfully tracked by the resources of Milton's maritime monody as it obsessively ranges across and under the sea, seeking its lost object, before finding and following a similar figure, if not a substitute. There is, moreover, another common factor in Milton and Byron's poems, aside from an identity as monodies and some shared personnel: in Milton's poem, a corrupt clergy is deplored, while in Byron's, envious calumniators of Sheridan, and implicitly of Byron himself, are the object of censure. Distinct passages are given over to this exercise in both poems, at ll. 59–88 in the *Monody* and at ll. 112–31 in *Lycidas*. Although these are monodies, they operate in stereo.

So, this emergent alternative blueprint envisages a theatre that might follow and encompass Byron as he goes, even as far as 'Hindostan', where Sheridan's rhetoric is declared to have followed Warren Hastings. There is thus a sense in which the new Drury launched in 1812 is being relaunched as a ship in 1816, as an extension of England that can travel to any clime. Along with Walter Scott's review of Canto III of *Childe*

Harold's Pilgrimage, which identifies Byron as a 'gallant vessel near the breakers', it is Drury Lane that, in the same year, puts the 'ship' into 'his Lordship'.[15] This equation between 'the wooden O' and 'the wooden world', already established by the naval extravaganzas at Sadler's Wells, is corroborated by at least three intriguing items of external evidence. The first item is that the arrangement at Sadler's Wells, whereby the theatre framed and contained ships, could be found in reversed form in the contemporary Royal Navy, as commanders, notably Nelson, encouraged amateur theatricals on their ships. Designed largely to alleviate the boredom produced by long periods at sea, the theatricals on just one ship could be as varied as those in the patent theatres in London: the *Royal George*, for example, in the Mediterranean in 1807, housed three acting companies, which catered to the entire social spectrum of the ship with their range of cultural offerings. Performing on alternate nights, the wardroom officers staged *Henry IV*, the midshipmen acted 'the genteel comedy' *The Poor Gentleman*, and the lower deck put on Foote's farce *The Mayor of Garratt*.[16] Although on-board amateur theatricals were not new in this period, the naval historian N.A.M. Rodger implies that they were required more urgently after 1793, when the Royal Navy was deployed to impose an economic blockade on France.[17] One effect of this form of economic warfare, and of the French retaliation in kind, was to extend naval tours of duty colossally, as ships spent so much more time at sea, disrupting the enemy's trade and protecting convoys sailing to and from British ports. Theatres could therefore be ships because ships were often theatres. While the former equation hovers implicitly within much contemporary writing about the theatre, it is sometimes formulated explicitly, as in the following account of Drury Lane in 1808, before its reconstruction: 'Over the stage is a double range of galleries, called flies, containing machinery, and where the greatest part of the scenery is worked; but which, from the number of blocks, wheels, and ropes crossing each other in every direction, give it very much the appearance of a ship's deck.'[18] The scenery is here the sails, taking us elsewhere.

Bearing more precisely on the equation that Byron's international Drury Lane intimates between itself and the ship is a third item of context. This context is a contemporaneous change in naval protocol: in 1811, the newly installed Regent proposed that His Majesty's ships should henceforth be launched by women.[19] While the national theatre at Drury Lane was launched in 1812 by Robert William Elliston, reciting Byron's address, this international theatre was launched in 1816 by Mrs Davison, delivering Byron's *Monody*. From the former theatre, Byron is absent; in the latter, he's as present as he ever is.

A pressing question transpires here. Since the inclusive, melodramatic, international Drury Lane is projected from within the analytical, comic, national Drury Lane, which judiciously creates and tests such doubles, can it be collapsed back into it in a moment of resolution and reconciliation? Is there a means of harmonizing the two blueprints within the first one? I think not. There are two impediments to such a resolution. The first is that the contradiction between these versions of Drury Lane replicates the polarization of Romantic theatre between so-called legitimate and illegitimate drama: just as the advertised national theatre is correlated with the literary drama of Shakespeare and Sheridan's plays, so a theatre encompassing scenes beyond the national boundaries and identity is generally associated with the vulgar forms of gothic drama and oriental melodrama. Although it is the elevated form of the monody, in the intersection of Byron and Milton's poems, that licenses an international perspective at Drury Lane, the kind of drama that is available to track Byron within that dimension is anything but exalted. Only a drama that would amplify, by its own conventions, those gothic and melodramatic properties already manifest in Byron's public persona could follow him to foreign parts.

One story that might be told to accommodate these two blueprints, specifically across this impediment of illegitimacy, is Moody's compelling argument that legitimate and illegitimate drama infiltrate one another in the post-Waterloo era of intense political consciousness. Applying this argument to this case would even benefit the argument itself, because this application would reveal the larger, international dimension of illegitimacy that contributes to the crisis in, though not of, legitimacy on London stages. It is the restoration of the monarchies at the Congress of Vienna that constitutes the broader European crisis pulsating within the theatres of London. How legitimate can the *ancien régime* now be? This historical argument about drama, however, cannot, in return for the broader context of illegitimacy afforded by Byron's addresses, defuse the tension between Byron's two Druries, because they can be seen to respond to different imperatives: the demand for private theatres is answered by the programme for a national theatre; this demand for a national theatre is in turn answered by the programme for an international theatre.

The second impediment to the reconciliation of Byron's blueprints is that the first impediment devolves on to the even larger cultural problem, posed by a prevalent cultural nationalism, of accommodating the extremes of the individual self and the further reaches of empire within the nation, as a common home. It is just such an urgent melodrama that seems to be invoked in the reference of Byron's *Monody* to the trial of Warren Hastings: the hero Sheridan appears to use English law to combat the villain Hastings on behalf of a broken oriental family, which is thus embraced. Yet there is powerful resistance to this cosy, melodramatic scenario, at the very juncture where the *Monody* goes international. Replaying Sheridan's triumphant speech at Hastings' impeachment, Byron's *Monody* deflects any implication that nation can be a remedy for the ills of its own empire. The passage in the *Monody* rendering this speech, which I quoted above, emphasizes the fact that Sheridan's response to the 'loud cry of trampled Hindostan' (l. 41) is universal in its authority and address. Rather than deriving from the laws of the nation, the authority of Sheridan's speech emanates directly from the deity, as 'the delegated voice of God' (l. 44). The addressees of the speech, furthermore, are not confined to Westminster Hall, at the heart of the nation, where the impeachment proceedings took place: they encompass, after all, not one but several 'Senates' (l. 46), and not one but several 'nations' (l. 45). In place of any claim that the British nation can bring the British empire to book, by making it responsible to the laws of the nation, there is in Byron's account of Sheridan's speech a distinct implication that such imperial crimes would not have been committed in the first place had those national laws been intrinsically adequate. This implication is partly prompted, and verified, by the fact that Hastings was ultimately acquitted. Self and empire are accordingly not permitted to come home to the nation at Byron's Drury Lane, and Byron's national and international models of the theatre thus remain apart.

So large is this second impediment posed by Byron's *Monody* to the reconciliation of these theatrical models that it figures prominently in others of Byron's works. Whereas Edgeworth and Scott's writings, as we have noted, trace just this convergence of self and empire, minus the venue of Drury Lane, Byron's verse abjures and reverses it; the norm of nation is analyzed back into its brilliant but sordid components of ego and empire. This recurrent Byronic critique would figure subsequently in *Don Juan*, especially in the Dedication and its relationship to the following cantos. Concentrating on part of the English literary establishment and its complicity with the political establishment, the Dedication ironizes that composite institution of the nation by asserting that England is effectively like the rest of Europe, as a product of raw historical forces:

Europe has slaves, allies, kings, armies still,
And Southey lives to sing them very ill.

Meantime, Sir Laureate, I proceed to dedicate
In honest simple verse this song to you. (*Don Juan* Dedication 16–17)

What ensues is a comic epic that, inter alia, atomizes English pretensions to superiority across a European canvas which features different manners but also many common impulses. There is a similar dissolution of England, and hence nation, also at the beginning of one of Byron's works, in *The Corsair*. Published in 1814, at a moment equidistant from the *Address* and the *Monody*, this romance opens as follows:

> O'er the glad waters of the dark blue sea,
> Our thoughts as boundless, and our souls as free,
> Far as the breeze can bear, the billows foam,
> Survey our empire and behold our home!
> These are our realms, no limits to their sway—
> Our flag the sceptre all who meet obey.
> Ours the wild life in tumult still to range
> From toil to rest, and joy in every change. (CPW III, 150; ll. 1–8)

Until the penultimate line, this verse is a compelling candidate to replace the national anthem. It certainly leaves Thomson's 'Rule Britannia' standing. Although the Preface to the poem, and the dedication to Thomas Moore, voice a distinct anti-colonialist sentiment, the poem proper begins with such driving ebullience that one might be swept, on a first reading, into a moment of patriotic romance, as just indicated. Once we reach that penultimate line, however, it is evident that what we might have imagined as the voice of the nation, in which we have a share, is in fact the raving of a band of pirates. England's proud nationhood is thus equated with indiscriminate, international buccaneering; rather than being organically centred in a single hallowed place or region, 'we' are cast as a ragged assortment of itinerant opportunists. The only hope for us is that these pirates are soon characterized as noble outlaws, and so we might be identified accordingly. There is a lurking implication, however, that we remain as different from these noble pirates as we originally supposed that we were from any kind of pirates; our very ignorance of our piratical identity convicts us as ignoble buccaneers.

early post-colonial tragedy?

Even as the polarization of Romantic theatre, between legitimate and illegitimate, prevents Byron's two blueprints from being reconciled, because together they express that polarization, the fact that they do so enables them to be a reflection on it, formulating this division and so imbuing Drury Lane with an acute consciousness of its own dialectical character. Charged with this awareness, Drury Lane becomes not just a ground contested between two agendas, but also the ground on which that contest is conducted; it is a debatable land,[20] especially since its scope is so potentially expansive, and also a debating chamber. After Byron's two addresses, this debate is enacted, very practically, both in the commitment of the theatre to the legitimate repertoire, despite adverse financial consequences, and in the increasing profile of oriental melodramas and gothic dramas, which depict a wider world of alien and exotic scenes. There is little in the way of oriental melodrama at Drury Lane until 1814, when Thomas Dibdin's *The Ninth Statue; or, the Irishman in Bagdad* was staged. Although this play effectively introduced a melodramatic phase at Drury Lane, there were rather more such plays produced at Covent Garden in this period, and far more at the Surrey Theatre. Given the contradictory imperatives of Byron's two addresses, the fact that there were fewer of these lucrative melodramas at Drury Lane, in the context of a heavy 'classical' repertoire from which the returns were much more modest, not only suggests that there is a meta-theatrical debate underway but also dramatizes it right there, within the theatre. Covent Garden struggles with the same predicament, but without the Byronic backdrop to bring it into theoretical relief.

It is to such melodramas that Elaine Hadley has attributed the capacity to constellate empire, self and nation in an intimate if fraught ménage.[21] Hadley's argument is that the oriental societies in these plays frame a critique of British aristocracy under the Regency by demonstrating a melodramatic investment in the bonds of family that is not shared by an increasingly decadent, distracted and therefore abstracted aristocracy. The oriental despots in these melodramas are obvious analogues of the Regent, and they are typically defeated and then displaced by the family reunion of their victims at the end. So alien has home become that abroad is more like home as it was and should be. By juxtaposing empire and nation, to reveal the shortcomings of the latter in particular, these melodramas constitute a variation on Byron's critique of imperialism and thereby dispel one of the two impediments to a reconciliation between Byron's theatrical agendas. The irony and comedy of the national theatre meet the melodrama of the international theatre in a critique of human bondage and a valorization of human bonding, and they meet, furthermore, in London theatres. Perfect. But the reconciliation still doesn't work, because these plays fall foul of the other impediment already considered: oriental melodramas such as Matthew Lewis's *Timour the Tartar* (1811) and John Kerr's *Histerkan* (1816), as productions low on words and high on spectacle, do not satisfy the stipulation of literary quality emphasized particularly in Byron's *Address*. Once again, the *Address* and the *Monody* make incommensurable demands.

There may, however, be one play and production that offers a resolution of national and international Druries. Byron's *Marino Faliero*, like the *Monody on the Death of Sheridan*, was written in Italy and performed at Drury Lane. Unlike the *Monody*, however, this play actually describes home as abroad and abroad as home. Voyaging geographically along the sea lanes of Britain's empire, *Marino Faliero* also travels historically, until it meets and retraces the sea lanes of that other maritime empire, Venice; the play then reverses its progress, back to England, and to Drury Lane, where it is produced by Elliston, who originally delivered Byron's opening *Address*. But there has been a crucial shift in genre in the meantime. Tragedy, rather than the comedy or melodrama of Byron's two Druries, is the mode in which empire returns palpably to the nation, as the Venetian and Assyrian emperors in Byron's plays discover: Faliero, Foscari and Sardanapalus all confront this tragedy of empire coming home.[22] Despite the evolving prevalence of tragedy in Byron's plays after *Manfred*, this twisting of genre continues within them: Marilyn Butler has persuasively reread *Sardanapalus* as an 'intellectual comedy', and I have argued elsewhere that almost all of the plays, as well as being political tragedies, are comedies of self-censorship.[23] Behind all of Byron's theatrically averse dramas, then, there stands a body of theory that is itself highly theatrical, and the generic contortions of these plays might well be read as a creative response to the contradictions in this theory that its theatrical immediacy engenders.

But what of *Marino Faliero*, where we left it? The play has sailed from England to Italy, after Byron, and then back again, into Elliston's production. But then, disaster strikes! Byron protests passionately, denouncing this theatrical doubling and summoning *Marino Faliero* back. Why? Well, this final destination of the play within the nation, on stage, upsets any equipoise between national and international Druries. Only by calling the play back, and thus reactivating its oscillation between national and international dimensions, between England and Italy, can Byron restore this tense equipoise. To summon the play is effectively to float and displace its theatre, so that Drury Lane modulates into a sea lane. If self and empire are ever to be theatrically accommodated within the nation, in the form of early post-colonial tragedy, that theatre must, indeed, be mobile. So Drury Lane may well be an address created by Byron's theatrical addresses, but it is not figured merely as a place, such as Covent Garden, and thus as a kind of Drury Land. This Theatre Royal also exists relationally and dynamically on a right of way; it is 'Drury Lane'.

notes

I thank Jane Stabler and Barbara Goff for their help with this chapter, Simon Bainbridge for a useful conversation, and Jeffrey Cox for assistance from behind the scenes.

1. See, for example, Burroughs 1997.
2. Hoeveler 1990, 162–8; Wolfson 1991; and Franklin 1992.
3. Stabler 2002, 64–96.
4. See Moody 2000.
5. See Hadley 1995; Hays and Nikolopoulou 1996.
6. 'Parenthetical Address, by Dr Plagiary'. *CPW* III, 32–3.
7. See Simpson 1999.
8. As Byron's *Address* recalls Dr Johnson's 'Prologue', which marks the opening of Garrick's Drury Lane in 1747.
9. Sheridan 1975.
10. See Carlson 1996.
11. Cobbett supplemented the larger *Register* with a pamphlet version.
12. See Soderholm 1996, 41–101.
13. Lansdown 1992, 20–3.
14. Reiman 1972, 1002–3.
15. Scott 1816, 206.
16. Rodger 2004, 505.
17. Rodger 2004, 526. There is still much scope for scholarly work on the nautical/naval connection with Romantic drama.
18. Ackermann 1808, 228–9.
19. See the section on 'Launch' on the Royal Navy website.
20. A term designating the Anglo-Scottish borderlands, popularized by Scott.
21. Hadley 1999.
22. Diego Saglia (2005) has recently proposed the next instalment of this trajectory, whereby 'historical verse tragedy' (99) in the 1820s articulates 'the fictional proto-liberal polity' and does so on the basis that 'Words are crucial to (its) foundation' (111). Over Byron's tragedies this argument falters. Only by sidelining the largely closeted manifestation of Byron's tragedies, along with the debates about that closeting, can Saglia's narrative proceed smoothly. If 'Words are crucial' in this matter, how words exist, between page and stage, and *where* they exist, must also be crucial.
23. Butler 1992 and Simpson 1998.

works cited and suggestions for further reading

Ackermann, R. *The Microcosm of London; or, London in Miniature*. Vol. 1. London: T. Bensley, 1808.

Baillie, Joanna. *A Series of Plays, 1798–1812*. Ed. D.H. Reiman. Vol. 3. New York: Garland, 1977.

Baker, David Erskine. *Biographia Dramatica*. London: Longman & Co, 1812.

Brewer, William D. 'Joanna Baillie and Lord Byron'. *Keats-Shelley Journal* 44 (1995): 165–81.

Burroughs, Catherine. *Closet Stages: Joanna Baillie and the Theater Theory of British Romantic Women Writers.* Philadelphia: University of Pennsylvania Press, 1997.

——, ed. *Women in British Romantic Theatre: Drama, Performance and Society 1790–1840.* Cambridge: Cambridge University Press, 2000.

Butler, Marilyn. 'John Bull's Other Kingdom: Byron's Intellectual Comedy'. *Studies in Romanticism* 31.3 (1992): 281–94.

Carlson, Julie A. *In the Theatre of Romanticism: Coleridge, Nationalism, Women.* Cambridge: Cambridge University Press, 1994.

——. 'Trying Sheridan's Pizarro'. *Texas Studies in Literature and Language* 38. 3–4 (1996): 359–78.

Christensen, Jerome. *Lord Byron's Strength: Romantic Writing and Commercial Society.* Baltimore and London: Johns Hopkins University Press, 1993.

Cobbett, William. *Cobbett's Weekly Political Register.* 89 vols. London: W. Cobbett, 1802–35.

Colman, George, the younger. *The poor gentleman; a comedy.* London: Longman & Co, 1806.

Cox, Jeffrey. 'The Ideological Tack of Nautical Melodrama'. *Melodrama: the Cultural Emergence of a Genre.* Eds Michael Hays and Anastasia Nikolopoulu. New York: St Martin's Press, 1996.

Cox, Jeffrey N. and Michael Gamer, eds. *The Broadview Anthology of Romantic Drama.* Peterborough: Broadview Press, 2003.

Davis, Tracy C. *The Economics of the British Stage, 1800–1914.* Cambridge: Cambridge University Press, 2000.

Dick, Alex. 'Romantic Drama and the Performative: A Reassessment'. *European Romantic Review* 14.1 (2001): 97–115.

Dibdin, Thomas. *The Ninth Statue; or, the Irishman in Bagdad.* London: John Miller, 1814.

Donkin, Ellen. *Getting into the Act: Women Playwrights in London 1776–1829.* London: Routledge, 1995.

Foote, Samuel. *The Mayor of Garratt: A farce.* London: W. Simpkin and R. Marshall, 1820.

Franklin, Caroline. *Byron's Heroines.* Oxford: Clarendon Press, 1992.

Genuine Rejected Addresses, Presented to the Committee of Management for Drury-Lane Theatre. London: B. McMillan, 1812.

Hadley, Elaine. *Melodramatic Tactics: Theatricalized Dissent in the English Marketplace, 1800–1885.* Stanford, CA: Stanford University Press, 1995.

——, 'Home as Abroad: Orientalism and Occidentalism in Early English Stage Melodrama'. *Texas Studies in Literature and Language* 41.4 (1999): 330–50.

Hays, Michael and Anastasia Nikolopoulou, eds. *Melodrama: the Cultural Emergence of a Genre.* New York: St Martin's Press, 1996.

Hoeveler, Diane Long. *Romantic Androgyny: The Women Within.* University Park: Pennsylvania State University Press, 1990.

Jewett, William. *Fatal Autonomy: Romantic Drama and the Rhetoric of Agency.* Ithaca, NY: Cornell University Press, 1997.

Johnson, Samuel .'Prologue spoken by Mr Garrick at the opening of the Theatre in Drury Lane 1747'. *Samuel Johnson.* Ed. Donald Greene. Oxford: Oxford University Press, 1984. 10–12.

Kerr, John. *Histerkan; or The Assassin of the Mountain.* London: John Osler, 1816.

Lansdown, Richard. *Byron's Historical Dramas*. Oxford: Clarendon Press, 1992.

Lewis, Matthew Gregory. *Timour the Tartar. A grand romantic melo-drama*. London: Lowndes & Hobbs, 1811.

Milton, John. *The Complete Poems*. Ed. John Leonard. London: Penguin, 1998.

Moody, Jane. *Illegitimate Theatre in London, 1770–1840*. Cambridge: Cambridge University Press, 2000.

Nicoll, Allardyce. *A History of English Drama, 1660–1900*. 6 vols. Cambridge: Cambridge University Press, 1952–9.

Reiman, Donald H., ed. *The Romantics Reviewed; Contemporary Reviews of British Romantic Writers*. Part B, Vol. 3. New York: Garland , 1972.

Rodger, N.A.M. *The Command of the Ocean: A Naval History of Britain 1649–1815*. London: Penguin , 2004.

Royal Navy website <http://www.royal.navy.uk>.

Saglia, Diego. 'Mediterranean Unrest: 1820s Verse Tragedies and Revolutions in the South'. *Romanticism* 11.1 (2005): 99–111.

Scott, Walter. Review of *Childe Harold's Pilgrimage*, Canto III, *Quarterly Review* 31 (October 1816): 172–208.

Sheridan, Richard Brinsley. 'Verses to the Memory of Garrick'. *The Plays and Poems of Richard Brinsley Sheridan*. Ed. R. Compton Rhodes. Vol. 3. Oxford: Blackwell, 1928. 211–16.

——. *Sheridan's Plays*. Ed. Cecil Price. Oxford: Oxford University Press, 1975.

Simpson, Michael. *Closet Performances: Political Exhibition and Prohibition in the Dramas of Byron and Shelley*. Stanford, CA: Stanford University Press, 1998.

——. 'Re-OPening After the Old Price Riots: War and Peace at Drury Lane'. *Texas Studies in Literature and Language* 41.4 (1999): 378–402.

Smith, James and Horace. *Rejected Addresses: or, the New Theatrum Poetarum*. London: John Murray, 1812.

Soderholm, James. *Fantasy, Forgery and the Byron Legend*. Lexington: University of Kentucky Press, 1996.

Stabler, Jane. *Burke to Byron, Barbauld to Baillie, 1790–1830*. Basingstoke: Palgrave, 2002.

Wolfson, Susan J. '"A Problem Few Dare Imitate": Sardanapalus and "Effeminate Character"'. *ELH* 58.4 (1991): 867–902.

10
byron and war
sketches of spain: love and war
in *childe harold's pilgrimage*

philip shaw

I

Freud's immediate response to the declaration of war was an unexpected one. One would have supposed that a pacific savant of fifty-eight would have greeted it with simple horror, as so many did. On the contrary, his first response was rather one of youthful enthusiasm, apparently a reawakening of the military ardours of boyhood ... He was quite carried away, could not think of any work, and spent his time discussing the events of the day with his brother Alexander ... He was excitable, irritable, and made slips of the tongue all day long.[1]

you know ... I am no *coward*, nor would I shrink from Danger on a proper occasion, indeed Life has too little valuable for me, to make Death horrible; I am not insensible to Glory, & even hope before I am at *Rest*, to see some service in a military Capacity, yet I cannot conquer my repugnance to a Life absolutely & exclusively devoted to Carnage, or bestow any appellation in my Idea applicable to a *mercenary* Soldier, but the *Slave of Blood* ... When you return from the Field bring me the *Scalp* of Massena, or the chin of Bonaparte.

BLJ I, 114, 118

there has been a *thirty years war* and a *Seventy years war*—was there ever a *Seventy or a thirty years peace*?—or was there even a day's *Universal* peace—except perhaps in China—where they have found out the miserable happiness of a stationary & unwarlike mediocrity?

BLJ IX, 30

Perhaps the first thing one notices on reading Byron's commentaries on war is the impetuous, contradictory, and provocative tone with which Byron writes. Like Freud, over one hundred years later, Byron is both attracted to and disgusted by war, impelled on the one hand by youthful 'ardour', constrained on the other by 'repugnance to a Life absolutely & exclusively devoted to Carnage'. In both cases, as the psychoanalytic critic Jacqueline Rose suggests, 'the familiar destructiveness of war represents not, as is commonly supposed, finality but uncertainty, a hovering on the edge of what, like death, can never be totally known'.[2] For Freud, the coming of war thus marks a return to the instability of adolescence; for Byron, it disrupts 'the miserable happiness of a stationary & unwarlike mediocrity'. Above all, and somewhat surprisingly, war is conceived as the antithesis of death or '*Rest*'.

In light of this last point, it is worth bearing in mind the critical judgement of Byron as a poet of movement. According to this view, no sooner has a position been attained, be it a truth claim, a moral proposition or a statement about the self, than the poetry moves forwards, allowing qualifications, modifications, and refutations to proliferate. 'For Byron,' as Jerome McGann observes, 'the dialectic of loss and gain is endless, nor does it culminate in any "higher order" or synthesis.'[3] His poetry, unlike that, say, of Wordsworth, seems dedicated to the art of self-contestation, dissolving certainties so that it may be truthful to flux. For Byron, the world simply is a place of doubt, uncertainty, and change. By remaining faithful to this truth, however arbitrary, the poet commits to life and not to death. But this leaves us with a peculiar ethical dilemma: is it paradoxical, even perverse, of Byron to regard war as a matter of life and not of death?

Freud's essay 'Why War?' written in 1932, confronts us with a similarly unpalatable proposition. While Freud is under no illusions about the futility of war, he remains convinced that war has its 'advantages' as well as its 'perils'; like the civilizing process, we owe to it 'the best of what we have become as well as a good part of what we suffer from'.[4] As Freud comments a little earlier in his essay, love and hate 'scarcely ever operate in isolation' (Freud 1985, 356), and the satisfaction of 'destructive impulses' is frequently 'facilitated by their admixture with others of an erotic and idealistic kind' (357). The destructive energies of war, in other words, are intimately bound with the procreative energies of love, whether this is seen in the sexualized metaphors applied to weaponry, in the rhetoric of father- and motherlands, or in the phenomenon of victors mourning the loss of their antagonists.

In Byron's war poetry, which comprises a significant portion of his corpus, we encounter a similar preoccupation with the intermixture of love and death. My focus in this chapter will be on the Spanish stanzas in Canto I of *Childe Harold's Pilgrimage*. Inspired by Byron's first-hand impressions of the Spanish struggle against French occupation during the summer of 1809, Canto I of *Childe Harold* has generated a significant amount of critical attention, from William Borst's *Lord Byron's First Pilgrimage* (1948) to Gordon Kent Thomas's *Lord Byron's Iberian Pilgrimage* (1983) and, most recently, from Diego Saglia's *Byron and Spain* (1996) and *Poetic Castles in Spain* (2000) to Richard Cronin's *The Politics of Romantic Poetry* (2000) and Simon Bainbridge's *British Poetry and the Revolutionary and Napoleonic Wars* (2003). Books by Jerome McGann (1968), Carl Woodring (1970) and Jerome Christensen (1993) have also looked in detail at Byron's treatment of the conflict in Spain.[5]

Central to these studies is a concern with Byron's alleged inconsistencies. William Borst, for example, maintains that 'It is vain ... to look for any completely consistent attitude toward the war in *Childe Harold*, for the first canto is a loosely connected series of reflections representing opinions held at several distinct times' (Borst 1948, 43). Carl Woodring and Jerome McGann have also drawn attention to Byron's 'ambiguous, even contradictory attitudes' (McGann 1968, 43), his 'indecisiveness' (Woodring 1970, 155) and 'growing sense of bafflement and helplessness' (McGann 1968, 53). And in *The Politics of Romantic Poetry*, Richard Cronin observes how the Peninsular War 'prompts reflections so various that they end in bewilderment' (Cronin 2000, 135).

In seeking to account for the poem's inconsistencies, most modern commentators follow William Borst's early focus on the complexities of Byron's political position, noting that as a supporter of the Whig party the poet was conditioned to oppose the Tory government's war with France, yet could see in the Spanish uprising a struggle for national independence and liberty worthy of his support. Byron's distrust of his country's war policy was confirmed by the disastrous outcome of the Convention of Cintra, which followed the defeat of the French at Vimeiro in Portugal. Signed on 30 August 1808, the peace treaty granted free passage to the French, leaving the Peninsula open to further threats of invasion. When, as predicted, Napoleon marched into Spain to stamp out resistance a few months later, Tories and Whigs alike were united in sympathy for the Spanish cause. But this initial period of enthusiasm was short-lived. In the wake of Wellesley's (later Lord Wellington) withdrawal from Spain into Portugal following his dubious victory at Talavera in July 1809, and the destruction of the Spanish forces at Thames and Ocana in November of that year, Byron, in common with many of his peers, came to regard the prosecution of the war as costly indulgence.[6] By 1811, however, Byron's attitude to the war and, in particular, to Wellesley, had again changed, as the following note, appended to *Childe Harold* confirms: 'The late exploits of Lord Wellington have effaced the follies of Cintra. He has, indeed, done wonders' (*CPW* II, 188).[7]

In one important sense, the poem's ideological uncertainties may be related to the Byronic investment in movement, in this case to the jerky, unpredictable rhythms of history. As Richard Cronin suggests, it is literally the case that Byron's journey through the Iberian Peninsula would not have been possible were it not for the early successes of the British forces. His stay in Seville and Cadiz in the summer of 1809, for example, could not have been accomplished six months earlier when the former town had fallen to the French and the latter was under siege. The composition of *Childe Harold's Pilgrimage* therefore owes its being to the progress of the war and any attempt to dissect its attitude to the conflict must take account of this underlying irony. As Cronin goes on to state, while Harold in Canto II 'affects indifference to military matters' and is left 'unmov'd' by 'Actium, Lepanto, fatal Trafalgar', delighting not 'in themes of bloody fray' (Cronin 2000, 129), the truth is that the 'space within which Harold savours his literary emotions is a space that has been won for him by the "well-reev'd guns" of the frigate that he is sailing on' (129–30).

While Cronin admits that it is 'his own position as an uninvolved spectator' that the poem 'eventually turns to scrutinize' (135–6), Simon Bainbridge goes further in claiming that Byron is 'critical of the "imaginative consumption of war" rather than representative of it' (Bainbridge 2003, 173). Together with Saglia, Bainbridge pays particular attention to the ways in which the war was presented to the British public in fictional forms such as drama and romance. Tory writers, for example, were apt to compare the struggle against Napoleon with the 'holy' war waged by Roderick against the Moors. Buoyed along by the rhetoric of chivalry, the leaders of the expeditionary force were described as 'Knights' defending the hierarchies of the *ancien régime* as well the contemporary claims of national liberty and independence.[8]

That the romance mode was widely accepted as a vehicle for the presentation of the war becomes clear when we consider that Byron's self-declared *Romaunt* was regarded by at least one reviewer as 'a perfect anomaly in the annals of chivalry'. For rather than celebrating the nation's prowess in arms, the Childe

> arraigns wars, generally and indiscriminately, confounding the just with the unjust, the defensive with the offensive, the preservative with the destructive, not with the judgement of a sage, but with the settled moroseness of a misanthrope; victories, though gained by courage exerted in the best of causes, excite only the sarcastic sneers of this querulous vagabond; and the profession of a soldier, deemed honourable by wise and good men, is the subject of his ridicule and contempt.[9]

As Bainbridge comments, in 'his anomalous romance, Byron had made the genre a vehicle for anti-war sentiment, and specifically ridiculed the failure of the British leaders to live up to the chivalric roles that were being scripted for them' (Bainbridge 2003, 171).

Bainbridge goes on to present a forceful and persuasive account of Byron's abilities as an anti-war poet, contrasting his example with the efforts of the establishment poets John Wilson Croker, Walter Scott, and Robert Southey, all of whom took up their pens in support of the Peninsular campaigns. Like Cronin, however, Bainbridge does not go on to consider that part of Byron's mind which remains half in love with the painful pleasures of war. As Tim Webb has noted, Byron, though frequently critical of the motivations and conduct of wars was not immune to dreams of military glory, from the young man who saw himself as the head of a military troop ('Byron's blacks') to the would-be combatant of the Greek war of independence. These glimpses of the man of action inform a number of Byron's letters and poems.[10] It is telling, for example, that the pirates in *The Corsair* commit to a 'wild life in tumult still to range / From toil to rest, and joy in every change' (*CPW* III, 150; ll. 7–8), regarding 'the approaching fight' as something to 'woo' (l. 17) and turning 'what some deem danger to delight' (l. 18). Might the contradictions of the Spanish stanzas be a product less of political confusion than of psychic ambiguity? To discover what Byron is all about in his treatment of war it seems necessary to recall the comparison with Freud with which I began. For both poet and analyst, war is, quite simply, a mode of contradiction involving the scandalous intertwining of opposing desires, chiefly love and hate. Thus, while opposition to war makes sense from a moral and/or political point of view, a part of the mind, call it the unconscious, remains in thrall to war's visceral charge.[11]

II

To understand the paradoxical consistency of *Childe Harold's Pilgrimage* Canto I, let us turn first of all to that section of the poem in which the anti-war sentiment is most evident. Here I will look specifically at stanzas 33–44, stanzas that chart a poet's passage from Portugal to Spain and a poem's journey from peace to war.

The river Guadiana, one of the longest streams in the Iberian Peninsula, flows westward through south-eastern Portugal and south-central Spain to the Atlantic Ocean. In Byron's poem it flows also through time: a 'bleeding stream' (I, 34, 9) linking the fate of 'Moor and knight' (I, 34, 6) in the medieval period with that of the Napoleonic and Allied forces in the present day. Blood flows through the poem, linking past conflicts with those of the present. In accordance with this long temporal view, the following stanza opens with an apostrophe to 'lovely Spain! renown'd, romantic land!' (I, 35, 1), and a recollection of the eighth-century Christian leader Pelayo, whose defeat of the Moors at Covadonga ushered in the 800 year holy war known as the Reconquest. Nested within this apparent celebration of the triumph of Christendom, however, is an allusion to one of the most mordant books of the Old Testament, the *Ecclesiastes* in which Solomon laments the fate of the wealthy and the wise, the weak and the strong; for 'time and chance happen to them all' (9.11). In Byron's version, both 'Paynim turban and the Christian crest' thus fall prey to sudden falls, 'Mix'd' alike (I, 34, 9) in time's sanguine flow. With its anticipation of contemporary carnage, the allusion offers a subtle corrective to the lazy parallelisms of John Wilson Croker, whose pro-war poem *The Battle of Talavera* (1809) seeks to conceal the horror of battle through allusion to the chivalric gloss of the Spanish Reconquest.[12]

Byron's attitude to the misappropriation of chivalry in the Napoleonic context is neatly conveyed in the stanzas that follow. Firstly, in stanza 36, he comments on how the epic dimensions of the hero's fate dwindle, over time, to a 'peasant's plaint' (I, 36, 4). When 'granite moulders' and 'records fail', when 'Volume, Pillar' or 'Pile' can no longer be relied on to preserve the amplitude of the great, *then* 'the Mighty shrink into a song!' (I, 36, 3–6). Jerome McGann notes an allusion here to 2 Samuel 1.19: 'Thy glory, O Israel, is slain upon thy high places! How are the mighty fallen!' In one sense, as Kelsall has argued, Byron's understanding of the cyclical nature of history reflects the dominant Whig ideology of the time.[13] But whilst with one part of his mind the poet appears to discern patterns in the chaos of history, with another he remains true to his paradoxical faith in flux. Thus, it is possible to read the poem's consciousness of the ends of empire, which extends in Canto II to the decline of ancient Greece, and in Canto III to the fall of Napoleonic France, as a reversal of the formal ascent from oral 'song' to written epic. The end of empire, in other words, marks a return to the fructifying compost of literary culture, and so to the fictive, unpredictable origins of imperial history.

In this stanza, then, Byron's sympathies are with the lyric remnants of history, with that which remains *after* the trumpets have sounded. But even as the spoils of war are counted amongst the vanities of human wishes, the poem attends to the enduring appeal of chivalric discourse. Chivalry, after all, is a potent tool of bellicist ideology, and the next stanza draws on one of its most commonly deployed devices, the rhetorical question: 'Say, is [Chivalry's] voice more feeble than of yore, / When her war-song was heard on Andalusia's shore?' (stanza 37, *passim*). If we read this line with the Wisdom of Solomon we might well reply that the voice of chivalry, in this modern context, is all too strong. The problem is not with the absence of chivalry but rather with its persistence, the fact that the everyday business of death and suffering, about to be practised on the plains of Talavera, continues to be overlaid by fantasies of glory.[14]

The epic tradition to which Byron responds does not deny the brute reality of loss. Indeed, martial verse lays great store in tragic reversals of fortune, as Homer shows in his unflinching depiction of the deaths of Patroclus and Achilles in the *Iliad*. Where Byron differs from Homer, and for that matter from the would-be Homerians Croker, Southey, and Scott, is in his refusal to find profit in such loss. There are no heroes in modern Spain, and consequently no heroic deaths. Each volley heard at Talavera tells merely of the fact, blunt and incomprehensible, 'that thousands cease to breathe' (I, 38, 7). In Byron's vision of war there seems to be no scope for pathos or redemption. The imagery, drawn from the book of *Revelation*, is one of apocalypse without millennium, a vision of the world at the end of time harried by Death on a 'pale horse' (6.8). Byron's vivid description of Death riding 'upon the sulphury Siroc' (I, 38, 8) is comparable with Benjamin West's painting *Death on a Pale Horse* (c. 1802). But where West counterbalances his vision of destruction with a portrayal of Christ the redeemer, Byron focuses on a terrifying portrait of the 'Giant' of war (I, 39), 'His blood-red tresses deep'ning in the sun, / With death-shot glowing in his fiery hands' (I, 39, 2–3). The stanza closes with an explicit reference to the sacrificial nature of war: 'For on this morn three potent nations meet, / To shed before his shrine the blood he deems most sweet' (I, 39, 8–9). Conflict, in other words, is regarded as a gross form of collective bloodletting, a means for 'potent' nations to vent their passion for destruction.

But what purpose exactly does this sacrifice fulfil, and what does it tell us about Byron's attitude to war? In *Violence and the Sacred*, the literary theorist René Girard writes

> Ritual violence is always less internal than the original violence. In assuming a mythico-ritual character, violence tends toward the exterior, and this tendency in turn assumes certain sacrificial characteristics; it conceals the site of the original violence, thereby shielding from this violence, and from the very knowledge of this violence, the elementary group whose very survival depends on the absolute triumph of peace … [through engaging in ritual violence] the groups agree never to be completely at peace, so that their members may find it easier to be at peace among themselves. We see here the principle behind all 'foreign' wars: aggressive tendencies that are potentially fatal to the cohesion of the group are redirected from within the community to outside it.[15]

Put more simply, war may be regarded as the attempt to project internal antagonisms, such as class conflict, on to the face of a belligerent foreign Other. Whilst some critics might regard this claim as insufficiently historicist, it is worth noting that, from the outset, the British conflict with Revolutionary and Imperial France was conceived as a struggle between competing ideologies. Edmund Burke's later writings, in particular his *Heads for Consideration on the Present State of Affairs* (1792) in which France is portrayed as a monstrous 'evil' threatening the heart of Europe, proved instrumental in persuading the Pitt government to regard the war with France as a fight for national identity.[16] With France fulfilling the role of malevolent Other, revolution could be defined now as a strictly foreign affair thus concealing, in Girard's words, 'the site of the original violence'. That the ideology of sacrifice should be instrumental to this violence is brought out in a fugitive comment from *The Times* in 1812: 'We are engaged in a war – a war of no common description – a war of system against system, in which no choice is left us, but victory or extirpation.' It was, moreover, impossible to engage in such a struggle, 'without sweat', and crucially, 'without a wound'. Blood must be shed, in other words, that the British 'system' might survive.[17]

Returning to *Childe Harold*, Girard's emphasis on the ritualistic nature of foreign war seems particularly relevant to the stress, in stanza 40, on the pseudo-chivalric aspects of Talavera. As Diego Saglia notes (2000, 132), Byron has in mind a particular passage from Croker's poem in which a chivalric framework is used to conceal an impending sense of horror:

> Waving ensigns, pennons light
> And glancing blades and bayonets bright,
> And eagles wing'd with gold;—
> And warrior bands of many a hue,
> Scarlet and white and blue.[18]

Here, a rhetoric of connection, 'And glancing ... And eagles ... And warrior bands', dazzles the eye with a sense of accumulated power. While Byron echoes Croker's fascination with the gaudy pageantry of war, the pleasure of looking is immediately undercut by parenthetical irony: 'By Heaven! It is a splendid sight to see / (For one who hath no friend, no brother there) / Their rival scarfs of mix'd embroidery' (I, 40, 1–3). Saglia's comments on 'the alternation of brutality and beauty' in this stanza are particularly astute, as is his view that the 'contradictions and ruptures' of the poem counter the establishment endeavour to cultivate a 'unitary perception' of Spain (Saglia 1996, 76). Where I depart from Saglia, however, is in his stress on 'the narrator's non-commitment', for while the attitudes presented in this stanza are undoubtedly 'diverse and contrasting' (76) it seems to me that the reflections on the glamour of war at the opening of the stanza are deliberately undercut by the emphasis on destruction at the stanza's close. The verse, in other words, must be read retrospectively to appreciate its enduring fascination with the underlying horror of war. As example, we may consider again stanza 40, where the association of 'rival' and 'mix'd' prefigures, brilliantly, the offensive ravelling of human tissue that is to come.

Prior to the fight, however, Byron relays, again with a glance towards the spectacular emphases of Croker's *Talavera*, a catalogue of ceremonial pomp:

> Three hosts combine to offer sacrifice;
> Three tongues prefer strange orisons on high;
> Three gaudy standards flout the pale blue skies;
> The shouts are France, Spain, Albion, Victory! (I, 41, 1–4)

The anaphora builds up sublime expectations, only to dash these with brute finality:

> The foe, the victim, and the fond ally
> That fights for all, but ever fights in vain,

Are met—as if at home they could not die—
To feed the crow on Talavera's plain,
And fertilize the field that each pretends to gain. (I, 41, 5–9)

The expected clash is elided, along with any potential for heroic description. In Byron's account, the armies 'Are met', only, in the space of a line, to become crow's fodder. There could be no more effective antidote to the poetics and politics of sublimity than this. As the dead of Talavera 'rot—Ambition's honour'd fools' (I, 42, 1), so too do the pretences of consensual loyalism. Where Croker draws on figures of continuity to raise a vision of national triumph Byron, through antithesis and oxymoron, presents a more conflicted view (see Saglia 2000, 132). As if to emphasize the futility of rhetorical claims to unanimity, Byron draws attention to another calamitous victory, the battle of Albuera, its 'glorious field of grief' (I, 43, 1) mourned by 'tears of triumph' (I, 43, 6). No doubt with Croker in mind, but also with a nod to the anonymous *The Battle of Albuerra, a Poem* (1811), the poem asserts that the name of Albuera shines merely 'in worthless lays, the theme of transient song!' (I, 43, 9).

Byron's dismissal of modern warfare and contemporary war culture concludes with a withering and, to some minds, ideologically incoherent attack on the motivations of the common soldier. Stanza 44 begins with a reminder of those 'thousands' whose lives are lost in the establishment's 'game of lives' (I, 44, 2–4). Byron then goes on, in line 5, to revive the archaic Spenserian diction of the poem's opening: 'In sooth 'twere sad to thwart their noble aim', only to thwart this restatement of chivalric intent with a reminder of the socio-economic reality of contemporary soldiering: 'blest hirelings!' (I, 44, 6). The stanza ends with a cynical comment on the true purpose of 'foreign' wars: by dying for the 'country's good', the poem notes, the professional soldier is preserved from the 'shame' of some 'domestic' act of theft or violence (I, 44, 6–8). Here again, with a memory of Byron's aversion to '*mercenary*' soldiering, war is identified as a political business, useful for directing attention away from discord on the home front.

The presentation of Talavera would appear to support the idea of Byron as an anti-war poet. While enthusiasm for martial display is a dominant motif in these stanzas, such enthusiasm is undermined by pointed reminders of how war impacts on the bodies of its participants. In the stanzas that follow, as we shall discover, the body remains the focus of Byron's interests. In this case, however, the emphasis is less on the horrors of war than on its paradoxical pleasures. Still following Byron's real and imaginary route through Spain, our attention turns now from one geographical locus, the battlefield, to another: the city.

III

Seville, where Byron stayed between 25-8 July, lies some 248 miles to the south of Talavera. As the battle raged in the north, the poet dedicated himself to amorous pursuits. The Seville cantos are, accordingly, centred on the pursuit of 'Love' (I, 46, 5). As yet, the city remains 'unconscious of the coming doom' (I, 46, 1)—its capture by the French in January 1810. But that of which the city is unconscious is precisely Byron's theme. And while the citizens of Seville indulge in 'feast', 'revel' and 'song' (I, 46, 2), the threat of death and destruction looms beyond the city bounds and is signified inside by lexis of 'wounds' (I, 46, 4), 'silent crimes' and 'tott'ring walls' (I, 46, 8–9). In these lines, the co-mingling of violence and sexual pleasure, with their portent of 'deeds to come' (I, 52, 1), provide an illuminating commentary on the conflicted nature of human desire.

In Seville, and later as we shall see in Cadiz, the intermingling of love and war leads to some disturbing transformations, not the least of which is its effect on gender distinctions. Here, for example, is the opening to stanza 54:

> Is it for this the Spanish maid, arous'd,
> Hangs on the willow her unstrung guitar,
> And, all unsex'd, the Anlace hath espus'd,
> Sung the loud song, and dar'd the deed of war? (I, 54, 1–4)

'Unsex'd' yet 'arous'd' the Spanish maid presents a confusing spectacle. While, as Saglia points out, Byron's portrayal of 'Spain's dark-glancing daughters' (I, 59, 7) owes much to contemporary cliché (Saglia 2000, 197), his treatment of female heroism in times of war indicates a darker fascination with the erotics of destruction. This fascination comes to a head with the description of Augustina de Aragón, the famed Maid of Zaragoza in stanzas 55 and 56. Known throughout Spain for her crucial intervention during the first siege of Zaragoza in October 1808, news of Augustina's heroism had reached England prior to Byron's departure. As Robert Southey records in his *History of the Peninsular War* (1827–28), she 'sprung forward over the dead and dying, snatched a match from the hand of a dead artilleryman, and fired off a six-and twenty pounder; then, jumping upon the gun, made a solemn vow never to quit it alive during the siege'.[19] Celebrated in graphic form in Goya's *Qué valor*, a print from the *Disasters of War* series (1810–12), the contemporary fascination with the Maid of Zaragoza comes in part from her association with Athena/Minerva, a goddess figure combining the attributes of nurturer and warrior. In the Greek Medusa legend, which forms the core of Byron's account, Perseus uses Athena's bronze shield as a mirror so that he may see the Gorgon without looking at her directly. The symbolic significance of this legend lies in its presentation of two competing aspects of feminine identity: beautiful and enabling on the one hand, monstrous and destructive on the other.[20]

In Byron's poem, the Maid of Zaragoza has a no less ambiguous status. Presented initially as she who 'Stalks with Minerva's step where Mars might quake' (I, 54, 9), the maid takes on many of the attributes of her monstrous opponent:

55.

Ye who shall marvel when you hear her tale,
Oh! Had you known her in her softer hour,
Mark'd her black eye that mocks her coal-black veil,
Heard her light, lively tones in Lady's bower,
Seen her long locks that foil the painter's power,
Her fairy form, with more than female grace,
Scarce would you deem that Saragoza's tower
Beheld her smile in Danger's Gorgon face,
Thin the clos'd ranks, and lead in Glory's fearful chase.

56.

Her lover sinks—she sheds no ill-tim'd tear;
Her chief is slain—she fills his fatal post;
Her fellows flee—she checks their base career;
The foe retires—she heads the sallying host:
Who can appease like her a lover's ghost?
Who can avenge so well a leader's fall?
What maid retrieve when man's flush'd hope is lost?
Who hang so fiercely on the flying Gaul,
Foil'd by a woman's hand, before a batter'd wall?

Key to this ambivalence is the significance of 'foil', a word repeated in both stanzas and later, as we shall discover in the bull fighting stanzas towards the end of the canto. The *OED* defines foil, in its verbal form, as a 'repulse, defeat' or 'baffling check'. While Byron goes to some lengths to emphasize the warrior woman's 'softer' aspects, the attributes he focuses on, in particular 'her black eye' and 'long locks' are Medusa-like in their ability to 'foil the painter's power'. With 'more than female grace', the image of the Maid thus veers towards a kind of excessive, monstrous femininity whilst at the same time her ability to 'foil' the painter's power recalls her primary identification with Medusa's adversary, the warrior goddess in possession of the mirror. Interestingly, the *OED* goes on to define foil as 'an amalgam of tinfoil and mercury placed behind the glass of a mirror, to produce a reflection'. Still further, a foil may also be defined as a sword, used in fencing. In his reading of this passage Jerome Christensen stresses that the invaders are 'Foil'd' not by a woman's 'gaze' but by a woman's 'hand', an important point since it 'assigns a much more active status to the woman, rendering her locks not as snakes but as swords'. It is not therefore

the image of the Gorgon, that infinitely various, phallicized head, that threatens paralysis; that image screens a more disturbing, preconscious awareness that the woman has arms of her own that she can wield in peace and in war, thus challenging the prevailing conventions by which things are ordered. (Christensen 1993, 74)

The capacity for defiance, for reflection, and for violence encoded in 'foil' leads to a multiplication of feminine attributes and ultimately to a collapse of the very idea of a fixed female identity.

With the Seville stanzas, Byron passes therefore from a fascination with war conceived as a scene of ritual dismemberment to a deeper concern with the instabilities of gender. Through the attribution of a symbolic phallus, the Maid gains in power and is transformed into a devouring, destructive figure. She thus maintains a dual function as an emblem of unbridled maternal power and as a symbol of the insubstantial, because transferable, nature of the phallus, a paradox brought out in Freud's problematic reading of the snaked-haired Medusa (1920).[21] The significance of this dual construction is given particular focus in Goya's image, which portrays a woman taking possession of a blatantly phallic canon. And in Byron too the Maid notably 'retrieve[s] when man's flush'd hope is lost' (I, 56, 7). Thus, while the gaze of the Gorgon petrifies the phallus, the abundance of her serpentine tresses offers the promise of restitution. As we shall go on to see, Byron's meditation on the horrors of war leads, ultimately, to an encounter with the traumatic origins of the self.

IV

Like Seville, Cadiz is presented as a city dedicated to self-gratification, in defiance of the self-denying rigours of war:

> Ah, Vice! How soft are thy voluptuous ways!
> While boyish blood is mantling who can 'scape
> The fascination of thy magic gaze?
> A Cherub-hydra round us dost thou gape,
> And mould to every taste thy dear delusive shape. (I, 65, 5–9)

Yet even here, the 'Cherub-hydra', with its echo of the snake-haired Medusa, qualifies the 'mantling of boyish blood', infusing its status as a figure of desire with intimations of loss. As the verse progresses, the ritualized worship of love ('A thousand altars rise, for ever blazing bright' (I, 66, 9)) thus turns, naturally enough, to a related mode of devotion: the worship of death. And here again, the war that the city would deny returns in symbolic form, in this case via the ritualized slaughter of the bullring. The point, as with the Talavera stanzas, is to highlight the role that destruction plays in the forging of identity.

Byron attended his first bullfight at Puerto de Santa Maria, near Cadiz, on 30 July 1809, a few days after the Allied victory at Talavera. As Diego Saglia notes, while the dead and wounded were plundered on the battlefield, their countrymen to the south indulged in 'a surrogate experience' of war (Saglia 2000, 133). To make the connection with the recent battle the stanzas begin with a further reflection on the significance of ritual, noting that the bullfight takes place on the Sabbath 'sacred to a solemn feast' (I, 68, 3). Instead of the body and blood of Christ, however, the meal to be consumed is man. The ensuing description is swift and brutal, and comes with a further allusion to the discredited rhetoric of chivalry: 'Hark! heard you not the forest-monarch's roar? / Crashing the lance, he snuffs the spouting gore / Of man and steed, o'erthrown beneath his horn' (I, 68, 4–6). In Burke's *Philosophical Enquiry into the Origin of our Ideas of the Sublime and Beautiful* (1757), the bull is presented as an example of the sublime.[22] To Burke's portrait of the animal's awe-inspiring destructiveness, Byron adds a further sexualized detail: the superior power, over the lance, of the death-dealing horn.

Significantly, the majority of the crowd in the surrounding arena is female: 'Here dons, grandees, but chiefly dames abound' (I, 72, 5). And once more, they are presented as immune, both to violence ('The throng'd Arena shakes with shouts for more; / Yells the mad crowd o'er

entrails freshly torn,' (I, 68, 7–8)) and to grief ('Nor shrinks the female
eye, nor ev'n affects to mourn,' (I, 68, 9)). As with the Seville stanzas the
female gaze seems poised between an ironic regard for romantic sacrifice
in the tiers ('Skill'd in the ogle of a roguish eye, / Yet ever well inclin'd
to heal the wound / None through their cold disdain are doom'd to die
… by Love's sad archery,' (I, 72, 6–9)) and a lust for destruction in the
arena. Within this space, literal and metaphoric violence substitute for
one another.

The connection between the specious pageantry of Talavera and the
sexual display within the arena is made explicit with the arrival of the
matadors:

> Hush'd is the din of tongues—on gallant steeds,
> With milk-white crest, gold spur, and light-pois'd lance,
> Four cavaliers prepare for venturous deeds,
> And lowly bending to the lists advance;
> Rich are their scarfs, their chargers featly prance. (I, 73, 1–5)

Here, as Christensen comments, the poet 'sardonically contrasts' the
sanguine sports of the Spaniards with 'the bloodless "fooleries" of the
English bourgeoisie' (I, 71, 1). At first the suburban pursuits of the English
('Some Richmond-hill ascend, some scud to Ware, / And many to the
steep of Highgate hie,' (I, 70, 3–4)) appear to lack the passion and the
power of the bullfight, ('the ungentle sport that oft invites / The Spanish
maid, and cheers the Spanish swain' (I, 80, 1–2)). And yet the English
too, on the same 'jubilee of man' (I, 69, 1), are no less devoted

> to the worship of the solemn Horn,
> Grasp'd in the holy hand of Mystery,
> In whose dread name both men and maids are sworn. (I, 70, 6–8)

The veneration of the hunting 'Horn' echoes the sacramental nature of the
bull's horn in stanza 68, suggesting that the anodyne pursuits of Byron's
countrymen are no less steeped in violent eroticism than the deadly 'play'
(stanza 78) of their Spanish counterparts. Thus, even as Byron condemns
the Spanish for 'theatricalizing suffering and "gloating in another's pain"'
(Christensen 1993, 71–2) the English claim to civilized detachment is
highly debatable. Indeed, as the poem goes on to suggest, those men
and maids gloating in the Spanish arena are no different from those
who, closer to home, indulge vicariously in the bloody spectacle of the

Peninsular War. What, after all, is the purpose of England's intervention in Spain if not to indulge a taste for sacrificial bloodletting?

As Diego Saglia has pointed out, the image of Spain as a vast bullring was widely disseminated throughout this period. In this, the ascription of artistic form is crucial. Unlike the open field, the arena imposes form on the shapeless event of killing, allowing carnage to be turned into sacrificial profit. Within the arena, the bull becomes a metonym for the imperial forces at large in Europe. Specifically, through the allusion to the animal's 'mad career' (I, 76, 4) the bull becomes identified with Napoleon. As the ensuing lines indicate, Byron, though opposed to the Emperor's oppression of Spain, is driven to identify with the epic dimensions of his rise and fall. Significantly, at this point in the poem the word 'foil' returns, materialized in this case as an object of death:

> Foil'd, bleeding, breathless, furious to the last,
> Full in the centre stands the bull at bay,
> Mid wounds, and clinging darts, and lances brast,
> And foes disabled in the brutal fray. (I, 78, 1–4)

While at first Byron appears to delight in the confrontation, the lines succumb to an overwhelming sense of pathos through identification, first with the defiance and then with the suffering of the bull. Christensen's claim that Byron finds in the bull a fitting object for his own sense of doom, both as an aristocrat in the public arena and as a writer subject to commercialism, is richly suggestive. As emblems of the heroic modes of war and culture, the Lord and the Emperor nevertheless become meaningful only within a system of aesthetic conventions. Poet, bull, and militarist are therefore sacrificed to the pitiless gaze of feminized consumption, 'sweet sight for vulgar eyes' (I, 79, 7). But the real atrocity, the one that remains out of view, 'scarce seen in dashing by', is that of the bull's 'dark bulk' (I, 79, 9). The literal object, the one that is actually sacrificed, whether it is conceived as 'corse' (I, 79, 7), country, or corps, is strategically ungraspable and must remain so if it is to remain serviceable as an object of desire.

Well aware of how aesthetics may be used to assist the political, Byron links the serviceability of the sacrificial object with the contemporary taste for historical prose narratives. Chief among his targets is Sir John Carr, whose *Descriptive Travels in the Southern and Eastern Parts of Spain and the Balearic Isles, In the Year 1809* (1811), helped foster British enthusiasm for the war. In Carr's hands the war becomes a matter of quantity: 'How many troops ycrossed the laughing main / That neer beheld the same return again / How many buildings are in such a place, / How many relics ...' (*CPW* II, 42). Most likely excised from the published text on account of the stanzas' less than flattering portrayal of the Wellesleys, the satirical tone in contrast to the bullfight stanzas is marked by the return of Spenserian archaisms and a calculated flatness of affect. Just as, in the commercial realm, money becomes the measure of all, so in the military sphere, quantity is valued over quality, a distinction that recalls Byron's earlier distaste for the '*mercenary*'.

But if the tendency to absorb statistical information while exercising a taste for romance is disparaged, does the ironic antidote to this taste fare any better? In the lyric 'To Inez', which replaced 'The Girl of Cadiz' between stanzas 84 and 85, the Childe speaks of a 'settled, ceaseless gloom', and of 'weariness' with 'pleasure'. Most tellingly, while others 'still of transport dream', the Childe believes himself to be 'awake' ('To Inez' ll, 849–63, *passim*). The lyric seems therefore to eschew romance in favour of a gloomy adjustment to the real. But while the Childe claims to be 'unmov'd' by life's pleasures, including such 'delights' as the 'scenes of vanish'd war', the poem itself seems driven to 'mark' both its own and its audience's investment in such pleasures (Canto II, stanza 40, *passim*). Like the Childe who 'cannot hope for rest' ('To Inez' l, 856), the poem dallies compulsively with the very forces that it would resist. War, in other words, is a passion, perhaps even an antidote to depression, that Byron and his audience cannot easily forego. Still, it is worth remembering that *Childe Harold's Pilgrimage* though subtitled 'A Romaunt' is a poem dedicated to the art of spoiling. Byron's version of romance, as we have seen, differs markedly from that of his establishment peers and the poem ends by noting that for 'all the blood at Talavera shed' (I, 90, 1) Spain yet remains in chains.

There is, however, a further sense in which Canto I seeks, finally, to resist the glorification of war. This is achieved through a turn to the elegiac mode in stanza 91. Here, the poem pauses to commemorate Byron's long-standing friend John Wingfield of the Coldstream Guards who, in anticipation of the poet's fate, died of a fever at Coimbra, Portugal, prior to the battle of May 1811. Significantly, Wingfield's death is described as 'unbleeding' (I, 91, 7) and 'bloodless' (I, 92, 7). Unlike those 'boasted slain' (I, 91, 7) whose bodies contribute to the red page of history, Wingfield's name, officially 'unlaurel'd' (I, 91, 5), lives on in poetic elegy. Just as, in the Waterloo stanzas of Canto III, Byron commemorates his cousin Frederick Howard whose death leaves a 'ghastly gap' (III, 31, 2), so here the recollection of a single name, otherwise 'forgotten' (I, 91, 6), speaks of a life beyond indifference. Until 'mourn'd and mourner lie united in repose' (I, 92, 9), elegy alone provides us with a glimpse of what it might be like to be released from war.[23] When pursued forward, however, to the equivalent acts of commemoration in Canto III, and then again to the mock heroic stanzas of *Don Juan*, the poet's elegy could just as easily be read as yet another variation on the relations between pleasure and pain.[24] For Freud, let us recall, what is common to both love and war is the desire for a return to a condition of premature unity and 'repose', a state of dissolution recalling the idealized fusion of mother and infant. Thus, whilst elegy does indeed suggest a route beyond war, the longing for reunion is predicated on a primal act of separation. The redemptive aspect of elegy in Byron's poem must therefore be conceived as a modality of the epic destruction of war; we cannot, in other words, love except as a consequence of loss.

notes

1. Ernest Jones, *Sigmund Freud: Life and Works*. Vol. 2, II, 189–92. For a stimulating commentary on psychoanalytic approaches to war see Daniel Pick, *War Machine: The Rationalisation of Slaughter in the Modern Age*, 211–57.
2. Jacqueline Rose, *Why War? – Psychoanalysis, Politics, and the Return to Melanie Klein*, 17.
3. Jerome J. McGann, *Byron and Romanticism*, 106.
4. Sigmund Freud, 'Why War?' (1933) in Sigmund Freud, *Civilization, Society and Religion: Group Psychology, Civilization and Its Discontents and Other Works*, ed. Albert Dickson, 361–2.
5. William A. Borst, *Lord Byron's First Pilgrimage*; Gordon Kent Thomas, *Lord Byron's Iberian Pilgrimage*; Diego Saglia, *Byron and Spain: Itinerary in the Writing of Place* and *Poetic Castles in Spain*; Richard Cronin, *The Politics of Romantic Poetry*, 128–36; Simon Bainbridge, *British Poetry and the Revolutionary and Napoleonic Wars*, 170–9; Jerome McGann, *Fiery Dust: Byron's Poetic Development*; Carl Woodring, *Politics in English Romantic Poetry*; Jerome Christensen, *Lord Byron's Strength: Romantic Writing and Commercial Society*, 65–78.
6. In a letter to his mother Byron writes: 'in England they would call it a victory – a pretty victory! Two hundred officers and five thousand men killed, all English, and the French in as great force as ever' *BLJ* I, 221.
7. Simon Bainbridge notes 'from mid-September 1809 Whig criticism of the war intensified ... it was not until July 1812 when Wellesley beat Marmont in the first decisive Allied victory in open battle that British criticism of the war against France was stilled'. See *Napoleon and English Romanticism*, 127.
8. See Bainbridge 1995, 95–133 and Saglia 1996, 2000.
9. From the *Anti-Jacobin Review*. Quoted in Donald H. Reiman, ed., *The Romantics Reviewed: Contemporary Reviews of British Romantic Writers, Part B: Byron and Regency Society Poets*. Vol. I, 11.
10. Timothy Webb, 'Byron and the Heroic Syllables'. *Keats-Shelley Review* 5 (1990): 42.

11. In an illuminating essay, Peter J. Manning suggests that in Byron 'love and war function identically'. Common to both experiences 'is an obliteration of detachment, and ... the prototype of this experience, erasing the outlines of the self, is the fusion of infant and mother'. But whilst it seems true to say that the appeal of war lies in its relations with the death drive, as outlined by Freud in *Beyond the Pleasure Principle* (1920), it is perhaps more accurate to regard war as a principle of *both* life *and* death. War, as it emerges in Byron, is an active force, albeit one that enables the self to die in its own way. See Peter J. Manning, *Reading Romantics: Text and Context*, 121.

12. Croker's publisher John Murray described the poem as having enjoyed a success greater 'than any short poem he knew'. By 1812 the poem had gone into nine editions, presenting comparison with that other Murray success *Childe Harold's Pilgrimage*. For further details and discussion, see Cronin 2000, 130, 212, and Saglia 2000, 130–1.

13. See Malcolm Kelsall, *Byron's Politics*.

14. Typical of the manner in which establishment writers responded to Spain is this passage from Thomas Bourke's *A Concise History of the Moors in Spain*, 216: 'the manners of the chivalrous ages, though lost to the rest of Europe, are still, to a certain degree, perceptible in various parts of Spain'. In his 'Addition to the Preface' to *Childe Harold's Pilgrimage* Byron responds to the charge of having written an unchivalric poem with the curt dismissal 'So much for chivalry. Burke need not have regretted that its days are over, though Marie Antoinette was quite as chaste most of those in whose honours lances were shivered, and knights unhorsed ... I fear a little investigation will teach us not to regret these monstrous mummeries of the middle ages' *CPW* II, 5–6. The poet has in mind here Edmund Burke's objection to the treatment of the French Queen in his *Reflections on the Revolution in France* (1790).

15. René Girard, *Violence and the Sacred*, trans. Patrick Gregory, 249.

16. Quoted by Conor Cruise O'Brien in his intro. to Edmund Burke's *Reflections on the Revolution in France and on the proceedings in Certain Societies in London relative to that event*, ed. Conor Cruise O' Brien, 60.

17. *The Times*, 15 February 1812. Cited in Clive Emsley, *British Society and the French Wars, 1793–1815*, 159–60.

18. Text taken from J.W. Croker, *Talavera. Ninth edition. To Which are Added, Other Poems*. Saglia notes that Byron knew the poem and that he owned an 1812 edition, which he sold on the first day of his 1816 book sale (Saglia 2000, 130). The volume is listed as item 158 in the sale catalogue. See *CMP* 237.

19. Quoted by Gordon Kent Thomas in *Lord Byron's Iberian Pilgrimage*, 36.

20. For a suggestive reading of the Medusa figure in Romanticism see Neil Hertz's essay 'Medusa's head: Male Hysteria under Political Pressure' in Hertz's collection *The End of the Line: Essays on Psychoanalysis and the Sublime*, 179–91.

21. Sigmund Freud, 'Medusa's Head' (1920) in James Strachey, ed., *The Standard Edition of the Complete Psychological Works of Sigmund Freud*. Vol. 18, 273–4.

22. Saglia 2000, 133. See Burke 1990, 60.

23. In support of this conclusion Simon Bainbridge argues that the elegy on Wingfield constitutes 'a meaningful way of responding to war and its desolations ... Byron reclaims the form from its uses for "the boasted slain", emphasizing the effect of one individual loss and act of remembrance over the anonymizing tributes of official culture'. Bainbridge 2003, 178. See also Philip Shaw, *Waterloo and the Romantic Imagination*, 186–91.

24. *Don Juan*, Canto VIII, stanzas 14–18, which focuses on the Russian Siege of Ismail (1790), touches on many of the issues addressed in this chapter, including the links between war and sexuality ('The troops ... they mounted one by one, / Cheerful as children climb the breast of mothers,' VIII, 15, 1–6) and the contrasting pleasures of epic and elegy: 'For fifty thousand heroes, name by name, / Though all deserving equally to turn / A couplet, or an elegy to claim, / Would form a lengthy lexicon of glory, / And what is worse still, a much longer story' (VIII, 17, 4–8).

The reading of an epic, like the waging of a war, is predicated on rapid transitions and abrupt turns. To derive pleasure from epic the reader must resist the temptation to dwell on the individual death. Yet even as the impulse to elegiac immobility is queried in *Don Juan*, there is sufficient satirical purpose in the poem, achieved via the interpolation of lengthy digressions, to prevent the reader from succumbing to the temptations of epic indifference.

works cited and suggestions for further reading

Bainbridge, Simon. *Napoleon and English Romanticism*. Cambridge: Cambridge University Press, 1995.

——. *British Poetry and the Revolutionary and Napoleonic Wars*. Oxford: Oxford University Press, 2003.

Bennett, Betty, ed. *British War Poetry in the Age of Romanticism 1793–1815*. New York and London: Garland, 1976.

Borst, William A. *Lord Byron's First Pilgrimage*. New Haven: Yale University Press, 1948.

Bourke, Thomas. *A Concise History of the Moors in Spain*. London: Rivington and Hatchard, 1811.

Burke, Edmund. *Reflections on the Revolution in France and on the proceedings in Certain Societies in London relative to that event*. Ed. Conor Cruise O' Brien. Harmondsworth: Penguin, 1968 (repr. 1990).

Christensen, Jerome. *Lord Byron's Strength: Romantic Writing and Commercial Society*. Baltimore, MD: Johns Hopkins University Press, 1993.

Cronin, Richard. *The Politics of Romantic Poetry*. Basingstoke: Macmillan, 2000.

Croker, J.W. *Talavera. Ninth edition. To Which are Added, Other Poems*. London: John Murray; Edinburgh: W. Blackwood, 1812.

Emsley, Clive. *British Society and the French Wars, 1793–1815*. London: Macmillan, 1979.

Favret, Mary A. 'Coming Home: the Public Spaces of Romantic War'. *Studies in Romanticism* 33.4 (Winter 1994): 539–48.

Freud, Sigmund. 'Medusa's Head' (1920). *The Standard Edition of the Complete Psychological Works of Sigmund Freud*. Ed. James Strachey. Vol. 18. London: Hogarth Press, 1953–74.

——. *Beyond the Pleasure Principle* (1920). *The Standard Edition of the Complete Psychological Works of Sigmund Freud*. Ed. James Strachey. Vol. 18. London: Hogarth Press, 1953–74.

——. *Civilization, Society and Religion: Group Psychology, Civilization and Its Discontents and Other Works*. Ed. Albert Dickson. Harmondsworth: Penguin, 1985.

Girard, René. *Violence and the Sacred*. Trans. Patrick Gregory. Baltimore, MD: Johns Hopkins University Press, 1979.

Hertz, Neil. *The End of the Line: Essays on Psychoanalysis and the Sublime*. New York: Columbia University Press, 1985.

Jones, Ernest. *Sigmund Freud: Life and Works*. 3 vols. London: Hogarth Press, 1953–7.

Kelsall, Malcolm. *Byron's Politics*. Brighton: Harvester, 1987.

Manning, Peter J. *Reading Romantics: Text and Context*. New York and Oxford: Oxford University Press, 1990.

McGann, Jerome J. *Fiery Dust: Byron's Poetic Development*. Chicago, IL: University of Chicago Press, 1968.

——. *Byron and Romanticism*. Cambridge: Cambridge University Press, 2002.

Pick, Daniel. *War Machine: The Rationalisation of Slaughter in the Modern Age*. New Haven and London: Yale University Press, 1993.

Reiman, Donald H., ed. *The Romantics Reviewed: Contemporary Reviews of British Romantic Writers, Part B: Byron and Regency Society Poets*. 5 vols. New York and London: Garland, 1972.

Rose, Jacqueline. *Why War? – Psychoanalysis, Politics, and the Return to Melanie Klein*. Oxford: Blackwell, 1993.

Saglia, Diego. *Byron and Spain: Itinerary in the Writing of Place*. Lewiston, NY: Edwin Mellen, 1996.

——. *Poetic Castles in Spain: British Romanticism and Figurations of Iberia*. Amsterdam and Atlanta, GA: Rodopi, 2000.

Scarry, Elaine. *The Body in Pain: The Making and Unmaking of the World*. Oxford: Oxford University Press, 1985.

Shapiro, Michael J. *Violent Cartographies: Mapping Cultures of War*. Minneapolis: University of Minnesota Press, 1997.

Shaw, Philip. 'Britain at War: The Historical Context'. *A Companion to Romanticism*. Ed. Duncan Wu. Oxford: Blackwell, 1998. 48–60.

——, ed. *Romantic Wars: Studies in Culture and Conflict, 1793–1822*. Aldershot: Ashgate, 2000.

——. *Waterloo and the Romantic Imagination*. Basingstoke: Palgrave, 2002.

Thomas, Gordon Kent. *Lord Byron's Iberian Pilgrimage*. Provo: Brigham Young University Press, 1983.

Watson, J.R. *Romanticism and War: A Study of British Romantic Period Writers and the Napoleonic Wars*. Basingstoke: Palgrave, 2003.

Webb, Timothy. 'Byron and the Heroic Syllables'. *Keats-Shelley Review* 5 (1990): 41–74.

Woodring, Carl. *Politics in English Romantic Poetry*. Cambridge, Mass.: Harvard University Press, 1970.

11
byron and intertextuality
laureate triumph in *childe harold* iv:
staël, hemans, hobhouse, byron

nanora sweet

I protest against & prohibit the *'laurels'*—which would be a most awkward assumption and anticipation of that which may never come to pass. ... *You* would like them naturally because the verses won't do without them—

BLJ V, 243 from La Mira, to Murray, 20 June 1817

That's what Byron protested, in words seldom reprinted, when his friend John Cam Hobhouse proposed 'a wreath about the brows' of a heroic bust he'd commissioned of the poet in Rome.[1] Byron's words indicate that his upcoming fourth and perhaps 'greatest' canto of *Childe Harold's Pilgrimage* (1818)—a poem he hadn't meant to write—might be read as a poem of laureate triumph.[2] In its 'verses', the poet speaks of aspiring to 'fame' and 'laurels' in his 'land's language': if the 'blight' on his 'fortunes' means that laurels 'light ... on a loftier head', so be it; 'awkward assumption' or not, he has expressed his interest (*CHP* IV, 9–10). The canto would emulate the progress of a laureate to Rome, retracing Byron's own steps, starting with a pilgrimage to places associated with laureate poets Petrarch and Tasso, and to Florence with its museums and Dantean associations, past places evoking Rome's republic and the laureate Horace, to Rome and all its sights. His poem would combine hope and despair over Italy's present captivity to Austria and enact a scene of laureate crisis in the Coliseum. Those laurels: the verses couldn't do without them.

Back in Venice after his visit to Rome, Byron wrote 126 stanzas of Canto IV in less than a month. On 31 July he welcomed Hobhouse to his home at La Mira outside Venice and kept on writing. When Hobhouse left for London in January, Byron had finished fifty-eight more stanzas, two short of the final 186, his longest poem to date. The canto reflects Hobhouse's interest in the troubled but laurelled careers of Roman and Italian statesmen and writers. Its sixty-four lengthy notes document his interest, all but eleven of them entirely by Hobhouse, and these spilled over into his separately published *Historical Illustrations of the Fourth Canto of Childe Harold*.[3] In January 1818 he delivered the poem to Byron's publisher John Murray in London. As if heralded – or condemned? – by Byron's new 'laureate' poem, Hobhouse began his own vexed career as a politician, spending months in Newgate prison and ultimately years in Parliament.

Once the schoolchild's introduction to the poet, with its climactic address to the ocean ('Roll on, thou deep and dark blue ocean—roll!' (IV, 179ff.)), Byron's *Pilgrimage* and its Italian canto have lost critical standing over the past century. A consensus emerged that the *Pilgrimage* belonged in a 'romantic' canon Byron left behind when he took up a comic mantle in 1818 with *Beppo* and *Don Juan*.[4] Byron abets this argument with remarks on his change in style.[5] Yet the argument depends on critical approaches no longer taken without question: a developmental approach to authorship (congruent with mid-century absorption in psychology) and a ready privileging of works that target a largely male audience.[6] Byron's critics contended with another difficulty in the case of the fourth canto, its purported 'looseness' of form. Uncertain of the poem's formal category, inclined to privilege imagistic and dramatic unity, critics laid this fault at Hobhouse's door.[7] Byron's new editor, Jerome McGann, went on the offensive, arguing in his critical study *Fiery Dust* that Hobhouse's influence was 'indirect' and that when Byron took Hobhouse's ideas into the canto, he 'worked' them in 'with evident purpose' and results 'Rich and Strange' (McGann 1968, 122). McGann's close readings are convincing, yet his magical words – Ariel's, from *The Tempest* – seem aimed at protecting Byron from outside influences like too much prose by the plodding Hobhouse.[8]

We have learned to read poets and non-poetic texts in new ways since the 1960s, to recover and follow links among texts diverse in gender and genre – intertextual links that an era devoted to unity had suppressed – in this case, links to women writers and a male writer whose boxy prose lacks the 'sex appeal' of Byronic comedy. Canto IV's form is laureate triumph, and it reads best in the context of companion works in that form.[9] Triumph requires the 'looseness', or inclusiveness, of *concordia discors*. Its model is a conquering processional with lots of booty and captives of different genders and origins.[10] Triumph fosters relations among texts, for many of its passages are booty from other people's work. After all, Byron was a poet for whom writing was a social experience made up of conversation and quotation. As serious as 'triumph' poetry can be, it has its inside jokes and ridiculous points and the writers know it. The fact is, Byron's contemporaries did contribute to the making of the *Childe Harold* IV – especially Germaine de Staël, who was a friend of Byron's and then Hobhouse's, and Felicia Hemans who had the same publisher as Byron, and Hobhouse too – 'because the verses won't do without them'.

Politics, literature, and art conspired to make laureate triumph the form of the moment in Napoleonic Europe: its rhythm of conquest and reversal; its props of chariot and arch, trophy and captive, Rome and the Capitol, laurels and getting them and giving them up. Napoleon had been defeated and lost his laurels; he'd been taken captive, twice. His opponent Madame de Staël, creator of the century's woman laureate 'Corinne', returned to Paris, recalling her father's re-entry there before the French Revolution. She'd wooed the English with her writing, especially her 1807 *Corinne or Italy* with its sober Scottish-British protagonist Oswald. They led the fight in taking back the Continent, but now old dynasties were triumphing. With Southey in office, the poet-laureateship of Britain seemed under-appointed for this moment. In the visual arts, a post-war triumph was playing itself out on the Continent. Napoleon and the French had taken hundreds of works from Italy, and many were being returned, the Apollo Belvedere, Laocoon, Dying Gladiator, Capitoline Wolf, Medici Venus, and the horses of St Mark's: these appear in Canto IV. Staël's *Corinne* was replete with commentary on these works, still in Italy when her novel opens (1793). In 1816, *The Restoration of the Works of Art to Italy* would be Felicia Hemans's first adult poem, portraying the return of art to Florence, Venice, and Rome.

Triumph does not appear in Stuart Curran's *Poetic Form and British Romanticism*, a 'law of genre' of sorts for Romanticism.[11] Tacit 'laws' of gender and nation may explain why Byron's critics note Germaine de Staël's influence without pursuing it in much detail – until the systematic comparisons by Joanne Wilkes in 1999.[12] Sonia Hofkosh and others argue persuasively that Byron tried to contain the influence of women on his writing.[13] Yet as an account of male and female captivity and its overturning, triumph incorporates 'laws' of gender and genre and their overturning and cannot honour these attempts.[14] A hybrid form, part lyric, part epic, triumph depends on a mix of poetry and prose and ingredients attractive to women and to men. It has its own veiled diplomatic and parliamentary designs on the world. Both Byron and Staël were 'rogue' diplomats for parts of their careers, and Hobhouse a Member of Parliament and Hemans the sister of a diplomatic secretary.[15] Petrarch too, who created triumph as a literary form in *Trionfi*, was a self-appointed diplomat, shuttling among capitals in an era of papal schism at Avignon and republican revolt in Rome. Better known for his sonnets to Laura, derided and yet imitated among British poets, Petrarch was praised and blamed by Byron himself, discounted by William Hazlitt, emulated by Percy Shelley, and valued by Thomas Campbell who catered readily to female readers and writers.[16]

Earlier twentieth-century criticism of *Childe Harold's Pilgrimage* and its fourth canto looked for *organic unity* in imagery and *dramatic unity* in narrative.[17] Seekers after organic unity sometimes found triumph-like patterns: Bernard Blackstone saw a Poundian Vorticism in Byron's 'loops of time',[18] Brian Wilkie 'long strokes on a large canvas'.[19] Robert Gleckner offered the term 'topographical',[20] and M.K. Joseph found structures in both poem and canto.[21] Later deconstructive critics saw triumph as figure if not form in Shelley's *The Triumph of Life*, but did not extend this to Byron.[22] Seekers after *dramatic unity* had the more difficult time: looking for irony dependent on distance between narrator and character, they were thwarted when the Pilgrim character disappeared after the middle of Canto III (to reappear briefly in Canto IV). This criticism found Childe Harold/Byron variously an existential, Miltonic, or Wordsworthian hero as befitted its time.[23]

With a resurgence of Romantic studies in the 1960s that privileged Wordsworth and sublimity, Jerome McGann offered the poet-figure's synthesizing of 'piecemeal' experience in St Peter's as an analogue to Wordsworth's at the Simplon Pass.[24] By 1990 a postmodern and feminist critique of Byron emerged, suspicious of unity and polite consensus[25] and leading to broad cultural studies that make Byron a real-world actor but emphasize compromises in his cosmopolitan liberalism: here Caroline Franklin and Jonathan David Gross took up his relations with Staël.[26] In the 1990s Jerome Christensen read Byron with Hobhouse; then Susan Wolfson opened a two-way textual connection between Byron and Hemans.[27]

Roman triumph and its legacy in Renaissance spectacle and literature were present for Byron and his contemporaries, whether through Livy or Gibbon or poems like Thomson's 'The Progress of Liberty' or Elijah's 'chariot of fire' assimilated to triumph in Dante's *Purgatorio* 29 (extending to Beatrice's triumph in *Paradiso*). More often, like Staël's Oswald in *Corinne*, they'd seen 'statesmen borne in triumph by the people';[28] less often, they'd read Petrarch's codification of the genre in *Trionfi*, although

Shelley studied it and Staël, Hobhouse, and Hemans refer to it.[29] Some knew the legends if not the works of Petrarch and Tasso: the former's crowning on Rome's Capitoline Hill in 1341, with an explication of Laura/ laurels, the latter's career troubled by madness, his crowning prevented by death. Perhaps they knew of the improvisatrice Corilla crowned at Rome in 1776.[30] Many, including Byron, Hemans, and Hobhouse, knew woman's triumph through *Corinne* (Oswald: 'for the first time, he was witness to such homage paid a woman'). Many knew of Napoleon's laurels and Arc de Triomphe.

Roman triumph brought the victorious general to Rome in a procession through arch or arches of senators and soldiers, captives and other 'trophies,' to the Temple of Jupiter on Capitoline Hill. In his chariot the conqueror was accompanied by a slave who whispered, 'Remember, you too are mortal': for the essence of triumph is its reversal, figured in the unstable roles of captive and captor. To reinforce this reminder, the scene is complemented by a killing of imprisoned slaves; then the laurels are gained, and then relinquished. It is this chiasmic power of reversal that triumph signifies, not an unrelieved vaunting of conquest.[31] Here triumph reflects the contentions of the gods, for Apollo grants the laurels and Jupiter compels their surrender.

In Petrarch's Christian temporality, triumph's reversals become a sequence, a progressive 'trumping' of love by chastity by death by fame by time by eternity. Thus Corinne passes from love through its disappointment to death but also fame. There are six 'triumphs' in Petrarch's terza rima *Trionfi*, a work begun in 1351 but still under revision at the poet's death in 1374. Figurally progressive, this vernacular lyric-epic forms a humanistic bridge, Rome to Italy; it extends from poetry to painting and spectacle. *Trionfi* drew Petrarch's other masterworks to it, for Laura of the sonnets is the crux here, and Scipio Africanus appears from the incomplete Latin epic that earned the poet his laurels; Petrarch's laureate acts are triumphs, especially his progress to welcome Rienzi, Rome's 'last tribune', as are the patriotic canzoni accompanying these acts. One canzone supplies the epigraph to *Corinne* and is echoed in lines from Ariosto that form Byron's epigraph for Canto IV. As Renaissance spectacle, triumph refers to an entrained *concordia discors*, one that is, as W.H. Herendeen writes, 'unencompassable', dissolving rather than ending; as Ricardo Quinones has said, it achieves a 'tandem extremity of vision'.[32]

Laureate poets like Rome's Horace give Hemans and Byron much of their undersong: each translates Horace and uses his rosy garland of *carpe diem*. McGann's notes to Canto IV reveal that Horace is his most echoed source alongside Shakespeare and Isaiah/the Psalms. The crowning of Petrarch and vicissitudes of Tasso preoccupy Staël, Hemans, and Byron.[33] An interpretive genre, triumph allows for emphasis on politics, literature, or art, for studies of time and a 'pilgrim's progress' from love to eternity, arguably Harold's course in Cantos I–IV. Hobhouse had a willing listener when (as it seems) he proposed that Harold's pilgrimage end in a Roman triumph. Both men were acquainted with triumph's Italianate variation through Staël, Byron through Hemans; Hobhouse studied Roman and Italian materials on the topic for his notes and *Illustrations*.

Staël and Byron were competitors as London's literary lions of 1813–14.[34] When her *De l'Allemagne* appeared in 1813, he pored over it, unable to put it down. His *The Bride of Abydos* makes unacknowledged use of two Goethe passages drawn from *De l'Allemagne* or *Corinne* or both: an analogy between painting and music and the lines from *Wilhelm Meister*, 'Kennst du das Land wo die Zitronen blühn', echoed in Corinne's ode at the Capitol and in Hemans's poetry. These passages are trophies, 'stolen', as Byron told the Countess of Blessington, by writers 'at third or fourth hand'.[35] His copy of *Corinne* appears in his sale catalogue of 1816, and we know he later teased Teresa Guiccioli for using the novel as a love manual. The book was by him, however, when in September 1816 Hobhouse read it concertedly before visiting Coppet: 'very good but prosy', Hobhouse wrote (pot calling kettle?), and kept Staël and her book in mind during the autumn, for praise, critique, and fact checking.[36] The only substantial note Byron will write for *Childe Harold* IV is a tribute to Staël that, according to Ann Gardiner, shows 'a close reading of *Corinne* on the part of Byron, whose *Childe Harold IV* appeared eleven years after de Staël's novel'.[37]

Caroline Franklin suggests Oswald as an alter ego for Harold/Byron, Jonathan David Gross suggests Corinne, crossing genders.[38] The half-English, lyric-heroic 'Corinne' is an ideal protagonist for triumph's hybrid form. But more evidently, Staël's book offers Byron the ground for his Pilgrim's progress – and means of its interpretation.[39] The parallel texts add up quickly if in different sequence: Corinne and Nelvil visit the Pantheon (Byron's stanzas: 146–7), Castel San Angelo (152), St Peter's (153–9), the Capitol (with prisons nearby; 163) and its approaches and Tarpeian Rock near the Forum with arches (110–12), the Coliseum (128–45), the *caritas romana* (148–51), the Palatine (106–7), Rienzi (180), the tomb of Metella (99–105), Egeria's fountain (115–27), the Vatican Museum (160–3). Stanzas on Rome not traceable in some measure to Staël look to Hemans on art and Hobhouse on Roman ruins and heroes.

Beyond persons and places, *Corinne* and Canto IV interpret laureate triumph through its lyric-epic properties. On the day of Corinne's crowning in Book II, Apollo shines with 'radiant beams'.[40] As Oswald, newly arrived in Rome, joins the buzzing throng, Corinne appears in 'triumphal procession', her 'chariot' led by noblemen and foreigners, already nearly a trophy herself ('reminiscent of Greek statuary'). She 'seemed at once a priestess of Apollo' in her approach to Jupiter's Capitol, an artist whose triumph 'had not cost a single tear' (for she herself is captive?). Ascending the stairway, received by conservators and the senator who will crown her, she is celebrated as 'Italy' ('we would be men as she is a woman') and asked to improvise on its glories: 'glory', she says in triumph's terms, 'who so often picks her victims from among the victors she has crowned'.

Her improvisation matches Petrarch's as a study of Italianate laurels gained, missed, withheld: 'the crown that Petrarch wore', the one 'left hanging from Tasso's funereal cypress tree', the one never offered Dante. These topics inform the poet's pilgrimage through Arqua and Ferraro in Canto IV, the sites of Petrarch's old age and tomb, Tasso's glory and imprisonment, Ariosto's easy success, the tombs of Florence (stanzas 30–41). Corinne's speech offers Byron his motif of Apollonian colour, for these poets' words 'are the prism of the universe', with Ariosto himself 'a rainbow': she knows the iridescent imagery that can sparkle in *Trionfi*.[41] Most happily, she says, Petrarch's love of learning moved in tandem with his love of Laura, his humanism giving 'secrets of ages past' to 'the future'.

Corinne refers to *Trionfi* when she says Petrarch 'was to share in the power of eternity to witness all of time' (29). She quotes the Northern poet's lines on Italy, Goethe's 'Do you know this land where the orange trees bloom?' Unnerved in the audience, Oswald comes to her notice; she addresses his Northern melancholy with Rome, 'the land of tombs', and the Coliseum, site of Byron's own perverse triumph, where he will acknowledge his laurels of misanthropy and relinquish them. She is crowned in 'myrtle and laurel', myrtle a hint that hers is a Triumph of Love and will run a course to Eternity through denial, death, and time. Within an instant, her crown falls, in what is after all its obligatory relinquishing, as Corinne turns, disrupted, to her fated love Oswald. His own crowning will come in oak and laurel, much later at Ancona, site of his heroism in Book I. As he is undone by her crowning, she will be by his, much more gravely. She will be abased 'like a condemned slave', 'hurled from the triumphal chariot to the unfathomable depths of woe'

(349, 347) but – those 'depths' are an Eternity that can be made over to Childe Harold.

It is Oswald who gives the book's triumph its 'dissolution', its 'extremity of vision', in Herrenden's term, at the end and the beginning; its Eternity. At book's end Oswald watches Corinne's funeral procession to its vanishing point (a motif replicated at the end of Hemans's *Restoration*). At the book's other 'extremity of vision' – in Book I – Oswald offers an emblem for eternity beyond love and its abasement; beyond death, fame, and time:

> the spectacle of that splendid ocean upon which man may never fix his mark. He may work the land, cut his roads through the mountains, lock rivers into canals to carry his wares. Yet though his ships furrow the waters, the billows come swiftly to erase this slight trace of servitude, leaving the sea once more as she was on the first day of creation. (12)

As Peter Vassallo, Jerome McGann, and others note, this is Byron's source for his Canto's most famous passage, now an integral part of the poem as triumph:[42]

> Roll on, thou deep and dark blue ocean—roll!
> Ten thousand fleets sweep over thee in vain;
> Man marks the earth with ruin—his control
> Stops with the shore... (IV, 179, 1–4)

This passage offers much more: '...Rome, Carthage, what are they?' referring to the great conquest epic of the Roman republic, the Punic Wars and Scipio Africanus of Petrarch's epic and in Hobhouse's studies. The ocean, Byron's self-confessed 'image of Eternity' (IV, 183, 6), has the 'unencompassable' sense of Petrarch's last triumph. This is trophy rhetoric in the genre's tradition: plunder burnished – and if Simone Balayé is right, plunder from Virgil forward.[43] Shakespeare is here, too, from Sonnet 116: 'It is an ever-fixèd mark'. Brilliantly, Byron relocates his Triumph of Eternity from Ancona on the Adriatic, scene of Oswald's heroism and laurels, to a site south of Rome nearer Virgil's home. Homer is invoked here and through the *Pilgrimage* in the epithet 'dark blue ocean'.

If Byron plundered Staël's trophies in ways foretold, Felicia Hemans follows her as a woman writing laureate verse on Italy: of Corinne, she wrote 'C'est moi' in her copy of the novel.[44] In an intertext including *Childe Harold*, her 1816 *The Restoration of the Works of Art to Italy* becomes all the more a triumph, with the processional and evanescent aesthetics of that genre.[45] M. Byron Raizis has called Hemans 'the most important English Haroldian', and the intertextual work of Susan Wolfson has set a pattern for Hemans-Byron relations.[46] Finding echoes of *Childe Harold* in Hemans's work after 1818 – his stanza 179 ('Roll on, ...') in her 'The Indian Woman's Death Song', his stanza 82 ('trebly hundred triumphs') in 'her Corinne at the Capitol' (1829) – Wolfson encourages attention to all these 'Haroldian' interactions, such as a Byronic epigraph Hemans removed when *Restoration* was given a second edition by his publisher.

In 1816–17 Hemans published her first adult books of poetry with Murray, two progress poems set in Europe's South, *Restoration* and *Modern Greece*. Murray sent Byron these pamphlet-poems; and on 30 September 1816 at Diodati, not long after Hobhouse had read *Corinne*, Byron read *Restoration* and planned to take it to Italy: '—it is a good poem—very', he wrote Murray (*BLJ* V, 108). Without *Restoration*, his next canto might have taken a different turn, for it gives him a processional of art vibrant with laureate imagery.[47] Byron's first thoughts on notes for Canto IV emphasized art work (*BLJ* V, 253); but because Byron generally spoke slightingly of painting and even sculpture, his sudden connoisseurship in *Childe Harold* IV has puzzled scholars.[48] Hemans's 'gallery' poem moved him in August 1816; and Stendhal reports that in a November 1816 tour of a Milan gallery, Byron showed a 'depth of sentiment' about a painting: 'electrified', he 'improvised for an hour, better ... than Madame de Stael'.[49]

Hemans's *Restoration* offers further ingredients to *Childe Harold* IV, including the Filicaja sonnet occupying stanzas 42–3, five lines of which Hemans cites in Italian as an epigraph.[50] Wilkes speaks of Staël translating this patriotic poem, then removing it from *Corinne* (supposing 'fear of censorship' by Napoleon (Wilkes 1999, 101)). Hemans translated the sonnet for her 1818 *Translations from Camoens*. In this poem, Italy is woman and her charms – like her art works – have been plundered. To protect these charms against rapine, Hemans's *Restoration* offers a series of female personifications, figuration that plays a surprising new role in *Childe Harold* IV.

To the art work mentioned in *Corinne*, Hemans brings the crucial Apollo Belvedere *and* Canto IV's aesthetic language. Central to triumph in its epic mode, the lord of laurels stands against the reigning Jupiter who compels laurel-abjuration. Hemans's language is aestheticized like Byron's, with an Apollonian *radiance* of *dyes*, *tints*, *gleams*, and especially *rays*; these are gathered by Byron to a *rainbow*, which hints at the hunting bow carried by Apollo and carries light in its spectrum. Read alongside Byron's poem,

Hemans's work with Apollo's charioteering comes clear in the sunrise of Italy's Orient: for her, St Mark's horses, now restored, 'still glow' as 'proud Racers of the Sun' (l. 231).[51] For him, the Sunset at La Mira outside Venice is 'one vast Iris of the West' (IV, 27, 6). In Hemans's words, 'Sunset gilds' a hero's tomb (l. 104), and a fearful night in epic simile gives way to 'the rich glories of expanding light' in Florence (l. 148). The 'Athens of Italy!' Florence has been a destination of East–West triumph in plundered art (l. 157). Here 'pure lightnings of exalted thought' invoke Jupiter's power, and Florence's Venus is 'Love's radiant Goddess' (ll. 186–8).

In Hemans's counter-triumph of reclaimed art, 'fallen Italy', the 'Land of departed Fame', is asked to 'rejoice', for womanhood is reclaimed as well, countering the abasement that threatens Corinne. Hemans would 'rouse once more the daring soul of song', 'the myrtle-vale, the laurel grove' (ll. 12, 25, 24). For the British army of reconquest, 'triumph' has meant no tomb but 'a field' and 'no sculptur'd trophy'. Still, 'triumph''s trophies 'throw / A veil of radiance' over 'half' the 'woe' of a still suffering land (ll. 62, 64, 86–90). Earthly loss looks to art's 'deathless fame' (l. 99); in an imagery reclaimed from fallen woman, Hemans invokes Triumphs of *Love, Chastity, Death,* and now *Fame*.[52]

Time and *Eternity*? In Venice, St Mark's horses are 'formed to bear / Heaven's car of triumph,' the sun's (ll. 233–4). In 'fleeting triumph', they figure *time* as wakening day, 'noontide and the setting sun' (ll. 260, 262). The poem's next stop is *Eternity*, the 'Eternal City' Rome (l. 275), her religiosity earned by triumph. Rome cannot regain her 'noon', 'her own triumphal crown' – for war's 'lightning' (Jove again) strikes 'thy honours' – still, the Apollo Belvedere's 'immortal' form 'sheds radiance round'— a poet reflecting 'one ... ray' (ll. 309, 305, 334–5, 338). Meanwhile, a broken torso, subject to 'Time', may be 'Mould of a Conqueror' – and the suffering Laocoon refers us to 'Heaven', to Eternity (ll. 352, 368, 406). In the prismatic aesthetic Corinne described, painting can make 'the noontide of eternity', combining all lights and times. Epic figuration returns, with a Jovian-Judean 'Eternal' ('in the thunder pealed') and triumph's Christ, 'the Conqueror of the grave' (ll. 430, 480, 489). Hemans turns to the brilliantly coloured *Transfiguration* of Raphael: like Petrarch's *Trionfi*, a work unfinished at its maker's death. In a note, she adds that the painting 'was carried before his body to the grave' (Hemans 2000, 33 n. 43). Painting and body have triumph's 'tandem' quality here; they manage an unfinished, continuing connection from time to an eternity whose 'excess of light' is Christ-like, Beatrice-like (l. 508).

This poem bears couplet sonnets to Italy, Florence, and Rome in its train, as Wolfson points out, furthering its Renaissance progress.[53] It forecasts the gathering of rays in Byron's radiant/rainbow sequence. Like his *Pilgrimage* III–IV, *Restoration* writes of 'Peopling each scene with beings worthy thee' (l. 326). Byron's language of 'peopling' begins in Canto III (stanza 73) and resumes in Canto IV (stanzas 4 and 19). The susceptible Byron may have echoed a woman writer in this phrase, strengthening his ability with triumph, its great thronging of people. Without a doubt, *Childe Harold* IV shows the aesthetic effect of a work he called 'a good poem—very'.

Susceptible as well to male texts, Byron drew in the worldly destinies of statesmen and authors from Hobhouse's Notes and *Illustrations*. John Cam Hobhouse brings the anxiety and melancholy of an Oswald to Byron's work – the persona that Byron will shape to his own ends in the Coliseum scene. One critic, Jerome Christensen, has taken Hobhouse on board. He concludes that, far from disunifying the canto, Hobhouse (and his notes and pressure on stanzas) places it under a regime of 'serial' (yet 'static', 'phallic') liberalism.[54] Christensen equates triumph and 'colonization' and flattens '"trophy"' into 'objectification' (Christensen 1993, 186). For him, Byron and Hobhouse are engaged in a post-aristocratic commodification that ensures a 'radical break' with poets of triumph like Tasso. Christensen finds Byron and Hobhouse post- (or terminally) liberal, capable only of deadly repetition in 'republican stereotypes' and 'platitudes' (195). Christensen would flatten the intertext of triumph; he is missing Staël and Hemans, but he does make Hobhouse a reality, one uncannily amenable to Foucauldian discipline and surveillance.

These motifs and themes arise from Hobhouse's fifty-three notes to the Canto and his *Historical Illustrations*, rife with triumph iconography: prisons and cells come early and often, and captives and slaves. The Bridge of Sighs in Byron's stanza one ('A palace and a prison on each hand') drew from Corinne one anecdote about judicial abuse, but Hobhouse offers a long and technically obsessive account, with his signature penchant for superstitious duality: 'Some of the detained appear to have offended against, and others to have belonged to, the sacred body...'.[55] His treatment of Tasso's cell is similarly protracted. As a sample of his ability to twist a point toward captivity, he argues that Venetians turn to the sea to avoid 'slavery' (n. 134). When the sexuality of Byron's Medici Venus embarrasses him, he turns to identifying slaves in statuary (n. 433). An anecdote on republicanism shows that its most loyal defenders may be those who emerge from its prisons (n. 506).

But it is through Hobhouse that we understand the epic dimensions of triumph. The laurel wreath, we understand from him, is a protection against lightning (n. 364). We know that Jupiter is the lightning god whose temple was on the Capitol; if we see that he is the discipliner of laureates, we begin to understand that laurels are a form of lightning rod, dually attracting and repelling punishment. Now Byron's curious passage on Ariosto, Canto IV, stanza 41, begins to come clear. The happy Ariosto, successful when Tasso was not (and rumoured to have fomented Tasso's failure), is 'disgraced' when lightning strikes the laurels of his bust:

> The lightning rent from Ariosto's bust
> The iron crown of laurel's mimic'd leaves;
> Nor was the ominous element unjust,
> For the true laurel-wreath which Glory weaves
> Is of the tree no bolt of thunder cleaves,
> And the false semblance but disgraced his brow;
> Yet still, if fondly Superstition grieves,
> Know, that the lightning sanctifies below
> Whate'er it strikes;—yon head is doubly sacred now. (IV, 41)

We know that, once gained, laurels are to be abjured (worn lightly?), certainly not laid on like iron. Jupiter's thunderbolt plays havoc with iron laurels, but not those from Apollo's 'true' laurel tree. But wait, this punishing strike is but a pharmakon, inextricably poison and remedy, for it 'sanctifies' whatever it 'strikes'.[56]

Another lightning rod is the oversize statue of Pompey, one of Hobhouse's favourite triumphators (n. 775), with its bloodstain of Caesar's death. As Hobhouse recounts, the statue was drawn into the Coliseum for a French Revolutionary pageant, with, to his peculiar taste, its right arm amputated for logistical purposes. We think again of the heroic bust by Thorwaldsen that helped launch Byron's canto, with or without the laurels of 'awkward assumption', and its awkward travel to England for a place of repose. Were the laurels Hobhouse tried to press on Byron part of his deeply learned superstition? Was the heroic bust? Elsewhere, Hobhouse depicts the wolf, 'sacred image of the Capital', struck by lightning and thrown into the Forum as damaged. Yet sick infants are taken to that site (n. 784): another pharmakon. Caesar would have his laurels, because he was bald (n. 1293), and so on. Hobhouse takes power and abasement to a different level in triumph. And here we have Byron's 'scorpion', a reminder, a 'token', 'this lightning of the mind' of self-torment (stanzas 23–4). In the melancholic poet, what were laurels have now become 'Nemesis' – again a figure Hobhouse writes about.

As Christensen suggests, Hobhouse is intrigued with a rhetoric of repetition and the vernacular, the secret of success for Boccaccio (n.

514) – as for Hobhouse's herald, Byron? The complement to fame is what we – and Hobhouse – call 'the proverbial': for instance, Trajan of the famous arch 'was proverbially the best of the Roman princes', a triumphator as fine as Pompey (n. 999). Hobhouse fights a running battle with arch-Catholic sources like John Chetwode Eustace and A.W. Schlegel, accusing Eustace of something like but not quite the same as a proverb: 'a mere compilation of former riches' (n. 1566) – perhaps an intertext? Fully (and fatally) armed within and without, bearing his notes and canto to their publisher (also his 'go to jail' card), Hobhouse fears pastiche and worships proverb.

His *Illustrations* seeks triumphal arches in Rome's rubble, as one would suspect. In these extraordinary commentaries, tendriled to just a few lines in the canto, the city makes and remakes itself like a Piranesi staircase. The record may be his (pair of) commentaries on Stanza 80 ('The Goth, the Christian, Time, War, Flood, and Fire'), which run for 112 pages in the *Illustrations*. Hobhouse imposes on us what triumph must be and teaches us that the slave murmuring in the conqueror's ear is that pharmakon called Nemesis: One must appease 'Nemesis, the perpetual attendant on good fortune, of whose power the Roman conquerors were also reminded by certain symbols [whips?] attached to their cars of triumph' (n. 1181).

Byron's achievement: this many stanzas must be managed in sections, more or less as M.K. Joseph has them.[57] Venice 1–29; the laureate route 30–61; past Punic settings, rainbowed falls, Horace's Soracte 62–77; to Rome 78–163; the Coda with Pilgrim, Charlotte, Ocean, farewell 164–86. Through these sections, two streams of triumph material maintain themselves: the motifs of triumph (Hobhouse is here: these are largely Roman and of metal or stone) and those of its interpretation (Hemans here: these are largely Italianate and of colour and light). Fully forty-seven stanzas use the Hobhousean language and armature of triumph: triumph, trophy, laurels, slaves, car and captive, lightning, arch, Capitol, gladiator, arena, Nemesis, Torture and Time, dungeon.

In miniature, stanza 16 provides one well-torsioned study of triumph: Athens fell at Syracuse, and 'fetter'd thousands bore the yoke of war'. The 'Attic Muse' rose up her voice,' the laureate ('the bard') as slave, leading to reversals in the triumphal 'car':

> See! As they chant the tragic hymn, the car
> Of the o'ermastered victor stops, the reins fall
> From his hands—his idle scimitar
> Starts from its belt—he rends his captive's chains,
> And bids him thank the bard for freedom and his strains.

The conqueror conquered, as we've grown to expect; but the weapon idle in war, active in peace? This stanza trades in the armature rather than the aesthetics of triumph – with the important, resolving exception of the muse-like bard – and is capable of surprising reversal.

Glances at others suggest similar powers. Stanza 50: Florence's art and its Goddess 'in stone' so discompose its viewers that 'Chain'd to the chariot of triumphal Art / We stand as captives' (IV, 50, 4–5). The Medici Venus, a trophy twice, or many times over, reverses in triumph and takes captives (but no tears are shed?). The canto is rife with variations on stony themes and laurel forms: Napoleon receives an interesting play in stanza 92. Tears and blood aplenty flow from his triumph, despite his 'arch'; such a flood as to evoke Noah's own and the wordplay, *arch/ark*. This flood 'ebbs but to reflow' in the direction of (re)conquest; to interrupt that, Byron invokes the rainbow of Noah's narrative, and Iris's too, and perhaps Newton's, in this sometimes prismatic world of Italianate triumph.

Another reading could see the canto's unusual progression of female figures, entirely unprecedented in Byron but familiar from Hemans's personifications. These are statues and *genii loci* and 'proverbial' figures à la Hobhouse: Venus, Niobe, Iris, Cecilia Metalla, Egeria, the *caritas romana* (or daughter nursing her father through his prison grate, a favourite with all camps!), Princess Charlotte.[58] These may be seen sexually or not, or both, as in the reversal around Egeria from 'nympholepsy' to 'the faculty divine' of reason (stanzas 115 and 127). Most produce extraordinary runs of stanzas. Read through the language of triumph, the Cecelia Metella stanzas (99–105) have their touches: 'A woman's grave' – nothing known of her, but the round fortress tower of her tomb sports the best of laurels, 'The garland of eternity...'. A site of speculation, she brings the poet to feel he's 'bodied forth the heated mind / Forms', 'planks' to 'Build me a little bark of hope' (IV, 104–5). This *bark* becomes *ark* (and *arch*), this 'hope' the rainbow (again arch).

Apollo brings rainbow and light to triumph iconography and its interpretation. Working against the stony hardware of Roman triumph in Canto IV is the aestheticized light of Italian art captured in time and movement and progress. Whether these works return to rest, or whether as Hemans suggests they have always been plunder and never can rest, they ally with Apollo's motion, the day and its cycles but also Eternity and its light, prismatic in poetry and art; and with Apollo's laurels, the perishable, renewable crown. Fully thirty-five stanzas refer here to hues and rays as Hemans uses them, to dyes and stars and the milky way too; to rainbows or the bubbles that bear them and the arches and bridges in their shape that serve, like them, to unify pictures; the sunset and

Iris. Iris as hope has an epic dimension, messenger of the gods, bringing hope to the battlefield. Hope in biblical and classical forms, the rainbow half, the iris whole.

It is Apollo in the Vatican whose laurels are the gold standard: 'the Lord of the unerring bow,' 'brow all radiant'. Hemans's Apollo Belvedere 'sheds radiance round', one's words but 'reflected ray[s]'. Byron's stood surrounded in thought, 'each conception ... / A ray of immortality' which, 'Starlike ... gathered to a god!' (stanzas 161–2). Then: the Pilgrim, whose 'halo' fades (IV, 165, 7), his ritually relinquished laurels. From aesthetic eternity, and over its Ocean, the wood and stone of human triumph beckon this poem back, as if with Hobhouse's hand: in stanza 181's 'rock-built cities', 'monarchs tremble in their capitals', and 'the oak leviathans' false capitals of the sea. The 'oak' of Oswald's laurels is a toy to the ocean. One might think that, as the indispensable scene of triumph, Rome at least would last, the 'Eternal City': Rome with its 'deep blue sky' mirroring the 'deep and dark blue ocean' and making up 'the Roman globe' (stanza 111); matching the rainbow-on-rainbow 'one vast Iris of the West' (IV, 27, 6).

The heart of the poem, still, must be the Coliseum scene (stanzas 128–45), for it is the melancholic laureate's Capitol, given Oswald by Corinne. She visits there twice in her novel, once with Oswald and once alone: the second time at night takes her further into the slavery that is Petrarch's Triumph of Love, his most fully developed and flagellated throng. There Hobhouse finds all the arches he wants, 'arches on arches', and his captives flex their muscles.[59] As well choose the Coliseum for a dark-horse laureate-chase as try the Capitol, for the Coliseum holds the greatest of trophies in some eyes: male bodies. The scene encompasses torture past (and present), is linked with Time's triumph in the lines now Byron's epitaph at St Mary's Hucknall (IV, 137, 4–5).

The figure before us has accepted Jovian lightning ('my brain seared'), but that has not after all served as pharmakon. He hears Nemesis, and like any other conqueror he must reverse course like the 'o'ermastered victor' in stanza 16. He has the laurels, but they are what burns, they have eaten into him like iron, recalling Ariosto's and the lightning ('let me not have worn / This iron in my soul in vain' (IV, 131, 8–9)), and he must lay them down: 'That curse shall be Forgiveness' (IV, 135, 1). Relinquishing the laurels of the misanthropic poet, he imagines death and time, and the Gladiator appears before him, figure of victory and captivity inextricable and death. An impulse to mobilize the Goths to revenge dies with Byron's voice; the moon and stars shine through the 'topmost arch', eternity 'through the loops of time' (IV, 144, 2–3). The laurels have reappeared on the Coliseum itself, a 'garland-forest' (IV, 144, 5), like that in the silly Hobhouse story about the bald Caesar, which is a note to this stanza. On this pleasantly ridiculous note, the scene passes.

On the eve of departure from Venice, Byron depicts an evening he and Hobhouse shared (stanzas 27–9). On the Brenta river, the sunset spreads its 'dyes' and 'hues', creating 'one vast Iris of the West' – hope, and the prismatic radiance of the eye's own coloured circle as now the laurels. Somehow, in the unencompassable way of triumph, in stanza 27 'the Day joins the past Eternity'. This emblem serves the rest of the poem, including the sequence of water and cascade at Terni, which combine the 'torture' and 'eternity' in triumph, as the Pilgrim passes battlefields from the Punic Wars (stanzas 65–71.) Iris reappears above the falls, 'Like Hope upon a death-bed,' 'Love watching Madness with unalterable mien' (IV, 72, 9): Tasso the mad poet is here, and the misanthropic poet figure that Byron carries within himself. But Byron did not carry the voices of male precursors only: the echoes of Staël, Hemans, and Hobhouse, which are just beginning to resound again, sing to us that the intertext of Romantic triumph is one genre in many imaginations.

notes

1. By Bertel Thorwaldsen: Samuel Smiles, *A Publisher and His Friends*, 2 vols. Vol. I, 391.
2. Jerome J. McGann, *Fiery Dust: Byron's Poetic Development*, 123.
3. Hobhouse's book appeared in 1818 from Murray, with 'An Essay on Italian Literature' anonymously by Ugo Foscolo and documents by Tasso and Rienzi. References here are to John Hobhouse, *Historical Illustrations of the Fourth Canto of Childe Harold*, 2nd edn. Vol. 1. Foscolo's role in the triumph intertext merits further research.
4. See Samuel C. Chew, Introduction, *Childe Harold's Pilgrimage and Other Romantic Poems*, ix–l. See Alan Rawes, *Byron's Poetic Experimentation: Childe Harold, the Tales, and the Quest for Comedy* and Drummond Bone, '*Childe Harold IV, Don Juan* and *Beppo*' in *The Cambridge Companion to Byron*, ed. Drummond Bone, 151–70.
5. Remarks laced with snobbery and misogyny: see Marlon B. Ross, *The Contours of Masculine Desire: Romanticism and the Rise of Women's Poetry*, 324 n.3.
6. On women as readers of early cantos of *Childe Harold*, see William St Clair, 'The Impact of Byron's Writing: An Evaluative Approach' in *Byron: Augustan and Romantic*, ed. Andrew Rutherford, 1–25.
7. Andrew Rutherford, 'The Influence of Hobhouse on *Childe Harold's Pilgrimage*, Canto IV', *Review of English Studies* n.s. 12 (1961): 394. McGann 1968, 122–38. Peter Vassallo, *Byron: The Italian Literary Influence*, 50.
8. For a recent critique of McGann's editing of *Childe Harold*, especially Cantos I–II, regarding social production, see Roger Poole, 'What Constitutes, and What is External to, the "Real" Text of Byron's *Childe Harold's Pilgrimage, A*

Romaunt: And Other Poems (1812)?' in *Lord Byron the European: Essays from the International Byron Society*, ed. R.A. Cardwell, Studies in British Literature. Vol. 31, 149–208.

9. For a related introduction to triumph, see my '"Under the subtle wreath": Louise Bogan, Felicia Hemans, and Petrarchan Poetics' in *The Transatlantic Poetess*, ed. Laura Mandell, *Romanticism on the Net* 29–30 March 2004, <http://www.erudit.org/revue/ron/2003/v/n29/007714ar.html>.

10. On *concordia discors* see W.H. Herendeen, 'Petrarch's *Trionfi* and the Rhetoric of Triumph' in *Petrarch's Triumphs: Allegory and Spectacle*, ed. Konrad Eisenbichler and Amilcare A. Iannucci, 88; see entire essay and collection *passim*.

11. But see Stuart Curran, *Poetic Form and British Romanticism*, 151–7.

12. See McGann, 'Rome and Its Romantic Significance' in *Roman Images*, ed. Annabel Patterson, 93, and Vassallo 1984, 17–20. Caroline Franklin, *Byron: A Literary Life*: the entire *Pilgrimage* forms 'a masculine response to the Romantic feminism' of *Corinne* (113). Joanne Wilkes, *Lord Byron and Madame de Staël: Born for Opposition*.

13. Sonia Hofkosh, 'The Writer's Ravishment: Women and the Romantic Author – The Example of Byron' in *Romanticism and Feminism*, ed. Anne K. Mellor, 93–114.

14. I paraphrase Jacques Derrida's study of literary boundaries as hymeneal 'law': 'La Loi du genre/The Law of Genre', trans. Avital Ronell, *Glyph* 7 (1980): 176–232.

15. See my '"The Inseparables": Hemans, the Brownes, and the Milan Commission', *Forum for Modern Language Studies* 39.2 (2003): 165–77.

16. See Richard F. Kennedy, 'Byron and Petrarch', *Byron Journal* 11 (1983): 52–3; *BLJ* II, 172; III, 240 on Petrarch and *passim*; excerpts in Beatrice Corrigan, ed., *Italian Poets and English Critics, 1755–1859*; Alan M. Weinberg, *Shelley's Italian Experience*; Thomas Campbell, 'The Life of Petrarch', *The Sonnets, Triumphs, and Other Poems of Petrarch*, cxxxvi.

17. On both unities, W. Paul Elledge, *Byron and the Dynamics of Metaphor*, 54, 62.

18. Bernard Blackstone, '"The Loops of Time": Spatio-Temporal Patterns in "Childe Harold"', *Ariel* 2.4 (October 1971): 5–17.

19. Brian Wilkie, 'Byron: Artistry and Style' in *Romantic and Victorian: Studies in Memory of William H. Marshall*, eds W. Paul Elledge and Richard L. Hoffman, 130–1.

20. Robert F. Gleckner, *Byron and the Ruins of Paradise*, 270–1.

21. M.K. Joseph, *Byron the Poet*.

22. See contributions by Paul de Man, Jacques Derrida, and J. Hillis Miller to *Deconstruction and Criticism*, ed. Harold Bloom.

23. See McGann 1968, 138; Wilkie 1971, 130; Mark Kipperman, *Beyond Enchantment: German Idealism and Romantic Poetry*, 179; Vincent Newey, 'Authoring the Self: *Childe Harold* III and IV' in *Byron and the Limits of Fiction*, eds Bernard Beatty and Vincent Newey, 184.

24. Byron, stanza 157. McGann 1968, 31–66. McGann emulates 'internalized quest romance'; see Harold Bloom and Geoffrey Hartman in *Romanticism and Consciousness*, ed. Harold Bloom.

25. See William H. Galperin, *The Return of the Visible in British Romanticism*, 139–40, 257, 270; and Ross 1989, 28–49.

26. Caroline Franklin, 'Cosmopolitan Masculinity and the British Female Reader of *Childe Harold's Pilgrimage*', *Lord Byron the European*, 105–25. Daryl S. Ogden, 'Byron, Italy, and the Poetics of Liberal Imperialism', *Keats-Shelley Journal* 49 (2000): 114–37. Jonathan David Gross, *Byron: The Erotic Liberal*.

27. Jerome Christensen, *Lord Byron's Strength*. Susan J. Wolfson, 'Hemans and the Romance of Byron' in *Felicia Hemans: Reimagining Poetry in the Nineteenth Century*, eds Nanora Sweet and Julie Melnyk, 155–80. On Hemans and Byron as epideictic writers, see my '"A darkling plain": Hemans, Byron, and The Sceptic; A Poem' in *The Sceptic: A Hemans-Byron Dialogue (1820)*, *A Romantic Circles Electronic Edition*, eds Nanora Sweet and Barbara Taylor, Jan. 2004, Romantic Circles, University of Maryland, <http://www.rc.umd.edu/editions/sceptic/index.html>.

28. Germaine de Staël, *Corinne, or Italy*, trans. Avriel H. Goldberger, 22. All references to *Corinne* use this edition.

29. Staël 1987, 29; Hobhouse, *CPW* II, 327 n.506; Hemans, 'The Magic Glass', *The Poems of Felicia Hemans*, 468.

30. See Paola Guili, 'Tracing Sisterhood: Corilla Olimpica as Corinne's Unacknowledged Alter Ego'. *The Novel's Seductions: Staël's 'Corinne' in Critical Inquiry*, ed. Karyna Szmurlo, 165–84.

31. H.S. Versuel, *Triumphus: An Inquiry into the Origin, Development and Meaning of the Roman Triumph*. On Roman and Petrarchan triumph, see Esther Nyholm, '"Triumph" as a Motif in the Poems of Petrarch and in Contemporary and Later Art' in *Medieval Iconography and Narrative: A Symposium*, eds Flemming G. Andersen et al., 70–99.

32. Ricardo J. Quinones, '"Upon this Bank and Shoal of Time'. *Time, Literature and the Arts: Essays in Honor of Samuel L. Macey*, 43; and *passim*.

33. Staël 1987, 244–5; Donelle R. Ruwe, 'The Canon-Maker: Felicia Hemans and Torquato Tasso's Sister' in *Comparative Romanticisms: Power, Gender, Subjectivity*, eds Larry H. Peer and Diane Long Hoeveler, 133–57; *CPW* II, 317: Canto IV a 'poetic parallel of Tasso's *Jerusalem Delivered*' in context of Byron's 1817 *The Lament of Tasso*.

34. See Robert C. Whitford, *Madame de Staël's Literary Reputation in England*, University of Illinois Studies in Language and Literature. Vol. 4, No. 1; Wilkes 1999, 1–9; and *BLJ passim* for this period.

35. On these readings and borrowings, see *CPW* III, 436 n.1 and n.179; *BLJ* III, 181, 231–2, 211, 184 n. and Staël 1987, 156. *Lady Blessington's Conversations of Lord Byron*, ed. Ernest J. Lovell, Jr., 186–7. See Franklin 'The Influence of Madame de Staël's Account of Goethe's Die Braut von Korinth in De l'Allemagne on the Heroine of Byron's Siege of Corinth', *Notes & Queries* n.s. 35.3 [233 o.s.] (September 1988): 307–10.

36. Vassallo 1984, 169 n.40. *BLJ* VI–VIII to Guiccioli *passim*. Lord Boughton [John Cam Hobhouse], *Recollections of a Long Life*, ed. Lady Dorchester, 12, 61–2, 69.

37. Ann Gardiner, 'The Gender of Fame: Remembering Santa Croce in *Corinne* and *Childe Harold's Pilgrimage*,' in *Corvey Women Writers on the Web Journal* 2 (2004): 9. Sheffield Hallam University <http://www2.shu.ac.uk/corvey/cw3journal/general%20issues/listofissues.html>.

38. Franklin 2000, 113; Gross 2001, 88.

39. Vassallo 1984, 17–20.

40. Referring *passim* to 'Corinne's Improvisation at the Capital' in *Corinne* 26–31.

41. As Cupid's wings: Petrarch *The Triumphs of Petrarch*, trans. Ernest Hatch Wilkins, 6.

42. Vassallo 1984, 180; *CPW* II, 340 n.1603–20: n. 1603 offers Thomas Campbell's 'On Leaving a Scene in Bavaria' as another source.

43. Balayé, *Les Carnets de voyage de Madame de Staël*, 162 n.188.

44. Henry F. Chorley, *Memoirs of Mrs. Hemans*. Vol. I, 304 n.

45. On Hemans and Staël see Ellen Peel and Nanora Sweet, 'Corinne in England: Hemans, Jewsbury, and Browning', *Novel's Seductions*, 207–11; Nanora Sweet, 'History, Imperialism, and the Aesthetics of the Beautiful: Hemans and the Post-Napoleonic Moment' in *At the Limits of Romanticism*, eds Mary A. Favret and Nicola J. Watson, 170–84.

46. M. Byron Raizis, 'Childe Harold's Offspring, English and American', *Byron Journal* 27 (1999): 28. Wolfson 2001, 155–80.

47. One wonders about the impact of her next poem, *Modern Greece*, which sings of a Harold-like 'wanderer' to Greece and now 'to Italia's' shores murmuring 'a wild farewell'. The poem chants, 'O ye blue waters!' and adds that the mighty vanish, 'E'en as their barks have left no traces on the tide'. Byron received the poem from Murray between 21 August and 4 September 1817. (Quoted from Hemans 2000, 35–6.) According to McGann, the poet's draft manuscript of Canto IV including stanza 179 was complete by 19 July (*CPW* II, 184). At the very least, these poets are resonating closely and drawing in common on Staël.

48. Joseph 1964, 87; Bruce Haley, 'The Sculptural Aesthetics of *Childe Harold* IV', *MLQ* 44 (1983): 254–5.

49. Stendhal quoted in Ernest J. Lovell, Jr., ed. *His Very Self and Voice*, 198–9. For the term 'gallery poem', see Grant F. Scott, 'The Fragile Image: Felicia Hemans and Romantic Ekphrasis', *Felicia Hemans: Reimagining Poetry in the Nineteenth Century*, 36–54.

50. They may have found this in a common source; Vassallo (21) suggests J.-C.-L. Sismondi's *De la littérature du Midi de l'Europe* (1813) which both read.

51. I quote *Restoration* by line from Hemans 2000, where it appears, with notes, pages 18–33.

52. Hemans is not above Byronic double entendre here: the 'Fair Florence' apostrophized in *Childe Harold* II.32 was Mrs. Spencer Smith, shipboard 'Calypso', remade here into a awakening dreamer (ll. 145–56), 'fond affection' Niobe-like 'bending o'er the dead'.

53. See Hemans 2000, 31 notes.

54. Christensen 1993, 195–7.

55. *CPW* II, 218 n.1. These notes occupy *CPW* II, 199–264. For the Bridge of Sighs in *Corinne*, see Staël 1987, 299.

56. In Plato's association of 'writing' with pharmakon (in *Phaedrus*), Jacques Derrida found a famous instance of undecidability as it operates within binaries (here, speech and writing) and 'disseminates' through them. See 'Plato's Pharmacy', *Dissemination*, trans. Barbara Johnson, 63–171. Triumph and its figures show a similar dissemination of undecidability, from Jupiter's lightning to the laurels he strikes, from the role of victor and to that of victim,

and so forth. Hobhouse's later attempt to distinguish proverb from pastiche replicates Plato's attempt to uncouple speech and writing.

57. Joseph 1964, Appendix B, 144–5.

58. See Fiona Wilson's just published '"Virt'ous Fraud": The Perverse Politics of the *Caritas Romana* Scene in *Childe Harold*', *Keats-Shelley Journal* 54 (2005): 93–112.

59. Wilkes explores the contrasting fortunes of Childe Harold/Byron and Corinne, especially in this setting.

works cited and suggestions for further reading

Balayé, Simone. *Les Carnets de voyage de Madame de Staël*. Geneva: Librairie Droz, 1971.

Blackstone, Bernard. '"The Loops of Time": Spatio-Temporal Patterns in "Childe Harold"'. *Ariel* 2.4 (October 1971): 5–17.

Bloom, Harold. Ed. *Romanticism and Consciousness*. New York: Norton, 1970.

—. ed. *Deconstruction and Criticism*. New York: Seabury, 1979.

Bone, Drummond. '*Childe Harold* IV, *Don Juan* and *Beppo*.' *The Cambridge Companion to Byron*. Ed. Drummond Bone. Cambridge: Cambridge University Press, 2004. 151–70.

Boughton, Lord [John Cam Hobhouse]. *Recollections of a Long Life*. Ed. Lady Dorchester. London: John Murray, 1909.

Campbell, Thomas. 'The Life of Petrarch'. *The Sonnets, Triumphs, and Other Poems of Petrarch*. Ed. Thomas Campbell. London: George Bell & Sons, 1901. v–cxl.

Chew, Samuel C. Introduction to *Childe Harold's Pilgrimage and Other Romantic Poems*. Ed. Samuel C. Chew. New York: Odyssey, 1936. ix–l.

Chorley, Henry F. *Memoirs of Mrs. Hemans*. 2 vols. London: Saunders and Otley, 1836.

Christensen, Jerome. *Lord Byron's Strength*. Baltimore, MD: Johns Hopkins University Press, 1993.

Corrigan, Beatrice. Ed. *Italian Poets and English Critics, 1755–1859*. Chicago, IL: University of Chicago Press, 1969.

Curran, Stuart. *Poetic Form and British Romanticism*. New York: Oxford University Press, 1986.

Derrida, Jacques. 'La Loi du genre/The Law of Genre'. Trans. Avital Ronell, *Glyph* 7 (1980): 176–232.

——. *Dissemination*. Trans. Barbara Johnson. Chicago, Il: University of Chicago Press, 1981.

Elledge, W. Paul. *Byron and the Dynamics of Metaphor*. Nashville: Vanderbilt University Press, 1968.

Franklin, Caroline. 'The Influence of Madame de Staël's Account of Goethe's Die Braut von Korinth in De l'Allemagne on the Heroine of Byron's Siege of Corinth'. *Notes & Queries* n.s. 35.3 [233 o.s.] (September 1988): 307–10.

——. 'Cosmopolitan Masculinity and the British Female Reader of *Childe Harold's Pilgrimage*'. *Lord Byron the European: Essays from the International Byron Society*. Ed. R.A. Cardwell. Studies in British Literature. Vol. 31. Lewiston, NY: Mellen, 1997. 105–25.

——. *Byron: A Literary Life*. Basingstoke: Macmillan, 2000.

Galperin, William H. *The Return of the Visible in British Romanticism*. Baltimore, MD: Johns Hopkins University Press, 1993.

Gardiner, Ann, 'The Gender of Fame: Remembering Santa Croce in *Corinne* and *Childe Harold's Pilgrimage*'. *Corvey Women Writers on the Web Journal* 2 (2004), Sheffield Hallam University <http://www2.shu.ac.uk/corvey/cw3journal/general%20issues/listofissues.html>.

Gleckner, Robert F. *Byron and the Ruins of Paradise*. Baltimore, MD: Johns Hopkins University Press, 1967.

Gross, Jonathan David. *Byron: The Erotic Liberal*. Lanham, MD: Rowan & Littlefield, 2001.

Guili, Paola. 'Tracing Sisterhood: Corilla Olimpica as Corinne's Unacknowledged Alter Ego'. *The Novel's Seductions: Staël's 'Corinne' in Critical Inquiry*. Ed. Karyna Szmurlo. Lewisburg, PA: Bucknell University Press 1999. 165–84.

Haley, Bruce. 'The Sculptural Aesthetics of Childe Harold IV'. *MLQ* 44 (1983): 254–5.

Hemans, Felicia. *The Poems of Felicia Hemans*. Edinburgh: Blackwood, 1854.

——. *Felicia Hemans, Selected Poems, Letters, Reception Materials*. Ed. Susan J. Wolfson. Princeton, NJ: Princeton University Press, 2000.

Herendeen, W.H. 'Petrarch's *Trionfi* and the Rhetoric of Triumph'. *Petrarch's Triumphs: Allegory and Spectacle*. Eds Konrad Eisenbichler and Amilcare A. Iannucci. Toronto: University of Toronto Press, 1990. 87–96.

Hobhouse, John. *Historical Illustrations of the Fourth Canto of Childe Harold*. 2nd edn. London: John Murray, 1818. Reprint, n.p.: Norwood, 1977.

Hofkosh, Sonia. 'The Writer's Ravishment: Women and the Romantic Author – The Example of Byron'. *Romanticism and Feminism*. Ed. Anne K. Mellor. Bloomington, IN: Indiana University Press, 1988. 93–114.

Joseph, M.K. *Byron the Poet*. London: Gallanz, 1964.

Kennedy, Richard F. 'Byron and Petrarch'. *Byron Journal* 11 (1983): 52–3.

Kipperman, Mark. *Beyond Enchantment: German Idealism and Romantic Poetry*. Philadelphia: University of Pennsylvania Press, 1986.

Lovell, Ernest J. Jr., ed. *His Very Self and Voice*. New York: Macmillan, 1954.

Lovell, Ernest J. Jr., ed. *Lady Blessington's Conversations of Lord Byron*. Princeton, NJ: Princeton University Press, 1969.

McGann, Jerome J. *Fiery Dust: Byron's Poetic Development*. Chicago, IL: University of Chicago Press, 1968.

——. 'Rome and Its Romantic Significance'. *Roman Images*. Ed. Annabel Patterson. Baltimore, MD: Johns Hopkins University Press, 1984. 83–104.

Newey, Vincent. 'Authoring the Self: *Childe Harold* III and IV'. *Byron and the Limits of Fiction*. Eds Bernard Beatty and Vincent Newey. Totowa, NJ: Barnes & Noble, 1988. 148–90.

Nyholm, Esther. '"Triumph" as a Motif in the Poems of Petrarch and in Contemporary and Later Art'. *Medieval Iconography and Narrative: A Symposium*. Eds Flemming G. Andersen et al. Odense: Odense University Press, 1980. 70–99.

Ogden, Daryl S. 'Byron, Italy, and the Poetics of Liberal Imperialism'. *Keats-Shelley Journal* 49 (2000): 114–37.

Peel, Ellen and Nanora Sweet. 'Corinne in England: Hemans, Jewsbury, and Browning'. *The Novel's Seductions: Staël's 'Corinne'. Critical Inquiry*. Ed. Karyna Szmurlo. Lewisburg, PA: Bucknell University Press, 1999. 207–11.

Petrarch. *The Triumphs of Petrarch*. Trans. Ernest Hatch Wilkins. Chicago, IL: University of Chicago Press, 1962.

Poole, Roger. 'What Constitutes, and What is External to, the "Real" Text of Byron's *Childe Harold's Pilgrimage*, A Romaunt: And Other Poems 1812?'. *Lord Byron the European: Essays from the International Byron Society*. Ed. R.A. Cardwell. Studies in British Literature. Vol. 31. Lewiston, NY: Mellen, 1997. 149–208.

Quinones, Ricardo J. 'Upon this Bank and Shoal of Time'. *Time, Literature and the Arts: Essays in Honor of Samuel L. Macey*. Victoria, BC: University of Victoria, 1994. 34–45.

Raizis, M. Byron. 'Childe Harold's Offspring, English and American'. *Byron Journal* 27 (1999): 26–37.

Rawes, Alan. *Byron's Poetic Experimentation: Childe Harold, the Tales, and the Quest for Comedy*. Aldershot: Ashgate, 2000.

Ross, Marlon B. *The Contours of Masculine Desire: Romanticism and the Rise of Women's Poetry*. New York: Oxford University Press, 1989.

Rutherford, Andrew. 'The Influence of Hobhouse on *Childe Harold's Pilgrimage*, Canto IV'. *Review of English Studies* n.s. 12 (1961): 391–7.

Ruwe, Donelle R. 'The Canon-Maker: Felicia Hemans and Torquato Tasso's Sister'. *Comparative Romanticisms: Power, Gender, Subjectivity*. Eds Larry H. Peer and Diane Long Hoeveler. Columbia, SC: Camden House, 1998. 133–57.

St Clair, William. 'The Impact of Byron's Writing: An Evaluative Approach'. *Byron: Augustan and Romantic*. Ed. Andrew Rutherford. London: Macmillan, 1990. 1–25.

Scott, Grant F. 'The Fragile Image: Felicia Hemans and Romantic Ekphrasis'. *Felicia Hemans: Reimagining Poetry in the Nineteenth Century*. Eds Nanora Sweet and Julie Melnyk. Basingstoke: Palgrave, 2001. 36–54.

Smiles, Samuel. *A Publisher and His Friends*. 2 vols. London: Murray, 1891.

Staël, Germaine de. *Corinne, or Italy*. Trans. Avriel H. Goldberger. New Brunswick, NJ: Rutgers University Press, 1987.

Sweet, Nanora. '"A darkling plain": Hemans, Byron, and The Sceptic; A Poem'. *The Sceptic: A Hemans-Byron Dialogue (1820), A Romantic Circles Electronic Edition*. Eds Nanora Sweet and Barbara Taylor, January 2004, Romantic Circles, University of Maryland <http://www.rc.umd.edu/editions/sceptic/index.html>.

——. 'History, Imperialism, and the Aesthetics of the Beautiful: Hemans and the Post-Napoleonic Moment'. *At the Limits of Romanticism*. Eds Mary A. Favret and Nicola J. Watson. Bloomington, IN: Indiana University Press, 1994. 170–84.

——. '"The Inseparables": Hemans, the Brownes, and the Milan Commission'. *Forum for Modern Language Studies* 39.2 (2003): 165–77.

——. '"Under the subtle wreath": Louise Bogan, Felicia Hemans, and Petrarchan Poetics'. *The Transatlantic Poetess*. Ed. Laura Mandell. *Romanticism on the Net* 29–30 March 2004 <http://www.erudit.org/revue/ron/2003/v/n29/007714ar.html>.

Vassallo, Peter. *Byron: The Italian Literary Influence*. London: Macmillan, 1984.

Versuel, H.S. *Triumphus: An Inquiry into the Origin, Development and Meaning of the Roman Triumph*. Leiden: E. Brill, 1970.

Weinberg, Alan M. *Shelley's Italian Experience*. New York: St Martin's Press, 1991.

Whitford, Robert C. *Madame de Staël's Literary Reputation in England*. University of Illinois Studies in Language and Literature. Vol. 4, no. 1. Urbana: University of Illinois Press, 1918.

Wilkes, Joanne. *Lord Byron and Madame de Staël: Born for Opposition*. Aldershot: Ashgate, 1999.

Wilkie, Brian. 'Byron: Artistry and Style'. *Romantic and Victorian: Studies in Memory of William H. Marshall*. Eds W. Paul Elledge and Richard L. Hoffman. Rutherford, NJ: Farleigh Dickinson University Press, 1971. 130–1.

Wilson, Fiona. '"Virt'ous Fraud": The Perverse Politics of the *Caritas Romana* Scene in *Childe Harold*'. *Keats-Shelley Journal* 54 (2005): 93–112.

Wolfson, Susan J. 'Hemans and the Romance of Byron'. *Felicia Hemans: Reimagining Poetry in the Nineteenth Century*. Eds Nanora Sweet and Julie Melnyk. Basingstoke: Palgrave, 2001. 155–80.

12
don juan and the shiftings of gender

susan j. wolfson

When the poet of *Don Juan* Canto XIV exhorts abolitionist William Wilberforce to teach all tyrants 'that "sauce for goose is sauce for gander", / And ask them how *they* like to be in thrall' (83), the adage hints at a sexual politics, too, in the apposition of tyrant with the gander-gender. But it is male thraldom that proves the warmer concern – no less so for Byron, especially in the arena in which this was most likely, the domestic affections. 'Indeed I do love Lord [Holland],' he assured Lady Blessington in 1823, the year Canto XIV saw print, in prelude to this sigh:

> though the pity I feel for his domestic thraldom has something in it akin to contempt. Poor dear man! he is sadly bullied by *Milady;* and, what is worst of all, half her tyranny is used on the plea of kindness and taking care of his health. Hang such kindness! say I. She is certainly the most imperious, dictatorial person I know—is always *en reine.*[1]

Hereby hangs the general tale of *Don Juan*: the ganders get better sauce, with Byron's wit the seductive co-conspirator in keeping females in thrall. For all her wry and canny critiques of male privilege, even Virginia Woolf (after an evening of enervation with Katherine Mansfield's *Bliss)* had to agree with her father about 'the able witty mind of [Byron's] thoroughly masculine nature' in *Don Juan,* and she found no little relief in Byron's decidedly 'male virtues'.[2]

That Woolf was 'ready ... to fall in love' with the poet of *Don Juan,* and felt a 'superb force' in his letters is connected to the way both archives reflect a liking for women cut of Lady Holland's cloth. Taking a breath after his grumble about her imperious behaviour, Byron tenders a sympathetic, even an exculpatory, supplement: if the Lady is always *en reine,* this stance, 'in her peculiar position, shows tact, for she suspects

257

that were she to quit the throne she might be driven to the antichamber' (Blessington 1969, 12). Admiring the Lady's skill on the field of her endeavours, the home front and its theatre of social warfare, Byron not only cheered her self-possession, but felt a twin in her rejection of 'cant' (in her case, on female propriety).[3]

Lady Holland and Lady Blessington are Lord Byron's social test cases: like him, they are aristocratic nonconformists not in thrall to what the world expects; unlike him, they live in a world in which a man's domestic thraldom is the exception that proves the rule. They are continuous with the women in the textual imaginary of *Don Juan* who exercise power, in figures from enthralling to appalling, for self-interest and against male autonomy. Writing *Don Juan* Byron turns again and again to the arbitrary grants of gender, to find both fun and serious reflection by vexing, sometimes unfixing, the sign-systems of difference – nowhere more so than in an array of transvestite forms. The gender play with 'feminine' and 'masculine' proves shifty, however. When power is at stake, the poet of *Don Juan* may appeal to customary patterns of privilege – male, aristocratic, European.[4] Yet across the cantos, these patterns can unfold into a complicated, often contradictory, patchwork of unpredictably vibrant effects. A heightened awareness of the artifice of gender generates a critical energy along the unstable edges.

the travesty of don juan

One edge is a homoerotic frisson.[5] Like the campy hetero-effeminate that fronts the gender play of *Sardanapalus,* the cross-dressings of *Don Juan* wink at the *sub*culture, subtexted in code words ('boy') and substitute figures. This is a poem, comments G. Wilson Knight, that continually romances the 'almost feminine beauty in its hero'.[6] Juan is a confection for male bemusement and gazing as well as female doting and desire, and in his transvestite parts evokes the homoerotic appeal of the boys in Shakespeare's theatre. Byron's most self-invested figure under wraps in *Don Juan* is Canto XIV's Lord Henry Amundeville, a Regency aristocrat with an Abbey and a hetero-flair that has the look of a coterie-legible act. For all his macho broadcasts – he's a 'handsome man', famed 'in each circumstance of love or war' to have 'preserved his perpendicular' (XIV, 71) – there is a static of estrangement: he kisses Lady Adeline 'less like a young wife than an aged sister' (XIV, 69). There is 'no connubial turmoil: / Their union was a model to behold, / Serene, and noble,—conjugal, but cold' (XIV, 86). The latest epitaph on Byron's marriage, this also models a code of 'truths ... better kept behind a screen' (XIV, 80), the screen at once disguising and advertising a secret. 'But there was something wanting on the whole—/ I don't know what, and therefore cannot tell—' the poet demurs (XIV, 71), then proposes that 'undefinable *"Je ne sçais quoi"'* that led Helen to prefer what Byron did, a 'Dardan boy' (XIV, 72). It is with a coy rhyme-pairing of *perplexes* and *sexes* that he plays out this Continental affectation of mystery:

> There is an awkward thing which much perplexes,
>   Unless like wise Tiresias we had proved
> By turns the difference of the several sexes:
>   Neither can show quite *how* they would be loved. (XIV, 73)

It is the phantasm Tiresias who not only experiences sexual difference, but does so beyond the binary of just two sexes, with something like homoerotic knowledge.

If Lord Henry suggests covert turns under normative wraps, slightly askew, it is in overt travesty that Byron found the master-trope for critical pressure on the gender system sustained by assumptions about *masculine* and *feminine*.[7] Thinking of rhetorical rupture, Hazlitt thought *travesty* the best term for *Don Juan* itself. Noting the 'great power' in 'the oddity of the contrast[s]', he recognized a crucial theatrical effect: 'You laugh and are surprised that any one should turn round and *travestie* himself: the drollery is in the utter discontinuity.'[8] Don Juan, the hero with a difference, is the meta-trope of this operation. The sole instance *travesty* in all Byron's poetry is Juan's 'odd travesty' of his compelled disguise, 'femininely all array'd' (V, 74, 80) for secretion in a harem – a critical figure through which not just Juan, but the entire social structure of 'feminine', is exposed as an array, not nature but a stylizing manageable by either sex.

Even the body is dubious text. The poet gives him to us as 'feminine in feature' (VIII, 52), 'a most beauteous Boy' (IX, 53), with a capacity for dancing away 'like a flying Hour' (XIV, 40). To the internal observers, the gender is double. Donna Julia's maid beholds a 'pretty gentleman' of 'half-girlish face' (I, 170, 171); Haidée dotes on 'a very pretty fellow', his 'cheek and mouth' like 'a bed of roses' (II, 148, 168) – a blazon a sonneteer might array for a lady love. In his debut in Empress Catherine's court, the very 'Man' has to be surmised:

> ... slight and slim,
> Blushing and beardless; and yet ne'ertheless
> There was a something in his turn of limb,

> And still more in his eye, which seemed to express
> That though he looked one of the Seraphim,
> There lurked a Man beneath the Spirit's dress. (IX, 47)

Byron arrays the *a*-rhymes so that the gender signifier *him* is just a verbal ghost in 'Seraphim'.[9]

Preening at Catherine's court, Juan is at his most theatrically self-possessed, managing his dress with dandy aplomb. Across the epic, however, this liberty alternates with a world of women (and latently here, Catherine) with designs on a rather more imperiled male body, especially when bereft of its male garbing. He is 'half-smother'd' (I, 165) in Julia's bedding as she hides him from her husband's posse, from which he flees 'naked' into the night (I, 188). Washed up naked, half-dead Juan is reborn as Haidée's dress-up boy-toy: she 'stripp'd her sables off' to make his bed, and for its covers, she and maid Zoe 'gave a petticoat apiece' (II, 133). Petticoat influence survives the clothes in which Haidée later 'dress'd' Juan: the apparel of those 'very spacious breeches' does not proclaim the man. Or it does another: absent patriarch Lambro (II, 160). For both Julia and Haidée, Juan is always a 'boy' – so too his charm for Empress Catherine's 'preference of a boy to men much bigger' (IX, 72).

Byron lightly exacerbates the crisis by letting all these women seem much bigger. Julia is of 'stature tall', with 'handsome eyes' (I, 60, 61). Haidée is 'Even of the highest for a female mould' (II, 116). Protecting Juan from Lambro's wrath, she 'threw herself her boy before; / Stern as her sire' (to sharpen the point, Byron revised *calm* to *stern*); 'She stood ... stern, she woo'd the blow; / And tall beyond her sex'; 'She drew up her height,' and 'with a fix'd eye scann'd / Her father's face'; 'How like they look'd! the expression was the same'; 'their features and / Their stature differing but in sex and years' (IV, stanzas 42–5 *passim*). In this mirroring, Haidée and sire differ less from each other than both from boy Juan – his cast throughout this episode (II, stanzas 144 and 174; IV, stanzas 19 and 38).

Gender reversals cast *Don Juan* into an edgy romance: 'Juan nearly died' in Julia's chamber (I, 168). It's a fatal 'she' – sea, just about to 'suck him back to her insatiate grave' (II, 108) that releases him to Haidée's isle. Rebirth as Haidée's boy-toy imperils not only Juan's manhood but, implicitly, his life in the world: her doting eyes are raven-fringed, 'black as death' (II, 117).[10] The threat is perpetual: Juan is 'half-kill'd' by Lambro's squad (IV, 74), and his Turkish travesty wins a Sultana's death warrant; ravenous Catherine all too soon reduces her 'beauteous' boy to 'a condition / Which augured of the dead' (X, 39). So, too, in his first brush with Fitz-Fulke's back-from-the-dead Black Friar-drag ('sable frock and dreary cowl'; XVI, 123), a she-comparison of freaked-out Juan to Medusa is no empowerment; he seems more like one of the Gorgon's unmanned, petrified victims:

> ... Juan gazed upon it with a stare,
>   Yet could not speak or move; but, on its base
> As stands a statue, stood: he felt his hair
>   Twine like a knot of snakes around his face;
> He taxed his tongue for words, which were not granted ... (XVI, 23)

The next morning they both look death-'pale' (XVI, 31) and, in a canto Byron didn't live to finish, there is a morning-after pallor of an apparently longer encounter, with Juan looking ever more 'wan and worn', and her Grace scarcely better, 'pale and shivered' (XVII, 14). A manuscript scrap indicates the agenda: 'The Shade of the/Friar/The Dth of J' (*CPW* V, 761n). To relinquish the gender grammar, even in farce, is to court a death sentence. If Juan's defaults are culpable, the women pay the fuller wage: all save the Duchess are humiliated; Julia is doomed to convent life-in-death; Haidée is bereft, prisoned, demented, pregnant, dead.

And yet, for all this sorting out, the power of *Don Juan* – both its popularity and its scandal – emanates from Byron's critical perspective on these ordering schemes.

double-cross-dressing

Back in 1705, Mary Astell complained that when male historians 'condescend to record the great and good Actions of Women', they usually give 'this wise Remark':

> That such Women *acted above their Sex*. By which one must suppose that they wou'd have their Readers understand, That they were not Women who did those Great Actions, but that they were men in Petticoats![11]

In order to sustain the habit of equating great and good actions with the male sex, extraordinary women get classed as cross-dressed men. Astell knows that in this wry reflection on the figure of women acting 'up' lies a more serious proposal: that 'men', too, are defined by how they act, and a man in petticoats is no figure of greatness. In the two episodes of cross-sex cross-dressing in *Don Juan*, Byron stages a theatre of mobility with these genres in play. Even as the narratives draw comic energy from their dress-reversals and structural dislocations of power, the fate of manhood in the new formations remains a nagging question. What is a man in a petticoat?

This wasn't theory for Byron; it was life as Teresa Guiccioli's Cavalier Servente. In the Italian culture of young wives and husbands much older, a *Servente* is a wife's socially tolerated 'escort'. Byron was capable of taking a wry perspective on the business. Here was a system of fathers tending daughters as goods ('shut up in a convent till she has attained a marriageable or marketable age') to be sold preferably 'under the market price' – that 'portion of his fortune [...] fixed by law for the dower' – to a suitor of riches or rank. Eligible bidders were sometimes older than father. La Guiccioli was married off in her teens to a rich noble of fifty or sixty (*BLJ* VI, 107, 173). The daughters rarely objected, because marriage was better than a life sentence to a convent. The young woman 'is too happy to get her liberty on any terms', and her husband to get 'her money or her person'. 'There is no love on either side,' Byron observed of this inevitably unhappy, corruptible, and 'preposterous connexion'.[12]

When, however, Byron reacted to his part in the system, the terms shift in correspondence to his degradation. Not only did a distinction between '*Cavalier Serventeism*' and that 'prostitution, where the women get all the money they can' in loveless business 'contracts' seemed a bit moot,[13] but serventism seemed less dignified than the frankly managed business. Teresa may have been a 'Woman on the Market' in Luce Irigaray's terms ('they always pass from one man to another'), and Byron may have practiced male privileges, in their crudest forms: 'He allows fathers & mothers to bargain with him for their daughters' (said P.B. Shelley in disgust in 1818), a practice 'common enough in Italy' but still distressing to 'an Englishman'.[14] But in Italy, Byron was also a commodity: his service and trophy value (a 'fetish object' for power-display[15]) was part of the Italienne culture of boy-toys. 'The *k*night-service of the Continent, with or without the *k*', is 'slavery', he groused to Medwin.[16] In Italy, Staël's Nelvil complains to Corinne, it almost seems 'que les femmes sont le sultan et les hommes le sérail'.[17] Unlike England, 'the *polygamy* is all on the female side,' Byron chimes in, the 'strange sensation' exacerbated by his 'effeminate way of life' in Italy (*BLJ* VI, 226, 210).

Having just ranted to Murray in April 1819 about not castrating the first two cantos of *Don Juan* – 'I will have none of your damned cutting & slashing' especially to please 'le femine' – (*BLJ* VI, 105-6), he swooned in first love to Teresa. She was already calling him in public 'Mio Byron', having known him scarcely a week, and busily arranging his life. 'I should not like to be frittered down into a regular Cicisbeo,' Byron sighed to

Hobhouse, but it was an elegiac case: 'What shall I do! I am in love—and tired of promiscuous concubinage' (*BLJ* VI, 108). By June he was helpless: 'The Lady does whatever she pleases with me' (*BLJ* VI, 162); he was 'completely *governed* by' her – 'every thing depends upon *her* entirely' (*BLJ* VI, 164). And by August he was a slave: 'this Cisisbean existence is to be condemned.—But I have neither the strength of mind to break my chain, nor the insensibility which would deaden it's weight' (*BLJ* VI, 214).

In Juan's Turkish episode, Byron sets out to govern in poetry what he can't manage in life. Polygamy gets put back on the male side and sexual property is female: the Sultan has a harem of 1500 and four wives (one of them Gulbeyaz). 'Turks and Eastern people manage these matters better,' he thought (reflecting on the 'fatal' fall of his *'beau idéal'* in his experience with worldly women); 'They lock them up, and they are much happier'—*they* and *them* gender-sorted at least in Eastern stages.[18] Not under such tight management, *Don Juan* finds an escape clause in cross-dressing. While Juan in drag is a farce, the genre doesn't dispel the critical effect: the denaturalizing and theatricalizing of gender as an 'act'.[19] Presented by Baba with his Princess array, Juan protests he is not 'in a masquerading mood' (V, 73). Well before Joan Riviere was theorizing 'Womanliness as a Masquerade' (1929) and Luce Irigaray was raising the stakes by identifying 'the *masquerade of femininity*' as a production for the male marketplace of desire,[20] Byron staged the question with Juan's protests that he is not 'in a masquerading mood' for this 'odd travesty' (V, 74). No 'perfect transformation', Juan's feminine masquerade is 'display'd' in a form that all but makes the Wollstonecraft case: the artifices to which females are routinely trained. Juan's costuming and coaching 'to stint / That somewhat manly majesty of stride' (V, 91), a dressing down for him, is every woman's schooling for success. It's the recurring figure in modern gender criticism. 'I don't mind drag', Gloria Steinem put the case plain; 'women have been female impersonators for some time'. 'Is drag the imitation of gender, or does it dramatize the signifying gestures through which gender itself is established?' asks Judith Butler in her preface to *Gender Trouble*.[21]

The artifices that gender critics theorized and Byron recognized are politicized by the harem site. This was a male Romantic trope for erotic paradise, a beau-idealizing with which Byron collaborated when he made the enslaved heroine of *The Giaour* 'Circassia's daughter' (*CPW* III, 56; l. 505). 'For my part,' Rousseau crooned in *Émile*, 'I would have a young Englishwoman cultivate her agreeable talents, in order to please her future husband, with as much care and assiduity as a young Circassian cultivates her's, to fit her for the Haram of an Eastern bashaw'. This

English is Wollstonecraft's text in *Rights of Woman*, the translation not only a convenience but also a point about the translation of ideology, whatever the other national antagonisms.[22] Keeping the woman French rather than rendering her English, Macaulay had cited the same passage in a 'Letter on Education' that began:

> Though the situation of women in modern Europe, ... when compared with that condition of abject slavery in which they have always been held in the east, may be considered as brilliant; yet if we withhold comparison, and take the matter in a positive sense, we shall have no great reason to boast of our privileges...[23]

This, because the privileges coincide 'with a total and absolute exclusion of every political right' (Macaulay 1780). Refusing the orientalizing, Macaulay and Wollstonecraft set harem as a trope for patriarchal system per se. It is no less the project of English culture, Wollstonecraft acidly remarks, to form girls into creatures 'only fit for a seraglio'.[24]

Yet for all this troping and travesty of she-training, *Don Juan* is most Byronic in its sidelining of the wrongs of woman for the wrongs of a feminized man.[25] Byron even thought to up the ante by having the Sultana 'carry [Juan] off from Constantinople',[26] sex-switching the usual ravishment. Fronting Byron's embarrassment about women's ways with him, haremized Juan is shocked (shocked!) to find himself eyed as sexual 'property' by an imperious woman: 'a glance on him she cast, /... merely saying, "Christian, canst thou love?"' (V, 116). 'A man actually becomes a piece of female property,' Byron ranted of his service to La Guiccioli (*BLJ* VII, 28); 'the system of *serventism* imposes a thousand times more restraint and slavery than marriage ever imposed'.[27] He felt particularly taxed by 'the defined duties of a Cavalier Servente, or Cavalier Schiavo' – that is, slave (*BLJ* VII, 195). It was virtual reverse *couverture*:

> 'Cavlier Servente' is the phrase
>   Used in politest circles to express
> This supernumerary slave, who stays
>   Close to the lady as a part of dress.
> Her word is the only law which he obeys.
>   His is no sinecure, as you may guess;
> Coach, servants, gondola, he goes to call,
> And carries fan, and tippet, gloves, and shawl. (*Beppo* 40)

Byron first wrote *gentleman*, then decided on *slave*. It's not just that a Servente carries his lady's accessories but that he is one of these, 'stays / Close to the lady as a part of dress' – the punning and sliding of *who stays* ('whose stays') reinforcing the complaint. Byron never developed his plan to extend Juan's career of cross-dressing into the 'ridicules' of this Italian role (*BLJ* VIII, 78), but he gives the lad an audition with the Sultana and then the Empress, when he compares 'the actual and official duties' of 'the Imperial Favourite's Condition' to those of a 'Cavalier Servente' (IX, 51; 52). When he later described Juan's 'station' as that of 'man-mistress to Catherine the Great', the compound spells the cost: as woman's property Juan is regendered.[28]

This status is not exactly a new one. He is Julia's boy-toy and Haidée's pet: 'her bird', 'her own, her ocean-treasure' (II, 168, 173), 'her beautiful, her own' (IV, 58), and always 'her boy' (II, 174; IV, 42). Rather than a radical transformation, slavery is the disenchanted variation: 'chain'd, so that he cannot move, / And all because a lady fell in love' (IV, 51). If erotic thrall hazards a loss of male social identity (Antony, too, a 'slave' to 'Love' [II, 205]), material slavery confirms it. The 'boy' Juan (V, 13), an 'odd male' (figuratively no less than numerically), gets paired with an 'odd female' in an allotment in which everyone else is linked 'Lady to lady', 'man to man' (IV, 91, 92). His gender in this odd couple – the female is as 'handsome' as he (IV, 95; V, 9) – falls to operatic theatricality: he keeps company with a strange soprano occasioning 'some discussion and some doubt' among the vendors if she 'might be deem'd to be male' (IV, 92), and a castrato of the '*third* sex' (IV, 86). Juan soon finds himself in a she-place, leered at and for sale. His 'intended bidder' eyes him more intently than 'lady e'er is ogled by a lover' (V, 26), like a woman whom 'wealth[y] lust / Buys ... in marriage' (II, 200). The gender-trade is completed when it turns out that the purchaser is a powerful she, by whom he will be 'eyed ... o'er and o'er' (V, 107). Byron joked to Lady Melbourne on the eve of his marriage to the first woman he expected to 'govern' him, 'I shall become Lord Annabella' (*BLJ* IV, 229).

Juan's slavery is more Byronic yet in its trace of the subjection of authors to the market and its female arbiters. At the end of Canto IV, the poet abandons the slaveship to muse on authorship and its love of 'fame'. This, too, is a self-correction: 'Byron's vanity, or to give it a milder, and, perhaps, more appropriate term, his love of fame' (Matthew Iley reports) 'was excessive.' *Don Juan* doses love with savage critique. A patently fickle she, 'fame is but a lottery, / Drawn by the blue-coat misses of a coterie', that is, the bluestocking arbiters of taste.[29] The winners are gender-contaminated, a 'ball-room bard, a foolscap, hot-press darling'

(IV, 109). The figures are cut from Byron's cloth: 'a ball-room bard—a *hot-pressed* darling,' he recalled his life in 1812.[30] By 1814 he had come to despise 'authorship' as a 'sign of effeminacy' (*BLJ* III, 220), and by 1819 he disdained the suit for public 'Estimation': 'I have never flattered their opinions,' he rages to Murray; 'Neither will I make "Ladies books" "al dilettar le femine e la plebe"—I have written from the fullness of my mind, from passion—from impulse—from many motives—but not for their 'sweet voices'" (*BLJ* VI, 105–6), he sneers in echo of Shakespeare's Coriolanus (II. iii. 111). He talks the talk, protesting the integrity of motives, mind and passion, independent of the idols of the marketplace.[31] In other letters to Murray, he scorns 'the bookmaking of women', both the commodity '*She* book' and the economic gamble (September 1820; *BLJ* VII, 183). Yet as with the disdain of fame, Byron concedes a onetime complicity, even a she-style – 'that false stilted trashy style which is a mixture of all the styles of the day' (*BLJ* VII, 182). Medwin thought he was still out 'to captivate all the ladies', hearing him say that he 'was more pleased with the fame my "Corsair" had, than with that of any other of my books. Why? for the very reason because it did shine, and in *boudoirs*. Who does not write to please the women?'[32] When in 1822 Shelley lamented the truckling to the 'vulgar' and 'the ephemeral demand of the day' in Murray's urging of Byron 'to resume [the] old "Corsair style, to please the ladies"', Byron conceded his part, but with an escape clause: 'Murray is right, if not righteous: all I have yet written has been for women-kind; you must wait until I am forty, their influence will then die a natural death, and I will show the men what I can do.'[33]

Byron's sensitivity to the choice between selling oneself to womankind and showing men what men can do (an emerging rhetoric for the self-constituting male writer in the nineteenth century) registers in Juan's Turkish career. The Sultana's 'blue eyes' (V, 116) link her 'passion and power' over Juan to those 'Benign ceruleans of the second sex' who 'make the fortunes of all books' (IV, 108) and who are the latest avatar of the fickle goddess herself. Such slavery is on the poet's mind in his return to enslaved Juan at the close of Canto IV: 'But to the narrative: the vessel bound / With slaves to sell off in the capital' (IV, 113). Before it is clear that 'the vessel bound' is a slaveship and not a book, and that the capital is Constantinople and not London, a common market terminology seems to cover feminized human slaves ('deck'd ... out in all the hues of heaven' for 'sale' [IV, 114]) and the hot-press darlings drawn in a lottery run by women. No wonder, then, that Byron works out renewed expressions of male power.

The agenda is cued by Juan's steadfast integrity: Byron allows him the dignity of protesting to his buyer, 'I'm not a lady', of worrying about his reputation if 'it e'er be told / That I unsexed my dress,' and of declaring, 'my soul loathes / The effeminate garb' (V, 73, 75, 76). It is only Baba's threat that petulance will leave him with more unsex'd than dress that effects nominal compliance. Lordly male character abides. Juan 'stood like Atlas' before the Sultana, refusing the command to 'kiss the lady's foot' (V, 104, 102): 'rather than descend / To stain his pedigree,' he hews to the Castilian custom that 'commands / The gentleman, to kiss the lady's hands' (V, 104, 105). Opposing abasement with chivalric courtesy is the polite correction. A slap more political comes in Juan's public refusal of the Sultana's 'imperial' advance:

> ... he was steel'd by sorrow, wrath, and pride:
> With gentle force her white arms he unwound,
>   And seated her all drooping by his side.
> Then rising haughtily he glanced around,
>   And looking coldly in her face, he cried,
> 'The prison'd eagle will not pair, nor I
> Serve a sultana's sensual phantasy....
>   . . .
>   Love is for the free!
>   . . .
>   Whate'er thy power, and great it seems to be,
> Heads bow, knees bend, eyes watch around a throne,
>   And hands obey—our hearts are still our own.' (V, 126–7)

In the mask of enslaved, cross-dressed Juan, Byron sings liberation, its theme continuous with his answer to Teresa's urging a love interest for *Sardanapalus*: it 'could scarcely exist in the social state of inferiority in which woman was placed in ancient civilization'.[34] He was repelled by modern atrocities, and helped rescue a thirteen-year old girl kidnapped by Kurdish mountaineers for sale at a bazaar, 'whence Constantinople is supplied with *women*, like *beasts of the field,* from a *cattle* market'. Byron hid her 'in boy's attire' and hoped to return her to her parents.[35] Yet *Don Juan* is not only less consolidated on this liberal thinking, but self-conflicted – and this by its tug of male self-interest. As Elaine Showalter remarks about *Tootsie,* '"feminist" speeches' by a man in drag (here, on the job market) 'are less a response to the oppression of women than an instinctive situational male reaction to being treated like a woman'.[36]

An allied male reaction, also *Tootsie* and also Byron, is a deflection into farce and patent cliché. 'This was a truth to us extremely trite,' the poet yawns at Juan's protest (V, 128) – *us*, the men who've heard it all, already, for whom Juan's passion is no great matter. The episode then plays out as farce, the genre of choice for male transvestitism in literary and theatrical tradition. Questions of female subjection are translated into camp and parody.[37] The Englishman who befriends Juan in the slave market gives the cue with a riff on Laertes's caution to Ophelia – 'Keep your good name' – and Juan plays along: '"Nay," quoth the maid, "the Sultan's self shan't carry me, / Unless his highness promises to marry me"' (V, 84). When the Sultan takes a shine to his beauty, Juan shows his skill at feminine mimicry: 'This compliment ... made her blush and shake' (V, 156). When Baba forces him into 'a suit / In which a Princess with great pleasure would / Array' (V, 73), the genre, and gender, turn into a drag act:

> sighing, on he slipp'd
> A pair of trowsers of flesh-colour'd silk,
> Next with a virgin zone he was equipp'd,
> Which girt a light chemise, as white as milk;
> But tugging on his petticoat he tripp'd ...
>
> And, wrestling both his arms into a gown,
> He paused and took a survey up and down....
>
> ... Baba found
> So many false long tresses all to spare,
> That soon his head was most completely crown'd,
> After the manner then in fashion there;
> And this addition with such gems was bound
> As suited the *ensemble* of his toilet ...
>
> And now being femininely all array'd,
> With some small aid from scissars, paint, and tweezers,
> He look'd in almost all respects a maid,
> And Baba smilingly exclaim'd 'You see, sirs,
> A perfect transformation here display'd.' (V, 77–80)

The spectacle 'see, sirs' is wryly rhymed with its device, 'tweezers'. Byron took the pattern of this transformation from female models: Lady Mary Wortley Montagu's 'habit' during her residence in Turkey with her ambassador husband, and its imprint on Haidée at festival: 'Her orange silk full Turkish trowsers'; 'azure, pink, and white ... her chemise'; 'Her hair's long auburn waves', 'starr'd with gems' (III, 70, 72, 73). The poet's pronouns – 'Her shape, her hair, her air, her every thing' (VI, 35) – cheerily abet, miming Shakespeare's besotted Troilus on 'fair Cressid' ('Her eyes, her hair, her cheek, her gait, her voice' [I. i. 54]). Of Juan's regendering the poet explains in an aside,

> (I say *her*, because
> The Gender still was Epicene, at least
> In outward show, which is a saving clause) (VI, 58)

Byron plays the grammatical sense of *epicene*, nouns designating both genders, into the theatrical one, female characters played by male actors. He's already epicened Juan's easy fit into the odalisques 'all clad alike; like Juan, too'; 'They formed a very nymph-like looking crew' (V, 99); 'His youth and features favour'd the disguise' (V, 115), and

> no one doubted on the whole, that she
> Was what her dress bespoke, a damsel fair,
> And fresh, and 'beautiful exceedingly.' (VI, 36)

The phrase in quotes further cross-dresses Juan as Coleridge's Geraldine in damsel guise (*Christabel* I, 68), like Juan, ready to vamp. Shelley joined this fun at least: 'The Don Juan is arrived,' he wrote in spring 1822 of a yacht he commissioned; 'nothing can exceed the admiration *she* has excited, for we must suppose the name [...] given her during the equivocation of sex which her godfather suffered in the Harem'.[38] The convention of she-ship, covered with a male name, is recast as a male in she-drag.

Across these transformations, the poem called *Don Juan* stays true to the 'manly' genre. Juan's feminine array ultimate bodes no unsexing. In a 'labyrinth of females' (VI, 57), a seraglio of 'a thousand bosoms there / Beating for love as the caged birds for air,' Juan 'in his feminine disguise' (VI, 26) is a newly potentiated male. No prisoner of sex, he now wields the gaze, 'ogling all their charms from breasts to backs' (VI, 29), and his masculinity remains so intact that 'Although they could not see through his disguise, / All felt a soft kind of concatenation, / Like Magnetism, or Devilism' of attraction (VI, 38) to 'Juanna' and want 'her' in their beds. Juan's dress proves the indirection by which to find directions out; as the only phallic woman in the harem, he gains a world of sexual opportunity.

Trading on a long-standing male fantasy, and familiar staple of sexual farce, Juan's phallic success upholds his status as an aristocratic European male, not in military but in erotic conquest of the East. Clothes make the man.

So much so, that Juan himself stages his next masquerade; and here, gender play, rather than abject travesty, is the flagrant trope. In an outrageous drag act, Juan makes his debut in Catherine's court, (cross?)-dressed as a military dandy. His couturist is she 'Art' (IX, 44):

> ... in a handsome uniform;
> A scarlet coat, black facings, a long plume,
> Waving, like sails new shivered in a storm,
> Over a cocked hat in a crowded room,
> And brilliant breeches, bright as a Cairn Gorme,
> Of yellow cassimere we may presume,
> White stocking drawn, uncurdled as new milk,
> O'er limbs whose symmetry set off the silk. (IX, 43)

This is right out of the book of Byron's Eastern masquerades. 'For ceremonial occasions abroad' (reports Doris Langley Moore of the he-artist of this scene), Byron 'had a cocked hat with plumes, and a scarlet suit embroidered with gold which was the full dress uniform of an aide-de-camp'.[39] Offering a similarly gaudy Albanian outfit (famous from Thomas Phillips's 1813 portrait) to Margaret Mercer Elphinstone for a masquerade the same year (*BLJ* IV, 112–13), Byron was the wry impresario of a layered transvestite spectacle: a Regency 'Beauty' decked out as an Albanian dandy, and a female impersonation of Phillips's 'Byron'.

Behind this Byronism in masquerade are long-standing psychological investments that pay off in male power plays. The psychological matrix is described by Otto Fenichel and Robert Stoller, who both read male transvestitism as a fantasy of phallic-woman.[40] Stoller proposes that the transvestite man believes in 'the biological and social "inferiority" of women, and also know[s] that within himself there is a propensity toward being reduced to this "inferior" state'. This reduction is legible in Juan's 'feminine' characteristics and serial enslavements, but it also goes in reverse, to become the motor for his phallic luck. The male transvestite, goes Stoller's argument, fantasizes himself a phallic woman, either to counter his feminine tendencies or to assert a superior presence in relations with strong women. The prototype for this strong figure, moreover, 'has actually existed in his life—that is, the fiercely dangerous and powerful woman who ... humiliated him as a child': mother, with whom the male transvestite at once identifies and supersedes.[41] This story may seem a myth of male-theorized, male-centred psychoanalytic lore, but for this very reason it illuminates Byron's gallery of imperious women: Juan's mother Donna Inez, the Sultana and Empress Catherine; and their prototype, the first Catherine, the 'Mrs. Byron furiosa' (*BLJ* I, 93–4) of Byron's letters – her character etched in an escalating series of Byron-rants written at about Juan's age (in 1805–6) to half sister (by their father) Augusta:[42]

> In former days she spoilt me, now she is altered to the contrary, for the most trifling thing, she upbraids me in a most outrageous manner.... she flies into a fit of phrenzy upbraids me as if I was the most undutiful wretch in existence.... Am I to call this woman mother? Because by natures law she has authority over me, am I to be trampled upon in this manner? ... Am I to be eternally subjected to this caprice! I hope not, indeed a few short years will emancipate me from the shackles I now wear. (*BLJ* I, 54, 56)

> I have never been so *scurrilously* and *violently* abused by any person, as by that woman, whom I think, I am to call mother. . . . such is my mother; *my mother.* (*BLJ* I, 66)

> this female Tisiphone, a name which your *Ladyship* will recollect to have belonged to one of the Furies.—... my tormentor whose *diabolical* disposition ... seems to increase with age, and to acquire new force with Time.... No Captive Negro, or Prisoner of war, ever looked forward to their emancipation, and return to Liberty, with more Joy, ... than I do to my escape from maternal bondage.... I have escaped the Trammels or rather *Fetters* of my domestic Tyrant Mrs Byron. (*BLJ* I, 74, 75–6, 79)

Wresting authority from nature's law, Byron casts Juan-the-phallic-woman to address (and redress) a psychic grievance in the form of 'a better woman than a biological female'.[43]

Because the female dictating Juan's travesty is a Sultana, Juan's status as phallic woman stages more than a psychic grievance. Noting transvestic sanction 'at carnival times, at masquerade parties', Stoller glances at a liberatory latency.[44] As Byron could discern from his own carnivalizing, transvestic play was risky business for status quo ante. Contesting the view of carnival as 'a safety valve' for 'conflicts within the system' that preserves 'the basic order', Natalie Davis proposes that festive and literary inversions of sex roles could excite 'new ways of thinking' and so undermine assent, especially through 'connections with everyday circumstances outside the privileged time of carnival and stage-play'. Carnival could even provide strategies. Aware that 'irrational' women were given some legal license for misbehaviour, men who wanted to act up cross-dressed. Female clothes and titles could even energize and 'validate disobedient and riotous behavior', Davis proposes, citing transvestite rioting in Britain from the 1450s to the 1840s. The market-women's march on Versailles in October 1789 involved 'men in the disguise of women', reports Tom Paine.[45] Scott's *Heart of Midlothian* (1818) staged the Edinburgh Porteous Riots of 1736, spearheaded by transvestite 'Madge Wildfire' – a 'stout Amazon' in the sorority of 'bold and bloody' Empress Catherine, a 'modern Amazon' (IX, 70; VI, 96). Byron knew all this and more. An opponent of capital punishment for frame-breaking, he was well aware of 'General Ludd's wives', two men in women's clothes who led a loom-smashing, factory-burning riot at Stockport in 1812.[46]

Juan in she-garb is obliquely masculinized by these affiliations, and directly so by Byron's determined reduction of the Sultana to a woman after all. Her 'mixture' of 'half-voluptuousness and half command' (V, 108) resolves into the body beautiful: 'Her presence was as lofty as her state; / Her beauty of that overpowering kind' (V, 97); 'Her form had all the softness of her sex' (V, 109). The poet happily derides her 'self-will' and everything 'haughty' in her, capping his critique with relief that 'She was a sultan's bride, (thank Heaven, not mine)' (V, 111). Outwitted, she collapses into a caricature of a woman scorned. Not outwittable, just escapable, Empress Catherine gets degraded by slander. While her sexual appetites match Byron's, she earns contempt as 'the greatest of all sovereigns and w-----s' (VI, 92), a word Byron spelled out in his manuscript (*CPW* V, 327), and over which his friend Douglas Kinnaird paused to question the unfair play:

> why call the <u>Katherine</u> a whore? She hired or whored others—She was never hired or whored herself—why blame her for liking fucking? If she had canted as well as cunted, then call her names as long as you please—But it is hard to blame her for following her natural inclinations. ... I looked for more liberality from you—You must not turn against rogering—even tho' you practice it seldomer.[47]

Kinnaird tweaks Byron with an illiberalism of geese and ganders, of not being able to imagine a natural woman with political power. The culpability of the Sultana in commanding Juan's sexual surrender or of the Empress's in hiring it, moreover, is not something Byron cares to impose on men who seize women's bodies: Canto XIII makes crude just of geriatric rape. After the sack of Ismail, some seventy-year-old virgins are raped, while 'widows of forty' were 'heard to wonder in the din / . . . "Wherefore the ravishing did not begin!"' (VIII, 130, 132). To whom is this *Playboy* humour 'very funny'? Mary Shelley refused to fair copy the couplet about the old virgins.[48] The guys at *Blackwood's Edinburgh Magazine* (July 1823) managed to have it both ways, lamenting the 'leering and impotent ... loinless drivelling ... where the poet (the *poet!*) is facetious at the state of females during the sack of a town*' – letting this asterisk point to a pageful of objectionable text (stanzas 128–34), with this loinless apology: 'it is a pity to reprint such things, but a single specimen here may do good by the disgust for the whole which it must create' (XIV, 89). Disgust or gusto? Let the reader decide.

The lustful woman with purchasing power is rebuked in the Sultana, and the lustful she with political power is travestied in the Empress; but a designing woman with social and theatrical savvy (a Byron in drag) opens the question for another hearing. Duchess Fitz-Fulke's turn as Friar-ghost recalls Byron's own donning of friar-robes for fraternity fun at his abbey (*BLJ* VII, 231), and then a masquerade at Almack's in 1814, as well as the adventures of Caro Lamb, who showed up in his rooms 'in the disguise of a carman' (Byron recalled to Medwin); 'My valet, who did not see through the masquerade, let her in', and when 'she put off the man, and put on the woman [...] Imagine the scene!'[49] Detoxified of Caro, Fitz-Fulke's 'man' is liberal fantasy. Like a female author in a male pseudonym, the Duchess dresses for success. She is Byronism cross-gendered, a modern woman, sexually self-possessed, socially adept, out to manipulate the system of representation to advantage.[50]

No less than Caro, restless female readers grasped the emancipatory lure of male guising – genius by another name. In 1833, *The Athenæum's* 'Paris Correspondence' (2 February) outed 'George Sand' as a cross-dressed 'young lady, who, some years back, distinguished herself at the age of thirteen, by an indomitable wish to escape from her parents and seek out Lord Byron'; and in true Byronic fashion, she became 'answerable for works that do more honour to her genius than her delicacy' (74). She-men in *Don Juan* are cast for contempt or hapless farce; but she-transvestites, driven by will, desire, and imagination, dress up to move up or move out. In a Gynocrasy ruling over not much more than gossip, social intrigue, and assistance to husbands' careers, the Duchess dons male garb for sexual initiative. Her gender game takes its cue from masquerade culture, in Venetian streets and London assembly rooms, in all its transgressive frisson, with an extra libertine thrill in the clerical garb. Monitors such as

Thomas Gisborne warned of masquerades giving 'scope for unbounded licence of speech and action ... in one promiscuous assemblage'.[51] With more liberal interest, Lady Mary Montagu noted that in Turkey, women go out *only* in disguise – a habiting that, while it looks like repression, operates as license: 'This perpetual Masquerade gives them entire Liberty of following their Inclinations without Danger of Discovery.'[52] From the gender shifts of the early cantos to the intuition of perpetual charade in the epic's evolution, *Don Juan* discovers its own liberty. If the masculine tradition that Byron inherited is famed for writing 'Woman' as other, and *Don Juan* intermittently signs on to the binaries of 'masculine' and 'feminine', the cross-dressings of Byron's imagination are increasingly attracted to unstable borderlines of definition.[53]

notes

1. Lady Marguerite Blessington, *Lady Blessington's 'Conversations of Lord Byron'*, ed. Ernest J. Lovell, Jr., 11–12.
2. Virginia Woolf, 7 August 1918; *A Writer's Diary*, ed. Leonard Woolf, 2–3.
3. Blessington 1969, 12. Lady Holland's divorce from her first husband and her illegitimate son by Lord Holland closed much of London society to her. 'The first dispute I ever had with lady Byron,' recalled Byron, 'was caused by my urging her visit Lady [Holland]' (12).
4. Leslie Marchand comments on the heterosexual hierarchy in *Byron: A Biography*, 3 vols, Vol. I, 330, and Louis Crompton on the hierarchical, aristocratic preference in homosexual relations – pederastic over comrade form in *Byron and Greek Love*, 239–40.
5. Crompton's is the foundational study of Byron's homosexual passions and pursuits.
6. G. Wilson Knight, 'The Two Eternities: An Essay on Byron', in *The Burning Oracle: Studies in the Poetry of Action*, 268.
7. *travesty, trans + vestre* (to clothe); the *OED* cites Don Juan's harem travesty.
8. William Hazlitt, 'Lord Byron' in *The Spirit of The Age; or Contemporary Portraits*. 2nd edn, 161.
9. I owe this observation to Jack Cragwall.
10. For the involvement of Julia with death, see Peter Manning: 'Enveloping protection becomes suffocation, and what were only undertones in Juan's affair with Julia become prominent'; *Byron and His Fictions*, 186.
11. To Ruth Perry, in *The Celebrated Mary Astell: An Early English Feminist*, 25, I owe this reference to Mary Astell, *The Christian Religion, As Profess'd by a Daughter of the Church of England*, 293.
12. Thomas Medwin, *Conversations of Lord Byron: Noted During a Residence with His Lordship at Pisa, in the Years 1821 and 1822*, 22. See also Thomas Moore's *Life of Byron*, which casts Italian mothers as bawds: Count Guiccioli's 'great opulence rendered him an object of ambition among the mothers of Ravenna, who, according to the too frequent maternal practice, were seen vying with each other in attracting so rich a purchaser for their daughters, and the young

Teresa Gamba, then only eighteen, and just emancipated from a convent, was the selected victim'; *The Works of Lord Byron: With His Letters and Journals, and His Life*, 17 vols, Vol. 4, 144.

13. Medwin 1824, 22.

14. Luce Irigaray, 'Le marché des femmes', 1978; trans. Catherine Porter and Carolyn Burke, 'Woman on the Market', in *This Sex Which is Not One*, 171; Percy Bysshe Shelley, *Letters*, ed. Frederick L. Jones, 2 vols, Vol. 2, 58. Mary Shelley deleted this report in her edition of the letters.

15. Irigaray 1985, 183.

16. Medwin 1824, 73–4.

17. Germaine de Staël, *Corinne ou l'Italie*, 1807, Book. 6, Ch. 3 (ed. Simone Balayé, 157).

18. Medwin 1824, 73; cf. Matthew Iley, *The Life, Writings, Opinions, and Times of the Right Hon. George Gordon Noel Byron, Lord Byron*, 'By an English Gentleman, in the Greek Military Service, and Comrade of His Lordship', 3 vols, Vol. 2, 237.

19. On Byron's tactics in defamiliarizing, by gender-switching, situations so habitual as to seem natural, see Katherine Kernberger, 'Power and Sex: The Implication of Role Reversal in Catherine's Russia', *Byron Journal* 8 (1980): 42–9.

20. Irigaray 1985, 'Questions', *This Sex Which is Not One*, 133–4.

21. Steinem's remark is noted by Marjorie Garber, who contends that '*All* women cross-dress as women when they produce themselves as artifice'. *Vested Interests: Cross-Dressing & Cultural Anxiety*, 65, 49; Judith Butler adds, 'drag implicitly reveals the imitative structure of gender itself – as well as its contingency'. *Gender Trouble: Feminism and the Subversion of Identity*, 137–8; her introduction is quoted from p. x.

22. Mary Wollstonecraft, *A Vindication of the Rights of Woman*, 1792, eds Lorne Macdonald and Kathleen Scherf, 208.

23. Catharine Macaulay, *Letters on Education, With Observations on Religious and Metaphysical Subjects*, 210–15; for 'French woman', see 213. Rousseau's remarks are in *Émile* Book V, 'Sophy' in *Émile ou de l'Education*, trans. Barbara Foxley, 374. Wollstonecraft reviewed Macaulay's *Letters* for the *Analytical Review* in 1790. In 1797, Mary Hays was still rebuking Rousseau's syllabus (*Monthly Magazine* 3, 193). For the orientalizing, see Alan Richardson, 'Escape from the Seraglio: Cultural Transvestism in *Don Juan*' in *Rereading Byron*, eds Alice Levine and Robert N. Keane, 175–85.

24. Wollstonecraft 1997, 113.

25. *Lara* even troped 'Slavery' as a she-tyrant (CPW III, 214; l. 2). Of the politics of Selim's enforced haremizing in *The Bride of Abydos*, see Manning 1978, 40.

26. Medwin 1824, 164.

27. Blessington 1969, 180; Teresa didn't mark this comment.

28. Medwin 1824, 165. Cecil Lang terms Juan Catherine's 'male whore', with *male* signalling the scandal. 'Narcissus Jilted: Byron, *Don Juan*, and the Biographical Imperative' in *Historical Studies and Literary Criticism*, ed. Jerome J. McGann, 158.

29. Iley 1825. Vol. 2, 355. The marketplace potency of women, Sonia Hofkosh argues, imperils the male writer's 'fantasy of self-creation and self-government'. *Sexual Politics and the Romantic Author*, 37. Byron's scorn of the professional writer as effeminate, no man of letters, tunes the blue-stocking mockeries

of *Beppo*: the virulence of the attack, argues Manning, registers 'the power of the woman-dominated society of salons and *cavaliere servente* for which Laura stands in the poem, and that of the audience of women readers outside it'. 'The Nameless Broken Dandy and the Structure of Authorship' in *Reading Romantics: Texts and Context*, 151–5.

30. Medwin 1824, 214.

31. The satires on sentiment in *Don Juan*, argues Anthony Vital, reflect Byron's early association of poetry with femininity. 'Lord Byron's Embarrassment: Poesy and the Feminine', *Bulletin of Research in the Humanities* 86 (1983–85): 269, 273. The English cantos' flirting with the woman-dominated genre of the novel, observes Malcolm Kelsall, courts the social structure of gynocracy, a 'transfer of power from the poet's Muse to the female salon', already registered in Canto IV's blue-stocking stanzas. 'Byron and the Women of the Harem' in Levine and Keane, eds 1993, 171. For the psycho-cultural dynamics of Byron's female readership, see Andrew Elfenbein, *Byron and the Victorians*, 59–74.

32. Medwin 1824, 214, 206.

33. E. J. Trelawny, *Recollections of the Last Days of Shelley and Keats*, 35–6.

34. Ernest J. Lovell, Jr., *His Very Self and Voice: Collected Conversations of Lord Byron*, 247.

35. Iley 1825. Vol. III, 123–6.

36. Elaine Showalter, 'Critical Cross-Dressing: Male Feminists and The Woman of The Year', *Raritan* 3/2 (Fall 1983): 138.

37. Jane Stedman distinguishes the Elizabethan convention of boys in serious female roles from the later transvestite theatrics of farce and grotesque parodies. 'From Dame to Woman: W.S. Gilbert and Theatrical Transvestism' in *Suffer and Be Still: Women in the Victorian Age*, ed. Martha Vicinus, 20.

38. 16 May 1822; Shelley 1964. Vol. 2, 421.

39. 'It was an admissible dress for peers being presented at foreign courts, and certainly it had a tremendous effect on certain pashas in Albania and Turkey'. Doris Langley Moore, 'Byronic Dress', *Costume* 5 (1971): Citing *Don Juan* IX, 43–5 and Moore's report, Lang reads a masked reference to Byron: like Juan, Byron piqued the sexual interest of a sixty-something potentate (Ali Pasha), who exercised a kind of feminizing erotic doting on his physical beauty (Lang 1985, 158–61).

40. Otto Fenichel, 'The Psychology of Transvestitism', 1930 in *The Collected Papers of Otto Fenichel, First Series*. Vol. 1, 169. This mode of transvestite, elaborates Stoller, is essentially butch, reveling in the male physiognamy under wraps and getting 'great pleasure in revealing that he is a male-woman'. *Sex and Gender: On the Development of Masculinity and Femininity*, 176–7. It's worth noting, however, that Stoller's frame is as much ideology as disinterested science: a father 'overly loving and "maternal" to his small children' earns the label 'effeminate', as does a man 'oversolicitous to other people and thrillingly responsive to the universe of art' (Stoller 1968, 179).

41. Stoller 1968, 215.

42. For the literary reverberations of Byron's relationship with his mother, see Manning 1978, 23–55, 177–99. To Jack Cragwall I owe the note on the name *Catherine*.

43. Stoller 1968, 177. Also referring to Stoller (and to Natalie Davis), Sandra Gilbert and Susan Gubar argue that transvestite episodes in modern literature,

charged by emerging social issues, recoil into restored, revitalized structures of male authority. *Sexchanges* in Vol. 2 of *No Man's Land: The Place of the Woman Writer in the Twentieth Century*, 333–5. Showalter invokes Stoller to discern a 'phallic woman' in the male feminist critics of the 1980s – a professional transvestite who usurps and in effect marginalizes the feminism he seems to endorse (Showalter 1983).

44. Stoller 1968, 186.
45. Natalie Davis, 'Women on Top', *Society and Culture in Early Modern France*, (130–1, 142–3, 147–50); Tom Paine, *The Rights of Man* (1791–1793). *Two Classics of the French Revolution*, 299.
46. For the Stockport riots, see E.P. Thompson, *The Making of the English Working Class*, 567; the riots in Walter Scott's *Heart of Midlothian* are in chapters 6 and 7.
47. Letter to Byron, 15 October 1822; Ms. in John Murray Archives; transcribed by Jane Stabler (2002, 182–3), to whom I am indebted for this reference.
48. For her refusal, see Steffan and Pratt 1957. Vol. 3, 177. Byron used such 'wit' in 1813 in *The Devil's Drive*: in the siege, 'an old maid, for years forsaken,' asks one invader, 'pray are the rapes beginning?' (stanza 9). It is Andrew Rutherford who calls the stanzas in *Don Juan* 'very funny', though he regrets Byron's 'flippant treatment of the rapes'. *Byron: A Critical Study*, 178–9. Even Jerome McGann tries to have it both ways, regarding these stanzas as a repellant nihilism, but willing to amuse an audience by rehearsing them. *Byron and Romanticism*, ed. James Soderholm, 136–7.
49. Marchand 1957. Vol. 2, 459 and *Byron's Poetry: A Critical Introduction*, 216–17.
50. For the masquerade as icon of a corrupt and duplicitous 'world', see G.J. Barker-Benfield, *The Culture of Sensibility: Sex and Society in Eighteenth-Century Britain*, 182–7.
51. Thomas Gisborne, *An Inquiry into the Duties of the Female Sex*. 1796; 7th edn, 152–3. Of the monkery, Garber comments, the 'scandal of cross-dressing and the scandal of religious impersonation, when present in the same transvestic figure, intensified the libertinism of the masquerade' (Garber 1992, 219).
52. To her sister, 1 April 1717. *The Complete Letters*, ed. Robert Halsband, 3 vols. Vol. 1, 328. All these sites, Terry Castle writes, flirted with 'female sexual freedom, and beyond that, female emancipation generally'; in the eighteenth-century novel, masquerade episodes stage a 'symbolic theater of female power', where women usurp not only male dress but also men's 'social and behavioral "freedoms"'. 'Eros and Liberty at the English Masquerade, 1710–90'. *Eighteenth-Century Studies* 17 (1983-84).
53. I am grateful to my editors at Stanford University Press for allowing me to redact this essay from a chapter in *Borderlines: The Shiftings of Gender in British Romanticism*. (Stanford, CA: Stanford University Press, 2006).

works cited and suggestions for further reading

Astell, Mary. *The Christian Religion, As Profess'd by a Daughter of the Church of England*. London: R. Wilkin, 1705.

Barker-Benfield, G.J. *The Culture of Sensibility: Sex and Society in Eighteenth-Century Britain*. Chicago, IL: University of Chicago Press, 1992.

Blessington, Marguerite Lady. *Lady Blessington's 'Conversations of Lord Byron'*. 1834. Ed. Ernest J. Lovell, Jr. Princeton, NJ: Princeton University Press, 1969.

Butler, Judith. *Gender Trouble: Feminism and the Subversion of Identity*. New York: Routledge, 1990.

Castle, Terry. 'Eros and Liberty at the English Masquerade, 1710-90'. *Eighteenth-Century Studies* 17 (1983–84): 156–76.

Crompton, Louis. *Byron and Greek Love*. Berkeley, CA: University of California Press, 1985.

Davis, Natalie Zemon. 'Women on Top'. *Society and Culture in Early Modern France*. Stanford, CA: Stanford University Press, 1975. 124–51.

Elfenbein, Andrew. *Byron and the Victorians*. Cambridge: Cambridge University Press, 1995.

Fenichel, Otto. 'The Psychology of Transvestitism'. 1930. *The Collected Papers of Otto Fenichel, First Series*. New York: Norton, 1953. Vol. 1, 167–80.

Garber, Marjorie. *Vested Interests: Cross-Dressing & Cultural Anxiety*. New York: Routledge, 1992.

Gilbert, Sandra M. and Susan Gubar. *Sexchanges*. Vol. 2 of *No Man's Land: The Place of the Woman Writer in the Twentieth Century*. New Haven: Yale University Press, 1989.

Gisborne, Thomas. *An Inquiry into the Duties of the Female Sex*. 1796; 7th edn. London: T. Cadell and W. Davies, 1806.

Hays, Mary. *Appeal to the Men of Great Britain in Behalf of Woman*. London: J. Johnson and J. Bell, 1798.

Hazlitt, William. 'Lord Byron'. *The Spirit of The Age; or Contemporary Portraits*. 2nd edn. London: Colburn, 1825. 149–68.

Hofkosh, Sonia. *Sexual Politics and the Romantic Author*. Cambridge: Cambridge University Press, 1998.

[Iley, Matthew.] 'By an English Gentleman, in the Greek Military Service, and Comrade of His Lordship'. *The Life, Writings, Opinions, and Times of the Right Hon. George Gordon Noel Byron, Lord Byron*. 3 vols. London: Matthew Iley, 1825.

Irigaray, Luce. 'Le marché des femmes'. 1978. Trans. Catherine Porter and Carolyn Burke, 'Woman on the Market'. *This Sex Which is Not One*. Ithaca, NY: Cornell University Press, 1985. 170–91.

——. 'Questions.' *This Sex Which is Not One*. Ithaca, NY: Cornell University Press, 1985. 119–69.

Kelsall, Malcolm. 'Byron and the Women of the Harem'. *Rereading Byron*. Eds. Alice Levine and Robert N. Keane. New York and London: Garland, 1993. 165–73.

Kernberger, Katherine. 'Power and Sex: The Implication of Role Reversal in Catherine's Russia'. *Byron Journal* 8 (1980): 42–9.

Knight, G. Wilson. 'The Two Eternities: An Essay on Byron'. *The Burning Oracle: Studies in the Poetry of Action*. London: Oxford University Press, 1939. 199–288.

Lang, Cecil. 'Narcissus Jilted: Byron, *Don Juan*, and the Biographical Imperative'. *Historical Studies and Literary Criticism*. Ed. Jerome J. McGann. Madison,WI: University of Wisconsin Press, 1985. 143–79.

Lovell, Ernest J. Jr. *His Very Self And Voice: Collected Conversations of Lord Byron*. New York: Macmillan, 1954.

Macaulay, Catharine (Graham). *Letters on Education, With Observations on Religious and Metaphysical Subjects*. London: C. Dilly, 1790.

Manning, Peter J. *Byron and His Fictions*. Detroit: Wayne State University Press, 1978.

——. 'The Nameless Broken Dandy and the Structure of Authorship'. *Reading Romantics: Texts and Contexts*. New York and London: Oxford University Press, 1990. 145–62.

Marchand, Leslie A. *Byron: A Biography*. 3 vols. New York: Knopf, 1957.

——. *Byron's Poetry: A Critical Introduction*. Cambridge, Mass.: Harvard University Press, 1968.

McGann, Jerome J. *Byron and Romanticism*. Ed. James Soderholm. Cambridge: Cambridge University Press, 2002.

Medwin, Thomas. *Conversations of Lord Byron: Noted During a Residence with His Lordship at Pisa, in the Years 1821 and 1822*. London: Henry Colburn, 1824.

Montagu, Lady Mary Wortley. *The Complete Letters*. Ed. Robert Halsband. 3 vols. Oxford: Clarendon Press, 1965–67.

Moore, Doris Langley. 'Byronic Dress'. *Costume* 5 (1971): 1–13.

Moore, Thomas. *The Works of Lord Byron: With His Letters and Journals, and His Life*. 17 vols. London: John Murray, 1832–34.

Paine, Thomas. *The Rights of Man (1791–1793)*. *Two Classics of the French Revolution*. New York: Anchor, 1973. 267–515.

Perry, Ruth. *The Celebrated Mary Astell: An Early English Feminist*. Chicago, IL: University of Chicago Press, 1986.

Richardson, Alan. 'Escape from the Seraglio: Cultural Transvestism in *Don Juan*'. *Rereading Byron*. Eds Alice Levine and Robert N. Keane. New York and London: Garland, 1993. 175–85.

Rousseau, Jean-Jacques. *Émile ou de l'Education*. Trans. Barbara Foxley. London: J.M. Dent and New York: E.P. Dutton, 1911.

Rutherford, Andrew. *Byron: A Critical Study*. Stanford, CA: Stanford University Press, 1961.

Scott, Walter. *The Heart of Midlothian*. 4 vols. Edinburgh: Archibald Constable, 1818.

Shelley, Mary, ed. *Essays, Letters from Abroad, Translations and Fragments by Percy Bysshe Shelley*. 2 vols. London: Edward Moxon, 1840 [1839]; Philadelphia: Lea and Blanchard, 1840.

Shelley, Percy Bysshe. *Letters*. Ed. Frederick L. Jones. 2 vols. Oxford: Clarendon Press, 1964.

Showalter, Elaine. 'Critical Cross-Dressing: Male Feminists and The Woman of The Year'. *Raritan* 3/2 (Fall 1983): 130-49.

Stabler, Jane. *Byron, Poetics and History*. Cambridge: Cambridge University Press, 2002.

Staël, Germaine de. *Corinne ou l'Italie*. 1807. Ed. Simone Balayé. France: Gallimard, 1985.

Stedman, Jane W. 'From Dame to Woman: W.S. Gilbert and Theatrical Transvestism'. *Suffer and Be Still: Women in the Victorian Age*. Ed. Martha Vicinus. Bloomington, IN: Indiana University Press, 1972. 20-37.

Steffan, Truman Guy and Willis W. Pratt, eds. *Byron's Don Juan, A Variorum Edition*. 4 vols. Austin: University of Texas Press, 1957.

Stoller, Robert J. *Sex and Gender: On the Development of Masculinity and Femininity*. New York: Science House, 1968.

Thompson, E.P. *The Making of the English Working Class*. London: Victor Gollancz, 1964.

Trelawny, E[dward] J[ohn]. *Recollections of the Last Days of Shelley and Keats*. Boston: Tricknor and Fields, 1858.

Vital, Anthony Paul. 'Lord Byron's Embarrassment: Poesy and the Feminine'. *Bulletin of Research in the Humanities* 86 (1983-85): 269-90.

Wollstonecraft, Mary. *A Vindication of the Rights of Woman*. 1792. Eds Lorne Macdonald and Kathleen Scherf. Peterborough, Ont.: Broadview Press, 1997.

Woolf, Virginia. *A Writer's Diary*. Ed. Leonard Woolf. New York: Harcourt Brace Jovanovich, 1954.

index

Individual Byron works are listed separately